D1121819

FICTION *The One-Handed Pianist* * *The Disappearance*

NONFICTION *A Critic's Journey* * *Gabriel García Márquez: The Early Years* * *The Hispanic Condition* * *Art and Anger* * *The Riddle of Cantinflas* * *Imagining Columbus* * *The Inveterate Dreamer* * *Octavio Paz: A Meditation* * *Bandido* * *On Borrowed Words* * *Spanglish* * *¡Lotería!* (with Teresa Villegas) * *Dictionary Days* * *Resurrecting Hebrew*

ANTHOLOGIES *The Norton Anthology of Latino Literature* * *Tropical Synagogues* * *The Oxford Book of Latin American Essays* * *Becoming Americans: Four Centuries of Immigrant Writing* * *Growing Up Latino* (with Harold Augenbraum) * *Mutual Impressions* * *The Oxford Book of Jewish Stories* * *Wáchale!* * *The Scroll and the Cross* * *The Schocken Book of Modern Sephardic Literature* * *Lengua Fresca* (with Harold Augenbraum)

CONVERSATIONS *Love and Language* (with Verónica Albin) * *With All Thine Heart* (with Mordecai Drache) * *Eight Conversations* (with Neal Sokol) * *Conversations with Ilan Stavans* * *What Is* la hispanidad? (with Iván Jaksić) * *Knowledge and Censorship* (with Verónica Albin)

CARTOONS *Latino USA* (with Lalo Alcaráz) * *Mr. Spic Goes to Washington* (with Roberto Weil)

TRANSLATIONS *Sentimental Songs* by Felipe Alfau

GENERAL *The Essential Ilan Stavans*

EDITIONS *The Collected Stories* by Calvert Casey * *The Poetry of Pablo Neruda* * *Collected Stories* by Isaac Bashevis Singer (three volumes) * *Encyclopedia Latina* (four volumes) * *Selected Writings* by Rubén Darío * *I Explain a Few Things* by Pablo Neruda * *Cesar Chavez: An Organizer's Tale* * *Spain, Take This Chalice from Me* by César Vallejo

THE FSG BOOK OF TWENTIETH-CENTURY LATIN AMERICAN POETRY

FARRAR STRAUS GIROUX   NEW YORK

AN ANTHOLOGY

edited by

ILAN STAVANS

the **FSG** *book of*

TWENTIETH-

CENTURY

LATIN

AMERICAN

POETRY

Farrar, Straus and Giroux
18 West 18th Street, New York 10011

Library of Congress Cataloging-in-Publication Data
The FSG book of twentieth-century Latin American poetry :
an anthology / edited by Ilan Stavans. — 1st ed.
    p. cm.
Poems in various Latin American languages (primarily Spanish and
Portuguese) with translations into English; introduction in English.
Includes index.
ISBN: 978-0-374-10024-7 (alk. paper)
    1. Latin American poetry—20th century. 2. Latin American poetry—
20th century—Translations into English. I. Stavans, Ilan.

PQ7087.E5F78 2011
861'.608098—dc22

                                                            2010039694

Designed by Quemadura
Flower illustrations by Raúl Peña

www.fsgbooks.com

1 3 5 7 9 10 8 6 4 2

PARA **EARL SHORRIS**, SURCADOR DE

TERRITORIOS INEXPLORADOS

Contents

Introduction

TRANSLATION AND POWER

ILAN STAVANS

This anthology has a double mission: to showcase the rich, multifarious poetic tradition in Latin America during the twentieth century; and to invite the reader to recognize the range of verbal possibilities of that tradition. The originals are, for the most part, in Spanish and Portuguese, but I have included poets communicating in indigenous tongues as well as pieces written in English and French, and descendants of immigrants who use the immigrant tongue as their conduit. In other words, this volume isn't only in but about translation.

To appreciate the nuances in the material that follows, it is important to think of language not only as a set of syntactical patterns per se but as the overall philosophical conception, in Wittgenstein's sense, of how a person processes thought, and how the syntactical patterns, as well as culture in general, shape that thought. What changed in Latin America the moment that Spanish and Portuguese arrived from the Iberian Peninsula at the end of the fifteenth century? What do we mean, in epistemological terms, when we say that the region became modern? What scar did the eclipse of the dozens of aboriginal tongues used until then leave on the way people approached life from colonial times onward?

It is seldom remembered that the Spanish and Portuguese that came from the Iberian Peninsula during the colonial enterprise were just around then consolidating their status as national languages. By "national" I mean an extremity of the state. *El español*, for instance, which in some countries is known as *el castellano*, is the tongue of the Castilian region. The fall of Granada and the success of *La Reconquista*, along with the political marriage of the Catholic monarchs Queen Isabella and King Ferdinand, saw it embraced as the nation's language and, in the lexicographer Antonio de Nebrija's words, it became *la compañera del imperio*, the empire's companion, in Spain's quest to expand its territories across the Atlantic. Spanish, the third most widely used language in the world now, has approximately four hundred million speakers worldwide, fewer than 10 percent of whom live in Spain. Portuguese, the seventh, is used by close to two hundred million, 95 percent of whom are Brazilians.

Yet in the Spanish- and Portuguese-speaking Americas, the official languages are but a mirage. In 1492 there were almost a hundred different aboriginal languages from what is now Mexico to Argentina. Scores perished but several dozen survive. Each of those surviving tongues is a worldview. And those worldviews, while in eclipse, continue to manifest themselves in myriad ways. Proof of this is the work of Humberto Ak'Abal from Guatemala, who is active in K'iche and Spanish today. His verses, while infused in the perplexities fostered by modernity, reach back to the pre-Columbian cosmogony of Mesoamerica. Similarly, Elicura Chihuailaf from Chile writes in Mapuche, and Natalio Hernández Xocoyotzin from Mexico in Náhuatl. Others such as Pura López Colomé have pre-Columbian ancestry. To write in an indigenous tongue nowadays might be to limit one's exposure. But these aboriginal languages are nonetheless part of the tableaux of Latin American poetry, which is far more pluralistic than is commonly understood. They are a reminder that beyond the surface there have always been other ways of looking at modernity.

The time frame for adopting Spanish and Portuguese as the region's official languages was rather short when one compares it to the natural span of linguistic formation: less than three centuries, between 1523, when Hernán Cortés defeated the Aztecs in the imperial city of Tenochtitlán, imposing a moral, social, religious, and economic system imported from the Iberian Peninsula, and the fever for self-determination that swept the emerging republics in the Americas from 1810 onward. As soon as they acquired their independence, the Latin American republics broke their political ties with the mother countries but kept their languages. In retrospect, such decisions appear obvious, even fated. After all, the colonizers had rejected the indigenous tongues as unworthy. The *criollo* intelligentsia, rather than pondering the issue, simply endorsed the verbal mores of the colonial period. They pushed for the language of Lope de Vega, Góngora, Quevedo, and Cervantes as their ticket to orderly life. With rather limited exceptions (say, Bolivia and Paraguay), Spanish and Portuguese went from weapons of conquest to tools of self-determination.

All this is to say that we the people of Latin America know, and not only unconsciously, what it means to live in an environment defined by superimposed verbal codes. Growing up in Mexico in the sixties, I was in constant contact with the aboriginal tongues spoken by the indigenous population in the nation's capital. For the most part these tongues were not taught at school. Families simply passed them from one generation to the next. Society approached their speakers with suspicion. They were *indios*, a derogative term denoting a primitive outlook. But the conquest had taken place almost five centuries earlier.

Arguably the region's first serious aesthetic break with Spain and its literature in modern times came about at the end of the nineteenth century through Modernismo. A kind of Romanticism but with stronger ideological commitments, it was this artistic movement, and the mentality it fostered, that made the region's population feel part of the modern world. The movement coincided with the arrival of the railroad, electricity, photography, and the telephone. It coincided with the embrace of science and with Positivism as a mode of thought. What is more, this era is known for its intense nationalist feelings.

Critics differ on the exact life span of Modernismo but it is safe to suggest that it emerged in 1885, when one of its leaders, Rubén Darío, published *Azul* . . . , a groundbreaking book that included poetry and prose, and it concluded in 1915, a few years before Darío's death. The movement (not to be confused with Modernism, which, roughly speaking, came about in the English-speaking world a couple of decades later and includes Woolf, Stein, Pound, and Joyce) is understood as a form of American Symbolism. Its mission was to move Latin American culture in another direction, away from the obscurantism of Iberian mores and into more refreshing styles. Another objective was to refine the Spanish language, making it more agile. Known as the Spanish-American bard, Darío is a complex, multifaceted figure whose influence continues to be felt in the present. From a small town in Nicaragua, he nurtured hemispheric dreams, allowing the language to acquire a distinctive refinement yet autochthonous taste. He used—to some, the word is abused—a series of motifs, such as the swan, China as the archetype of exoticism, and the poet as divine messenger, to make the hemispheric literature less isolated, more cosmopolitan.

Also led by the Cuban activist and man of letters José Martí, who died in 1895 in the battlefield, the Modernistas were influenced, in various degrees, by Parnassianism, Symbolism, and other French artistic trends. In fact, as Iberian patterns were pushed aside, French culture became the model to emulate. Figures such as Rimbaud, Verlaine, and Victor Hugo were idealized. Several poems by Darío adopt foreign figures, such as snow, swans, and the princess. The bunch was attracted to Orientalism and the grotesque, and through these rubrics, to a type of eroticism that stresses the mysterious. And it was fascinated by *lo auténtico*, that which is native to the Americas. Darío, for one, wrote a poem celebrating Caupolicán, a leader of the Mapuches in Chile in their struggle against the Spaniards. And Martí's most famous songs, *Versos sencillos*, are about peasant life in the tropics.

I've included an array of Modernista poets from the Spanish-language world in this anthology: not only Martí and Darío but José Asunción Silva from Colombia, Ricardo Jaimes Freire from Bolivia, Leopoldo Lugones from Argentina, José Santos Chocano from Peru, Julio Herrera y Reissig and Delmira Agustini from Uruguay, and Amado Nervo and Enrique González Martínez from Mexico. Within the Modernismo ranks there were unavoidable tensions. The reader will recognize these tensions in a number of places, including González Martínez's attack on Darío in his poem "Tuércele el cuello al cisne. . . ." In Brazil, the Modernista aesthetics found its most lucid exponent in José Oswald de Andrade, best known for his *Manifesto antropófago*, published in 1928, a call for Brazilian nationalism through the arts. Andrade's strong patriotic sentiments were not unique to him: Darío and Martí eulogized their own countries as a way to emphasize their difference from Spain. Equally influential was Mário de Andrade, a Brazilian poet as well as cultural critic, photographer, and, most important, an ethnomusicologist, whose book *Paulicéia desvairada*, released in 1922, is a tribute to São Paulo, and whose short, syncopated poems have been enormously influential in Brazil.

Darío and Martí's revolution gave place to a number of avant-garde paths, including Vanguardismo, one of the trends linked to the French avant-garde that was always hungry to experiment, formally and in terms of content, and was exemplified by César Vallejo, the politically driven Catholic poet from Peru who died in Spain during that nation's civil war; and Creacionismo, which purported to animate—that is, locate the anima in—the items the poet wrote about, exemplified by the Chilean dandy Vicente Huidobro, author of the book *Altazor*. Vallejo died in Paris (of hiccups, according to some accounts) but he never wrote in French. Huidobro, instead, befriended European avant-gardists such as Picasso, Miró, and Éluard, to the degree that he composed his own poetry in French. A sample of it is included in this volume. Their poetry pushed the Latin American poetic tradition in myriad directions.

Arguably the four most famous post-Modernistas in Latin America, and the driving force of twentieth-century poetry—*los cuatro grandes*—are Jorge Luis Borges, Carlos Drummond de Andrade, Pablo Neruda, and Octavio Paz. Each digested the aesthetic revolution that preceded him in a different way. That effort at processing what had come before entailed a connection with different cultures. Since childhood, Borges, who might well be the most famous Argentine of the twentieth century, was marked by the presence of the English language at his home, since his maternal side of the family hailed from England. In his "Autobiographical Essay" he relates how he first read *Don Quixote of La Mancha* in English. His closeness to the Anglo-Saxon world defines his vision as a poet. Such was Borges's infatuation that he agreed to incorporate into his *Obras completas* a couple of strange poems, called, without obfuscation, "Two English Poems." Throughout his life, Borges taught himself other languages, among them French, German, Italian, Latin, Anglo-Saxon, Nordic, and some Hebrew. The access Borges had to them allowed him to expand his intellectual horizons. His multilingual correspondence has survived. And he wrote a couple of book prologues in French.

Modernismo in Brazil was adapted in its own idiosyncratic fashion. Carlos Drummond de Andrade, at once a socialist and a metaphysician who owed a debt to the other two Andrades, is known as Brazil's poet laureate. In other words, he infused his poetry with elements at the core of the Antropofagists: nationalism and aestheticism. Although he refused to be connected with a particular trend (he was widely known as a shy person), Drummond de Andrade followed Whitman's free verse but was influenced by T. S. Eliot's *The Waste Land*. His oeuvre is inward-looking, exploring the solitude of the modern man in the universe, traits that are present in another post-Modernista: Neruda won the Nobel

Prize in 1970, three years before his death. No poet from Latin America is more popular. No one sells more books.

Born in the small town of Parral, he learned from Modernismo a political lesson: to be an engaged poet, using his words to describe labor turmoil in history and denouncing oppression whenever he found it. But Neruda wasn't a propagandist. His wide-ranging talents allow for epic vistas, as is the case of his magnum opus, *Canto general*, which stands in sharp contrast to his moments of intense intimacy, as shown in early efforts such as *Veinte poemas de amor y una canción desesperada* and in the mature material included in *Los versos del capitán*. Neruda's oeuvre exemplifies perhaps better than that of anyone else the tension at the heart of twentieth-century Latin American poetry between, on one side, the inward, personal attempt to explore human emotions and their connection to the landscape, and the desire to find existential answers to human dilemmas, and on the other side, the use of words as instruments of protest against oppression and in search of justice and equality.

As the reader will find in this selection, the pendulum between the private and the epic, between using the word to verbalize emotion in sublime fashion and as a mechanism to change the order of things political in the world, is constantly swinging. The truth is that most fine poets don't drink from a single well. Their work juxtaposes elements from both sides. There are, of course, some more ideologically driven than others, such as Efraín Huerta and Roque Dalton, but their universe is far from one-dimensional. For instance, in his poem "Amén de mariposas," Pedro Mir uses a tragic incident in the history of his native Dominican Republic, the "mysterious" assassination, on November 25, 1960, of the militant Mirabal sisters Patria Mercedes, María Argentina Minerva, and Antonia María Teresa, by the dictatorial regime of Rafael Leónidas Trujillo. In a region where tyranny, torture, and repression are de rigueur, it can't be surprising to encounter a mass of committed poetry. But in their search for answers to urgent social questions they find themselves in an assortment of situations and their response is invariably to humanize the dehumanized portion of humanity, to grant it the right to have its own voice. Likewise, poets such as Xavier Villaurrutia, Gonzalo Rojas, and Roberto Juarróz, portrayed at times as dilettantes, evidence the need to insert their aesthetic quest in precise historical coordinates, looking for ways to ground themselves on solid ground.

And then there is the uniform obsession with language as universe unto itself and the desire to branch out to other linguistic realms. Neruda, a polyglot, was fascinated with translation as a creative endeavor. Some Modernistas produced Spanish versions of Rimbaud, Baudelaire, Verlaine, and Maeterlinck. Just as Borges translated into Spanish the work of Kafka, Faulkner, Wilde, and Woolf, among others, he translated *Romeo and Juliet*. Another champion of translingual voyages was Octavio Paz, *el mexicano global*, born a decade after Neruda and also the recipient of a Nobel Prize. Paz was a tireless translator who rendered into Spanish the work of French, English, Portuguese, Mandarin, and Sanskrit writers, among others. He made the avant-garde his banner. Always restless as an intellectual, he produced poems and essays that point in multiple directions at once: to Mexico's pre-Columbian past and colonial poets such as the seventeenth-century nun Sor Juana Inés de la Cruz, the Spanish Golden Age, Surrealism, Eliot and Pound, and so-called *provincianos* such as his fellow *mexicano* Ramón López Velarde, author of *Suave patria*. Through *Plural* and *Vuelta*, the monthly magazines Paz edited for decades, he brought, from the sixties onward, a broad intellectual sophistication into the Spanish-speaking world.

It's mesmerizing to see how, through the eighty-plus poets featured here in chronological order by the author's date of birth, the syntax of *el español* changes throughout the century. In 1892, in his condemnation of Christopher Columbus, Darío seeks to purify the language from fin de siècle Iberian indulgences. Almost half a century later, Nicolás Guillén takes the reverse approach in "Negro bembón" and "Tú no sabe inglé," wanting to make the language elastic to allow for Afro-Caribbean slang.

Guillén was a leader of Negrista poetry, an aesthetics that sought to explore the rhythms and motifs of Afro-Caribbean culture. The tension between cleanliness and contamination persists today as Spanglish, practiced by the Puerto Rican poet Giannina Braschi among others, becomes a force to reckon with. This characteristic is a prism through which to understand race in Latin American poetry.

Needless to say, there are other leading voices in twentieth-century Latin American poetry taking the tradition in alternative directions: Gabriela Mistral's feminist impulse (she is known as *"la madre de Chile,"* and since the turn of the millennium her lesbianism has complicated her status, turning her in the eyes of some into a menacing icon), the Concretismo of poets such as Haroldo de Campo that uses words to create graphic designs on the page, and Nicanor Parra's antipoetry. But Borges, Drummond de Andrade, Neruda, and Paz, at times having elements in common and at others pushing as far away from the rest as possible, sum up the region's poetic possibilities in this period: a cosmopolitanism that might verge on disdain for the urgent problems of society, contrasted with an ideological compromise that runs the risk of becoming pamphleteering.

Indeed, one of the features that strike me as recurrent is the porosity of the poetic tradition these masters have shaped, a quality that is obviously a trademark of modernity: no author is capable of being an island and the region itself is never disconnected from global trends. Authors are constantly in dialogue with other linguistic traditions, recycling ideas, adapting them to local needs. I venture to think that the originality of post-Modernista Latin American poetry is precisely its spongelike quality: to be like Pierre Menard, adapting other works, making them acquire a new authenticity.

This characteristic goes further. To me one of the intriguing vicissitudes of this effort—call it Menardismo—is the deliberate verbal switch by some poets, an act (an art, too) of automatically inserting oneself in another tradition. Borges's experiments with English and Huidobro's with French abound in the Latin American poetic tradition. One instance among many is Julia de Burgos, a Puerto Rican in New York City (although, like Braschi, not quite a *nuyorriqueña*), who wrote her existential salvo "Farewell from Welfare Island" in English. And, of course, there is the verbal promiscuity, such as the Gallicisms that abound from Darío's work to that of the Argentine María Negroni, as well as the ubiquity of Anglicisms in almost every practitioner, a natural component when one considers the impact, since World War II, of U.S. popular culture in Latin America's everyday life.

Then there's travel as a poet's lifestyle. Poets, like other moderns (maybe more?), constantly move back and forth, physically and figuratively, serving as communicating vessels. The dialogue that results from this exchange is substantial. The Cuban poet Heberto Padilla, who was at the center of a political storm in the late seventies that came to be known as "*el caso Padilla*," a political affair in which Fidel Castro's government made him publicly apologize for crimes against the state enjoyed trotting around, not only in the world but through the past. His poems "Ana Frank" and "Retrato del poeta como un duende joven" are proof of his affinity. Alberto Blanco, from Mexico, not only surveys remote, at times imaginary societies, but cartography as an intellectual endeavor, in poems such as "Mapas."

Another major force that defines Latin American poetry in the twentieth century is immigration, and its effects are palpable in poetry. A compendium of immigrant writers to the region, from Italy, Japan, Russia, France, Germany, and the United States, not to mention Spain, is still unavailable. I'm not referring to literary travelers, of which there are a zillion, but to full-fledged migrants, refugees, and exiles, people who after a while adapt themselves, willingly and otherwise, to the prevailing mores. There is a unique Latin American literature in languages such as Afrikaans, Cantonese, and Yiddish.

These examples, along with indigenous poets featured in this anthology, and those looking at them for inspiration such as Alfonso Reyes, not only serve as a reminder of linguistic dimensions that prevail as undercurrents in the region's poetry but as a manifestation of another dimension: religion as a constant theme. The function of poetry in pre-Columbian Latin America was, first and foremost, as a theological conduit. During the colonial period it served to express religious feelings. It was with the age of independence, as secularism acquired a unifying societal role, that the topic became suspect among poets. However, this suspicion, as it turns out, was an excuse for spirituality to mutate into other religious manifestations. Darío's Catholic views are patent in "Lo fatal," and César Vallejo's in "Masa" are profound. (Thomas Merton called Vallejo "a modern Dante.") Ak'Abal explores Mayan theology and Myriam Moscona is fascinated with Jewish mysticism.

Parallel to this exploration is the sexual explicitness to be found in the Latin American poetic tradition. While the Hispanic world in the sixties underwent a revolution of social conventions, it never came close to its north-of-the-border Beatnik equivalent. Yet precisely because of the repression that Catholicism has exerted, an erotic component in the region has been evident, especially in the pen of women, since colonial times. Sor Juana Inés de la Cruz wrote the sonnet "Detente, sombra . . . ," a diatribe on the unstoppable needs of the flesh. The uninhibitedness of Delmira Agustini's "Fiera de amor" is equally significant.

Since the Spanish-American War of 1898, Latin America has maintained a love-hate relationship with the United States. It is seen as an intrusive force as well as a fountain of inspiration. The ambivalence is clear among the Modernistas, especially Darío, who looked at Theodore Roosevelt as a menace and English as a pervasive presence in daily parlance. José Enrique Rodó, a crucial essayist of Darío's generation, in his book *Ariel*, cautioned the Spanish-speaking youth of the Americas not to let the materialism of the neighboring north colonize their idealistic side. Neruda was more nuanced. In the segment from "Que despierte el leñador," included in this volume, he celebrates the average American as a sibling. The duality is patent in the way twentieth-century Latin American poets admire antiestablishment models such as Walt Whitman, Emily Dickinson, Robert Frost, William Carlos Williams, and Allen Ginsberg. They see in them a lesson in courage as well as an antidote to the imperial disdain of the United States.

Translating this work into English is an attempt to bridge the geographical, cultural, and linguistic divide to which poets are permanently calling attention. It is an endeavor that reaches back to the dusk of pre-Modernista times, after the Monroe Doctrine. Yet it became a favorite activity in the second half of the twentieth century, as an expected reaction to the Good Neighbor Policy. The translator must make the text come alive in the receiving language: not the equivalent words, but magic, ought to be the outcome. To some degree, that means betraying the original in some respect, making it malleable, and a trampoline. There's a plethora of fresh English renditions done specially for this anthology.

I have also embraced an army of superb translators whose versions are available. For instance, we owe W. S. Merwin the capacity to read the early Neruda in crystalline form. Similarly, Mark Strand not only translates, but re-creates, the stanzas of Carlos Drummond de Andrade. Richard Wilbur's versions of Borges and Vinícius de Moraes are inspiring. James Wright makes Cecilia Meireles have a Harlem groove and Achy Obejas translates Nicolás Guillén not into English but into Ebonics. Equally César Vallejo's difficult syntax isn't lost, but reconfigured, in Margaret Sayers Peden's renditions. The reader is likely to welcome other pairings, such as Elizabeth Bishop connecting with Octavio Paz, and Galway Kinnell with João Cabral de Melo Neto. Then there's Samuel Beckett, whose spoken Spanish was, as he himself acknowledged, quite limited, but who rendered some early twentieth-century Mexican poets into English in astonishing fashion. In my view, several of his translations are unsurpassable. And Giannina Braschi locates her poetry in the very act of translation, neither here nor there.

This anthology, in short, refuses to accept Robert Frost's dictum that poetry is what gets lost in translation. Just the opposite: poetry refurbishes itself through translation because translation is power.

THE FSG BOOK OF TWENTIETH-CENTURY LATIN AMERICAN POETRY

DE **VERSOS SENCILLOS**

I

Yo soy un hombre sincero
De donde crece la palma,
Y antes de morirme quiero
Echar mis versos del alma.

Yo vengo de todas partes,
Y hacia todas partes voy;
Arte soy entre las artes,
En los montes, monte soy.

Yo sé los nombres extraños
De las yerbas y las flores,
Y de mortales engaños,
Y de sublimes dolores.

Yo he visto en la noche oscura
Llover sobre mi cabeza
Los rayos de lumbre pura
De la divina belleza.

JOSÉ MARTÍ

Cuba **1853–1895**

FROM SIMPLE VERSES

I

I am an honest man
from where the palm tree grows,
and I want, before I die,
to cast these verses from my soul.

I come from all places
and to all places go:
I am art among the arts
and mountain among mountains.

I know the strange names
of flowers and herbs
and of fatal deceptions
and magnificent griefs.

In night's darkness I've seen
raining down on my head
pure flames, flashing rays
of beauty divine.

Alas nacer vi en los hombros
De las mujeres hermosas:
Y salir de los escombros
Volando las mariposas.

He visto vivir a un hombre
Con el puñal al costado,
Sin decir jamás el nombre
De aquella que lo ha matado.

Rápida, como un reflejo,
Dos veces vi el alma, dos:
Cuando murió el pobre viejo,
Cuando ella me dijo adiós.

Temblé una vez,—en la reja,
A la entrada de la viña,—
Cuando la bárbara abeja
Picó en la frente a mi niña.

Gocé una vez, de tal suerte
Que gocé cual nunca:—cuando
La sentencia de mi muerte
Leyó el alcaide llorando.

Oigo un suspiro, a través
De las tierras y la mar,
Y no es un suspiro,—es
Que mi hijo va a despertar.

Wings I saw springing
from fair women's shoulders,
and from beneath rubble
I've seen butterflies flutter.

I've seen a man live
with a knife in his side,
never speaking the name
of the woman who killed him.

Quick, as a reflection,
I saw the soul, twice:
When the poor old man died,
and when she told me good-bye.

Once I trembled, at the bars
of the vineyard gate—
when a savage bee stung
the forehead of my little girl.

Once I reveled in a destiny
like no other joy I'd known:
when the warden—reading
my death sentence—wept.

I hear a sigh that passes
over lands and seas,
and it is not a sigh—it is
my son, awakening from sleep.

Si dicen que del joyero
Tome la joya mejor,
Tomo a un amigo sincero
Y pongo a un lado el amor.

Yo he visto al águila herida
Volar al azul sereno,
Y morir en su guarida
La víbora del veneno.

Yo sé bien que cuando el mundo
Cede, lívido, al descanso,
Sobre el silencio profundo
Murmura el arroyo manso.

Yo he puesto la mano osada,
De horror y júbilo yerta,
Sobre la estrella apagada
Que cayó frente a mi puerta.

Oculto en mi pecho bravo
La pena que me lo hiere:
El hijo de un pueblo esclavo
Vive por él, calla, y muere.

Todo es hermoso y constante,
Todo es música y razón,
Y todo, como el diamante,
Antes que luz es carbón.

If I'm told to choose
the jeweler's finest gem,
I'll leave love aside
and take an honest friend.

I've seen the wounded eagle
soar through serene azure;
I've watched the viper die
of venom in its lair.

I know that when the world
surrenders, pallid, to repose,
the murmur of a tranquil stream
through the deep silence flows.

I've set my daring hand
stiff with horror and exultation,
upon a fallen star
that lay lifeless at my door.

In my bold breast I hide
the pain that ever wounds it:
the son of a people enslaved
lives for them, falls silent, dies.

All is beautiful and unceasing,
all is music and reason,
and all, like the diamond,
is carbon first, then light.

Yo sé que el necio se entierra
Con gran lujo y con gran llanto,—
Y que no hay fruta en la tierra
Como la del camposanto.

Callo, y entiendo, y me quito
La pompa del rimador:
Cuelgo de un árbol marchito
Mi muceta de doctor.

AMOR DE CIUDAD GRANDE

De gorja son y rapidez los tiempos.
Corre cual luz la voz; en alta aguja,
Cual nave despeñada en sirte horrenda,
Húndese el rayo, y en ligera barca
El hombre, como alado, el aire hiende.
¡Así el amor, sin pompa ni misterio
Muere, apenas nacido, de saciado!
¡Juala es la villa de palomas muertas
Y ávidos cazadores! Si los pechos
¡Se rompen de los hombres, y las carnes
Rotas por tierra ruedan, no han de verse
Dentro más que frutillas estrujadas!

Se ama de pie, en las calles, entre el polvo
De los salones y las plazas; muere
La flor que nace. Aquella virgen
Trémula que antes a la muerte daba
La mano pura que a ignorado mozo;

I know that fools are buried
with much luxury and wailing—
and that no fruit on earth can rival
the cemetery's crop.

I fall silent, and understand,
and drop my rhymester's show:
Upon a barren tree I hang
my fine scholar's robes.

*Translated by
Esther Allen*

LOVE IN THE BIG CITY

Times of gorge and rush are these:
Voices fly like light; lightning,
like a ship hurled upon dread quicksand,
plunges down the high rod, and in delicate craft
man, as if winged, cleaves the air.
And love, without splendor or mystery,
dies when newly born, of glut!
The city is a cage of dead doves
and avid hunters! If men's bosoms
were to open and their torn flesh
fall to the earth, inside would be
nothing but a splatter of small, crushed fruit!

Love happens in the street, standing in the dust
of saloons and public squares: the flower
dies the day it's born. The trembling
virgin who would rather death
have her than some unknown youth;

El goce de temer; aquel salirse
Del pecho el corazón; el inefable
Placer de merecer; el grato susto
De caminar de prisa en derechura
Del hogar de la amada, y a sus puertas
Como un niño feliz romper en llanto;—
Y aquel mirar, de nuestro amor al fuego,
Irse tiñendo de color las rosas,—
¡Ea, que son patrañas! Pues ¿quién tiene
tiempo de ser hidalgo? ¡Bien que sienta
Cual áureo vaso o lienzo suntuoso,
Dama gentil en casa de magnate!
¡O si se tiene sed, se alarga el brazo
Y a la copa que pasa se la apura!
Luego, la copa turbia al polvo rueda,
¡Y el hábil catador,—manchado el pecho
De una sangre invisible,—sigue alegre,
Coronado de mirtos, su camino!
¡No son los cuerpos ya sino desechos,
Y fosas, y jirones! ¡Y las almas
No son como en el árbol fruta rica
En cuya blanda piel la almíbar dulce
En su sazón de madurez rebosa,—
Sino fruta de plaza que a brutales
Golpes el rudo labrador madura!

¡La edad es ésta de los labios secos!
¡De las noches sin sueño! ¡De la vida
Estrujada en agraz! ¿Qué es lo que falta
Que la ventura falta? Como liebre
Azorada, el espíritu se esconde,
Trémulo huyendo al cazador que ríe,

the joy of trepidation; that feeling of heart
set free from chest; the ineffable
pleasure of deserving; the sweet alarm
of walking quick and straight
from your love's home and breaking
into tears like a happy child;—
and that gazing of our love at the fire,
as roses slowly blush a deeper color,—
Bah, it's all a sham! Who has the time
to be noble? Though like a golden
bowl or sumptuous painting
a genteel lady sits in the magnate's home!
But if you're thirsty reach out your arm,
and drain some passing cup!
The dirtied cup rolls to the dust, then,
and the expert taster—breast blotted
with invisible blood—goes happily,
crowned with myrtle, on his way!
Bodies are nothing now but trash,
pits, and tatters! And souls
are not the tree's lush fruit
down whose tender skin runs
sweet juice in time of ripeness,—
but fruit of the marketplace, ripened
by the hardened laborer's brutal blows!

It is an age of dry lips!
Of undreaming nights! Of life
crushed unripe! What is it that we lack,
without which there is no gladness? Like a startled
hare in the wild thicket of our breast,
fleeing, tremulous, from a gleeful hunter,

cual en soto selvoso, en nuestro pecho;
Y el deseo, de brazo de la fiebre,
Cual rico cazador recorre el soto.

¡Me espanta la ciudad! ¡Toda está llena
De copas por viciar, o huecas copas!
¡Tengo miedo ¡ay de mí! de que este vino
Tósigo sea, y en mis venas luego
Cual duende vengador los dientes clave!
¡Tengo sed,—mas de un vino que en la tierra
No se sabe beber! ¡No he padecido
Bastante aún, para romper el muro
Que me aparta ¡oh dolor! de mi viñedo!
¡Tomad vosotros, catadores ruines
De vinillos humanos, esos vasos
Donde el jugo de lirio a grandes sorbos
Sin compasión y sin temor se bebe!
¡Tomad! ¡Yo soy honrado, y tengo miedo!

DOS PATRIAS

Dos patrias tengo yo: Cuba y la noche.
¿O son una las dos? No bien retira
Su majestad el sol, con largos velos
Y un clavel en la mano, silenciosa
Cuba cual viuda triste me aparece.
¡Yo sé cuál es ese clavel sangriento
Que en la mano le tiembla! Está vacío
Mi pecho, destrozado está y vacío

the spirit takes cover;
and desire, on fever's arm,
beats the thicket, like the rich hunter.

    The city appals me! Full
Of cups to be emptied, and empty cups!
I fear—ah me!—that this wine
May be poison, and sink its teeth,
Vengeful imp, in my veins!
I thirst—but for a wine that none on earth
knows how to drink! I have not yet
endured enough to break through the wall
that keeps me—ah grief!—from my vineyard!
Take, oh squalid tasters
of humble human wines, these cups
from which, with no fear or pity,
you swill the lily's juice!
Take them! I am honorable, and I am afraid!

*Translated by
Esther Allen*

TWO HOMELANDS

    I have two homelands: Cuba and the night.
Or are they one and the same? No sooner
does his majesty, the sun, retire, than Cuba, with long veils,
and a carnation in hand, silent,
like a sad widow, appears before me.
I know that bleeding carnation
Trembling in her hand! It's empty,
my chest is destroyed and empty,

En donde estaba el corazón. Ya es hora
De empezar a morir. La noche es buena
Para decir adiós. La luz estorba
Y la palabra humana. El universo
Habla mejor que el hombre.

                           Cual bandera
Que invita a batallar, la llama roja
De la vela flamea. Las ventanas
Abro, ya estrecho en mí. Muda, rompiendo
Las hojas del clavel, como una nube
Que enturbia el cielo, Cuba, viuda, pasa . . .

where the heart once was. It's time
to begin dying. The night is right
to say good-bye. The light is bothersome
and the word is human. The universe
speaks better than man.
                              Like a flag
inviting us to battle, the candle's
red flame flickers. I open the windows
overwhelmed inside. Mute, plucking
the carnation's leaves, like a cloud
darkening the sky, Cuba, a widow, passes by . . .

Translated by
Ilan Stavans

UN POEMA

Soñaba en ese entonces en forjar un poema,
de arte nervioso y nuevo obra audaz y suprema;

escogí entre un asunto grotesco y otro trágico,
llamé a todos los ritmos con un conjuro mágico

y los ritmos indóciles vinieron acercándose,
juntándose en las sombras, huyéndose y buscándose,

ritmos sonoros, ritmos potentes, ritmos graves,
unos cual choques de armas, otros cual cantos de aves,

de Oriente hasta Occidente, desde el Sur hasta el Norte
de metros y de formas se presentó la corte.

Tascando frenos áureos bajo las riendas frágiles
cruzaron los tercetos, como corceles ágiles;

abriéndose ancho paso por entre aquella grey
vestido de oro y púrpura llegó el soneto rey,

JOSÉ ASUNCIÓN SILVA

Colombia 1865–1896

A POEM

I dreamed in those days of fashioning a poem
of nervous and novel art, daring and superior labor;

I chose between one matter, grotesque; another, tragic;
I called all rhythms with magic invocation

and the untamed rhythms came,
gathering in the shadows, running away and seeking each other,

echoing rhythms, vigor-filled rhythms, solemn rhythms,
some from the clash of weapons, others from the songs of birds,

from East to West, from South to North,
meters and forms came to royal court.

Hammering golden frames below the fragile reins
tercets crossed, like agile stallions;

breaking open a wide walkway, for among that herd,
garbed in gold and purple, the royal sonnet stepped in,

y allí cantaron todos . . . Entre la algarabía,
me fascinó el espíritu, por su coquetería

alguna estrofa aguda que excitó mi deseo
con el retintín claro de su campanilleo.

Y la escogí entre todas . . . Por regalo nupcial
le di unas rimas ricas, de plata y de cristal.

En ella conté un cuento, que huyendo lo servil,
tomó un carácter trágico, fantástico y sutil,

era la historia triste, desprestigiada y cierta
de una mujer hermosa, idolatrada y muerta,

y para que sintieran la amargura, exprofeso
junté sílabas dulces como el sabor de un beso,

bordé las frases de oro, les di música extraña,
como de mandolinas que un laúd acompaña,

dejé en una luz vaga las hondas lejanías
llenas de nieblas húmedas y de melancolías

y por el fondo oscuro, como en mundana fiesta
cruzan ágiles máscaras al compás de la orquesta,

envueltas en palabras que ocultan como un velo,
y con caretas negras de raso y terciopelo,

cruzar hice en el fondo las vagas sugestiones
de sentimientos místicos y humanas tentaciones . . .

and all that sang there ... Within the racket,
the spirit rapt me, with its flirting

one witty stanza goaded my longing
with its clear, chimed ringing.

And I picked it among the rest ... As a wedding gift,
I gave it rich rhymes, of silver and crystal.

In it I sang a tale which, far from servile,
staged a tragic man, fantastic and subtle,

it was the sad story, disreputable and true,
of a beautiful woman, worshipped and departed,

and so my readers might feel the bitter-felt grief, I aimed
to join sweet syllables as with the taste of a kiss,

I embroidered expressions with gold, gave them eccentric music,
like mandolins accompanied by a lute,

I set a nebulous light in the deep distances
full of dampened mists and melancholies

and in the dark depths, as in a dreary festivity
agile masks cross paths, following the orchestra's compass,

wrapped in words obscure as veils,
and with black masks of satin and velvet

I joined in the background vague insinuations
of mystical sentiments and human temptations ...

Complacido en mis versos, con orgullo de artista,
les di olor de heliotropos y color de amatista . . .

Le mostré mi poema a un crítico estupendo . . .
y lo leyó seis veces y me dijo . . . ¡No entiendo!

Pleased with my verse, with artist's pride,
I gave it the scent of heliotrope and the shade of amethyst . . .

I showed my poem to a marvelous critic . . .
and he read it six times and said, "I don't understand it."

Translated by
David Francis

A ROOSEVELT

Es con voz de la Biblia, o verso de Walt Whitman,
que habría de llegar hasta ti, Cazador,
primitivo y moderno, sencillo y complicado,
con un algo de Washington y cuatro de Nemrod.

Eres los Estados Unidos,
eres el futuro invasor
de la América ingenua que tiene sangre indígena,
que aún reza a Jesucristo y aún habla en español.

Eres soberbio y fuerte ejemplar de tu raza;
eres culto, eres hábil; te opones a Tolstoy.
Y domando caballos, o asesinando tigres,
eres un Alejandro-Nabucodonosor.
(Eres un profesor de energía,
como dicen los locos de hoy.)

Crees que la vida es incendio,
que el progreso es erupción,

RUBÉN DARÍO

Nicaragua **1867–1916**

TO ROOSEVELT

The voice that would reach you, Hunter, must speak
with biblical tones, or in the poetry of Walt Whitman.
You are primitive and modern, simple and complex;
you are one part George Washington and one part Nimrod.

You are the United States,
future invader of our naïve America
with its Indian blood, an America
that still prays to Christ and still speaks Spanish.

You are a strong, proud model of your race;
you are cultured and able; you oppose Tolstoy.
You are an Alexander-Nebuchadnezzar,
breaking horses and murdering tigers.
(You are a professor of energy,
as the current lunatics say.)

You think that life is a fire,
that progress is an irruption,

que en donde pones la bala
el porvenir pones.
    No.

    Los Estados Unidos son potentes y grandes.
Cuando ellos se estremecen hay un hondo temblor
que pasa por las vértebras enormes de los Andes.
Si clamáis, se oye como el rugir del león.
Ya Hugo a Grant lo dijo: Las estrellas son vuestras.
(Apenas brilla, alzándose, el argentino sol
y la estrella chilena se levanta . . .) Sois ricos.
Juntáis al culto de Hércules el culto de Mammón;
y alumbrando el camino de la fácil conquista,
a Libertad levanta su antorcha en Nueva York.

    Mas la América nuestra, que tenía poetas
desde los viejos tiempos de Netzahualcóyotl,
que ha guardado las huellas de los pies del gran Baco,
que el alfabeto pánico en un tiempo aprendió;
que consultó los astros, que conoció la Atlántida
cuyo nombre nos llega resonado en Platón,
que desde los remotos momentos de su vida
vive de luz, de fuego, de perfume, de amor,
la América del grande Moctezuma, del Inca,
la América fragante de Cristóbal Colón,
la América católica, la América española,
la América en que dijo el noble Guatemoc:
"Yo no estoy en un lecho de rosas"; esa América
que tiembla de huracanes y que vive de amor,
hombres de ojos sajones y alma bárbara, vive.
Y sueña. Y ama, y vibra, y es la hija del Sol.
Tened cuidado. ¡Vive la América española!

that the future is wherever
your bullet strikes.
      No.

   The United States is grand and powerful.
Whenever it trembles, a profound shudder
runs down the enormous backbone of the Andes.
If it shouts, the sound is like the roar of a lion.
And Hugo said to Grant: The stars are yours.
(The dawning Argentine sun barely shines;
the star of Chile is rising . . .) A wealthy country,
joining the cult of Mammon to the cult of Hercules;
while Liberty, lighting the path
to easy conquest, raises her torch in New York.

   But our own America, which has had poets
since the ancient times of Nezahualcóyotl,
which preserved the footprints of great Bacchus,
and learned the Panic alphabet once,
and consulted the stars; which also knew Atlantis
(whose name comes ringing down to us in Plato)
and has lived, since the earliest moments in life,
in light, in fire, in fragrance, and in love—
the America of Moctezuma and Atahualpa,
the aromatic America of Columbus,
Catholic America, Spanish America,
the America where noble Cuauhtémoc said:
"I am not on a bed of roses"—our America,
trembling with hurricanes, trembling with love:
O men with Saxon eyes and barbarous souls,
our America lives. And dreams. And loves and pulsates,
and it is the daughter of the Sun. Be careful.
Long live Spanish America!

Hay mil cachorros sueltos del León Español.
Se necesitaría, Roosevelt, ser, por Dios mismo,
el Riflero terrible y el fuerte Cazador,
para poder tenernos en vuestras férreas garras.

Y, pues contáis con todo, falta una cosa: ¡Dios!

SONATINA

La princesa está triste . . . ¿Qué tendrá la princesa?
Los suspiros se escapan de su boca de fresa
que ha perdido la risa, que ha perdido el color.
La princesa está pálida en su silla de oro,
está mudo el teclado de su clave sonoro,
y en un vaso olvidada se desmaya una flor.

El jardín puebla el triunfo de los pavos reales;
parlanchina, la dueña dice cosas banales,
y vestido de rojo piruetea el bufón.
La princesa no ríe, la princesa no siente;
la princesa persigue por el cielo de Oriente
la libélula vaga de una vaga ilusión.

¿Piensa acaso en el príncipe de Golconda o de China
O en el que ha detenido su carroza argentina
para ver de sus ojos la dulzura de luz?
¿O en el rey de las islas de las rosas fragantes,
o en el que es soberano de los claros diamantes,
o en el dueño orgulloso de las perlas de Ormuz?

A thousand cubs of the Spanish lion are roaming free.
Roosevelt, you must become, by God's own will,
the deadly Rifleman and the dreadful Hunter
before you can clutch us in your iron claws.

And though you have everything, you are lacking one thing: God!

*Translated by
Lysander Kemp*

SONATINA

The princess is sad. What ails the princess?
Nothing but sighs escape from her lips,
which have lost their smile and their strawberry red.
The princess is pale in her golden chair,
the keys of her harpsichord gather dust,
and a flower, forgotten, droops in its vase.

The garden is bright with the peacocks' triumph,
the duenna prattles of commonplace things,
the clown pirouettes in his crimson and gold;
but the princess is silent, her thoughts are far-off:
the princess traces the dragonfly course
of a vague illusion in the eastern sky.

Are her thoughts of a prince of Golconda or China?
Of a prince who has halted his silver coach
to see the soft light that glows in her eyes?
Of the king of the fragrant isle of roses,
or the lord who commands the clear-shining diamonds,
or the arrogant lord of the pearls of Ormuz?

¡Ay! la pobre princesa de la boca de rosa
quiere ser golondrina, quiere ser mariposa,
tener alas ligeras, bajo el cielo volar,
ir al sol por la escala luminosa de un rayo,
saludar a los lirios con los versos de Mayo,
o perderse en el viento sobre el trueno del mar.

Ya no quiere el palacio, ni la rueca de plata,
ni el halcón encantado, ni el bufón escarlata,
ni los cisnes unánimes en el lago de azur.
Y están tristes las flores por la flor de la corte;
los jazmines de Oriente, los nelumbos del Norte,
de Occidente las dalias y las rosas del Sur.

¡Pobrecita princesa de los ojos azules!
Está presa en sus oros, está presa en sus tules,
en la jaula de mármol del palacio real;
el palacio soberbio que vigilan los guardas,
que custodian cien negros con sus cien alabardas,
un lebrel que no duerme y un dragón colosal.

¡Oh, quién fuera hipsipila que dejó la crisálida!
(La princesa está triste. La princesa está pálida.)
¡Oh visión adorada de oro, rosa y marfil!
¡Quién volara a la tierra donde un príncipe existe
(La princesa está pálida. La princesa está triste.)
más brillante que el alba, más hermoso que Abril!

Calla, calla, princesa—dice el hada madrina—
en caballo con alas hacia acá se encamina,
en el cito la espada y en la mano el azor,

Alas, the poor princess, whose mouth is a rose,
who wants to be a swallow, a butterfly,
would skim on light wings, or mount to the sun
on the luminous stair of a golden sunbeam;
would greet the lilies with the verses of May,
or be lost in the wind on the thundering sea.

She is tired of the palace, the silver distaff,
the enchanted falcon, the scarlet buffoon,
the swans reflected on the azure lake.
And the flowers are sad for the flower of the court:
the jasmines of the east, the water lilies of the north,
the dahlias of the west, and the roses of the south.

The poor little princess with the wide blue eyes
is imprisoned in her gold, imprisoned in her tulle,
in the marble cage of the royal palace,
the lofty palace that is guarded by sentries,
by a hundred Negroes with a hundred halberds,
a sleepless greyhound, and the monstrous dragon.

Oh to be a butterfly leaving its cocoon!
(The princess is sad. The princess is pale.)
Oh, adorable vision of gold, marble, and rose!
Oh to fly to the land where there is a prince—
(The princess is pale. The princess is sad.)—
more brilliant than daybreak, more handsome than April!

"Hush, Princess, hush," says her fairy godmother;
"the joyous knight who adores you unseen
is riding this way on his wingèd horse,

el feliz caballero que te adora sin verte,
y que llega de lejos, vencedor de la Muerte,
a encenderte los labios con su beso de amor.

AMA TU RITMO ...

Ama tu ritmo y ritma tus acciones
bajo su ley, así como tus versos;
eres un universo de universos
y tu alma una fuente de canciones.

La celeste unidad que presupones
hará brotar en ti mundos diversos,
y al resonar tus números dispersos
pitagoriza en tus constelaciones.

Escucha la retórica divina
del pájaro del aire y la nocturna
irradiación geométrica adivina;

mata la indiferencia taciturna
y engarza perla y perla cristalina
en donde la verdad vuelca su urna.

Translated by
Lysander Kemp

a sword at his waist and a hawk on his wrist,
and comes from far-off, having conquered Death,
to kindle your lips with a kiss of true love!"

LOVE YOUR RHYTHM . . .

Love your rhythm and rhythmize your deeds.
Obey its laws, as in your poetry.
You're a cosmos in a cosmos set free.
Be the fountain of songs that your soul needs.

The celestial oneness you surely are
will make worlds sprout in you that are diverse,
and if your meters start to sound dispersed,
use Pythagoras to unite your stars.

Hear divine rhetoric in each feather
of every bird that takes to air, and learn
nighttime geometric heat and weather.

Kill all indifference that is taciturn
and string pearl on crystal together
in the place where truth tips over its urn.

Translated by
Greg Simon and
Steven F. White

LO FATAL

A René Pérez

Dichoso el árbol que es apenas sensitivo,
y más la piedra dura, porque ésa ya no siente,
pues no hay dolor más grande que el dolor de ser vivo,
ni mayor pesadumbre que la vida consciente.

Ser, y no saber nada, y ser sin rumbo cierto,
y el temor de haber sido y un futuro terror . . .
Y el espanto seguro de estar mañana muerto,
y sufrir por la vida y por la sombra y por

lo que no conocemos y apenas sospechamos,
y la carne que tienta con sus frescos racimos,
y la tumba que aguarda con sus fúnebres ramos,
¡y no saber adónde vamos,
ni de dónde venimos! . . .

LO FATAL

To René Pérez

The tree is happy for it is barely sentient,
and all the more the hard rock for it feels nothing.
There's no greater pain than being alive,
no bigger despair than conscious life.

To be and not to know, to be without a path,
the dread of having been and a terror to come ...
The sure fright of being dead tomorrow,
to suffer for life, through darkness, and for

that which we know not and barely suspect,
the flesh that tempts with its new fruit,
the tomb that awaits with its funeral sprays,
not to know where we go,
nor where we came from ... !

*Translated by
Ilan Stavans*

EL ALBA

Las auroras pálidas,
Que nacen entre penumbras misteriosas,
Y enredados en las orlas de sus mantos
Llevan jirones de sombra,
Iluminan las montañas,
Las crestas de las montañas, rojas;
Bañan las torres erguidas,
Que saludan su aparición silenciosa,
Con la voz de sus campanas
Soñolienta y ronca;
Ríen en las calles
Dormidas de la ciudad populosa,
Y se esparcen en los campos
Donde el invierno respeta las amarillentas hojas.
Tienen perfumes de Oriente
Las auroras;
Los recogieron al paso, de las florestas ocultas
De una extraña flora.
Tienen ritmos y músicas harmoniosas,
Porque oyeron los gorjeos y los trinos de las aves

RICARDO JAIMES FREIRE

Bolivia 1868–1933

THE DAWN

Colorless dawns,
born among mysterious penumbras,
carry shreds of darkness with them
tangled in the fringes of their cloaks;
they illuminate the mountains,
the crests of the mountains, reddish;
they wash across the proud towers,
which salute their silent manifestation
with the sleepy and hoarse
voice of their bells;
they laugh through the drowsy
streets of the crowded city
and disperse across the fields
where winter honors the yellowing leaves.
The dawns contain
perfumes of the Orient,
having gathered them, in passing, from the secret forests
of an unfamiliar flora.
They bring a rhythmic, harmonious music,
for they have heard the trills and warbles

35

Exóticas.
De pronto, un terremoto mueve las casas viejas
y la gente en los patios y calles se arrodilla

medio desnuda y clama: "¡Santo Dios! ¡Santo fuerte!
¡Santo inmortal!" La tierra tiembla a cada momento.
¡Algo de apocalíptico mano invisible vierte! . . .

La atmósfera es pesada como plomo. No hay viento.
Y se diría que has pasado la Muerte
ante la impasibilidad del firmamento.

of exotic birds.
When suddenly an earthquake shakes the old houses,
and the people kneel to pray in the streets and patios,

    half naked, crying: "Dear God! Powerful God!
Immortal God!" The earth trembles each moment,
as if it were shaken by some invisible and apocalyptic hand—

    The air is heavy as lead. There is no wind.
And it could be said that Death has passed this way
under the impassivity of the firmament.

*Translated by
Víctor Tulli*

Y TÚ, ESPERANDO . . .

Pasan las hoscas noches cargadas de astros,
pasan los cegadores días bermejos,
pasa el gris de las lluvias, huyen las nubes
. . . ¡y tú, esperando!

¡Tú, esperando y las horas no tienen prisa!
¡Con qué pereza mueven las plantas torpes!
Las veinticuatro hermanas llevar parecen
zuecos de plomo.

Esa rosa encendida ya se presiente
entre los gajos verdes de su justillo.
Entre los gajos verdes su carne santa
es un milagro.

¡Pero cuándo veremos la rosa abierta!
Dios eterno, Tú nunca te precipitas;
mas el hombre se angustia porque es efímero.
¡Señor, cuándo veremos la rosa abierta!

AMADO NERVO

Mexico 1870-1919

AND THOU, EXPECTANT . . .

Fraught with stars the dark nights come and go
and come and go the dazzling coral days
and the grey of the rains and the fleeting clouds
. . . and thou, expectant.

Thou expectant and the lingering hours!
How languidly they stir, the torpid plants!
It seems the four-and-twenty sisters are shod
with clogs of lead.

This incandescent rose impends already
within the verdant clusters of its bodice.
Within the verdant clusters the wonder lurks
of its sacred flesh.

But when shall we behold the open rose!
Eternal God, thou never makest haste,
but man is anxious, being ephemeral.
Lord, when shall we behold the open rose!

*Translated by
Samuel Beckett*

39

TUÉRCELE EL CUELLO AL CISNE . . .

Tuércele el cuello al cisne de engañoso plumaje
que da su nota blanca al azul de la fuente:
él pasea su gracia no más, pero no siente
el alma de las cosas ni la voz del paisaje.

Huye de toda forma y de todo lenguaje
que no vayan acordes con el ritmo latente
de la vida profunda . . . y adora intensamente
la vida, y que la vida comprenda tu homenaje.

Mira al sapiente búho cómo tiende las alas
desde el Olimpo, deja el regazo de Palas
y posa en aquel árbol el vuelo taciturno . . .

Él no tiene la gracia del cisne, mas su inquieta
pupila, que se clava en la sombra, interpreta
el misterioso libro del silencio nocturno.

ENRIQUE GONZÁLEZ MARTÍNEZ

Mexico 1871–1952

WRING THE SWAN'S NECK . . .

Wring the swan's neck who with deceiving plumage
inscribes his whiteness on the azure stream;
he merely vaunts his grace and nothing feels
of nature's voice or of the soul of things.

Every form eschew and every language
whose processes with deep life's inner rhythm
are out of harmony . . . and greatly worship
life, and let life understand your homage.

See the sapient owl who from Olympus
spreads his wings, leaving Athena's lap,
and stays his silent flight on yonder tree.

His grace is not the swan's, but his unquiet
pupil, boring into the gloom, interprets
the secret book of the nocturnal still.

Translated by
Samuel Beckett

HISTORIA DE MI MUERTE

Soñé la muerte y era muy sencillo:
una hebra de seda me envolvía,
y a cada beso tuyo,
con una vuelta menos me ceñía.
Y cada beso tuyo
era un día;
y el tiempo que mediaba entre dos besos
una noche. La muerte es muy sencilla.
Y poco a poco fue desenvolviéndose
la hebra fatal. Ya no la retenía
sino por sólo un cabo entre los dedos . . .
Cuando de pronto te pusiste fría,
y ya no me besaste . . .
Y solté el cabo, y se me fue la vida.

LEOPOLDO LUGONES

Argentina **1874–1938**

STORY OF MY DEATH

I dreamed of death and it was quite simple:
a silk thread enwrapped me,
and each kiss of yours
with a turn unraveled me.
And each of your kisses
was a day;
and the time between two kisses,
a night. Death is quite simple.
And little by little the fatal thread
unwrapped itself. I no longer controlled it
but for a single bit between my fingers . . .
Then, suddenly, you became cold,
and no longer kissed me . . .
I let the thread go, and my life vanished.

*Translated by
Ilan Stavans*

EL REGRESO

La tierra ofrece el ósculo de un saludo paterno . . .
Pasta un mulo la hierba mísera del camino
y la montaña luce, al tardo sol del invierno,
como una vieja aldeana, su delantal de lino.

Un cielo bondadoso y un céfiro tierno . . .
La zagala descansa de codos bajo el pino,
y densos los ganados, con paso paulatino,
acuden a la música sacerdotal del cuerno.

Trayendo sobre el hombro leña para la cena,
el pastor, cuya ausencia no dura más de un día,
camina lentamente rumbo de la alquería.

Al verlo la familia le da la enhorabuena . . .
Mientras el perro, en ímpetus de lealtad amena,
describe coleando círculos de alegría.

JULIO HERRERA Y REISSIG

Uruguay **1875–1910**

THE RETURN

Earth offers its greeting, with a paternal kiss . . .
A mule grazes in the meager vegetation,
and in the late winter sun the mountain displays
her snowy apron, like a village matron.

A kindly sky, a gentle zephyr . . .
A shepherd-girl rests under a pine in the hollow
and in thick rows, with gradual steps, the cattle
come, obeying the priestly music of her horn.

Carrying wood to cook the evening meal,
the shepherd, whose absence from his house lasts
no more than a day, walks slowly toward the farm.

His family hurries to see him, and welcome . . .
Even the dog, who wags his lively tail,
inscribing fast circles of joy in the air.

*Translated by
Andrew Rosing*

BLASÓN

Soy el cantor de América autóctono y salvaje;
mi lira tiene un alma, mi canto un ideal.
Mi verso no se mece colgado de un ramaje
con un vaivén pausado de hamaca tropical . . .

Cuando me siento inca, le rindo vasallaje
al Sol, que me da el cetro de su poder real;
cuando me siento hispano y evoco el Coloniaje,
parecen mis estrofas trompetas de cristal . . .

Mi fantasía viene de un abolengo moro:
los Andes son de plata, pero el León de oro;
y las dos castas fundo con épico fragor.

La sangre es española e incaico es el latido;
¡y de no ser Poeta, quizás yo hubiese sido
un blanco Aventurero o un indio Emperador!

JOSÉ SANTOS CHOCANO

Peru 1875-1934

A MANIFESTO

I sing America, in its wild and autochthonous state;
my lyre has a soul, and my song has an ideal.
My poem does not hang from a branch,
calmly swinging like a tropical hammock . . .

When I feel Incan, I honor that king,
the Sun, who offers me the scepter of his royal power;
when I feel Spanish, I invoke the empire;
my strophes seem like crystal trumpets . . .

My imagination comes from ancient Moorish blood:
the Andes are of silver, but León is of gold;
I fuse both races with a noise like thunder.

My blood is Spanish and Incan in its throb;
if I were not a poet, I might have had the job
of a white adventurer, or Incan emperor!

Translated by
Andrew Rosing

47

FIERA DE AMOR

Fiera de amor, yo sufro hambre de corazones.
De palomos, de buitres, de corzos o leones,
No hay manjar que más tiente, no hay más grato sabor,
Había ya estragado mis garras y mi instinto,
Cuando erguida en la casi ultratierra de un plinto,
Me deslumbró una estatua de antiguo emperador.

 Y crecí de entusiasmo; por el tronco de piedra
Ascendió mi deseo como fulmínea hiedra
Hasta el pecho, nutrido en nieve al parecer;
Y clamé al imposible corazón . . . la escultura
Su gloria custodiaba serenísima y pura,
Con la frente en Mañana y la planta en Ayer.

 Perenne mi deseo, en el tronco de piedra
Ha quedado prendido como sangrienta hiedra;
Y desde entonces muerdo soñando un corazón
De estatua, presa suma para mi garra bella;

DELMIRA AGUSTINI

Uruguay **1886–1914**

FIERA DE AMOR

Beast of love, I suffer hunger for hearts.
Of pigeons, vultures, roe deer, or lions,
There is no more tempting prey, no more gratifying tastes,
It has already strangulated my claws and instinct,
When erected in an almost ethereal plinth,
I was fascinated by a statue of antique emperor.

And I grew in enthusiasm; through the stone stem
My desire ascended like fulminous ivy,
Up to the chest, seemingly nurtured in snow;
And I clamored to the impossible heart . . . the statue,
A custodian of its glory, pure and serene,
With its forehead in Tomorrow and its feet in Yesterday.

My perennial desire, the stone stem
Has been suspended like bloody ivy;
And since then I bite my heart while dreaming
Of the statue, supreme prisoner of my beautiful claw;

No es ni carne ni mármol: una pasta de estrella
Sin sangre, sin calor y sin palpitación . . .

¡Con la esencia de una sobrehumana pasión!

It is neither flesh nor marble: a star paste
Bloodless, with neither warmth nor palpitation . . .

With the essence of a superhuman passion!

Translated by
Ilan Stavans

LA SUAVE PATRIA

PROEMIO

Yo que sólo canté de la exquisita
partitura del íntimo decoro,
alzo hoy la voz a la mitad del foro,
a la manera del tenor que imita
la gutural modulación del bajo,
para cortar a la epopeya un gajo.

Navegaré por las olas civiles
con remos que no pesan, porque van
como los brazos del correo chuan
que remaba la Mancha con fusiles.

Diré con una épica sordina:
la Patria es impecable y diamantina.

Suave Patria: permite que te envuelva
en la más honda música de selva
con que me modelaste por entero

RAMÓN LÓPEZ VELARDE

Mexico **1888-1921**

SUAVE PATRIA: SWEET LAND

INTROIT

I who have sung only the exquisite
score of personal decorum,
today, at center stage, raise my voice
in the manner of a tenor's imitations
of the bass's deep-throated tones
to carve an ode from an epic poem.

I shall navigate through civil waves
with weightless oars, like that
patriot of yore who, with only a rifle,
rowed across the English Channel.

In a muted epic I shall tell that
our land is diamantine, impeccable.

Sweet Land: let me engulf you
in the deepest music of the jungle,
music that molded my expressions,

al golpe cadencioso de las hachas,
entre risas y gritos de muchachas
y pájaros de oficio carpintero.

PRIMER ACTO

Patria: tu superficie es el maíz,
tus minas el palacio del Rey de Oros,
y tu cielo, las garzas en desliz
y el relámpago verde de los loros.

El Niño Dios te escrituró un establo
y los veneros del petróleo el diablo.

Sobre tu Capital, cada hora vuela
ojerosa y pintada, en carretela;
y en tu provincia, del reloj en vela
que rondan los palomos colipavos,
las campanadas caen como centavos.

Patria: tu mutilado territorio
se viste de percal y de abalorio.

Suave Patria: tu casa todavía
es tan grande, que el tren va por la vía
como aguinaldo de juguetería.

Y en el barullo de las estaciones,
con tu mirada de mestiza, pones
la inmensidad sobre los corazones.

sounds of the rhythmic cadences of axes,
young girl's cries and laughter,
and birds of the carpenter profession.

ACT ONE

Patria: your surface is the gold of maize,
below, the palace of gold medallion kings,
your sky is filled with the heron's flight
and green lightening of parrot's wings.

God-the-Child deeded you a stable,
lust for oil was the gift of the devil.

Above your capital the hours soar,
hollow-eyed and roughed, in a coach-and-four,
while in your provinces the hours
roll like *centavos* from insomniac
clocks with fantail dove patrols.

Patria: your maimed terrain
is clothed in beads and bright percale.

Sweet Land: your house is still
so vast that the train rolling by seems
only a diminutive Christmas toy.

And in the tumult of the stations,
your brown-skinned face imparts
that immensity to every heart.

¿Quién, en la noche que asusta a la rana,
no miró, antes de saber del vicio,
del brazo de su novia, la galana
pólvora de los fuegos de artificio?

Suave Patria: en tu tórrido festín
luces policromías de delfín,
y con tu pelo rubio se desposa
el alma, equilibrista chuparrosa,
y a tus dos trenzas de tabaco sabe
ofrendar aguamiel toda mi briosa
raza de bailadores de jarabe.

Tu barro suena a plata, y en tu puño
su sonora miseria es alcancía;
y por las madrugadas del terruño,
en calles como espejos, se vacía
el santo olor de la panadería.

Cuando nacemos, nos regalas notas,
después, un paraíso de compotas,
y luego te regalas toda entera,
suave Patria, alacena y pajarera.

Al triste y al feliz dices que sí,
que en tu lengua de amor prueben de ti
la picadura del ajonjolí.

¡Y tu cielo nupcial, que cuando truena
de deleites frenéticos nos llena!
Trueno de nuestras nubes, que nos baña
de locura, enloquece a la montaña,

Who, on a dark and ominous night
has not, before he knew wrong, held
tight his sweetheart's arm to watch
the splendor of a fireworks display?

Patria: in your tropical abundance
you shimmer with the dolphin's iridescence;
the soul, an aerialist hummingbird,
plights its troth with your golden hair,
and, as offering to your tobacco braids,
my lively race of *jarabe* dancers
bring their honeymooned maguey waters.

Your soil rings of silver, and in your hand
even poetry's piggy bank rattles a tune,
and in early mornings across the land,
through streets like mirrors, spread
the blessed aromas of fresh-baked bread.

When we are born, you give us notes,
and compotes worthy of Paradise,
then, Sweet Land, your whole being,
all the bounty of earth and air.

To the sad and the joyful you say *sí*,
that on your loving tongue they savor
your tangy flavor of sesame.

When it thunders, your nuptial sky
fills us with frenzy and delight.
Thunderous clouds, that drench us
with madness, madden the mountain,

requiebra a la mujer, sana al lunático,
incorpora a los muertos, pide el Viático,
y al fin derrumba las madererías
de Dios, sobre las tierras labrantías.

Trueno del temporal: oigo en tus quejas
crujir los esqueletos en parejas,
oigo lo que se fue, lo que aún no toco
y la hora actual con su vientre de coco,
y oigo en el brinco de tu ida y venida,
oh trueno, la ruleta de mi vida.

INTERMEDIO

CUAUHTÉMOC

Joven abuelo: escúchame loarte,
único héroe a la altura del arte.

Anacrónicamente, absurdamente,
a tu nopal inclínase el rosal;
al idioma del blanco, tú lo imantas
y es surtidor de católica fuente
que de responsos llena el victorial
zócalo de ceniza de tus plantas.

No como a César el rubor patricio
te cubre el rostro en medio del suplicio:
tu cabeza desnuda se nos queda,
hemisféricamente, de moneda.

mend the lunatic, woo the woman,
raise the dead, demand the viaticum,
and then, finally, fling God's lumber
across tilled fields shaken with thunder.

Thunderous storm: I hear in your groans
the rattling of coupled skeletons,
I hear the past and what is to come,
I hear the present with its coconut drum,
and in the sound of your coming and going
I hear my life's roulette wheel, spinning, spinning . . .

INTERMISSION

CUAUHTÉMOC

Forever-young grandfather, hear my praise
for the only hero worthy of art.

Anachronistic, farcical,
the rose bows to your nopal;
you magnetize the Spaniard's language,
the spout from which flow Catholic prayers
to fill the triumphant *zócalo* where
the soles of your feet were scorched to ash.

Unlike Caesar, no patrician flush
suffused your face during your pain;
today, your unwreathed head appears,
hemispherically, on a coin.

Moneda espiritual en que se fragua
todo lo que sufriste: la piragua
prisionera, el azoro de tus crías,
el sollozar de tus mitologías,
la Malinche, los ídolos a nado,
y por encima, haberte desatado
del pecho curvo de la emperatriz
como del pecho de una codorniz.

SEGUNDO ACTO

Suave Patria: tú vales por el río
de las virtudes de tu mujerío;
tus hijas atraviesan como hadas,
o destilando un invisible alcohol,
vestidas con las redes de tu sol,
cruzan como botellas alambradas.

Suave Patria: te amo no cual mito,
sino por tu verdad de pan bendito,
como a niña que asoma por la reja
con la blusa corrida hasta la oreja
y la falda bajada hasta el huesito.

Inaccesible al deshonor, floreces;
creeré en ti, mientras una mejicana
en su tápalo lleve los dobleces
de la tienda, a las seis de la mañana,
y al estrenar su lujo, quede lleno
el país, del aroma del estreno.

A spiritual coin upon which is etched
all you suffered: the hollowed-out pirogue
of your capture, the chaos of your creatures,
the sobbing of your mythologies,
the swimming idols, and the Malinche,
but most to bewail is your having been severed
from the curved breast of the empress
as from the breast of a quail.

SECOND ACT

Suave Patria, this is your omen:
the river of virtues of your women.
Your daughters move like sylphs, or,
distilling an invisible alcohol,
webbed in the netting of your sun,
file by like graceful demijohns.

Patria, I love you not as myth
but for the communion of your truth,
as I love the child peering over the rail,
in a blouse buttoned up to her eartips
and skirt to her ankle of fine percale.

Impervious to dishonor, you flower.
I shall believe in you as long as
at the dawn hour one Mexican woman
carries home dough in her shawl,
and from the oven of its inauguration
the aroma spreads across the nation.

Como la sota moza, Patria mía,
en piso de metal, vives al día,
de milagro, como la lotería.

Tu imagen, el Palacio Nacional,
con tu misma grandeza y con tu igual
estatura de niño y de dedal.

Te dará, frente al hambre y al obús,
un higo San Felipe de Jesús.

Suave Patria, vendedora de chía:
quiero raptarte en la cuaresma opaca,
sobre un garañón, y con matraca,
y entre los tiros de la policía.

Tus entrañas no niegan un asilo
para el ave que el párvulo sepulta
en una caja de carretes de hilo,
y nuestra juventud, llorando, oculta
dentro de ti el cadáver hecho poma
de aves que hablan nuestro mismo idioma.

Si me ahogo en tus julios, a mí baja
desde el vergel de tu peinado denso
frescura de rebozo y de tinaja,
y si tirito, dejas que me arrope
en tu respiración azul de incienso
y en tus carnosos labios de rompope.

Por tu balcón de palmas bendecidas
el Domingo de Ramos, yo desfilo
lleno de sombra, porque tú trepidas.

Like a Queen of Hearts, *Patria*, tapping
a vein of silver, you live miraculously,
for the day, like the national lottery.

Your image is the Palacio Nacional,
the same grandeur, and the identical
stature of a boy and a thimble.

In the face of hunger and mortar, Felipe de Jesús,
saint and martyr, will give you a fig.

Suave Patria, gentle vendor of *chía*,
I want to bear you away in the dark of Lent,
riding a fiery stallion, disturbing
the peace and dodging shots from police.

Patria, your heart will always have room
for the bird a youngster tenderly
entombs in an empty spool box;
yes, in you our young hide, weeping,
the dried-apple cadavers
of birds that speak our own tongue.

If I am stifling in your July, send me
from the orchard of your hair the cool air
that brings shawls and dripping clay pitchers;
then, if I shiver, let me draw warmth
from your plump rum-punch lips
and your blue-incense breath.

Before your blessed-palm-draped balcony
I pass with heavy heart, knowing
you tremble on this Palm Sunday.

Quieren morir tu ánima y tu estilo,
cual muriéndose van las cantadoras
que en las ferias, con el bravío pecho
empitonando la camisa, han hecho
la lujuria y el ritmo de las horas.

Patria, te doy de tu dicha la clave:
sé siempre igual, fiel a tu espejo diario;
cincuenta veces al igual el *Ave*
taladrada en el hilo del rosario,
y es más feliz que tú, Patria suave.

Sé igual y fiel; pupilas de abandono;
sedienta voz, la trigarante faja
en tus pechugas al vapor; y un trono
a la intemperie, cual una sonaja:
¡la carreta alegórica de paja!

Your spirit and style are dying out,
like the vanishing goddess of song
in a country fair—indomitable bosom
challenging straining bodice—
who evoked lust along with life's rhythm.

Patria, I give you the key to happiness:
be faithful forever to your likeness:
fifty repeats of the *Ave* are carved
on the beads of the rosary, and it is
more fortunate than you, *Patria suave*.

Be constant, be true; your glory,
your eyes of abandon and thirsting voice;
tricolor sash across misty breasts,
and an open-air throne like a resonant timbrel:
allegory's straw cart!

*Translated by
Margaret Sayers Peden*

LA OLA DEL SUEÑO

A Queta Regules

La marea del sueño
comienza a llegar
desde el Santo Polo
y el último mar.

Derechamente viene,
a silbo y señal;
subiendo el mundo viene
en blanco animal.

Ha pasado Taitao,
Niebla y Chañaral,
a tu puerta y tu cuna
llega a acabar . . .

Sube del viejo Polo,
eterna y mortal.
Viene del mar Antártico
y vuelve a bajar.

GABRIELA MISTRAL

Chile 1889-1957

THE SLEEP-WAVE

To Queta Regules

It's rising now,
the tide of sleep
from the sacred south
and the final sea.

It comes straight
to whistle and call,
climbing the world,
a white animal.

It's passed Taitao,
Niebla, Chañaral,
at your door, your cradle
it's going to fall.

It rises from the ancient pole
mortal and eternal,
from the Antarctic sea
it comes, and sinks again.

67

La ola encopetada
se quiebra en el umbral.
Nos busca, nos halla
y cae sin hablar.

En cuanto ya te cubra
dejas de ronronear;
y en llegándome al pecho,
yo dejo de cantar.

Donde la casa estuvo,
está ella no más.
Donde tú mismo estabas,
ahora ya no estás.

Está la ola del sueño,
espumajeo y sal
y la Tierra inocente,
sin bien y sin mal.

La marea del sueño
comienza a llegar
desde el Santo Polo
y el último mar.

The lofty wave
breaks on our door.
It seeks us, finds us,
and silently falls.

As it covers you
you cease murmuring,
when it's up to my breast
I cease to sing.

Where the house was
it is no more.
Where you were
nobody's there:

There's only the sleep-wave's
salt foaming flood
and the innocent Earth
without evil or good.

It's rising now,
the tide of sleep
from the sacred south
and the final sea.

Translated by
Ursula K. Le Guin

LA MEDIANOCHE

Fina, la medianoche.
Oigo los nudos del rosal:
la salvia empuja subiendo a la rosa.

Oigo
las rayas quemadas del tigre
real: no le dejan dormir.

Oigo
la estrofa de uno,
y le crece en la noche
como la duna.

Oigo
a mi madre dormida
con dos alientos.
(Duermo yo en ella,
de cincos años.)

Oigo el Ródano
que baja y que me lleva como un padre
ciego de espuma ciega.

Y después nada oigo
sino que voy cayendo
en los muros de Arlés,
llenos de sol . . .

THE MIDNIGHT

Subtle, the midnight.
I hear the joints of the rosebush:
sap pushing upward to the rose.

I hear
the scorched stripes of the royal
tiger: they do not let him sleep.

I hear
somebody's song
and it spreads out in the night
like the sand dune.

I hear
my mother sleeping
breathing two breaths.
(I sleep in her,
these five years.)

I hear the Rhône,
carrying me down with it like a father
blinded with blind foam.

Then I hear nothing
but I'm falling
onto the sunny
walls of Arles . . .

*Translated by
Ursula K. Le Guin*

LA FLOR DEL AIRE

A Consuelo Salera

Yo la encontré por mi destino,
de pie a mitad de la pradera,
gobernadora del que pase,
del que le hable y que la vea.

Y ella me dijo: "Sube al monte.
Yo nunca dejo la pradera,
y me cortas las flores blancas
como nieves, duras y tiernas."

Me subí a la ácida montaña,
busqué las flores donde albean,
entre las rocas existiendo
medio-dormidas y despiertas.

Cuando bajé, con carga mía,
la hallé a mitad de la pradera,
y fui cubriéndola frenética,
con un torrente de azucenas.

Y sin mirarse la blancura,
ella me dijo: "Tú acarrea
ahora sólo flores rojas.
Yo no puedo pasar la pradera."

Trepé las peñas con el venado,
y busqué flores de demencia,

AIRFLOWER

To Consuelo Salera

My fate brought me to her
standing in the middle of the meadow,
mistress of all who pass her
or speak to her or see her.

And she told me, "Climb the mountain.
I never leave the meadow.
And pick white flowers for me,
snow-white, harsh, and tender."

I climbed the bitter mountain
and looked for the white of flowers
where among the rocks
they half-slept or wakened.

When I came down with my arms full
I found her there in the meadow,
and I poured out over her
a wild white flood of lilies.

Not looking at the whiteness,
she said to me, "Now, bring me
red flowers only.
I cannot leave the meadow."

I climbed the cliffs beside the deer,
and looked for flowers of madness,

las que rojean y parecen
que de rojez vivan y mueran.

Cuando bajé se las fui dando
con un temblor feliz de ofrenda,
y ella se puso como el agua
que en ciervo herido se ensangrienta.

Pero mirándome, sonámbula,
me dijo: "Sube y acarrea
las amarillas, las amarillas.
Yo nunca dejo la pradera."

Subí derecho a la montaña
y me busqué las flores densas,
color de sol y de azafranes,
recién nacidas y ya eternas.

Al encontrarla, como siempre,
a la mitad de la pradera,
segunda vez yo fui cubriéndola,
y la dejé como las eras.

Y todavía, loca de oro,
me dijo: "Súbete, mi sierva,
y cortarás las sin color,
ni azafranadas ni bermejas."

"Las que yo amo por recuerdo
de la Leonora y la Ligeia,
color del Sueño y de los sueños.
Yo soy Mujer de la pradera."

those that blossom red, that seem
to live and die of redness.

I came down and gave them to her,
shivering with the joy of giving,
and she turned as red as water
a wounded stag has bloodied.

But looking at me from her trance
she said, "Go up and bring me
the yellow ones, the yellow ones.
I never leave the meadow."

I went straight up the mountain
and looked for the crowded flower
color of sun and saffron,
just born, already everlasting.

Coming upon her as before
in the middle of the meadow,
I showered her with yellow
till she was like a threshing-floor.

And still, crazy with goldness,
she said, "Go up, my servant,
cut me the colorless flowers,
not saffron, not crimson:

the ones I love in memory
of Leonora and Ligeia,
sleep-color, dream-color.
I am the woman of the meadow."

Me fui ganando la montaña,
ahora negra como Medea,
sin tajada de resplandores,
como una gruta vaga y cierta.

Ellas no estaban en las ramas,
ellas no abrían en las piedras
y las corté del aire dulce,
tijereteándolo ligera.

Me las corté como si fuese
la cortadora que está ciega.
Corté de un aire y de otro aire,
Tomando el aire por mi selva . . .

Cuando bajé de la montaña
y fui buscándome a la reina,
ahora ella caminaba,
ya no era blanca ni violenta;

ella se iba, ola sonámbula,
abandonando la pradera,
y yo siguiéndola y siguiéndola
por el pastal y la alameda,

cargada así de tantas flores,
con espaldas y mano aéreas,
siempre cortándolas del aire
y con los aires como siega . . .

Ella delante va sin cara;
ella delante va sin huella,

I went high on the mountain,
now black as Medea,
without a trace of shining,
like a dim, constant cavern.

They did not grow on branches
or bloom among the stones:
I cut them from the soft air,
snipping it lightly.

I cut them as if I were
the blind thread-cutter.
Taking the air for my forest,
I cut them from one air and another.

When I came down from the mountain
and went to find the queen,
I saw her walking:
not white now, not fierce;

she went along, sleepwalking,
going away from the meadow,
and I followed her, followed her,
through pastures and poplars,

carrying all those flowers
with airy hands and arms
and still cutting them from the air
and with the winds for harvest.

Faceless she goes on before,
trackless she goes on before,

y yo la sigo todavía
entre los gajos de la niebla,

con estas flores sin color,
ni blanquecinas ni bermejas,
hasta mi entrega sobre el límite,
cuando mi Tiempo se disuelva . . .

UNA PALABRA

Yo tengo una palabra en la garganta
y no la suelto, y no me libro de ella
aunque me empuje su empellón de sangre.
Si la soltase, quema el pasto vivo,
sangra al cordero, hace caer al pájaro.

Tengo que desprenderla de mi lengua,
hallar un agujero de castores
o sepultarla con cales y cales
porque no guarde como el alma el vuelo.

No quiero dar señales del que vivo
mientras que por mi sangre vaya y venga
y suba y baje por mi loco aliento.
Aunque mi padre Job la dijo, ardiendo
no quiero darle, no, mi pobre boca
porque no ruede y la hallen las mujeres
que van al río, y se enrede a sus trenzas
y al pobre matorral tuerza y abrase.

and still I follow after her
among the wisps of fog,

    with these colorless flowers,
not white, not crimson,
till my surrender at the border
when my time may melt away . . .

Translated by
Ursula K. Le Guin

A WORD

I have a word inside my mouth
and don't let it get out and don't get rid of it,
though its blood-gush pushes at me.
If I let it out it would scorch the bright grass,
drain blood from lambs, drop birds from air.

I have to untangle it from my tongue,
find a rat-hole for it,
bury it under heaps of quicklime,
so it can't keep flying, as the soul does.

I can't show any signs of life
while it's coming and going through my blood,
and rising and falling with my crazy breathing.
My father Job spoke it as he burned,
but I can't let it use my poor mouth, no,
because it'll roll on; women will find it
as they go down to the river, it'll twist into their hair
and wither poor dry thickets up in fire.

79

Yo quiero echarle violentas semillas
que en una noche la cubran y ahoguen
sin dejar de ella el cisco de una sílaba.
O rompérmela así, como a la víbora
que por mitad se parte con los dientes.

Y volver a mi casa, entrar, dormirme,
cortada de ella, rebanada de ella,
y despertar después de dos mil días
recién nacida de sueño y olvido.

¡Sin saber más que tuve una palabra
de yodo y piedra-alumbre entre los labios
ni saber acordarme de una noche,
de una morada en país extranjero,
de la celada y el rayo a la puerta
y de mi carne marchando sin su alma!

LA OTRA

Una en mí maté:
yo no la amaba.

Era la flor llameando
del cactus de montaña;
era aridez y fuego;
nunca se refrescaba.

Piedra y cielo tenía
a pies y a espaldas

I want to sow it with seeds that grow so wild
they'll cover it overnight and swallow it
and not leave the shred of a syllable of it.
Or sever it like this, like biting
a snake in half with my teeth.

And then go home, go in, and go to sleep,
cut free from it, sliced off from it,
and wake up after a couple of thousand days
newborn out of sleep and forgetting.

Not knowing that I'd had between my lips
a word of iodine and saltpeter,
and not remembering a night,
a house in a foreign country,
the ambush, the lightning at the door,
and my body going on without its soul.

Translated by
Ursula K. Le Guin

THE OTHER WOMAN

I killed a woman in me.
I didn't love her.

She was the flower flaming
from the mountain cactus,
she was dryness and fire;
nothing could cool her.

Stone and sky she had
underfoot and around her;

81

y no bajaba nunca
a buscar "ojos de agua."

Donde hacía su siesta,
las hierbas se enroscaban
de aliento de su boca
y brasa de su cara.

En rápidas resinas
se endurecía su habla,
por no caer en linda
presa soltada.

Doblarse no sabía
la planta de montaña,
y al costado de ella,
yo me doblaba ...

La dejé que muriese,
robándole mi entraña.
Se acabó como el águila
que no es alimentada.

Sosegó el aletazo,
se dobló, lacia,
y me cayó a la mano
su pavesa acabada ...

Por ella todavía
me gimen sus hermanas,
y las gredas de fuego
al pasar me desgarran.

never did she kneel
to seek the gaze of water.

Where she lay down to rest
she withered the grass
with the heat of her breath,
the ember of her face.

Her speech hardened
quick as pitch,
so no soft charm
could be released.

She couldn't bow,
the mountain plant,
while I beside her
bowed and bent.

I left her to die,
robbing her of my heart.
She ended like that,
an eagle starved.

Her wings stopped beating,
she bowed down, spent,
and her quenched spark
dropped in my hand.

Her sisters still
mourn her, accuse me,
and the burning quicklime
claws me as I pass.

Cruzando yo les digo:
—Buscad por las quebradas
y haced con las arcillas
otra águila abrasada.

Si no podéis, entonces,
¡ay!, olvidadla.
Yo la maté. ¡Vosotras
también matadla!

Going by I tell them:
"Look in the creekbeds,
from their clays
make another fire-eagle.

If you can't,
well then, forget her!
I killed her. You, too,
you kill her!"

Translated by
Ursula K. Le Guin

Translator's note: the gaze of water: "ojos de agua," water-eyes, dialectical for springs
of water, in quotes in the original.

YERBAS DE TARAHUMARA

Han bajado los indios tarahumaras,
que es señal de mal año
y de cosecha pobre en la montaña.

Desnudos y curtidos,
duros en la lustrosa piel manchada,
denegridos de viento y sol, animan
las callas de Chihuahua,
lentos y recelosos,
con todos los resortes del miedo contraídos,
como panteras mansas.

Desnudos y curtidos,
bravos habitadores de la nieve
—como hablan de tú—
contestan siempre así la pregunta obligada:
—"Y tú ¿no tienes frío en la cara?"

Mal año en la montaña,
cuando el grave deshielo de las cumbres

ALFONSO REYES

Mexico **1889-1959**

TARAHUMARA HERBS

The Tarahumara Indians have come down,
sign of a bad year
and a poor harvest in the mountains.

Naked and tanned,
hard in their daubed lustrous skins,
blackened with wind and sun, they enliven
the streets of Chihuahua,
slow and suspicious,
all the springs of fear coiled,
like meek panthers.

Naked and tanned,
wild denizens of the snow,
they—for they thee and thou—
always answer thus the inevitable question:
"And is thy face not cold?"

A bad year in the mountains
when the heavy thaw of the peaks

escurre hasta los pueblos la manada
de animales humanos con el hato a la espalda.

La gente, al verlos, gusta
aquella desazón tan generosa
de otra belleza que la acostumbrada.

Los hicieron católicos
los misioneros de la Nueva España
—esos corderos de corazón de león.
Y, sin pan y sin vino,
ellos celebran la función cristiana
con su cerveza-chica y su pinole,
que es un polvo de todos los sabores.

Beben tesgüino de maíz y peyote,
yerba de los portentos,
sinfonía lograda
que convierte los ruidos en colores;
y larga borrachera metafísica
los compensa de andar sobre la tierra,
que es, al fin y a la postre,
la dolencia común de las razas de hombres.
Campeones del Maratón del mundo,
nutridos en la carne ácida del venado,
llegarán los primeros con el triunfo
el día que saltemos la muralla
de los cinco sentidos.

A veces, traen oro de sus ocultas minas,
y todo el día rompen los terrones,

drains down to the villages the drove
of human beasts, their bundles on their backs.

The people, seeing them, experience
that so magnanimous antipathy
for beauty unlike that to which they are used.

Into Catholics
by the New Spain missionaries they were turned
—these lion-hearted lambs.
And, without bread or wine,
they celebrated the Christian ceremony
with their chica beer and their pinole,
which is a powder of universal flavor.

They drink spirits of maize and peyote,
herb of portents,
symphony of positive aesthetics
whereby into colors forms are changed;
and ample metaphysical ebriety
consoles them for their having to tread the earth,
which is, all said and done,
the common affliction of all humankind.
The finest Marathon runners in the world,
nourished on the bitter flesh of deer,
they will be first with the triumphant news
the day we leap the wall
of the five senses.

Sometimes they bring gold from their hidden mines
and all the livelong day they break the lumps,

sentados en la calle,
entre la envidia culta de los blancos.
Hoy sólo traen yerbas en el hato,
las yerbas de salud que cambian por centavos:
yerbaniz, limoncillo, simonillo,
que alivian las difíciles entrañas,
junto con la orejuela de ratón
para el mal que la gente llama "bilis";
la yerba del venado, el chuchupaste
y la yerba del indio, que restauran la sangre;
el pasto del ocotillo de los golpes contusos,
contrayerba para las fiebres pantanosas,
la yerba de la víbora que cura los resfríos;
collares de semillas de ojo de venado,
tan eficaces para el sortilegio;
y la sangre de grado, que aprieta las encías
y agarra en la raíz los dientes flojos.

(Nuestro Francisco Hernández
—el Plinio Mexicano de los Mil y Quinientos—
logró hasta mil doscientas plantas mágicas
de la farmacopea de los indios.
Sin ser un gran botánico,
don Felipe Segundo
supo gastar setenta mil ducados,
¡para que luego aquel herbario único
se perdiera en la incuria y en el polvo!
Porque el padre Moxó nos asegura
que no fue culpa del incendio
que en el siglo décimo séptimo
aconteció en el Escorial.)

squatting in the street,
exposed to the urbane envy of the whites.
Today they bring only herbs in their bundles,
herbs of healing they trade for a few nickels:
mint and cuscus and birthroot,
that relieve unruly innards,
not to mention mouse-ear
for the evil known as "bile";
sumac and chuchupaste and hellebore
that restore the blood;
pinesap for contusions
and the herb that counters marsh fevers,
and viper's grass that is a cure for colds;
canna seeds strung in necklaces,
so efficacious in the case of spells;
and dragon's blood that tightens the gums
and binds fast the roots of loose teeth.

(Our Francisco Hernández
—the Mexican Pliny of the Cinquecento—
acquired no fewer than one thousand two hundred
magic plants of the Indian pharmacopoeia.
Don Philip the Second,
though not a great botanist,
contrived to spend twenty thousand ducats
in order that this unique herbarium
might disappear beneath neglect and dust!
For we possess the Reverend Father Moxó's
assurance that this was not due to the fire
that in the seventeenth century occurred
in the Palace of the Escorial.)

Con la paciencia munda de la hormiga,
los indios van juntando sobre el suelo
la yerbecita en haces
—perfectos en su ciencia natural.

With the silent patience of the ant
the Indians go gathering their herbs
in heaps upon the ground—
perfect in their natural science.

Translated by
Samuel Beckett

BIBLIOTECA NACIONAL

A Criança Abandonada
O doutor Coppelius
Vamos com Êle
Senhorita Primavera
Código Civil Brasileiro
A arte de ganhar no bicho
O Orador Popular
O Pólo em Chamas

RECLAME

Fala a graciosa atriz
Margarida Perna Grossa

Linda côr—que admirável loção
Considero lindacor o complemento
Da toalete fermina da mulher

OSWALD DE ANDRADE

Brazil 1890–1954

NATIONAL LIBRARY

The Abandoned Child
Doctor Coppelius
Let Us Go with Him
Miss Spring
Brazilian Code of Civil Law
How to Win the Lottery
Public Speaking for Everyone
The Pole in Flames

Translated by
Jean R. Longland

ADVERTISEMENT

Says the dainty actress
Margaret Piano Leg

Pretty tint—what a splendid lotion
I consider prettytint the complement
of woman's feminine toilette

Pelo seu perfume agradável
E como tônico do cabelo garçone
Se entendam tôdas com Seu Fagundes
Único depositório
Nos E. U. do Brasil

PROCISSÃO DO ENTÊRRO

A Verônica estende os braços
E canta
O pálio parou
Todos escutam
A voz na noite
Cheia de ladeiras acesas

for its agreeable odor
and as a tonic for the boyish bob
All women—deal with Mr. Fagundes
sole distributor
in the United States of Brazil

*Translated by
Jean R. Longland*

FUNERAL PROCESSION

The Veronica extends her arms
and sings
The baldachin has stopped
All listen
to the voice in the night
full of lighted hills

*Translated by
Jean R. Longland*

Translator's note: "Veronica," a woman who carries the holy sudarium in the processions of the burial of Christ; "pálio," a portable baldachin carried in processions, covering the honored person or the priest who holds the monstrance.

CUADRADOS Y ÁNGULOS

Casas enfiladas, casas enfiladas,
casas enfiladas.
Cuadrados, cuadrados, cuadrados.
Casas enfiladas.
Las gentes ya tienen el alma cuadrada,
ideas en fila
y ángulo en la espalda.
Yo misma he vertido ayer una lágrima,
Dios mío, cuadrada.

HOMBRE PEQUEÑITO

Hombre pequeñito, hombre pequeñito,
suelta a tu canario que quiere volar . . .
yo soy el canario, hombre pequeñito,
déjame saltar.

ALFONSINA STORNI

Switzerland **1892-1938**

SQUARES AND ANGLES

Lined houses, lined houses,
lined houses.
Squares, squares, squares.
Lined houses.
People already have a squared soul,
lined ideas
and their back in an angle.
Yesterday I myself spilled a tear:
my God, it is square.

VERY LITTLE MAN

Very little man, very little man,
let your canary free since it wants to fly . . .
I am the canary, very little man,
let me out.

*Translated by
Ilan Stavans*

Estuve en tu jaula, hombre pequeñito,
hombre pequeñito que jaula me das.
Digo pequeñito porque no me entiendes,
ni me entenderás.

Tampoco te entiendo, pero mientras tanto
ábreme la jaula, que quiero escapar;
hombre pequeñito, te amé media hora,
no me pidas más.

I was in your cage, very little man,
what a cage you have given me, very little man.
I say very little because you don't get what I say,
nor will you understand.

I don't understand you either, but meanwhile,
open the cage for me, for I want to escape;
very little man, I loved you for half an hour;
don't ask for more.

*Translated by
Ilan Stavans*

LOS HERALDOS NEGROS

Hay golpes en la vida, tan fuertes . . . ¡Yo no sé!
Golpes como del odio de Dios; como si ante ellos,
la resaca de todo lo sufrido
se empozara en la alma . . . ¡Yo no sé!

Son pocos; pero son . . . Abren zanjas oscuras
en el rostro más fiero y en el lomo más fuerte.
Serán talvez los potros de bárbaros atilas;
o los heraldos negros que nos manda la Muerte.

Son las caídas hondas de los Cristos del alma,
de alguna fe adorable que el Destino blasfema.
Esos golpes sangrientos son las crepitaciones
de algún pan que en la puerta del horno se nos quema.

Y el hombre . . . Pobre . . . ¡pobre! Vuelve los ojos, como
cuando por sobre el hombro nos llama una palmada;
vuelve los ojos locos, y todo lo vivido
se empoza, como charco de culpa, en la mirada.

Hay golpes en la vida, tan fuertes . . . ¡Yo no sé!

CÉSAR VALLEJO

Peru **1892-1938**

BLACK HERALDS

There are blows in life, so formidable . . . I don't know!
Blows as if from God's hatred; as if when struck
the undertow from everything ever suffered
were forming wells in your soul . . . I don't know!

They were few, but they are . . . they are open dark gullies
in the fiercest face and strongest back.
Perhaps they are the colts of barbarous Attilas;
or the black heralds sent to us by Death.

They are profound abysses of the Christs of the soul,
of some exalted faith that Destiny blasphemes.
Those blood-soaked blows are crepitations
from bread burning at the oven door.

And man . . . Poor . . . creature! His eyes turn back, as
when someone claps us on the shoulder;
his crazed eyes turn back, and all that he has lived
forms a well, like a pool of guilt, in his gaze.

There are blows in life, so formidable . . . I don't know!

*Translated by
Margaret Sayers Peden*

MASA

Al fin de la batalla,
y muerto el combatiente, vino hacia él un hombre
y le dijo: "No mueras, te amo tanto!"
Pero el cadáver ¡ay! siguió muriendo.

Se le acercaron dos y repitiéronle:
"No nos dejes! ¡Valor! ¡Vuelve a la vida!"
Pero el cadáver ¡ay! siguió muriendo.

Acudieron a él veinte, cien, mil, quinientos mil,
clamando: "Tanto amor, y no poder nada contra la muerte!"
Pero el cadáver ¡ay! siguió muriendo.

Le rodearon millones de individuos,
con un ruego común: "¡Quédate, hermano!"
Pero el cadáver ¡ay! siguió muriendo.

Entonces, todos los hombres de la tierra
le rodearon; les vio el cadáver triste, emocionado;
incorporóse lentamente,
abrazó al primer hombre; echóse a andar . . .

MASS

After the battle,
when the fighter was dead, a man came toward him
and said: "Don't die! I love you so much!"
But oh! The dead man just kept dying.

Two more approached him, repeating:
"Don't leave us! Have courage! Come back to life!"
But oh! The dead man just kept dying.

Twenty, a hundred, a thousand, five hundred thousand came,
clamoring: "So much love, powerless against death!"
But oh! The dead man just kept dying.

Millions surrounded him
with a common plea: "Stay, brother!"
But oh! The dead man just kept dying.

Then all the people of the earth
surrounded him; the dead man looked at them, sad, overwhelmed;
sat up slowly,
embraced the first man; began to walk . . .

*Translated by
Martín Espada*

¡CUÍDATE, ESPAÑA, DE TU PROPIA ESPAÑA! ...

¡Cuídate, España, de tu propia España!
¡Cuídate de la hoz sin el martillo,
cuídate del martillo sin la hoz!
¡Cuídate de la víctima apesar suyo,
del verdugo apesar suyo
y del indiferente apesar suyo!
¡Cuídate del que, antes de que cante el gallo,
negárate tres veces,
y del que te negó, después, tres veces!
¡Cuídate de las calaveras sin las tibias,
y del las tibias sin las calaveras!
¡Cuídate de los nuevos poderosos!
¡Cuídate del que come tus cadáveres,
del que devora muertos a tus vivos!
¡Cuídate del leal ciento por ciento!
¡Cuídate del cielo más acá del aire
y cuídate del aire más allá del cielo!
¡Cuídate de los que te aman!
¡Cuídate de tus héroes!
¡Cuídate de tus muertos!
¡Cuídate de la República!
¡Cuídate del futuro! ...

BE WARY, SPAIN, OF
YOUR OWN SPAIN! . . .

Be wary, Spain, of your own Spain!
Be wary of the sickle without the hammer,
Be wary of the hammer without the sickle!
Be wary of the victim who did not choose to be,
of the executioner who did not choose to be,
and of the indifferent who did not choose to be!
Be wary of he who, before the cock crows,
may deny you three times,
and of he who later did deny you three times!
Be wary of skulls without tibias,
and of tibias without skulls!
Be wary of the newly powerful!
Be wary of he who eats your corpses,
of he who devours, dead, your living!
Be wary of the one hundred percent loyal!
Be wary of the sky beyond the air
and be wary of the air beyond the sky!
Be wary of those who love you!
Be wary of your heroes!
Be wary of your dead!
Be wary of the Republic!
Be wary of the future!

Translated by
Margaret Sayers Peden

ESPAÑA, APARTA

DE MÍ ESTE CÁLIZ

Niños del mundo,
si cae España—digo, es un decir—
si cae
del cielo abajo su antebrazo que asen,
en cabestro, dos láminas terrestres;
niños, ¡qué edad la de las sienes cóncavas!
¡qué temprano en el sol lo que os decía!
¡qué pronto en vuestro pecho el ruido anciano!
¡qué viejo vuestro 2 en el cuaderno!

¡Niños del mundo, está
la madre España con su vientre a cuestas;
está nuestra maestra con sus férulas,
está madre y maestra,
cruz y madera, porque os dio la altura,
vértigo y división y suma, niños;
está con ella, padres procesales!

Si cae—digo, es un decir—si cae
España, de la tierra para abajo,
niños, ¡cómo vais a cesar de crecer!
¡Cómo va a castigar el año al mes!
¡Cómo van a quedarse en diez los dientes,
en palote el diptongo, la medalla en llanto!
¡Cómo va el corderillo a continuar
atado por la pata al gran tintero!
¡Cómo vais a bajar las gradas del alfabeto
hasta la letra en que nació la pena!

SPAIN, TAKE THIS

CHALICE FROM ME

Children of the world,
if Spain falls—I mean, you hear that said—
if her arm,
her forearm, falls from the heavens, caught
in a halter lead between two terrestrial plates;
children, how old the age of sunken temples!
How early in the sun what I was telling you!
How soon in your breast the ancient noise!
How old your 2 in the notebook!

Children of the world, Mother Spain
is here with the burden of her womb;
our teacher is here with her ferules,
mother and teacher is here,
cross and wood, for she gave you height,
vertigo and division and sums, children;
she is with herself, judgment fathers!

If she falls—I mean, you hear that said—if Spain
falls down from the Earth,
children, how you will stop growing!
How the year will chastise the month!
How your teeth will stay at ten,
the diphthong in block letters, the medal in tears!
How the young lamb will still be
tied by the foot to the large inkwell!
How you will descend the steps of the alphabet
to the letter that gave birth to pain!

Niños,
hijos de los guerreros, entre tanto,
bajad la voz, que España está ahora mismo repartiendo
la energía entre el reino animal,
las florecillas, los cometas y los hombres.
¡Bajad la voz, que está
con su rigor, que es grande, sin saber
qué hacer, y está en su mano
la calavera hablando y habla y habla,
la calavera, aquélla de la trenza,
la calavera, aquélla de la vida!

   ¡Bajad la voz, os digo;
bajad la voz, el canto de las sílabas, el llanto
de la materia y el rumor menor de las pirámides, y aún
el de las sienes que andan con dos piedras!
¡Bajad el aliento, y si
el antebrazo baja,
si las férulas suenan, si es la noche,
si el cielo cabe en dos limbos terrestres,
si hay ruido en el sonido de las puertas,
si tardo,
si no veis a nadie, si os asustan
los lápices sin punta, si la madre
España cae—digo, es un decir—
salid, niños del mundo; id a buscarla! . . .

Children,
sons of warriors, in the meantime,
speak softly, for at this very moment Spain is distributing
energy among the animal kingdom,
the flowers, the comets, and man.
Speak softly, for she is here
in all her rigor, which is great, not knowing
what to do, and in her hand
is the skull, speaking, it speaks and speaks,
the skull, the one with the braid,
the skull, the one from life!

Speak softly, I say to you:
speak softly, the song of syllables, the sobbing
of matter and the lesser murmur of the pyramids, and even
that of your temples walking with two stones!
Breathe softly, and if
a forearm falls,
if ferules clatter, if it is night,
if the sky can be held within two terrestrial limbs,
if there is noise in the sound of doors,
if I am late,
if you see no one, if you are frightened
by pencils with dull points, if Mother
Spain falls—I mean, you hear that said—
go forth, children of the world; go out to seek her!

Translated by
Margaret Sayers Peden

GLOBE-TROTTER

Ton regard bleu
        ton regard bleu
Tant de vagues, tant de rochers
        Où va-t-on?
Dans quel port laisserai-je ma chanson?
Le vent fait tourner les étoiles
Et le navire s'éloigne
Sur ton regard qui tremble

Par ici ont passé
Mes vers et mes années

Dans cette mer douce prairie
Broutée tous les printemps
Dans cette mer ont fait naufrage
Toutes mes barques fleuries

Matelot du couchant
        regardons les girouettes
Je n'irai jamais aux plages sans mouettes

VICENTE HUIDOBRO

Chile **1893-1948**

GLOBE-TROTTER

Your blue glance
      your blue glance
Many waves, many rocks
        Where do they all go?
In what port will I leave behind my song?
The wind makes the stars rotate
And the sailboat departs
In your trembling glance

My verse and years
Have wandered through here

In this sweet prairie sea
Where all springs make peace
All my flower boats
Have shipwrecked on this sea

Mariner of decline
      let us look at the sails
I shall never go to beaches without seagulls

Toujours debout
Matelot au fond du ciel
Avec les bras ouverts dans la proue

La fumée de ta pipe a gonflé les nuages
Et tout le ciel sent ton tabac

Regarde là-bas
Matelot triste
D'être un Christ
Sur les mâts

Levons les bras
Vers le ciel qui naît de l'eau
Vers cette aube oubliée par les oiseaux

Le vent fait tourner les étoiles
Et je suis ses yeux poissons natales
Entre les doigts un peu d'azur
Ecume de mer sur les chaussures

Le point de l'horizon est mon chapeau
Et sur toutes les plages
Ma cravate au vent est un drapeau

Globe-trotter
Je suis loin de moi-même
Au fond de ce brouillard je me souviens
(Un souvenir qui luit comme une lanterne
Orange dans la main)

Always standing
Mariner at the bottom of the sky
With open arms on the prow

The smoke of your pipe has inflated the clouds
And all the sky smells your tobacco

Look beyond
Sad mariner
From being a Christ
On the masts

Let us raise our arms
Toward the sky born from water
Until that dawn forgotten by birds

The wind makes the stars rotate
And I am her newborn-fish eyes
Between the fingers a bit of azure
Sea foam on the shoes

The line of the horizon is my hat
And on all the beaches
My tie is a flag in the wind

Globe-trotter
I'm far from myself
Inside this fog I recall
(A memory that shines like a lamp
Orange in the hand)

J'étais au collège, j'étais interne
Et je passais l'été
Au bord de tes yeux bleus

DE **ALTAZOR**

CANTO III

Romper las ligaduras de las venas
Los lazos de la respiración y las cadenas

De los ojos senderos de horizontes
Flor proyectada en cielos uniformes

El alma pavimentada de recuerdos
Como estrellas talladas por el viento

El mar es un tejado de botellas
Que en la memoria del marino sueña

Cielo es aquella larga cabellera intacta
Tejida entre manos de aeronauta

Y el avión trae un lenguaje diferente
Para la boca de los cielos de siempre

Cadenas de miradas nos atan a la tierra
Romped romped tantas cadenas

Translated by
Ilan Stavans

I was at school, I was interned
And the summer went by
On the edge of your blue eyes.

FROM **ALTAZOR**

CANTO III

Break the loops of veins
The links of breath and the chains

Of eyes paths of horizons
Flower screened on uniform skies

Soul paved with recollections
Like stars carved by the wind

The sea is a roof of bottles
That dreams in the sailor's memory

The sky is that pure flowing hair
Braided by the hands of the aeronaut

And the airplane carries a new language
To the mouth of the eternal skies

Chains of glances tie us to the earth
Break them break so many chains

Vuela el primer hombre a iluminar el día
El espacio se quiebra en una herida

Y devuelve la bala al asesino
Eternamente atado al infinito

Cortad todas las amarras
De río mar o de montaña

De espíritu y recuerdo
De ley agonizante y sueño enfermo

Es el mundo que torna y sigue y gira
En una última pupila

Mañana el campo
Seguirá los galopes del caballo

La flor se comerá a la abeja
Porque el hangar será colmena

El arcoíris se hará pájaro
Y volará a su nido contando

Los cuervos se harán planetas
Y tendrán plumas de hierba

Hojas serán las plumas entibiadas
Que caerán de sus gargantas

Las miradas serán ríos
Y los ríos heridas en las piernas del vacío

The first man flies to light the sky
Space bursts open in a wound

And the bullet returns to the assassin
Forever tied to the infinite

Cut all the links
Of river sea and mountain

Of spirit and memory
Of dying law and fever dreams

It is the world that turns and goes on and whirls
In the last eyeball

Tomorrow the countryside
Will follow the galloping horses

The flower will suck the bee
For the hangar will be a hive

The rainbow will become a bird
And fly singing to its nest

Crows will become planets
And sprout feathers of grass

Leaves will be loose feathers
Falling from their throats

Glances will be rivers
And the rivers wounds in the legs of space

Conducirá el rebaño a su pastor
Para que duerma el día cansado como avión

Y el árbol se posará sobre la tórtola
Mientras las nubes se hacen roca

Porque todo es como es en cada ojo
Dinastía astrológica y efímera
Cayendo de universo en universo

Manicura de la lengua es el poeta
Mas no el mago que apaga y enciende
Palabras estelares y cerezas de adioses vagabundos
Muy lejos de las manos de la tierra
Y todo lo que dice es por él inventado
Cosas que pasan fuera del mundo cotidiano
Matemos al poeta que nos tiene saturados

Poesía aún y poesía poesía
Poética poesía poesía
Poesía poética de poético poeta
Poesía
Demasiada poesía
Desde el arcoíris hasta el culo pianista de la vecina
Basta señora poesía bambina
Y todavía tiene barrotes en los ojos
El juego es juego y no plegaria infatigable
Sonrisa o risa y no lamparillas de pupila
Que ruedan de la aflicción hasta el océano
Sonrisa y habladurías de estrella tejedora
Sonrisa del cerebro que evoca estrellas muertas
En la mesa mediúmnica de sus irradiaciones

The flock will guide its shepherd
So the day can doze drowsy as an airplane

And the tree will perch on the turtledove
While the clouds turn to stone

For everything is as it is in every eye
An ephemeral astrological dynasty
Falling from universe to universe

The poet is a manicurist of language
Not the magician who lights and douses
Stellar words and the cherries of vagabond good-byes
Far from the hands of the earth
And everything he says is his invention
Things that move outside the ordinary world
Let us kill the poet who gluts us

Poetry still and poetry poetry
Poetical poetry poetry
Poetical poetry by poetical poets
Poetry
Too much poetry
From the rainbow to the piano-bench ass of the lady next door
Enough poetry bambina enough lady
It still has bars across its eyes
The game is a game and not an endless prayer
Smiles or laughter not the eyeball's little lamps
That wheel from affliction toward the sea
Smiles and gossip of the weaver star
Smiles of a brain evoking dead stars
On the séance table of its radiance

Basta señora arpa de las bellas imágenes
De los furtivos comos iluminados
Otra cosa otra cosa buscamos
Sabemos posar un beso como una mirada
Plantar miradas como árboles
Enjaular árboles como pájaros
Regar pájaros como heliótropos
Tocar un heliótropo como una música
Vaciar una música como un saco
Degollar un saco como un pingüino
Cultivar pingüinos como viñedos
Ordeñar un viñedo como una vaca
Desarbolar vacas como veleros
Peinar un velero como un cometa
Desembarcar cometas como turistas
Embrujar turistas como serpientes
Cosechar serpientes como almendras
Desnudar una almendra como un atleta
Leñar atletas como cipreses
Iluminar cipreses como faroles
Anidar faroles como alondras
Exhalar alondras como suspiros
Bordar suspiros como sedas
Derramar sedas como ríos
Tremolar un río como una bandera
Desplumar una bandera como un gallo
Apagar un gallo como un incendio
Bogar en incendios como en mares
Segar mares como trigales
Repicar trigales como campanas
Desangrar campanas como corderos
Dibujar corderos como sonrisas

Enough lady harp of the beautiful images
Of furtive illuminated "likes"
It's something else we're looking for something else
We already know how to dart a kiss like a glance
Plant glances like trees
Cage trees like birds
Water birds like heliotropes
Play a heliotrope like music
Empty music like a sack
Decapitate a sack like a penguin
Cultivate penguins like vineyards
Milk a vineyard like a cow
Unmast cows like schooners
Comb a schooner like a comet
Disembark comets like tourists
Charm tourists like snakes
Harvest snakes like almonds
Undress an almond like an athlete
Fell athletes like cypresses
Light cypresses like lanterns
Nestle lanterns like skylarks
Heave skylarks like sighs
Embroider sighs like silks
Drain silks like rivers
Raise a river like a flag
Pluck a flag like a rooster
Douse a rooster like a fire
Row through fires like seas
Reap seas like wheat
Ring wheat like bells
Bleed bells like lambs
Draw lambs like smiles

Embotellar sonrisas como licores
Engastar licores como alhajas
Electrizar alhajas como crepúsculos
Tripular crepúsculos como navíos
Descalzar un navío como un rey
Colgar reyes como auroras
Crucificar auroras como profetas
Etc. etc. etc.
Basta señor violín hundido en una ola ola
Cotidiana ola de religión miseria
De sueño en sueño posesión de pedrerías

Después del corazón comiendo rosas
Y de las noches del rubí perfecto
El nuevo atleta salta sobre la pista mágica
Jugando con magnéticas palabras
Caldeadas como la tierra cuando va a salir un volcán
Lanzando sortilegios de sus frases pájaro

Agoniza el último poeta
Tañen las campanas de los continentes
Muere la luna con su noche a cuestas
El sol se saca del bolsillo el día
Abre los ojos el nuevo paisaje solemne
Y pasa desde la tierra a las constelaciones
El entierro de la poesía

Todas las lenguas están muertas
Muertas en manos del vecino trágico
Hay que resucitar las lenguas
Con sonoras risas
Con vagones de carcajadas

Bottle smiles like wine
Set wine like jewels
Electrify jewels like sunsets
Man sunsets like battleships
Uncrown a battleship like a king
Hoist kings like dawns
Crucify dawns like prophets
Etc. etc. etc.
Enough sir violin sunk in a wave wave
Everyday wave of misery religion
Of dream after dream possession of jewels

After the heart-eating roses
And the nights of the perfect ruby
The new athlete leaps on the magic track
Frolicking with magnetic words
Hot as the earth when a volcano rises
Hurling the sorceries of his bird phrases

The last poet withers away
The bells of the continents chime
The moon dies with the night on its back
The sun pulls the day out of its pocket
The solemn new land opens its eyes
And moves from earth to the stars
The burial of poetry

All the languages are dead
Dead in the hands of the tragic neighbor
We must revive the languages
With raucous laughter
With wagonloads of giggles

Con cortacircuitos en las frases
Y cataclismo en gramática
Levántate y anda
Estira las piernas anquilosis salta
Fuegos de risa para el lenguaje tiritando de frío
Gimnasia astral para las lenguas entumecidas
Levántate y anda
Vive vive como un balón de fútbol
Estalla en la boca de diamantes motocicleta
En ebriedad de sus luciérnagas
Vértigo sí de su liberación
Una bella locura en la vida de la palabra
Una bella locura en la zona del lenguaje
Aventura forrada de desdenes tangibles
Aventura de la lengua entre dos naufragios
Catástrofe preciosa en los rieles del verso

Y puesto que debemos vivir y no nos suicidamos
Mientras vivamos juguemos
El simple sport de los vocablos
De la pura palabra y nada más
Sin imagen limpia de joyas
(Las palabras tienen demasiada carga)
Un ritual de vocablos sin sombra
Juego de ángel allá en el infinito
Palabra por palabra
Con luz propia de astro que un choque vuelve vivo
Saltan chispas del choque y mientras más violento
Más grande es la explosión
Pasión del juego en el espacio
Sin alas de luna y pretensión
Combate singular entre el pecho y el cielo

With circuit breakers in the sentences
And cataclysm in the grammar
Get up and walk
Stretch your legs limber the stiff joints
Fires of laughter for the shivering language
Astral gymnastics for the numb tongues
Get up and walk
Live live like a football
Burst in the mouth of motorcycle diamonds
In the drunkenness of its fireflies
The very vertigo of its liberation
A beautiful madness in the life of the word
A beautiful madness in the zone of language
Adventure lined with tangible disdain
The adventure of language between two wrecked ships
A delightful catastrophe on the rails of verse

And since we must live and not kill ourselves
As long as we live let us play
The simple sport of words
Of the pure word and nothing more
Without images awash with jewels
(Words carry too much weight)
A ritual of shadowless words
An angel game there in the infinite
Word by word
By the light of a star that a crash brings to life
Sparks leap from the crash and then more violent
More enormous is the explosion
Passion of the game in space
With no moon-wings no pretense
Single combat between chest and sky

Total desprendimiento al fin de voz de carne
Eco de luz que sangra aire sobre el aire

Después nada nada
Rumor aliento de frase sin palabra

Total severance at last of voice and flesh
Echo of light bleeding air into the air

Then nothing nothing
Spirit whisper of the wordless phrase

Translated by
Eliot Weinberger

ODE AO BURGUÊS

Eu insulto o burguês! O burguês-níquel,
o burguês-burguês!
A digestão bem feita de São Paulo!
O homem-curva! o homen-nádegas!
O homem que sendo francês, brasileiro, italiano,
é sempre um cauteloso pouco-a-pouco!

Eu insulto as aristocracias cautelosas!
Os barões lampiões! os condes Joões! os duques zurros!
que vivem dentro de muros sem pulos;
e gemem sangues de alguns mil-réis fracos
para dizerem que as filhas da senhora falam o francês
e tocam o "Printemps" com as unhas!

Eu insulto o burguês-funesto!
O indigesto feijão com toucinho, dono das tradições!
Fora os que algarismam os amanhãs!
Olha a vida dos nossos setembros!
Fará Sol? Choverá? Arlequinal!

MÁRIO DE ANDRADE

Brazil 1893-1945

ODE TO THE BOURGEOIS GENTLEMAN

I insult the bourgeois! The money-grabbing bourgeois,
the bourgeois-bourgeois!
The well-made digestion of São Paulo!
The man-belly! The man-buttocks!
The man who being French, Brazilian, Italian,
is always a cautious little take-your-time!

I insult the cautious aristocracies!
The kerosene lamp barons! The Count Johns! The jackass-braying
    dukes!
Who live inside walls never scaled;
and lament the blood of a few puny pennies
to say that their lady's daughters speak French
and play the "Printemps" with their fingernails!

I insult the fatal-bourgeois!
The undigested beans and bacon, guardian of traditions!
Down with those who count out their tomorrows!
Behold the life of our Septembers!
Will the sun shine? Will it rain? Harlequinate!

131

Mas à chuva dos rosais
o êxtase fará sempre Sol!

Morte à gordura!
Morte às adiposidades cerebrais!
Morte ao burguês-mensal!
ao burguês-cinema! ao burguês-tílburi!
Padaria Suissa! Morte viva ao Adriano!
"—Ai, filha, que te darei pelos teus anos?
—Um colar . . . —Conto e quinhentos!!!
Mas nós morremos de fome!"

Come! Come-te a ti mesmo, oh! gelatina pasma!
Oh! *purée* de batatas morais!
Oh! cabelos nas ventas! oh! carecas!
Ódio aos temperamentos regulares!
Ódio aos relógios musculares! Morte e infâmia!
Ódio à soma! Ódio aos secos e molhados!
Ódio aos sem desfalecimentos nem arrependimentos,
sempiternamente as mesmices convencionais!
De mãos nas costas! Marco eu o compasso! Eia!
Dois a dois! Primeira posição! Marcha!
Todos para a Central do meu rancor inebriante!

Ódio e insulto! Ódio e raiva! Ódio e mais ódio!
Morte ao burguês de giolhos,
cheirando religião e que não crê em Deus!
Ódio vermelho! Ódio fecundo! Ódio cíclico!
Ódio fundamento, sem perdão!

Fora! Fú! Fora o bom burguês! . . .

But in the rain of the rose gardens
ecstasy will always make the sun shine!

Death to flabbiness!
Death to cerebral adiposities!
Death to the monthly bourgeois!
to the movie-bourgeois! to the tilbury-bourgeois!
Swiss Bakery! Living death to the Café Adriano!
"Oh, sweetheart, what shall I give you for your birthday?"
"A necklace . . ." "Fifteen hundred bucks!!!
But we're starving to death!"

Eat! Oh, eat yourself up! Stupefied gelatin!
Oh, moral mashed potatoes!
Oh, hairs in the nostrils! Oh, bald pates!
Hatred to regulated temperaments!
Hatred to muscular clocks! Death and infamy!
Hatred to calculation! Hatred to grocery stores!
Hatred to those without weakness or repentance,
ever and eternally the conventional sameness!
Hands at their backs! I'll beat the rhythm! Hey!
Columns of two! First position! March!
All to the Central Jail of my inebriating rancor!

Hatred and execration! Hatred and rage! Hatred and more hatred!
Death to the bourgeois on his knees,
smelling of religion and not believing in God!
Scarlet hatred! Fecund hatred! Cyclical hatred!
Fundamental hatred, without pardon!

Down and away! Boo! Away with the good bourgeois gentleman! . . .

*Translated by
Jack E. Tomlins*

DOMINGO

Missas de chegar tarde, em rendas,
e dos olhares acrobáticos ...
Tantos telégrafos sem fio!
Santa Cecília regorgita de corpos lavados
e de sacrilégios picturais ...
Mas Jesus Cristo nos desertos,
mas o sacerdote no "Confiteor" ... Contrastar!
—Futilidade, civilização ...

Hoje quem joga? ... O Paulistano
Para o Jardim América das rosas e dos ponta-pés!
Friedenreich fez goal! Corner! Que juiz!
Gostar de Bianco? Adoro. Qual Bartô ...
E o meu xará maravilhoso! ...
—Futilidade, civilização ...

Mornamente em gasolinas ... Trinta e cinco contos!
Tens dez milreis? vamos ao corso ...
E filar cigarros a quinzena inteira ...
Ir ao corso é lei. Viste Marília?
E Filis? Que vestido: pele só!
Automóveis fechados ... Figuras imóveis ...
O bocejo do luxo ... Entêrro.
E tambem as famílias dominicais por atacado,
entre os convenientes perenemente ...
—Futilidade, civilização.

Central. Drama de adultério.
A Bertini arranca os cabelos e morre.

SUNDAY

Late arrivals at Mass, in lace,
exchanging acrobatic glances . . .
So much wireless telegraphy!
St. Cecilia exudes from washed bodies
and pictorial sacrileges . . .
But Jesus Christ in the wilderness,
but the priest at the Confiteor . . . Contrast!
"Futility, civilization . . ."

Who's playing today? . . . The Paulistano team.
Off to America Garden of the roses and kick-offs!
Friedenreich scored a goal! Corner! What a referee!
Do I like Bianco? Crazy about him. Better than Barto . . .
And my wonderful fellow-Mário! . . .
"Futility, civilization . . ."

Warmly in gasoline . . . Thirty-five thousand!
Do you have ten bucks? Let's go make the main drag . . .
And mooch cigarettes for two weeks on end . . .
You've got to go down to the main drag. Did you see Marilla?
And Phyllis! What a dress: practically naked!
Closed automobiles . . . Motionless figures . . .
The yawn of luxury . . . Burial.
And also the wholesale Sunday families,
among the perennially proper . . .
"Futility, civilization . . ."

Central Jail. A drama of adultery.
Bertini tears her hair and dies.

Fugas ... Tiros ... Tom Mix!
Amanhã fita alemã ... de beiços ...
As meninas mordem os beiços pensando em fita alemã ...
As romas de Petronio ...
E o leito virginal ... Tudo azul e branco!
Descansar ... Os anjos ... Imaculado!
As meninas sonham masculinidades ...
—Futilidade, civilização.

ANHANGABAÚ

Parques do Anhangabaú nos fogaréus da aurora ...
Oh larguezas dos meus itinerários! ...
Estátuas de bronze nu correndo eternamente,
num parado desdém pelas velocidades ...
O carvalho votivo escondido nos orgulhos
do bicho de mármore parido no *Salón* ...
Prurido de estesias perfumando em rosais
o esqueleto trêmulo do morcego ...
Nada de poesia, nada de alegrias! ...

E o contraste boçal do lavrador
que sem amor afia a foice ...

Estes meus parques do Anhangabaú ou de Paris,
onde as tuas águas, onde as mágoas dos teus sapos?
"Meu pai foi rei!
—Foi. —Não foi. —Foi. —Não foi."
Onde as tuas bananeiras?

Getaways . . . Hold-ups . . . Tom Mix!
Tomorrow a German film . . . for free!
The young girls are disturbed from thinking about German films . . .
The Romes of Petronius . . .
And the virgin's bed . . . All blue and white!
Rest . . . The angels . . . Immaculate!
The young girls dream masculinities . . .
"Futility, civilization . . ."

Translated by
Jack E. Tomlins

ANHANGABAÚ

Parks of the Anhangabaú in the conflagrations of the dawn . . .
Oh, expanses of my wanderings! . . .
Nude bronze statues eternally coursing,
in a fixed disdain for velocities . . .
The votive oak concealed in the hauteurs
of the marble beast birthed in the *salon* . . .
Itch of the aesthesias in rose gardens perfuming
the tremulous skeleton of the bat . . .
No poetry whatsoever, no joys whatsoever!

And the coarse contrast of the farmer
lovelessly honing his scythe . . .

These my parks of the Anhangabaú or of Paris,
where are your waters, where the sorrows of your toads?
"My father was a king!"
"He was." "He was not." "He was." "He was not."
Where are your banana trees?

Onde o teu rio encanecido pelos nevoeiros,
contando histórias aos sacis? . . .

Meu querido palimpsesto sem valor!
Crônica em mau latim
cobrindo uma écloga que não seja de Virgilio! . . .

T U

Morrente chama esgalga,
mais morta inda no espírito!
Espírito de fidalga,
que vive dum bocejo entre dois galanteois
e de longe em longe uma chávena da treva bem forte!

Mulher mais longa
que os pasmos alucinados
das tôrres de São Bento!
Mulher feita de asfalto e de lamas de várzea,
toda insultos nos olhos,
toda convites nessa boca louca de rubores!

Costureirinha de São Paulo,
italo-franco-luso-brasílico-saxônica,
gosto dos teus ardores crepusculares,
crepusculares e por isso mais ardentes,
bandeirantemente!

Lady Macbeth feita de névoa fina,
pura neblina da manhã!

Where is your river grizzled by the mists
telling tales to the forest imps?

My beloved and worthless palimpsest!
Chronicle in faulty Latin
overlying an eclogue that may not be from Virgil! . . .

Translated by
Jack E. Tomlins

Y O U

A dying flame grows thin,
deader yet in the spirit!
Spirit of a patrician lady,
who lives on a yawn between two gallantries
and only rarely on a cup of good strong gloom!

A woman taller
than the hallucinated awe
of the towers of São Bento!
Woman made of asphalt and marsh mud,
all insults in the eyes,
all invitations on that mouth mad with blushes!

Little seamstress from São Paulo,
italo-franco-luso-brasilico-saxon,
I like your crepuscular ardors,
crepuscular and therefore more ardent,
pioneer-wise!

Lady Macbeth made of fine mist,
pure morning haze!

Mulher que és minha madrasta e minha irmã!
Trituração ascencional dos meus sentidos!
Risco de aeroplano entre Mogí e Paris!
Pura neblina da manhã!

Gosto dos teus desejos de crime turco
e das tuas ambições retorcidas como roubos!
Amo-te de pesadelos taciturnos,
materialização da Canaan do meu Poe!
Nevermore!

Emílio de Menezes insultou a memória do meu Poe . . .

Oh! Incendiária dos meus alens sonoros!
Tu és meu gato preto!
Tu te esmagaste nas paredes do meu sonho!
Este sonho medonho! . . .

E serás sempre, morrente chama esgalga,
meio fidalga, meio barregã,
as alucinações crucificantes
de todas as auroras de meu jardim!

Woman who is my stepmother and my sister!
Ascending pulverization of my senses!
Line of the airplane between Mogí and Paris!
Pure morning haze!

I like your Turkish crime desires
and your ambitions twisted as swindles!
I love you with taciturn nightmares,
materialization of the Canaan of my Poe!
Nevermore!

Emílio de Menezes insulted the memory of my Poe . . .

Oh! Incendiary of my vibrant beyonds!
You are my black cat!
You were shattered on the walls of my dream!
This frightened dream! . . .

And you will always be, dying flame growing thin,
half lady, half whore,
the crucifying hallucinations
of all the dawns of my garden!

Translated by
Jack E. Tomlins

LA LUNA BLANCA

La luna blanca . . . y el frío . . .
y el dulce corazón mío
tan lejano . . . tan lejano . . .

¡Tan distante su mano . . . !

La luna blanca, y el frío
y el dulce corazón mío
tan lejano . . .

Y vagas notas del piano . . .
Del bosque un aroma arcano . . .
Y el remurmurar del río . . .

¡Y el dulce corazón mío
tan lejano . . . !

LEÓN DE GREIFF

Colombia **1895–1976**

WHITE MOON

White moon . . . and cold . . .
and my sweet heart
secluded . . . secluded . . .

Your hand, eluded!

White moon, and cold
my sweet heart
secluded . . .

The vague piano notes . . .
From the forest an arcane aroma . . .
And a river, resounded . . .

My sweet heart,
secluded . . . !

*Translated by
Ilan Stavans*

VIDA-GARFIO

Amante: no me lleves, si muero, al camposanto.
A flor de tierra abre mi fosa, junto al riente
Alboroto divino de alguna pajarera
O junto a la encantada charla de alguna fuente.

A flor de tierra, amante. Casi sobre la tierra
Donde el sol me caliente los huesos, y mis ojos,
Alargados en tallos, suban a ver de nuevo
La lámpara salvaje de los ocasos rojos.

A flor de tierra, amante. Que el tránsito así sea
Más breve. Yo presiento
La lucha de mi carne por volver hacia arriba,
Por sentir en sus átomos la frescura del viento.

Yo sé que acaso nunca allá abajo mis manos
Podrán estarse quietas.
Que siempre como topos arañarán la tierra.
En medio de las sombras estrujadas y prietas.

JUANA DE IBARBOUROU

Uruguay 1895-1979

LIFE-HOOK

Love: if I die don't take me to the cemetery.
Dig my grave just at ground level, near the laughing
Divine disturbance of a birdhouse.
Or by a fountain's haunting talk.

Just at ground level, my love. And almost above earth
Where the sun can heat the bones, and my eyes,
Extended, as if into stalks, rise to see again
The savage lamp of the setting sun.

Just at ground level, my love. So the passage
    Will be even shorter. I sense
Already my flesh fighting, trying to return
To feel the atoms of a freshening wind.

I know my hands
    May never stay still down there.
That like moles they will scrape the earth
In the middle of dark, compacted shadows.

Arrójame semillas. Yo quiero que se enraícen
En la greda amarilla de mis huesos menguados.
¡Por la parda escalera de las raíces vivas
Yo subiré a mirarte en los lirios morados!

Cover me with seeds. I want them to root
In the yellow chalk of my diminishing bones.
Up the gray staircase of living roots
I will rise to watch you. I'll be the purple lilies.

Translated by
Sophie Cabot Black
and María Negroni.

ESSA NEGRA FULÔ

Ora, se deu que chegou
(isso já faz muito tempo)
no bangüê dum meu avô
uma negra bonitinha
chamada negra Fulô.

Essa negra Fulô!
Essa negra Fulô!

Ó Fulô! Ó Fulô!
(Era a fala da Sinhá)
—Vai forrar a minha cama,
pentear os meus cabelos,
vem ajudar a tirar
a minha roupa, Fulô!

Essa negra Fulô!

Essa negrinha Fulô,
ficou logo pra mucama,

JORGE DE LIMA

Brazil 1895-1953

THAT YOUNG BLACK GIRL FULÔ

Now, it happened that there came
(this occurred so long ago)
to my grandfather's plantation
a young, pretty, black sensation
who was called Black Girl Fulô.

That young black girl Fulô!
That young black girl Fulô!

Oh Fulô! Oh Fulô!
(You could hear the missus call.)
—Go and freshen up my bed,
get the brush and comb my hair,
come and help me get undressed,
take off my clothing, Fulô!

That young black girl Fulô!

That young black girl named Fulô
soon became a servant girl,

para vigiar a Sinhá
pra engomar pro Sinhô!

Essa negra Fulô!
Essa negra Fulô!

Ó Fulô! Ó Fulô!
(Era a fala da Sinhá.)
Vem me ajudar, ó Fulô,
vem abanar o meu corpo
que eu estou suada, Fulô!
Vem coçar minha coceira,
vem me catar cafuné,
vem balançar minha rede,
vem me contar uma história,
que eu estou com sono, Fulô!
Essa negra Fulô!

"Era um dia uma princesa
que vivia num castelo
que possuía um vestido
com os peixinhos do mar.
Entrou na perna dum pato
saiu na perna dum pinto
o Rei-Sinhô me mandou
que vos contasse mais cinco."

Essa negra Fulô!
Essa negra Fulô!

Ó Fulô? Ó Fulô?
Vai botar para dormir

she would take care of the missus
she would starch the master's clothes!

That young black girl Fulô!
That young black girl Fulô!

Oh Fulô! Oh Fulô!
(You could hear the missus call.)
Come and help me, oh Fulô,
come and fan my body quickly
'cause I'm sweaty, oh Fulô!
Come and scratch me where it itches,
come and stroke and rub my head,
come and swing my hammock gently,
come and tell a bedtime story,
'cause I'm sleepy now, Fulô!
That young black girl Fulô!

"Once there was a lovely princess
who was living in a castle
where she owned a pretty dress
with the fishes of the sea.
She entered the leg of a duck
came out through the leg of a quail
the Lord-King commands me to say
five times I must tell you a tale."

That young black girl Fulô!
That young black girl Fulô!

Oh Fulô? Oh Fulô?
Go and get those children ready,

esses meninos, Fulô!
"Minha mãe me penteou
minha madrasta me enterrou
pelos figos da figueira
que o sabiá beliscou."

Essa negra Fulô!
Essa negra Fulô!

Fulô? Ó Fulô?
(Era a fala da Sinhá
chamando a negra Fulô.)
Cadê meu frasco de cheiro
que teu Sinhô me mandou?
—Ah! foi você que roubou!
Ah! foi você que roubou!

O Sinhô foi ver a negra
levar couro do feitor.
A negra tirou a roupa.

O Sinhô disse: Fulô!
(A vista se escureceu
que nem a negra Fulô.)

Essa negra Fulô!
Essa negra Fulô!

Ó Fulô? Ó Fulô?
Cadê meu lenço de rendas
cadê meu cinto, meu broche,
cadê meu terço de ouro

for it's bedtime, oh Fulô!
"Mother combed and brushed my hair
stepmother buried me out there
where the figs grow on our trees
eaten by the birds and bees."

That young black girl Fulô!
That young black girl Fulô!

Fulô? Oh Fulô?
(You could hear the missus call
for that young black girl Fulô.)
Where's my bottle of perfume
which your master sent to me?
—Ah! So you're the thief, I see!
Ah! So you're the thief, I see!

Master went to see the black girl
get a whipping at the post.
Black girl took off all her clothing.

Master whispered: Oh Fulô!
(Things went black before his eyes,
black as young black girl Fulô.)

That young black girl Fulô!
That young black girl Fulô!

Oh Fulô? Oh Fulô?
Where's my white and lacy hankie,
where's my belt, and where's my broach,
where's my golden rosary

que teu Sinhô me mandou?
Ah! foi você que roubou.
Ah! foi você que roubou.

Essa negra Fulô!
Essa negra Fulô!

O Sinhô foi açoitar
sozinho a negra Fulô.
A negra tirou a saia
e tirou o cabeção,
de dentro dele pulou
nuinha a negra Fulô.

Essa negra Fulô!
Essa negra Fulô!

Ó Fulô? Ó Fulô?
Cadê, cadê teu Sinhô
que nosso Senhor me mandou?
Ah! foi você que roubou,
foi você, negra Fulô?

Essa negra Fulô!

which your master sent to me?
Ah! So you're the thief, I see.
Ah! So you're the thief, I see.

 That young black girl Fulô!
 That young black girl Fulô!

Master went alone this time
for the whipping of Fulô.
Black girl stepped out of her skirt,
pulled the collar o'er her head,
from within her camisole
out popped naked black Fulô!

 That young black girl Fulô!
 That young black girl Fulô!

Oh Fulô? Oh Fulô?
Where, oh where'd your master go
whom our Lord had sent to me?
Ah! So you're the thief, I see,
was it you, Black Girl Fulô?

 That young black girl Fulô!

Translated by
Frederick G. Williams

PRELUDIO EN BORICUA

Tuntún de pasa y grifería
y otros parejeros tuntunes.
Bochinche de ñañiguería
donde sus cálidos betunes
funde la congada bravía.

Con caraceo de maraca
y sordo gruñido de gongo,
el telón isleño destaca
una aristocracia macaca
a base de funche y mondongo.

Al solemne palalúa haitiano
opone la rumba habanera
sus esguinces de hombro y cadera,
mientras el negrito cubano
doma la mulata cerrera.

De su bachata por las pistas
vuela Cuba, suelto el velamen,

LUIS PALÉS MATOS

Puerto Rico 1898–1959

PRELUDE IN PUERTO RICAN

A knock-knock of knots, nappy hair,
and other sassy drumbeats,
The gossip of ju-ju affairs
where their fiery jet-black heat
the conga-convened wild prepare.

In the maraca's crackling key
and muffled grunts of the grongo,
behind the isle's curtain you see
a pseudoaristocracy
nourished on *funche* and *mondongo*.

To Haiti's grave *papalua*
Havana's rumba opposes
its shoulder teases, hip poses,
as the fly-black Cuban's allure
mulatta's zest tames as she closes.

Cuba from street dancing glides,
billowing sail on the wind,

recogiendo en el caderamen
su áureo niágara de turistas.

(Mañana serán accionistas
de cualquier ingenio cañero
y cargarán con el dinero . . .)

Y hacia un rincón—solar, bahía,
malecón o siembra de cañas—
bebe el negro su pena fría
alelado en la melodía
que le sale de las entrañas.

Jamaica, la gorda mandinga,
reduce su lingo a gandinga.
Santo Domingo se endominga
y en cívico gesto imponente
su numen heroico respinga
con cien odas al Presidente.

Con su batea de ajonjolí
y sus blancos ojos de magia
hacia el mercado viene Haití.
Las antillas barloventeras
pasan tremendas desazones;
espantándose los ciclones
con matamoscas de palmeras.

¿Y Puerto Rico? Mi isla ardiente,
para ti todo ha terminado.
En el yermo de un continente,
Puerto Rico, lúgubremente,
bala como cabro estofado.

with swiveling hips reeling in
its blond Niagara tourist tides.

(Tomorrow shareholders besides
of any sugar plantation,
taking profits sans cessation . . .)

And in a corner—tenement,
canefield, dock, jetty, or pier—
the black swallows his bitter tear,
bemused by the music that's sent
from deep in his gut to his ear.

Jamaica, the tubby Mandinga,
reduces her language to lingua.
San Domingo's in Sunday array
and the civically grandest of modes
as its genius it bolts to display
in a hundred president's odes.

With a sesame seed basket tray
and the magical white that's her eyes,
Haiti comes selling her merchandise.
The Antilles that to windward ease
all go through terrible pains,
brushing away hurricanes
with a whisk of swaying palm trees.

And Puerto Rico? My ardent
isle, for you it's all been written.
On the rim of a continent,
Puerto Rico in funeral torment
writhes like a slow-dying goat.

159

Tuntún de pasa y grifería,
este libro que va a tus manos
con ingredientes antillanos
compuse un día . . .

. . . y en resumen, tiempo perdido,
que me acaba en aburrimiento.
Algo entrevisto o presentido,
poco realmente vivido
y mucho de embuste y de cuento.

MULATA-ANTILLA

En ti ahora, mulata,
me acojo al tibio mar de las Antillas.
Agua sensual y lenta de melaza,
puerto de azúcar, cálida bahía,
con la luz en reposo
dorando la onda limpia,
y en el soñoliento zumbo de colmena
que cuajan los trajines de la orilla.

En ti ahora, mulata,
cruzo el mar de las islas.
Eléctricos mininos de ciclones
en tus curvas se alargan y se ovillan,
mientras sobre mi barca va cayendo
la noche de tus ojos, pensativa.

A knotted, unfair-haired knock-knock,
this book that goes to your hands
with scraps from Antillean lands
did one day I concoct . . .

   . . . in sum, time wasted and glib,
that finally ends in ennui.
Something you glimpse or foresee,
little that's truly been lived,
and much of pure story and fib.

Translated by
Roberto Márquez

MULATTA-ANTILLES

   In you now, Mulatta,
I find welcome in the warm Antillean sea.
Waters sensual and molasses-slow,
a sugar port, sultry bay,
with a soft, lazing light
that gilds the crystal wave,
and the sleepy beehive hum
the shoreside bustle thickens.

   In you, Mulatta, now
I cross the sea of islands.
Electric kitten hurricanes
into your curves sinuous stretch and curl,
as the night in your eyes descends, slowly,
pensively, upon my little boat.

En ti ahora, mulata . . .
¡oh despertar glorioso en las Antillas!
Bravo color que el do de pecho alcanza,
música al rojo vivo de alegría,
y calientes cantáridas de aroma
—limón, tabaco, piña—
zumbando a los sentidos
sus embriagadas voces de delicia.

Eres ahora, mulata,
todo el mar y la tierra de mis islas.
Sinfonía frutal cuyas escalas
rompen furiosamente en tu catinga.
He aquí en su verde traje la guanábana
con sus finas y blandas pantaletas
de muselina; he aquí el caimito
con su leche infantil; he aquí la piña
con su corona de soprano . . . Todos
los frutos ¡oh mulata! tú me brindas,
en la clara bahía de tu cuerpo
por los soles del trópico bruñida.

Imperio tuyo, el plátano y el coco,
que apuntan su dorada artillería
al barco transeúnte que nos deja
su rubio contrabando de turistas.
En potro de huracán pasas cantando
tu criolla canción, prieta walkiria,
con centelleante espuela de relámpagos
rumbo al verde Walhalla de las islas.

Eres inmensidad libre y sin límites,
eres amor sin trabas y sin prisas;

In you, Mulatta, now . . .
Oh, glorious stir in the Antilles!
Powerful tone that a high C can scale,
a music sizzling with gaiety's glow,
hot Spanish-fly aromas
—pineapple, lemon, tobacco—
buzzing 'round the senses
their drunken voices of delight.

You, Mulatta, are now
all the land and sea of my islands.
A symphony of fruit whose movements
break furiously on your effluvium.
The guava is here in her green dress,
with her fine, soft muslin underwear,
the star fruit's here with her infant's milk;
here the pineapple with her soprano crown . . .
You offer me,
Mulatta, all of the fruits
in your luminous body's bay
tanned dark by tropic suns.

Your empire, the plantain and the coconut
that aim their gilded artillery
at the passing ship which leaves us
its blond contraband of tourists.
You ride by on a pony hurricane,
a dark Valkyrie, singing your Creole song,
spurs of lightning flashing,
on your way to the islands' green Valhalla.

You are a vastness free and limitless,
love without constraint or urgency;

en tu vientre conjugan mis dos razas
sus vitales potencias expansivas.
Amor, tórrido amor de la mulata,
gallo de ron, azúcar derretida,
tabonuco que el tuétano te abrasa
con aromas de sándalo y de mirra.
Con voces del Cantar de los Cantares,
eres morena porque el sol te mira.
Debajo de tu lengua hay miel y leche
y ungüento derramado en tus pupilas.
Como la torre de David, tu cuello,
y tus pechos gemelas cervatillas.
Flor de Sarón y lirio de los valles,
yegua de Faraón, ¡oh Sulamita!

    Cuba, Santo Domingo, Puerto Rico,
fogosas y sensuales tierras mías.
¡Oh los rones calientes de Jamaica!
¡Oh fiero calalú de Martinica!
¡Oh noche fermentada de tambores
del Haití impenetrable y voduista!
Dominica, Tortola, Guadalupe,
¡Antillas, mis Antillas!
Sobre el mar de Colón, aupadas todas,
sobre el Caribe mar, todas unidas,
soñado y padeciendo y forcejeando
contra pestes, ciclones y codicias,
y muriéndose un poco por la noche,
y otra vez a la aurora, redivivas,
porque eres tú, mulata de los trópicos,
la libertad cantando en mis Antillas.

in your womb my two races commingle
their vital, effervescent force.
Love, Mulatta's torrid love,
a flask of rum, a liquefying sugar,
a *tabonuco* beam sears to the marrow
with its fragrance of sandalwood and myrrh.
In the words of the Song of Songs,
you are swarthy because touched by the sun.
Milk and honey are under your tongue,
anointing oils the liquid in your eyes.
Your neck is like the tower of David,
your twin breasts are two fawns.
A rose of Sharon, a lily of the valley,
a pharaoh's mare, oh, Shulamith!

Cuba, Santo Domingo, Puerto Rico,
my fiery sensual lands.
Oh, the hot rums of Jamaica!
Martinique's wild callaloo!
Oh, fermenting night of the drums
of unplumbed, voodoo Haiti!
Dominica, Tortola, Guadeloupe,
Antilles, my Antilles!
On Columbus's sea, exalted all,
on the Caribbean Sea, all united,
dreaming, suffering, struggling
against plagues, cyclones, and greed,
dying a little each night,
and again at dawn, reborn,
for, Mulatta of the tropics, you are
freedom singing in my Antilles.

*Translated by
Roberto Márquez*

PÁGINA PARA RECORDAR

AL CORONEL SUÁREZ,

VENCEDOR EN JUNÍN

Qué importan las penurias, el destierro,
la humillación de envejecer, la sombra creciente
del dictador sobre la patria, la casa en el Barrio del Alto
que vendieron sus hermanos mientras guerreaba, los días inútiles
(los días que uno espera olvidar, los días que uno sabe que olvidará),
si tuvo su hora alta, a caballo,
en la visible pampa de Junín como en un escenario para el futuro,
como si el anfiteatro de montañas fuera el futuro.

Qué importa el tiempo sucesivo si en él
hubo una plenitud, un éxtasis, una tarde.

Sirvió trece años en las guerras de América. Al fin la suerte lo llevó
    al Estado Oriental, a campos del Río Negro.
En los atardeceres pensaría

JORGE LUIS BORGES

Argentina **1899–1986**

A PAGE TO COMMEMORATE

COLONEL SUÁREZ,

VICTOR AT JUNÍN

What do they matter now, the deprivations,
exile, the ignominies of growing old,
the dictator's shadow spreading across the land, the house
in Barrio del Alto, which his brothers sold while he fought,
the pointless days (days one hopes to forget,
days one knows are forgettable),
when he had at least his burning hour on horseback
on the plateau of Junín, a stage for the future,
as if that mountain stage itself were the future?

What is time's monotony to him, who knew
that fulfillment, that ecstasy, that afternoon?

Thirteen years he served in the Wars of Independence. Then fate
    took him to Uruguay, to the banks of the Río Negro.
In the dying afternoons he would think

que para él había florecido esa rosa:
la encarnada batalla de Junín, el instante infinito
en que las lanzas se tocaron, la orden que movió la batalla,
la derrota inicial, y entre los fragores
(no menos brusca para él que para la tropa)
su voz gritando a los peruanos que arremetieran,
la luz, el ímpetu y la fatalidad de la carga,
el furioso laberinto de los ejércitos,
la batalla de lanzas en la que no retumbó un solo tiro,
el *godo* que atravesó con el hierro,
la victoria, la felicidad, la fatiga, un principio de sueño,
y la gente muriendo entre los pantanos,
y Bolívar pronunciando palabras sin duda históricas
y el sol ya occidental y el recuperado sabor del agua y del vino,
y aquel muerto sin cara porque la pisó y borró la batalla . . .

Su bisnieto escribe estos versos y una tácita voz
desde lo antiguo de la sangre le llega:
—Qué importa mi batalla de Junín si es una gloriosa memoria,
una fecha que se aprende para un examen o un lugar en el atlas.
La batalla es eterna y puede prescindir de la pompa
de visibles ejércitos con clarines;
Junín son dos civiles que en una esquina maldicen a un tirano,
o un hombre oscuro que se muere en la cárcel.

of his moment that had flowered like a rose—
the crimson battle of Junín, the enduring moment
in which the lances crossed, the order of battle,
defeat at first, and in the uproar
(as astonishing to him as to the army)
his voice urging the Peruvians to the attack,
the thrill, the drive, the decisiveness of the charge,
the seething labyrinth of cavalries,
clash of the lances (not a single shot fired),
the Spaniard he ran through with his spear,
the headiness of victory, exhaustion, drowsiness descending,
and men dying in the marshes,
and Bolívar uttering words earmarked no doubt for history,
and the sun in the west by now, and water and wine
tasted as for the first time, and that dead man
whose face the battle had trampled on and obliterated . . .

His great-grandson is writing these lines,
and a silent voice comes to him out of the past,
out of the blood:
"What does my battle at Junín matter if it is only
a glorious memory, or a date learned by rote
for an examination, or a place in the atlas?
The battle is everlasting and can do without
the pomp of actual armies and of trumpets.
Junín is two civilians cursing a tyrant
on a street corner,
or an unknown man somewhere, dying in prison."

Translated by
Alistair Reid

LA NOCHE CÍCLICA

A Sylvina Bullrich

Lo supieron los arduos alumnos de Pitágoras:
Los astros y los hombres vuelven cíclicamente;
Los átomos fatales repetirán la urgente
Afrodita de oro, los tebanos, las ágoras.

En edades futuras oprimirá el centauro
Con el casco solípedo el pecho del lapita;
Cuando Roma sea polvo, gemirá en la infinita
Noche de su palacio fétido el minotauro.

Volverá toda noche de insomnio: minuciosa.
La mano que esto escribe renacerá del mismo
Vientre. Férreos ejércitos construirán el abismo.
(David Hume de Edimburgo dijo la misma cosa.)

No sé si volveremos en un ciclo segundo
Como vuelven las cifras de una fracción periódica;
Pero sé que una oscura rotación pitagórica
Noche a noche me deja en un lugar del mundo

Que es de los arrabales. Una esquina remota
Que puede ser del norte, del sur o del oeste,
Pero que tiene siempre una tapia celeste,
Una higuera sombría y una vereda rota.

Ahí está Buenos Aires. El tiempo que a los hombres
Trae el amor o el oro, a mí apenas me deja

THE CYCLICAL NIGHT

To Sylvina Bullrich

They knew it, the fervent pupils of Pythagoras:
That stars and men revolve in a cycle,
That fateful atoms will bring back the vital
Gold Aphrodite, Thebans, and agoras.

In future epochs the centaur will oppress
With solid uncleft hoof the breast of the Lapith;
When Rome is dust the Minotaur will moan
Once more in the endless dark of its rank palace.

Every sleepless night will come back in minute
Detail. This writing hand will be born from the same
Womb, and bitter armies contrive their doom.
(Edinburgh's David Hume made this very point.)

I do not know if we will recur in a second
Cycle, like numbers in a periodic fraction;
But I know that a vague Pythagorean rotation
Night after night sets me down in the world

On the outskirts of this city. A remote street
That might be either north or west or south,
But always with a blue-washed wall, the shade
Of a fig tree, and a sidewalk of broken concrete.

This, here, is Buenos Aires. Time, which brings
Either love or money to men, hands on to me

Esta rosa apagada, esta vana madeja
De calles que repiten los pretéritos nombres

De mi sangre: Laprida, Cabrera, Soler, Suárez . . .
Nombres en que retumban (ya secretas) las dianas,
Las repúblicas, los caballos y las mañanas.
Las felices victorias, las muertes militares.

Las plazas agravadas por la noche sin dueño
Son los patios profundos de un árido palacio
Y las calles unánimes que engendran el espacio
Son corredores de vago miedo y de sueño.

Vuelve la noche cóncava que descifró Anaxágoras;
Vuelve a mi carne humana la eternidad constante
Y el recuerdo ¿el proyecto? de un poema incesante:
"Lo supieron los arduos alumnos de Pitágoras . . ."

EL GOLEM

Si (como el griego afirma en el Cratilo)
El nombre es arquetipo de la cosa,
En las letras de *rosa* está la rosa
Y todo el Nilo en la palabra *Nilo*.

Y, hecho de consonantes y vocales,
Habrá un terrible Nombre, que la esencia
Cifre de Dios y que la Omnipotencia
Guarde en letras y sílabas cabales.

Only this withered rose, this empty tracery
Of streets with names recurring from the past

In my blood: Laprida, Cabrera, Soler, Suárez . . .
Names in which secret bugle calls are sounding,
Invoking republics, cavalry, and mornings,
Joyful victories, men dying in action.

Squares weighed down by a night in no one's care
Are the vast patios of an empty palace,
And the single-minded streets creating space
Are corridors for sleep and nameless fear.

It returns, the hollow dark of Anaxagoras;
In my human flesh, eternity keeps recurring
And the memory, or plan, of an endless poem beginning:
"They knew it, the fervent pupils of Pythagoras . . ."

*Translated by
Alistair Reid*

THE GOLEM

If, as the Greek maintains in the *Cratylus*,
a name is the archetype of a thing,
the rose is in the letters that spell *rose*
and the Nile entire resounds in its name's ring.

So, composed of consonants and vowels,
there must exist one awe-inspiring word
that God inheres in—that, when spoken, holds
Almightiness in syllables unslurred.

Adán y las estrellas lo supieron
En el Jardín. La herrumbre del pecado
(Dicen los cabalistas) lo ha borrado
Y las generaciones lo perdieron.

Los artificios y el candor del hombre
No tienen fin. Sabemos que hubo un día
En que el pueblo de Dios buscaba el Nombre
En las vigilias de la judería.

No a la manera de otras que una vaga
Sombra insinúan en la memoria
Aún está verde y viva la memoria
De Judá León, que era rabino en Praga.

Sediento de saber lo que Dios sabe,
Judá León se dio a permutaciones
De letras y a complejas variaciones
Y al fin pronunció el Nombre que es la Clave,

La Puerta, el Eco, el Huésped y el Palacio,
Sobre un muñeco que con torpes manos
Labró, para enseñarle los arcanos
De las Letras, del Tiempo y del Espacio.

El simulacro alzó los soñolientos
Párpados y vio formas y colores
Que no entendió, perdidos en rumores
Y ensayó temerosos movimientos.

Gradualmente se vio (como nosotros)
Aprisionado en esta red sonora

174

Adam knew it in the Garden, so did the stars.
The rusty work of sin, so the cabbalists say,
obliterated it completely;
no generation has found it to this day.

The cunning and naïveté of men
are limitless. We know there came a time
when God's people, searching for the Name,
toiled in the ghetto, matching rhyme to rhyme.

One memory stands out, unlike the rest—
dim shapes always fading from time's dim log.
Still fresh and green the memory persists
of Judah León, a rabbi once in Prague.

Thirsty to know things known only to God,
Judah León shuffled letters endlessly,
trying them out in subtle combinations
till at last he uttered the Name that is the Key,

the Gate, the Echo, the Landlord, and the Mansion,
over a dummy which, with fingers wanting grace,
he fashioned, thinking to teach it the arcane
of Words and Letters and of Time and Space.

The simulacrum lifted its drowsy lids
and, much bewildered, took color and shape
in a floating world of sounds. Following this,
it hesitantly took a timid step.

Little by little it found itself, like us,
caught in the reverberating weft

De Antes, Después, Ayer, Mientras, Ahora,
Derecha, Izquierda, Yo, Tú, Aquellos, Otros.

(El cabalista que ofició de numen
A la vasta criatura apodó Golem;
Estas verdades las refiere Scholem
En un docto lugar de su volumen.)

El rabí le explicaba el universo
"Esto es mi pie; esto el tuyo; esto la soga."
Y logró, al cabo de años, que el perverso
Barriera bien o mal la sinagoga.

Tal vez hubo un error en la grafía
O en la articulación del Sacro Nombre;
A pesar de tan alta hechicería,
No aprendió a hablar el aprendiz de hombre.

Sus ojos, menos de hombre que de perro
Y harto menos de perro que de cosa,
Seguían al rabí por la dudosa
Penumbra de las piezas del encierro.

Algo anormal y tosco hubo en el Golem,
Ya que a su paso el gato del rabino
Se escondía. (Ese gato no está en Scholem
Pero, a través del tiempo, lo adivino.)

Elevando a su Dios manos filiales,
Las devociones de su Dios copiaba
O, estúpido y sonriente, se ahuecaba
En cóncavas zalemas orientales.

of After, Before, Yesterday, Meanwhile, Now,
You, Me, Those, the Others, Right and Left.

That cabbalist who played at being God
gave his spacey offspring the nickname Golem.
(In a learned passage of his volume,
these truths have been conveyed to us by Scholem.)

To it the rabbi would explain the universe—
"This is my foot; this yours; this is a clog"—
year in, year out, until the spiteful thing
rewarded him by sweeping the synagogue.

Perhaps the Sacred Name had been misspelled
or in its uttering been jumbled or too weak.
The potent sorcery never took effect:
man's apprentice never learned to speak.

Its eyes, less human than doglike in their look,
and even less a dog's than eyes of a thing,
would follow every move the rabbi made
about a confinement always gloomy and dim.

Something coarse and abnormal was in the Golem,
for the rabbi's cat, as soon as it moved about,
would run off and hide. (There's no cat in Scholem
but across the gulf of time I make one out.)

Lifting up to its God its filial hands,
it aped its master's devotions—even the least—
or, with a stupid smile, would bend far over
in concave salaams the way men do in the East.

El rabí lo miraba con ternura
Y con algún horror. *¿Cómo* (se dijo)
Pude engendrar este penoso hijo
Y la inacción dejé, que es la cordura?

¿Por qué di en agregar a la infinita
Serie un símbolo más? ¿Por qué a la vana
Madeja que en lo eterno se devana,
Di otra causa, otro efecto y otra cuita?

En la hora de angustia y de luz vaga,
En su Golem los ojos detenía.
¿Quién no dirá las cosas que sentía
Dios, al mirar a su rabino en Praga?

POEMA CONJETURAL

El doctor Francisco Laprida, asesinado el día
22 de setiembre de 1829 por los montoneros
de Aldao, piensa antes de morir:

Zumban las balas en la tarde última.
Hay viento y hay cenizas en el viento,
se dispersan el día y la batalla
deforme, y la victoria es de los otros.
Vencen los bárbaros, los gauchos vencen.
Yo, que estudié las leyes y los cánones,
yo, Francisco Narciso de Laprida,
cuya voz declaró la independencia

The rabbi watched it fondly and not a little
alarmed as he wondered: "How could I bring
such a sorry creature into this world
and give up my leisure, surely the wisest thing?

What made me supplement the endless series
of symbols with one more? Why add in vain
to the knotty skein always unraveling
another cause and effect, with not one gain?"

In this hour of anguish and uncertain light,
upon his Golem his eyes would come to rest.
Who is to say what God must have been feeling,
Looking down and seeing His rabbi so distressed?

CONJECTURAL POEM

*Francisco Laprida, assassinated on the
22 of September 1829 by the revolutionaries
from Aldao, reflects before his death:*

Bullets whine on that last afternoon.
There is wind; and there is ash on the wind.
Now they subside, the day and the disorder
of battle, victory goes to the others,
to the barbarians. The gauchos win.
I, Francisco Narciso de Laprida,
who studied law and the civil canon,
whose voice proclaimed the independence

de estas crueles provincias, derrotado,
de sangre y de sudor manchado el rostro,
sin esperanza ni temor, perdido,
huyo hacia el Sur por arrabales últimos.
Como aquel capitán del Purgatorio
que, huyendo a pie y ensangrentado el llano,
fue cegado y tumbado por la muerte
donde un oscuro río pierde el nombre,
así habré de caer. Hoy es el término.
La noche lateral de los pantanos
me acecha y me demora. Oigo los cascos
de mi caliente muerte que me busca
con jinetes, con belfos y con lanzas.

Yo que anhelé ser otro, ser un hombre
de sentencias, de libros, de dictámenes,
a cielo abierto yaceré entre ciénagas;
pero me endiosa el pecho inexplicable
un júbilo secreto. Al fin me encuentro
con mi destino sudamericano.
A esta ruinosa tarde me llevaba
el laberinto múltiple de pasos
que mis días tejieron desde un día
de la niñez. Al fin he descubierto
la recóndita clave de mis años,
la suerte de Francisco de Laprida,
la letra que faltaba, la perfecta
forma que supo Dios desde el principio.
En el espejo de esta noche alcanzo
mi insospechado rostro eterno. El círculo
se va a cerrar. Yo aguardo que así sea.

of these harsh provinces, am now defeated,
my face smeared with mingled blood and sweat,
lost, feeling neither hope nor fear,
in flight to the last outposts in the south.
Like that captain in the *Purgatorio*
who, fleeing on foot, leaving a bloodstained trail,
where some dark stream obliterates his name,
so must I fall. This day is the end.
The darkness spreading across the marshes
pursues me and pins me down. I hear the hooves
of my hot-breathing death hunting me down
with horsemen, whinnying, and lances.

I who dreamed of being another man,
well-read, a man of judgment and opinion,
will lie in a swamp under an open sky;
but a secret and inexplicable joy
makes my heart leap. At last I come face to face
with my destiny as a South American.
The complicated labyrinth of steps
that I have traced since one day in my childhood
led me to this disastrous afternoon.
At last I have discovered
the long-hidden secret of my life,
the destiny of Francisco de Laprida,
the missing letter, the key, the perfect form
known only to God from the beginning.
In the mirror of this night I come across
my eternal face, unknown to me. The circle
is about to close. I wait for it to happen.

Pisan mis pies la sombra de las lanzas
que me buscan. Las befas de mi muerte,
los jinetes, la crines, los caballos,
se ciernen sobre mí . . . Ya el primer golpe,
ya el duro hierro que me raja el pecho,
el íntimo cuchillo en la garganta.

My feet tread on the shadows of the lances
that point me out. The jeering at my death,
the riders, the tossing manes, the horses
loom over me . . . Now comes the first thrust,
now the harsh iron, ravaging my chest,
the knife, so intimate, opening my throat.

Translated by
Alistair Reid

TWO ENGLISH POEMS

To Beatriz Bibiloni Webster de Bullrich

The useless dawn finds me in a deserted streetcorner; I have outlived
the night.
Nights are proud waves: darkblue topheavy waves laden with all hues
of deep spoil, laden with things unlikely and desirable.
Nights have a habit of mysterious gifts and refusals, of things half
given away, half withheld, of joys with a dark hemisphere. Nights
act that way, I tell you.
The surge, that night, left me the customary shreds and odd ends:
some hated friends to chat with, music for dreams, and the smoking
of bitter ashes. These things my hungry heart has no use for.
The big wave brought you.
Words, any words, your laughter; and you so lazily and incessantly
beautiful. We talked and you have forgotten the words.
The shattering dawn finds me in a deserted street of my city.
Your profile turned away, the sounds that go to make your name, the lilt
of your laughter: these are the illustrious toys you have left me.
I turn them over in the dawn, I lose them, I find them; I tell them to the
few stray dogs and to the few stray stars of the dawn.

JORGE LUIS BORGES

Your dark rich life . . .

I must get at you, somehow: I put away those illustrious toys you have
   left me, I want your hidden look, your real smile—that lonely,
   mocking smile your cool mirror knows.

II

What can I hold you with?

I offer you lean streets, desperate sunsets, the moon of the ragged
   suburbs.

I offer you the bitterness of a man who has looked long and long at
   the lonely moon.

I offer you my ancestors, my dead men, the ghosts that living men
   have honoured in marble; my father's father killed in the frontier
   of Buenos Aires, two bullets through his lungs, bearded and
   dead, wrapped by his soldiers in the hide of a cow; my mother's
   grandfather—just twenty-four—heading a charge of three
   hundred men in Peru, now ghosts on vanished horses.

I offer you whatever insight my books may hold, whatever manliness
   or humour my life.

I offer you the loyalty of a man who has never been loyal.

I offer you that kernel of myself that I have saved, somehow—the
   central heart that deals not in words, traffics not with dreams and
   is untouched by time, by joy, by adversities.

I offer you the memory of a yellow rose seen at sunset, years before
   you were born.

I offer you explanations of yourself, theories about yourself, authentic
   and surprising news of yourself.

I can give you my loneliness, my darkness, the hunger of my heart;
   I am trying to bribe you with uncertainty, with danger, with defeat.

SPINOZA

Las traslúcidas manos del judío
Labran en la penumbra los cristales
Y la tarde que muere es miedo y frío.
(Las tardes a las tardes son iguales.)
Las manos y el espacio de jacinto
Que palidece en el confín del Ghetto
Casi no existen para el hombre quieto
Que está soñando un claro laberinto.
No lo turba la fama, ese reflejo
De sueños en el sueño de otro espejo,
Ni el temeroso amor de las doncellas.
Libre de la metáfora y del mito
Labra un arduo cristal: el infinito
Mapa de Aquél que es todas Sus estrellas.

BORGES Y YO

Al otro, a Borges, es a quien le ocurren las cosas. Yo camino por Buenos Aires y me demoro, acaso ya mecánicamente, para mirar el arco de un zaguán y la puerta cancel; de Borges tengo noticias por el correo y veo su nombre en una terna de profesores o en un diccionario biográfico. Me gustan los relojes de arena, los mapas, la tipografía del siglo XVIII, las etimologías, el sabor del café, y la prosa de Stevenson; el otro comparte esas preferencias, pero de un modo vanidoso que las convierte en atributos de un actor. Sería exagerado afirmar que nuestra relación es hostil; yo vivo, yo me dejo vivir, para que Borges pueda

SPINOZA

Here in the twilight the translucent hands
Of the Jew polishing the crystal glass.
The dying afternoon is cold with bands
Of fear. Each day the afternoons all pass
The same. The hands and space of hyacinth
Paling in the confines of the ghetto walls
Barely exists for the quiet man who stalls
There, dreaming up a brilliant labyrinth.
Fame doesn't trouble him (that reflection of
Dreams in the dream of another mirror), nor love,
The timid love of women. Gone the bars,
He's free, from metaphor and myth, to sit
Polishing a stubborn lens: the infinite
Map of the One who now is all His stars.

Translated by
Willis Barnstone

BORGES AND I

The other one, Borges, is to whom things happen. I walk through
Buenos Aires, stop, maybe a bit mechanically, to look at the arch of an
entryway and a grillwork door; I have news of Borges by mail or when
I see his name in a list of professors or in a biographical dictionary.
I like hourglasses, maps, eighteenth-century typography, the taste of
coffee, and Stevenson's prose; the other shares those preferences but
with a vanity that turns them into an actor's attributes. It would be an
exaggeration to affirm that our relationship is hostile; I live, I let my-
self live, so that Borges can plot his literature and that literature justi-

tramar su literatura y esa literatura me justifica. Nada me cuesta confesar que ha logrado ciertas páginas válidas, pero esas páginas no me pueden salvar, quizá porque lo bueno ya no es de nadie, ni siquiera del otro, sino del lenguaje o la tradición. Por lo demás, yo estoy destinado a perderme, definitivamente, y sólo algún instante de mí podrá sobrevivir en el otro. Poco a poco voy cediéndole todo, aunque me consta su perversa costumbre de falsear y magnificar. Spinoza entendió que todas las cosas quieren perseverar en su ser; la piedra eternamente quiere ser piedra y el tigre un tigre. Yo he de quedar en Borges, no en mí (si es que alguien soy), pero me reconozco menos en sus libros que en muchos otros o que en el laborioso rasgueo de una guitarra. Hace años yo traté de librarme de él y pasé de las mitologías del arrabal a los juegos con el tiempo y con lo infinito, pero esos juegos son de Borges ahora y tendré que idear otras cosas. Así mi vida es una fuga y todo lo pierdo y todo es del olvido, o del otro.

No sé cuál de los dos escribe esta página.

fies me. It doesn't cost me anything to confess he has achieved a few valid pages, but those pages can't save me, perhaps because what's good no longer belongs to anyone, not even to the other, but to language and tradition. In any case, I'm destined to be lost, definitively, and just some instant of me will survive in the other. Little by little I cede everything, even though I'm aware of his perverse tendency to falsify and pontificate. Spinoza understood that all things want to be preserved in their being: the stone eternally wants to be a stone and the tiger a tiger. I shall remain in Borges, not in myself (if I am someone), but I recognize myself less in his books than in many others or in the laborious strumming of a guitar. Years ago I tried freeing myself from him and went from the mythologies of the suburbs to the games with time and the infinite, but those games are Borges's now and I shall come up with other things. Thus my life is a flight and I lose everything and everything belongs to oblivion, or to the other.

I don't know which of the two writes this page.

Translated by
Ilan Stavans

VIGÍLIA

Como o companheiro é morto,
todos juntos morreremos
um pouco.

O calor de nossas lágrimas
sôbre quem perdeu a vida,
não é nada.

Amá-lo, nesta tristeza,
é suspiro numa selva
imensa.

Por fidelidade reta
ao companheiro perdido,
que nos resta?

Deixar-nos morrer um pouco
por aquêle que hoje vemos
todo morto.

CECILIA MEIRELES

Brazil **1901–1964**

VIGIL

As the companion is dead,
so we must all together die
somewhat.

Shed for him who lost his life,
our tears are worth
nothing.

Love for him, within this grief,
is a faint sigh lost in a vast
forest.

Faith in him, the lost
companion—what but that
is left?

To die ourselves somewhat
through him we see today
quite dead.

*Translated by
James Merrill*

191

O CAVALO MORTO

Vi a névoa de madrugada
deslizar seus gestos de prata,
mover densidade de opala
naquele pórtico de sono.

Na fronteira havia um cavalo morto.

Grãos de cristal rolavam pelo
seu flanco nítido: e algum vento
torcia-lhe as crinas, pequeno,
level arabesco, triste adôrno.

—e movia a cauda ao cavalo morto.

As estrêlas ainda viviam
e ainda não eram nascidas
ai! as flôres daquele dia . . .
—mas era um canteiro o seu corpo:

um jardim de lírios, o cavalo morto.

Muitos viajantes contemplaram
a fluida música, a orvalhada
das grandes môscas de esmeralda
chegando em rumoroso jôrro.

Adernava triste, o cavalo morto.

E viam-se uns cavalos vivos,
altos como esbeltos navios,

THE DEAD HORSE

I saw the early morning mist
make silver passes, shift
densities of opal
within sleep's portico.

On the frontier, a dead horse.

Crystal grains were rolling down
his lustrous flank, and the breeze
twisted his mane in a littlest,
lightest arabesque, sorry adornment

—and his tail stirred, the dead horse.

Still the stars were shining
and that day's flowers, sad to say,
had not yet come to light
—but his body was a plot,

garden of lilies, the dead horse.

Many a traveler took note
of fluid music, the dewfall
of big emerald flies
arriving in a noisy gush.

He was listening sorely, the dead horse.

And some live horses could be seen
slender and tall as ships,

galopando nos ares finos,
com felizes perfis de sonho.

Branco e verde via-se o cavalo morto,

no campo enorme e sem recurso
—e devagar girava o mundo
entre as suas pestanas, turvo
como em luas de espelho roxo.

Dava o sol nos dentes do cavalo morto.

Mas todos tinham muita pressa,
e não sentiram como a terra
procurava, de légua em légua,
o ágil, o imenso, o etéreo sôpro
que faltava àquele arcabouço.

Tão pesado, o peito do cavalo morto!

galloping through the keen air
in profile, joyously dreaming.

White and green the dead horse

in the enormous field without recourse
—and slowly the world between
his eyelashes revolved, all blurred
as in red mirror moons.

Sun shone on the teeth of the dead horse.

But everybody was in a frantic rush
and could not feel how earth
kept searching league upon league
for the nimble, the immense, the ethereal breath
which had escaped that skeleton.

O heavy breast of the dead horse!

*Translated by
James Merrill*

OS OMBROS

SUPORTAM O MUNDO

Chega um tempo em que não se diz mais: meu Deus.
Tempo de absoluta depuração.
Tempo em que não se diz mais: meu amor.
Porque o amor resultou inútil.
E os olhos não choram.
E as mãos tecem apenas o rude trabalho.
E o coração está seco.

Em vão mulheres batem à porta, não abrirás.
Ficaste sozinho, a luz apagou-se
mas na sombra teus olhos resplandecem enormes.
És todo certeza, já não sabes sofrer.
E nada esperas de teus amigos.

Pouco importa venha a velhice, que é a velhice?
Teus ombros suportam o mundo

CARLOS DRUMMOND
DE ANDRADE

Brazil 1902-1987

YOUR SHOULDERS

HOLD UP THE WORLD

A time comes when you no longer can say: my God.
A time of total cleaning up.
A time when you no longer can say: my love.
Because love proved useless.
And the eyes don't cry.
And the hands do only rough work.
And the heart is dry.

Women knock at your door in vain, you won't open.
You remain alone, the light turned off,
and your enormous eyes shine in the dark.
It is obvious you no longer know how to suffer.
And you want nothing from your friends.

Who cares if old age comes, what is old age?
Your shoulders are holding up the world

e ele não pesa mais que a mão de uma criança.
As guerras, as fomes, as discussões dentro dos edifícios
provam apenas que a vida prossegue
e nem todos se libertaram ainda.
Alguns, achando bárbaro o espetáculo
prefeririam (os delicados) morrer.
Chegou um tempo em que não adianta morrer.
Chegou um tempo em que a vida é uma ordem.
A vida apenas, sem mistificação.

O ELEFANTE

Fabrico um elefante
de meus poucos recursos.
Um tanto de madeira
tirado a velhos móveis
talvez lhe dê apoio.
E o encho de algodão,
de paina, de doçura.
A cola vai fixar
suas orelhas pensas.
A tromba se enovela,
é a parte mais feliz
de sua arquitetura.

Mas há também as presas,
dessa matéria pura
que não sei figurar.
Tão alva essa riqueza
a espojar-se nos circos

and it's lighter than a child's hand.
Wars, famine, family fights inside buildings
prove only that life goes on
and not everybody has freed himself yet.
Some (the delicate ones) judging the spectacle cruel
will prefer to die.
A time comes when death doesn't help.
A time comes when life is an order.
Just life, without any escapes.

Translated by
Mark Strand

THE ELEPHANT

I make an elephant
from the little
I have. Wood
from old furniture
holds him up, and I fill him
with cotton, silk,
and sweetness.
Glue keeps his heavy
ears in place.
His rolled-up trunk
is the happiest part
of his architecture.

And his tusks are made
of that rare material
I cannot fake.
A white fortune
rolling around in circus dust

sem perda ou corrupção.
E há por fim os olhos,
onde se deposita
a parte do elefante
mais fluida e permanente,
alheia a toda fraude.

Eis meu pobre elefante
pronto para sair
à procura de amigos
num mundo enfastiado
que já não crê nos bichos
e duvida das coisas.
Ei-lo, massa imponente
e frágil, que se abana
e move lentamente
a pele costurada
onde há flores de pano
e nuvens, alusões
a um mundo mais poético
onde o amor reagrupa
as formas naturais.

Vai o meu elefante
pela rua povoada,
mas não o querem ver
nem mesmo para rir
da cauda que ameaça
deixá-lo ir sozinho.

É todo graça, embora
as pernas não ajudem

without being lost or stolen.
And finally there are
the eyes, where the most
fluid and permanent
part of the elephant
stays, free of dishonesty.

Here's my poor elephant
ready to leave,
to find friends
in a tired world
that no longer believes in animals
and doesn't trust in things.
Here he is: an imposing
and fragile hulk, who shakes his head
and moves slowly,
his hide stitched
with cloth flowers
and clouds—allusions
to a more poetic world
where love reassembles
the natural forms.

My elephant goes
down a crowded street,
but nobody looks,
not even to laugh
at his tail, which threatens
to leave him.

He is all grace, except
his legs don't help

e seu ventre balofo
se arrisque a desabar
ao mais leve empurrão.
Mostra com elegância
sua mínima vida,
e não há na cidade
alma que se disponha
a recolher em si
desse corpo sensível
a fugitiva imagem,
o passo desastrado
mas faminto e tocante.

Mas faminto de seres
e situações patéticas,
de encontros ao luar
no mais profundo oceano,
sob a raiz das árvores
ou no seio das conchas,
de luzes que não cegam
e brilham através
dos troncos mais espessos.
Esse passo que vai
sem esmagar as plantas
no campo de batalha,
à procura de sítios,
segredos, episódios
não contados em livro,
de que apenas o vento,
as folhas, a formiga
reconhecem o talhe,
mas que os homens ignoram,

and his swollen belly
will collapse
at the slightest touch.
He expresses
with elegance
his minimal life
and no one in town
is willing to take
to himself
from that tender body
the fugitive image,
the clumsy walk.

Easily moved, he yearns
for sad situations,
unhappy people,
moonlit encounters
in the deepest ocean,
under the roots of trees,
in the bosom of shells;
he yearns for lights
that don't blind
yet shine through
the thickest trunks.
He walks the battlefield
without crushing plants,
searching for places,
secrets, stories
untold in any book,
whose style only the wind,
the leaves, the ant
recognize, but men ignore

pois só ousam mostrar-se
sob a paz das cortinas
à pálpebra cerrada.

E já tarde da noite
volta meu elefante,
mas volta fatigado,
as patas vacilantes
se desmancham no pó.
Ele não encontrou
o de que carecia,
o de que carecemos,
eu e meu elefante,
em que amo disfarçar-me.
Exausto de pesquisa,
caiu-lhe o vasto engenho
como simples papel.
A cola se dissolve
e todo o seu conteúdo
de perdão, de carícia,
de pluma, de algodão,
jorra sobre o tapete,
qual mito desmontado.
Amanhã recomeço.

since they dare show themselves
only under a veiled peace
and to closed eyes.

And now late at night
my elephant returns,
but returns tired out,
his shaky legs
break down in the dust.
He didn't find
what he wanted,
what we wanted,
I and my elephant,
in whom I love to disguise myself.
Tired of searching,
his huge machinery
collapses like paper.
The paste gives way
and all his contents,
forgiveness, sweetness,
feathers, cotton,
burst out on the rug
like a myth torn apart.
Tomorrow I begin again.

*Translated by
Mark Strand*

DESAPARECIMENTO

DE LUÍSA PORTO

Pede-se a quem souber
do paradeiro de Luísa Porto
avise sua residência
à Rua Santos Óleos, 48.
Previna urgente
solitária mãe enferma
entrevada há longos anos
erma de seus cuidados.

Pede-se a quem avistar
Luísa Porto, de 37 anos,
que apareça, que escreva, que mande dizer
onde está.
Suplica-se ao repórter-amador,
ao caixeiro, ao mata-mosquitos, ao transeunte,
a qualquer do povo e da classe média,
até mesmo aos senhores ricos,
que tenham pena de mãe aflita
e lhe restituam a filha volatilizada
ou pelo menos dêem informações.
É alta, magra,
morena, rosto penugento, dentes alvos,
sinal de nascença junto ao olho esquerdo,
levemente estrábica.
Vestidinho simples. Óculos.
Sumida há três meses.
Mãe entrevada chamando.

THE DISAPPEARANCE

OF LUISA PORTO

Ask anyone who knows
the whereabouts of Luisa Porto
to please notify her residence
at 48 Santos Oleos Street.
Immediately advise
her poor sick mother
for many years a cripple
now beside herself with grief.

If you happen to come across
Luisa Porto, age 37, make her
come home, get her to write
or send word where she is.
Ask some amateur reporter,
a passing stranger, salesclerk, exterminator,
anybody at all, from whatever class,
even the well-to-do,
to have pity on a worried mother
and bring back her daughter
or at least some news.
Luisa's tall, thin,
dark hair, downy complexion, white teeth,
a beauty mark by her left eye,
rather nearsighted.
Plainly dressed, glasses.
Disappeared three months ago.
A sickly mother's appeal.

Roga-se ao povo caritativo desta cidade
que tome em consideração um caso de família
digno de simpatia especial.
Luísa é de bom gênio, correta,
meiga, trabalhadora, religiosa.
Foi fazer compras na feira da praça.
Não voltou.

Levava pouco dinheiro na bolsa.
(Procurem Luísa.)
De ordinário não se demorava.
(Procurem Luísa.)
Namorado isso não tinha.
(Procurem. Procurem.)
Faz tanta falta.

Se todavia não a encontrarem
nem por isso deixem de procurar
com obstinação e confiança que Deus sempre recompensa
e talvez encontrem.
Mãe, viúva pobre, não perde a esperança.
Luísa ia pouco à cidade
e aqui no bairro é onde melhor pode ser pesquisada.
Sua melhor amiga, depois da mãe enferma,
é Rita Santana, costureira, moça desimpedida,
a qual não dá notícia nenhuma,
limitando-se a responder: Não sei.
O que não deixa de ser esquisito.

Somem tantas pessoas anualmente
numa cidade como o Rio de Janeiro
que talvez Luísa Porto jamais seja encontrada.

Call upon the charitable people in our city
to assist in a family matter
worthy of special concern.
Luisa's a good girl, affectionate,
religious, hardworking, proper.
She left to do some shopping at the corner market
and never came back.

She had so little money in her pocket.
(Find Luisa.)
She's not the type to come home late.
(Find Luisa.)
She didn't have any boyfriend.
(Find her, find her.)
It's unbearable without her.

If in the meantime you can't find her,
don't just give up looking;
with persistence and faith, God will reward you,
you're bound to spot her sooner or later.
Her mother, a poor widow, never loses hope;
remember that Luisa seldom went downtown
so it's best to start right here in the neighborhood.
Her closest friend (not counting her mother)
is the seamstress Rita Santana, a frivolous girl
who apparently can shed no light on the matter
and limits herself to repeating: I don't know, I don't know!
Which, to say the least, is odd.

So many people disappear, year after year,
in a city like Rio,
Luisa Porto may never be found.

Uma vez, em 1898
ou 9,
sumiu o próprio chefe de polícia
que saíra à tarde para uma volta no Largo do Rocio
e até hoje.
A mãe de Luísa, então jovem,
leu no *Diário Mercantil*,
ficou pasma.
O jornal embrulhado na memória.
Mal sabia ela que o casamento curto, a viuvez,
a pobreza, a paralisia, o queixume
seriam, na vida, seu lote
e que sua única filha, afável posto que estrábica,
se diluiria sem explicação.

Pela última vez e em nome de Deus
todo-poderoso e cheio de misericórdia
procurem a moça, procurem
essa que se chama Luísa Porto
e é sem namorado.
Esqueçam a luta política,
ponham de lado preocupações comerciais,
percam um pouco de tempo indagando,
inquirindo, remexendo.
Não se arrependerão. Não
há gratificação maior do que o sorriso
de mãe em festa
e a paz íntima
conseqüente às boas e desinteressadas ações,
puro orvalho da alma.

Não me venham dizer que Luísa suicidou-se.
O santo lume da fé

Once, in 1898
or 9,
the chief of police vanished from sight
after stepping out one night to have a look around Rossio Square,
and till this very day . . .
Luisa's mother, at the time a young girl,
read it in the *Merchants Daily*
and was astonished,
the headline printed across her memory.
How could she have guessed that a brief marriage, then widowhood,
poverty, paralysis, and regret
would prove her lot in life;
that her only daughter, as sweet as she was nearsighted,
would vanish without explanation.

For the last time, and in the name of God
all-powerful in His goodness and mercy,
find the poor girl, the one
called Luisa Porto,
the one without a boyfriend.
Forget politics for a moment,
set aside materialistic concerns
and devote some time to searching,
making inquiries, nosing around.
You won't regret it. There's no
satisfaction greater than the smile
of a joyous mother
or the inner peace
that comes from simple acts of charity,
pure ablution to the soul.

Don't try to tell me that Luisa committed suicide.
The holy fire of faith

ardeu sempre em sua alma
que pertence a Deus e a Teresinha do Menino Jesus.
Ela não se matou.
Procurem-na.
Tampouco foi vítima de desastre
que a polícia ignora
e os jornais não deram.
Está viva para consolo de uma entrevada
e triunfo geral do amor materno
filial
e do próximo.

Nada de insinuações quanto à moça casta
e que não tinha, não tinha namorado.
Algo de extraordinário terá acontecido,
terremoto, chegada de rei,
as ruas mudaram de rumo,
para que demore tanto, é noite.
Mas há de voltar, espontânea
ou trazida por mão benigna,
o olhar desviado e terno,
canção.

A qualquer hora do dia ou da noite
quem a encontrar avise a Rua Santos Óleos.
Não tem telefone.
Tem uma empregada velha que apanha o recado
e tomará providências.

Mas
se acharem que a sorte dos povos é mais importante
e que não devemos atentar nas dores individuais,

burned within her soul
devoted to God and the Blessed Mother of our little Lord Jesus.
She would never take her life.
You've got to find her.
She could hardly be the victim of a disaster
if the police know nothing
and the press is uninformed.
The child lives for the consolation of her crippled mother
bearing witness to the absolute triumph of maternal love,
Christian piety,
filial duty.

And no insinuation regarding her virtue:
she did not, I repeat, did not have a boyfriend.
Something extraordinary will turn out to have happened:
an earthquake or the advent of a king;
the streets must have changed directions
for her to take so long; it's dark!
But I know she'll come back, either by herself
or led by a generous hand,
looking sheepish and tender
as a song.

At any hour of the day or night
whoever finds her, please advise Santos Oleos Street.
There's no telephone,
only an old housekeeper you can give your message to
and she'll take care of the rest.

But
should you decide that the fate of nations is far more important,
that we mustn't waste time on particular griefs;

se fecharem ouvidos a este apelo de campainha,
não faz mal, insultem a mãe de Luísa,
virem a página:
Deus terá compaixão da abandonada e da ausente,
erguerá a enferma, e os membros perclusos
já se desatam em forma de busca.
Deus lhe dirá:
Vai,
procura tua filha, beija-a e fecha-a para sempre em teu coração.

Ou talvez não seja preciso esse favor divino.
A mãe de Luísa (somos pecadores)
sabe-se indigna de tamanha graça.
E resta a espera, que sempre é um dom.
Sim, os extraviados um dia regressam
ou nunca, ou pode ser, ou ontem.
E de pensar realizamos.
Quer apenas sua filhinha
que numa tarde remota de Cachoeiro
acabou de nascer e cheira a leite,
a cólica, a lágrima.
Já não interessa a descrição do corpo
nem esta, perdoem, fotografia,
disfarces de realidade mais intensa
e que anúncio algum proverá.
Cessem pesquisas, rádios, calai-vos.
Calma de flores abrindo
no canteiro azul
onde desabrocham seios e uma forma de virgem
intata nos tempos.
E de sentir compreendemos.
Já não adianta procurar

if you've shut your ears to the ringing of the bell,
that's all right, insult Luisa's mother,
turn the page:
God will show compassion for the lost, the forsaken,
will minister to the lame, whose limbs
will unbend in the form of a quest.
God Himself will say:
Go,
find your only daughter, kiss her, and forever hold her to your heart.

Or perhaps that heavenly favor won't be needed after all.
Luisa's mother (all of us are sinners)
would feel unworthy of such grace.
And hope remains, which is itself a gift.
Yes, the stray lambs one day return
or never, or maybe, or always.
And by thinking we understand.
All she wants is her child
who on a distant afternoon, back in Cachoeiro,
had just been born and smelled of milk,
colic, and tears.
There's no need for more description
or this—forgive me—photograph:
vague shadows of a living being
that hardly tell you anything.
No more searching. Silence the radios.
The calm of petals opening
in a blue garden
where hearts are unburdened, and the figure of a virgin
untouched for all time.
And through feeling we comprehend.
There's no use looking any longer

minha querida filha Luísa
que enquanto vagueio pelas cinzas do mundo
com inúteis pés fixados, enquanto sofro
e sofrendo me solto e me recomponho
e torno a viver e ando,
está inerte
cravada no centro da estrela invisível
Amor.

RETRATO DE FAMÍLIA

Este retrato de família
está um tanto empoeirado.
Já não se vê no rosto do pai
quanto dinheiro ele ganhou.

Nas mãos dos tios não se percebem
as viagens que ambos fizeram.
A avó ficou lisa, amarela,
sem memórias da monarquia.

Os meninos, como estão mudados.
O rosto de Pedro é tranqüilo,
usou os melhores sonhos.
E João não é mais mentiroso.

O jardim tornou-se fantástico.
As flores são placas cinzentas.
E a areia, sob pés extintos,
é um oceano de névoa.

for my dear daughter Luisa, who
—while I wander through the ashes of the world
with these useless limbs affixed to me, while I suffer
and by suffering I release and reconcile myself
and return to life, and walk—
looms motionless
caught in the heart of that invisible star
Love.

Translated by
Thomas Colchie

FAMILY PORTRAIT

Yes, this family portrait
is a little dusty.
The father's face doesn't show
how much money he earned.

The uncles' hands don't reveal
the voyages both of them made.
The grandmother's smoothed and yellowed;
she's forgotten the monarchy.

The children, how they've changed.
Peter's face is tranquil,
that wore the best dreams.
And John's no longer a liar.

The garden's become fantastic.
The flowers are gray badges.
And the sand, beneath dead feet,
is an ocean of fog.

No semicírculo de cadeiras
nota-se certo movimento.
As crianças trocam de lugar,
mas sem barulho: é um retrato.

Vinte anos é um grande tempo.
Modela qualquer imagem.
Se uma figura vai murchando,
outra, sorrindo, se propõe.

Esses estranhos assentados,
meus parentes? Não acredito.
São visitas se divertindo
numa sala que se abre pouco.

Ficaram traços da família
perdidos no jeito dos corpos.
Bastante para sugerir
que um corpo é cheio de surpresas.

A moldura deste retrato
em vão prende suas personagens.
Estão ali voluntariamente,
saberiam—se preciso—voar.

Poderiam sutilizar-se
no claro-escuro do salão,
ir morar no fundo de móveis
ou no bolso de velhos coletes.

A casa tem muitas gavetas
e papéis, escadas compridas.

In the semicircle of armchairs
a certain movement is noticed.
The children are changing places,
but noiselessly! It's a picture.

Twenty years is a long time.
It can form any image.
If one face starts to wither,
another presents itself, smiling.

All these seated strangers,
my relations? I don't believe it.
They're guests amusing themselves
in a rarely opened parlor.

Family features remain
lost in the play of bodies.
But there's enough to suggest
that a body is full of surprises.

The frame of this family portrait
holds its personages in vain.
They're there voluntarily,
they'd know how—if need be—to fly.

They could refine themselves
in the room's chiaroscuro,
live inside the furniture
or the pockets of old waistcoats.

The house has many drawers,
papers, long staircases.

Quem sabe a malícia das coisas,
quando a matéria se aborrece?

O retrato não me responde,
ele me fita e se contempla
nos meus olhos empoeirados.
E no cristal se multiplicam

os parentes mortos e vivos.
Já não distingo os que se foram
dos que restaram. Percebo apenas
a estranha idéia de família

viajando através da carne.

PROCURA DA POESIA

Não faças versos sobre acontecimentos.
Não há criação nem morte perante a poesia.
Diante dela, a vida é um sol estático,
não aquece nem ilumina.
As afinidades, os aniversários, os incidentes pessoais não contam.
Não faças poesia com o corpo,
esse excelente, completo e confortável corpo, tão infenso à efusão
    lírica.
Tua gota de bile, tua careta de gozo ou de dor no escuro
são indiferentes.
Nem me reveles teus sentimentos,

When matter becomes annoyed,
who knows the malice of things?

The portrait does not reply,
it stares; in my dusty eyes
it contemplates itself.
The living and dead relations

multiply in the glass.
I don't distinguish those
that went away from those
that stay. I only perceive
the strange idea of family

traveling through the flesh.

*Translated by
Elizabeth Bishop*

LOOKING FOR POETRY

Don't write poems about what's happening.
Nothing is born or dies in poetry's presence.
Next to it, life is a static sun
without warmth or light.
Friendships, birthdays, personal matters don't count.
Don't write poems with the body,
that excellent, whole, and comfortable body objects to lyrical
    outpouring.
Your anger, your grimace of pleasure or pain in the dark
mean nothing.
Don't show off your feelings

221

que se prevalecem do equívoco e tentam a longa viagem
O que pensas e sentes, isso ainda não é poesia.

Não cantes tua cidade, deixa-a em paz.
O canto não é o movimento das máquinas nem o segredo das casas.
Não é música ouvida de passagem: rumor do mar nas ruas junto à
    linha de espuma.
O canto não é a natureza
nem os homens em sociedade.
Para ele, chuva e noite, fadiga e esperança nada significam.
A poesia (não tires poesia das coisas)
elide sujeito e objecto.

Não dramatizes, não invoques,
não indagues. Não percas tempo em mentir.
Não te aborreças.
Teu iate de marfim, teu sapato de diamante,
vossas mazurcas e abusões, vossos esqueletos de família
desaparecem na curva do tempo, é algo imprestável.

Não recomponhas
tua sepultada e merencória infância.
Não osciles entre o espelho e a
memória em dissipação.
Que se dissipou, não era poesia.
Que se partiu, cristal não era.

Penetra surdamente no reino das palavras.
Lá estão os poemas que esperam ser escritos.
Estão paralisados, mas não há desespero,
há calma e frescura na superfície intata.
Ei-los sós e mudos, em estado de dicionário.

that are slow in coming around and take advantage of doubt.
What you think and feel are not poetry yet.

Don't sing about your city, leave it in peace.
Song is not the movement of machines or the secret of houses.
It is not music heard in passing, noise of the sea in the streets that
    skirt the borders of foam.
Song is not nature
or men in society.
Rain and night, fatigue and hope, mean nothing to it.
Poetry (you don't get it from things)
leaves out subject and object.

Don't dramatize, don't invoke,
don't question, don't waste time lying.
Don't get upset.
Your ivory yacht, your diamond shoe,
your mazurkas and tirades, your family skeletons,
all of them worthless, disappear in the curve of time.

Don't bring up
your sad and buried childhood.
Don't waver between the mirror
and a fading memory.
What faded was not poetry.
What broke was not crystal.

Enter the kingdom of words as if you were deaf.
Poems are there that want to be written.
They are dormant, but don't be let down,
their virginal surfaces are fresh and serene.
They are alone and mute, in dictionary condition.

Convive com teus poemas, antes de escrevê-los.
Tem paciência, se obscuros. Calma, se te provocam.
Espera que cada um se realize e consuma
com seu poder de palavra
e seu poder de silêncio.
Não forces o poema a desprender-se do limbo.
Não colhas no chão o poema que se perdeu.
Não adules o poema. Aceita-o
como ele aceitará sua forma definitiva e concentrada
no espaço.

Chega mais perto e contempla as palavras.
Cada uma
tem mil faces secretas sob a face neutra
e te pergunta, sem interesse pela resposta
pobre ou terrível, que lhe deres:
Trouxeste a chave?

Repara:
ermas de melodia e conceito,
elas se refugiaram na noite, as palavras.
Ainda úmidas e impregnadas de sono,
rolam num rio difícil e se transformam em desprezo.

Live with your poems before you write them.
If they're vague, be patient. If they offend, be calm.
Wait until each one comes into its own and demolishes
with its command of words
and its command of silence.
Don't force poems to let go of limbo.
Don't pick up lost poems from the ground.
Don't fawn over poems. Accept them
as you would their final and definitive form,
distilled in space.

Come close and consider the words.
With a plain face hiding thousands of other faces
and with no interest in your response,
whether weak or strong,
each word asks:
Did you bring the key?

Take note:
words hide in the night
in caves of music and image.
Still humid and pregnant with sleep,
they turn in a winding river and by neglect are transformed.

Translated by
Mark Strand

NEGRO BEMBÓN

¿Po qué te pone tan brabo,
cuando te disen negro bembón,
si tiene la boca santa,
negro bembón?

Bembón así como ere
tiene de tó;
Caridá te mantiene,
te lo da tó.

Te queja todavía,
negro bembón;
sin pega y con harina,
negro bembón,
majagua de drí blanco,
negro bembón;
sapato de dó tono,
negro bembón . . .

NICOLÁS GUILLÉN

Cuba **1902-1989**

BIG-LIPPED NIGGA

Why you get so mad
when they call you big-lipped nigga,
when ya mouth's divine,
negro bembón?

Big-lipped as you iz,
you got everythin;
you live off grace,
you got everythin.

An still you bitch,
negro bembón;
in the thick of everythin,
negro bembón,
stiff white drill suit,
negro bembón;
two-toned shoes,
negro bembón.

Bembón así como ere,
tiene de tó;
Caridá te mantiene,
te lo da tó.

TÚ NO SABE INGLÉ

Con tanto inglé que tú sabía,
Bito Manué,
con tanto inglé, no sabe ahora
desí ye.

La mericana te buca,
y tú le tiene que huí:
tu inglé era de etrái guan,
de etrái guan y guan tu tri.

Bito Manué, tú no sabe inglé,
tú no sabe inglé,
tú no sabe inglé.

No te namore ma nunca,
Bito Manué,
si no sabe inglé,
si no sabe inglé.

Translated by
Achy Obejas

Big-lipped as you iz,
you got everythin;
you live off grace,
you got everythin.

YOU DON' KNOW NO ENGLISH

Considerin how much English y'uze ta know,
Bito Manué,
such fine English, now you cain't even say:
yeah

That 'merican woman's lookin fo you,
an ya hafta hide.
Ya English use to be: strai guan—
strike one—an guan tu tri.

Bito Manué, you don' know no English,
you don' know no English,
you don' know no English.

Don't fall in love no mo,
Bito Manué,
if you don' know no English,
if you don' know no English!

Translated by
Achy Obejas

PEQUEÑA ODA A UN NEGRO

BOXEADOR CUBANO

Tus guantes
puestos en la punta de tu cuerpo de ardilla,
y el punch de tu sonrisa.

El Norte es fiero y rudo, boxeador.
Ese mismo Broadway,
que en actitud de vena se desangra
para chillar junto a los rings
en que tú saltas como un moderno mono elástico,
sin el resorte de las sogas,
ni los almohadones del clinch:
ese mismo Broadway
que unta de asombro su boca de melón
ante tus puños explosivos
y tus actuales zapatos de charol;
ese mismo Broadway,
es el que estira su hocico con una enorme lengua húmeda,
para lamer glotonamente
toda la sangre de nuestro cañaveral.

De seguro que tú
no vivirás al tanto de ciertas cosas nuestras,
ni de ciertas cosas de allá,
porque el training es duro y el músculo traidor,
y hay que estar hecho un toro,
como dices alegremente, para que el golpe duela más.
Tu inglés,

BRIEF ODE TO A

BLACK CUBAN BOXER

Your gloves,
the tip of your squirrel pose
and the punch of your smile.

The north is fierce and rude, boxer.
That same Broadway,
which like a vein bleeds
and screams next to the ring
where you leap about like a latter-day elastic monkey,
without the ropes as a safety net,
nor a cushioning clinch;
that same Broadway
which smears its melon mouth with awe
before your explosive fists
and your genuine patent leather shoes;
that same Broadway,
that's the one that lengthens its snout like an enormous wet tongue,
to greedily lick up
all the blood from our sugar plantations.

Surely you don't live
keeping track of certain things here,
nor certain things there,
because training is tough and muscles treasonous,
and one must be strong as a bull,
as you gleefully say, to make the blow hurt so.
Your English,

un poco más precario que tu endeble español,
sólo te ha de servir para entender sobre la lona
cuanto en su verde slang
mascan las mandíbulas de los que tú derrumbas
jab a jab.

En realidad acaso no necesitas otra cosa,
porque como seguramente pensarás,
ya tienes tu lugar.
Es bueno, al fin y al cabo,
hallar un punching bag,
eliminar la grasa bajo el sol,
saltar,
sudar,
nadar,
y de la suiza al shadow boxing,
de la ducha al comedor,
salir pulido, fino, fuerte,
como un bastón recién labrado
con agresividades de blackjack.

Y ahora que Europa se desnuda
para tostar su carne al sol
y busca en Harlem y en La Habana
jazz y son,
lucirse negro mientras aplaude el bulevar,
y frente a la envidia de los blancos
hablar en negro de verdad.

a bit more precarious than your feeble Spanish,
is only good enough to help you understand
the lewd slang on the canvas
from the moving jaws of those you've destroyed
jab after jab.

In truth, you don't need much else,
because as you must certainly realize,
you've already attained your place.
It's good, in the long run,
to have a punching bag,
to work off the fat under the sun,
to leap,
to sweat,
to swim,
and go from jump rope to shadow boxing,
from the shower to the table,
to emerge polished, elegant, strong,
like a staff that's newly carved
and an attitude like a blackjack.

And now that Europe disrobes
to toast its flesh under the sun
and looks to Harlem and Havana
for jazz and *son*,
looking black as the boulevard applauds,
and facing white envy head-on,
that, that is black indeed.

Translated by
Achy Obejas

EL ESPEJO

Este espejo colgado a la pared,
donde a veces me miro de pasada . . .
es un estanque muerto que han traído
a la casa.
Cadáver de un estanque es el espejo:
Agua inmóvil y rígida que guarda
dentro de ella colores todavía,
remembranzas
de sol, de sombra . . .—filos de horizontes
movibles, de la vida que arde y pasa
en derredor y vuelve y no se quema
nunca . . .—Vaga
reminiscencia que cuajó en el vidrio
y no puede volverse a la lejana
tierra donde arrancaron el estanque,
aún blancas
de luna y jazmín, aún temblorosas
de lluvias y de pájaros, sus aguas . . .
Esta es agua amansada por la muerte:
Es fantasma

DULCE MARÍA LOYNAZ

Cuba 1902-1997

THE MIRROR

The mirror hanging on the wall,
where I sometimes see myself in passing . . .
is a dead pond brought
into the house.
Corpse of a pond is the mirror:
Still, rigid water containing
in itself remnants of color,
remembrances
of the sun, of shadow—movable
edges of the horizon burning, passing by
in circles, returning, never
burning up—vague
reminiscence that coalesced in the glass
and cannot return to the distant
land from where the pond was torn up,
still white
of moon and jasmine, still trembling
of rain and birds, its waters . . .
This is water tamed by death:
It's a ghost

de un agua viva que brillara un día,
libre en el mundo, tibia, soleada . . .
¡Abierta al viento alegre que la hacía
bailar! . . . No baila
más el agua; no copiará los soles
de cada día. Apenas si la alcanza
el rayo mustio que se filtra por
la ventana.
¿En qué frío te helaron tanto tiempo
estanque vertical, que no derramas
tu chorro por la alfombra, que no vuelcas
en la sala
tus paisajes remotos y tu luz
espectral? Agua gris cristalizada,
espejo mío donde algunas veces
tan lejana
me vi, que tuve miedo de quedarme
allí dentro por siempre . . . Despegada
de mí misma, perdida en ese légamo
de ceniza de estrellas apagadas . . .

AMOR ES . . .

Amar la gracia delicada
del cisne azul y de la rosa rosa;
amar la luz del alba
y la de las estrellas que se abren
y la de las sonrisas que se alargan . . .
Amar la plenitud del árbol,

of a living water that shone one day,
free in the world, lukewarm, suntanned . . .
Open to the happy wind that
made her dance . . . ! The water doesn't dance
anymore; it will not reflect
the suns of each day. It is barely reached
by the withered ray filtered through
the window.
In what cold did they freeze you for so long,
vertical pond, no longer spilling
your stream over the carpet, no longer
emptying your remote landscapes
in the living room and your spectral
light? Gray, crystallized water,
my mirror, where I saw myself
so distant
sometimes, where I feared being kept
inside forever . . . Detached
from myself, lost in the mud
of ash made of limbering stars . . .

Translated by
Ilan Stavans

LOVE IS . . .

To love the delicate grace
of the blue swan and the pink rose;
to love the light of dawn
and the stars opening up
and the smiles prolonging themselves . . .
To love the tree's plentitude,

amar la música del agua
y la dulzura de la fruta
y la dulzura de las almas
dulces . . . , amar lo amable, no es amor:
Amor es ponerse de almohada
para el cansancio de cada día;
es ponerse de sol vivo en el ansia
de la semilla ciega que perdió
el rumbo de la luz, aprisionada
por su tierra, vencida por su misma
tierra . . . Amor es desenredar marañas
de caminos en la tiniebla:
¡Amor es ser camino y ser escala!
Amor es este amar lo que nos duele,
lo que nos sangra
por dentro . . .
Es entrarse en la entraña
de la noche y adivinarle
la estrella en germen . . . ¡La esperanza
de la estrella! . . . Amor es amar
desde la raíz negra.
Amor es perdonar; y lo que es más
que perdonar, es comprender . . .
Amor es apretarse a la cruz, y clavarse
a la cruz,
y morir y resucitar . . .

¡Amor es resucitar!

to love the music of water
and the sweetness of fruit
and the sweetness of sweet
souls . . . , to love what's lovable isn't love:
love is to turn oneself into a pillow
for the tiredness of every day;
to put the living sun in the anxious,
blind seed that lost its path
searching for light, imprisoned
in its soil, defeated
by its own soil . . . Love is to untangle spiderwebs
of roads in darkness:
Love is this loving of what pains us,
what makes us bleed
inside . . .
It is to enter the heart
of night and guess
which is the star in gestation . . . The star's
hope! . . . To love is loving from the black root.
Love is to forgive, and more than
to forgive, to understand . . .
Love is holding tight to the cross, and nailing
oneself to the cross,
and dying and resurrecting . . .

Love is to resurrect!

Translated by
Ilan Stavans

YO SOÑABA EN CLASIFICAR ...

Yo soñaba en clasificar
el Bien y el Mal, como los sabios
clasifican las mariposas:
Yo soñaba en clavar el Bien y el Mal
en el oscuro terciopelo
de una vitrina del cristal ...
Debajo de la mariposa
blanca, un letrero que dijera: "EL BIEN."
Debajo de la mariposa
negra, un letrero que dijera: "EL MAL."
Pero la mariposa blanca
no era el bien, ni la mariposa negra
era el mal ... ¡Y entre mis dos mariposas,
volaban verdes, áureas, infinitas,
todas las mariposas de la tierra! ...

I dreamed of classifying
Good and Evil, as the wise men
classify butterflies:
I dreamed of pinning down Good and Evil
in the dark velvet
of a glass box . . .
Under the white
butterfly, a sign would read: "GOOD."
Under the black
butterfly, a sign would read: "EVIL."
But the white butterfly
didn't represent good, nor did the black butterfly
represent evil . . . And between my two butterflies,
green, golden, infinite, were flying
all the butterflies on earth! . . .

Translated by
Ilan Stavans

NOCTURNO GRITO

Tengo miedo de mi voz
y busco mi sombra en vano.

¿Será mía aquella sombra
sin cuerpo que va pasando?
¿Y mía la voz perdida
que va la calle incendiando?

¿Qué voz, qué sombra, qué sueño
despierto que no he soñado
serán la voz y la sombra
y el sueño que me han robado?

Para oír brotar la sangre
de mi corazón cerrado,
¿pondré la oreja en mi pecho
como en el pulso la mano?

Mi pecho estará vacío
y yo descorazonado
y serán mis manos duros
pulsos de mármol helado.

XAVIER VILLAURRUTIA

Mexico 1903–1950

NOCTURNE: THE SCREAM

I'm afraid of my own voice.
Uselessly I search for my shadow.

That shadow with no body
passing by—is that one mine?
Or that voice, lost,
wandering the streets setting fires?

What voice, what shadow, what waking
dream I've yet to dream
could be the voice, the shadow,
the dream they've stolen from me?

To hear the blood burst
from my sealed heart,
will I put my ear to my chest
like fingers on a pulse?

My chest will be empty
and I disheartened
and my hands hard pulses
of chilly marble.

*Translated by
Eliot Weinberger*

POEMA XX: PUEDO ESCRIBIR

Puedo escribir los versos más tristes esta noche.

Escribir, por ejemplo: "La noche está estrellada,
y tiritan, azules, los astros, a lo lejos."

El viento de la noche gira en el cielo y canta.

Puedo escribir los versos más tristes esta noche.
Yo la quise, y a veces ella también me quiso.

En las noches como ésta la tuve entre mis brazos.
La besé tantas veces bajo el cielo infinito.

Ella me quiso, a veces yo también la quería.
Cómo no haber amado sus grandes ojos fijos.

Puedo escribir los versos más tristes esta noche.
Pensar que no la tengo. Sentir que la he perdido.

Oír la noche inmensa, más inmensa sin ella.
Y el verso cae al alma como al pasto el rocío.

PABLO NERUDA

Chile 1904–1973

POEM XX: TONIGHT I CAN WRITE

Tonight I can write the saddest lines.

Write, for example, "The night is starry
and the stars are blue and shiver in the distance."

The night wind revolves in the sky and sings.

Tonight I can write the saddest lines.
I loved her, and sometimes she loved me too.

Through nights like this one I held her in my arms.
I kissed her again and again under the endless sky.

She loved me, sometimes I loved her too.
How could one not have loved her great still eyes.

Tonight I can write the saddest lines.
To think that I do not have her. To feel that I have lost her.

To hear the immense night, still more immense without her.
And the verse falls to the soul like dew to the pasture.

Qué importa que mi amor no pudiera guardarla.
La noche está estrellada y ella no está conmigo.

Eso es todo. A lo lejos alguien canta. A lo lejos.
Mi alma no se contenta con haberla perdido.

Como para acercarla mi mirada la busca.
Mi corazón la busca, y ella no está conmigo.

La misma noche que hace blanquear los mismos árboles.
Nosotros, los de entonces, ya no somos los mismos.

Ya no la quiero, es cierto, pero cuánto la quise.
Mi voz buscaba el viento para tocar su oído.

De otro. Será de otro. Como antes de mis besos.
Su voz, su cuerpo claro. Sus ojos infinitos.

Ya no la quiero, es cierto, pero tal vez la quiero.
Es tan corto el amor, y es tan largo el olvido.

Porque en noches como ésta la tuve entra mis brazos,
mi alma no se contenta con haberla perdido.

Aunque éste sea el último dolor que ella me causa,
y éstos sean los últimos versos que yo le escribo.

What does it matter that my love could not keep her.
The night is starry and she is not with me.

This is all. In the distance someone is singing. In the distance.
My soul is not satisfied that it has lost her.

My sight tries to find her as though to bring her closer.
My heart looks for her, and she is not with me.

The same night whitening the same trees.
We, of that time, are no longer the same.

I no longer love her, that's certain, but how I loved her.
My voice tried to find the wind to touch her hearing.

Another's. She will be another's. As she was before my kisses.
Her voice, her bright body. Her infinite eyes.

I no longer love her, that's certain, but maybe I love her.
Love is so short, forgetting is so long.

Because through nights like this one I held her in my arms
my soul is not satisfied that it has lost her.

Though this be the last pain that she makes me suffer
and these the last verses that I write for her.

*Translated by
W. S. Merwin*

PIDO SILENCIO

Ahora me dejen tranquilo.
Ahora se acostumbren sin mí.

Yo voy a cerrar los ojos.

Y sólo quiero cinco cosas,
cinco raíces preferidas.

Una es el amor sin fin.

Lo segundo es ver el otoño.
No puedo ser sin que las hojas
vuelen y vuelvan a la tierra.

Lo tercero es el grave invierno,
la lluvia que amé, la caricia
del fuego en el frío silvestre.

En cuarto lugar el verano
redondo como una sandía.

La quinta cosa son tus ojos.
Matilde mía, bienamada,
no quiero dormir sin tus ojos,
no quiero ser sin que me mires:
yo cambio la primavera
por que tú me sigas mirando.

I ASK FOR SILENCE

Now they can leave me in peace,
and grow used to my absence.

I am going to close my eyes.

I want only five things,
five chosen roots.

One is an endless love.

Two is to see the autumn.
I cannot exist without leaves
flying and falling to earth.

The third is the solemn winter,
the rain I loved, the caress
of fire in the rough cold.

My fourth is the summer,
plump as a watermelon.

And fifth, your eyes.
Matilde, my dear love,
I will not sleep without your eyes,
I will not exist but in your gaze.
I adjust the spring
for you to follow me with your eyes.

Amigos, eso es cuanto quiero.
Es casi nada y casi todo.

Ahora si quieren se vayan.

He vivido tanto que un día
tendrán que olvidarme por fuerza,
borrándome de la pizarra:
mi corazón fue interminable.

Pero porque pido silencio
no crean que voy a morirme:
me pasa todo lo contrario:
sucede que voy a vivirme.

Sucede que soy y que sigo.

No será, pues, sino que adentro
de mí crecerán cereales,
primero los granos que rompen
la tierra para ver la luz,
pero la madre tierra es oscura:
y dentro de mí soy oscuro:
soy como un pozo en cuyas aguas
la noche deja sus estrellas
y sigue sola por el campo.

Se trata de que tanto he vivido
que quiero vivir otro tanto.

Nunca me sentí tan sonoro,
nunca he tenido tantos besos.

That, friends, is all I want.
Next to nothing, close to everything.

Now they can go if they wish.

I have lived so much that someday
they will have to forget me forcibly,
rubbing me off the blackboard.
My heart was inexhaustible.

But because I ask for silence,
don't think I'm going to die.
The opposite is true;
it happens that I'm going to live.

To be, and to go on being.

I will not be, however, if, inside me,
the crop does not keep sprouting,
the shoots first, breaking through the earth
to reach the light;
but the mothering earth is dark,
and, deep inside me, I am dark.
I am a well in the water of which
the night leaves stars behind
and goes on alone across fields.

It's a question of having lived so much
that I want to live so much more.

I never felt my voice so clear,
never have been so rich in kisses.

Ahora, como siempre, es temprano.
Vuela la luz con sus abejas.

Déjenme solo con el día.
Pido permiso para nacer.

TU RISA

Quítame el pan, si quieres,
quítame el aire, pero
no me quites tu risa.

No me quites la rosa,
la lanza que desgranas,
el agua que de pronto
estalla en tu alegría,
la repentina ola
de plata que te nace.

Mi lucha es dura y vuelvo
con los ojos cansados
a veces de haber visto
la tierra que no cambia,
pero al entrar tu risa
sube al cielo buscándome
y abre para mí todas
las puertas de la vida.

Amor mío, en la hora
más oscura desgrana

Now, as always, it is early.
The light is a swarm of bees.

Let me alone with the day.
I ask leave to be born.

YOUR LAUGHTER

Deprive me of bread, if you want,
deprive me of air, but
don't deprive me of your laughter.

Don't deprive me of the rose,
the stick you thresh the grains with,
the water splashing
swiftly in your joy,
the sudden silver wave
born in you.

My struggle is painful. As I return
with my eyes sometimes tired
from watching
the unchanging earth,
your laughter enters
and raises to heaven
in search of me,
to open all the doors of life.

My loved one, in the darkest hour,
unsheath your laughter,

253

tu risa, y si de pronto
ves que mi sangre mancha
las piedras de la calle,
ríe, porque tu risa
será para mis manos
como una espada fresca.

Junto al mar en otoño,
tu risa debe alzar
su cascada de espuma,
y en primavera, amor,
quiero tu risa como
la flor que yo esperaba,
la flor azul, la rosa
de mi patria sonora.

Ríete de la noche,
del día, de la luna,
ríete de las calles
torcidas de la isla,
ríete de este torpe
muchacho que te quiere,
pero cuando yo abro
los ojos y los cierro,
cuando mis pasos van,
cuando vuelven mis pasos,
niégame el pan, el aire,
la luz, la primavera,
pero tu risa nunca
porque me moriría.

and if suddenly
you see my blood staining
the cobblestones,
laugh, for your laughter
will be for my hands
like an unsullied sword.

Near the sea in autumn,
your laughter must rise
in its cascade of foam,
and in spring, my love,
I want your laughter
to be like the flower I anticipated,
the blue flower, the rose
of my resonant homeland.

Laugh at the night,
at the last day, at the moon,
laugh at the twisted
streets of the island,
laugh at this clumsy
young man who loves you.
Yet when I open my eyes
and close them,
when my steps go,
when my steps return,
deny me bread, air,
light, spring,
but never your laughter
for I would die.

Translated by
Ilan Stavans

DE QUE DESPIERTE

EL LEÑADOR

... Y tú, Capharnaum, que hasta los cielos estás levantada,
hasta los infiernos serás abajada ... SAN LUCAS, 10:15

I

Al oeste de Colorado River
hay un sitio que amo.
Acudo allí con todo lo que palpitando
transcurre en mí, con todo
lo que fui, lo que soy, lo que sostengo.
Hay unas altas piedras rojas, el aire
salvaje de mil manos
las hizo edificadas estructuras:
el escarlata ciego subió desde el abismo
y en ellas se hizo cobre, fuego y fuerza.
América extendida como la piel del búfalo,
aérea y clara noche del galope,
allí hacia las alturas estrelladas,
bebo tu copa de verde rocío.

Sí, por agria Arizona y Wisconsin nudoso,
hasta Milwaukee levantada contra el viento y la nieve
o en los enardecidos pantanos de West Palm,
cerca de los pinares de Tacoma, en el espeso
olor de acero de tus bosques,
anduve pisando tierra madre,
hojas azules, piedras de cascada,

FROM **I WISH THE WOODCUTTER**

WOULD WAKE UP

... And thou, Capernaum, which art exalted to heaven,
shall be thrust down to hell ... LUKE 10:15

I

West of the Colorado River
there's a place I love.
I take refuge there with everything alive
in me, with everything
that I have been, that I am, that I believe in.
Some high red rocks are there, the wild
air with its thousand hands
has turned them into human buildings.
The blind scarlet rose from the depths
and changed in these rocks to copper, fire, and energy.
America spread out like a buffalo skin,
light and transparent night of galloping,
near your high places covered with stars
I drink down your cup of green dew.

Yes, through acrid Arizona and Wisconsin full of knots,
as far as Milwaukee, raised to keep back the wind and the snow,
or in the burning swamps of West Palm,
near the pine trees of Tacoma, in the thick odor
of your forests which is like steel,
I walked weighing down the mother earth,
blue leaves, waterfalls of stones,

huracanes que temblaban como toda la música,
ríos que rezaban como los monasterios,
ánades y manzanas, tierras y aguas,
infinita quietud para que el trigo nazca.

Allí pude, en mi piedra central, extender al aire
ojos, oídos, manos, hasta oír
libros, locomotores, nieve, luchas,
fábricas, tumbas, vegetales pasos,
y de Manhattan la luna en el navío,
el canto de la máquina que hila,
la cuchara de hierro que come tierra,
la perforadora con su golpe de cóndor
y cuanto corta, oprime, corre, cose:
seres y ruedas repitiendo y naciendo.

Amo el pequeño hogar del *farmer*. Recientes madres duermen
aromadas como el jarabe del tamarindo, las telas
recién planchadas. Arde
el fuego en mil hogares rodeados de cebollas.
(Los hombres cuando cantan cerca del río tienen
una voz ronca como las piedras del fondo:
el tabaco salió de sus anchas hojas
y como un duende del fuego llegó a estos hogares.)
Missouri adentro venid, mirad el queso y la harina,
las tablas olorosas, rojas como violines,
el hombre navegando la cebada,
el potro azul recién montado huele
el aroma del pan y de la alfalfa:
campanas, amapolas, herrerías,
y en los destartalados cinemas silvestres
el amor abre su dentadura
en el sueño nacido de la tierra.

hurricanes vibrating as all music does,
rivers that muttered prayers like monasteries,
geese and apples, territories and waters,
infinite silence in which the wheat could be born.

I was able there, in my deep stony core, to stretch
my eyes, ears, hands, far out into the air until I heard
books, locomotives, snow, battles,
factories, cemeteries, footsteps, plants,
and the moon on a ship from Manhattan,
the song of the machine that is weaving,
the iron spoon that eats the earth,
the drill that strikes like a condor,
and everything that cuts, presses, sews:
creatures and wheels repeating themselves and being born.

I love the farmer's small house. New mothers are asleep
with a good smell like the sap of the tamarind, clothes
just ironed. Fires are burning in a thousand homes,
with drying onions hanging around the fireplace.
(When they are singing near the river the men's voices
are deep as the stones at the river bottom;
and tobacco rose from its wide leaves
and entered these houses like a spirit of the fires.)
Come deeper into Missouri, look at the cheese and the flour,
the boards aromatic and red as violins,
the man moving like a ship among the barley,
the blue-black colt just home from a ride smells
the odor of bread and alfalfa:
bells, poppies, blacksmith shops,
and in the run-down movies in the small towns
love opens its mouth full of teeth
in a dream born of the earth.

Es tu paz lo que amamos, no tu máscara.
No es hermoso tu rostro de guerrero.
Eres hermosa y ancha, Norte América.
Vienes de humilde cuna como una lavandera,
junto a tus ríos, blanca.
Edificada en lo desconocido,
es tu paz de panal lo dulce tuyo.

Amamos tu hombre con las manos rojas
de barro de Oregón, tu niño negro
que te trajo la música nacida
en su comarca de marfil: amamos
tu ciudad, tu substancia,
tu luz, tus mecanismos, la energía
del Oeste, la pacífica
miel, de colmenar y aldea,
el gigante muchacho en el tractor,
la avena que heredaste
de Jefferson, la rueda rumorosa
que mide tu terrestre Oceanía,
el humo de una fábrica y el beso
número mil de una colonia nueva:
tu sangre labradora es la que amamos:
tu mano popular llena de aceite.

Bajo la noche de las praderas hace ya tiempo
reposan sobre la piel del búfalo en un grave
silencio las sílabas, el canto
de lo que fui antes de ser, de lo que fuimos.
Melville es un abeto marino, de sus ramas
nace una curva de carena, un brazo
de madera y navío. Whitman innumerable
como los cereales. Poe en su matemática

What we love is your peace, not your mask.
Your warrior's face is not handsome.
North America, you are handsome and spacious.
You come, like a washerwoman, from
a simple cradle, near your rivers, pale.
Built up from the unknown,
what is sweet in you is your hivelike peace.

We love the man with his hands red
from the Oregon clay, your Negro boy
who brought you the music born
in his country of tusks: we love
your city, your substance,
your light, your machines, the energy
of the West, the harmless
honey from hives and little towns,
the huge farm boy, on his tractor,
the oats which you inherited
from Jefferson, the noisy wheel
that measures your oceanic earth,
the factory smoke and the kiss,
the thousandth, of a new colony:
what we love is your workingman's blood:
your unpretentious hand covered with oil.

For years now under the prairie night
in a heavy silence on the buffalo skin
syllables have been asleep, poems
about what I was before I was born, what we were.
Melville is a sea fir, the curve of the keel
springs from his branches, an arm
of timber and ship. Whitman impossible to count
as grain, Poe in his mathematical

tiniebla, Dreiser, Wolfe,
frescas heridas de nuestra propia ausencia,
Lockridge reciente, atados a la profundidad,
cuántos otros, atados a la sombra:
sobre ellos la misma aurora del hemisferio arde
y de ellos está hecho lo que somos.
Poderosos infantes, capitanes ciegos,
entre acontecimientos y follajes amedrentados a veces,
interrumpidos por la alegría y por el duelo,
bajo las praderas cruzadas de tráfico,
cuántos muertos en las llanuras antes no visitadas:
inocentes atormentados, profetas recién impresos,
sobre la piel del búfalo de las praderas.

De Francia, de Okinawa, de los atolones
de Leyte (Norman Mailer lo ha dejado escrito),
del aire enfurecido y de las olas,
han regresado casi todos los muchachos.
Casi todos . . . Fue verde y amarga la historia
de barro y sudor: no oyeron
bastante el canto de los arrecifes
ni tocaron tal vez sino para morir en las islas, las coronas
de fulgor y fragancia:
                    sangre y estiércol
los persiguieron, la mugre y las ratas,
y un cansado y desolado corazón que luchaba.
Pero ya han vuelto,
                los habéis recibido
en el ancho espacio de las tierras extendidas
y se han cerrado (los que han vuelto) como una corola
de innumerables pétalos anónimos
para renacer y olvidar.

darkness, Dreiser, Wolfe,
fresh wounds of our own absence,
Lockridge more recently, all bound to the depths,
how many others, bound to the darkness:
over them the same dawn of the hemisphere burns,
and out of them what we are has come.
Powerful foot soldiers, blind captains,
frightened at times among actions and leaves,
checked in their work by joy and by mourning,
under the plains crossed by traffic,
how many dead men in the fields never visited before:
innocent ones tortured, prophets only now published,
on the buffalo skin of the prairies.

From France, and Okinawa, and the atolls
of Leyte (Norman Mailer has written it out)
and the infuriated air and the waves,
almost all the men have come back now,
almost all . . . The history of mud and sweat
was green and sour; they did not hear
the singing of the reefs long enough
and perhaps never touched the islands, those wreaths of brilliance
    and perfume,
except to die:
                dung and blood
hounded them, the filth and rats,
and a fatigued and ruined heart that went on fighting.
But they have come back,
                    you have received them
into the immensity of the open lands
and they have closed (those who came back) like a flower
with thousands of nameless petals
to be reborn and forget.

*Translated by
Robert Bly*

EL HIJO

Ay hijo, sabes, sabes
de dónde vienes?

De un lago con gaviotas
blancas y hambrientas.

Junto al agua de invierno
ella y yo levantamos
una fogata roja
gastándonos los labios
de besarnos el alma,
echando al fuego todo,
quemándonos la vida.

Así llegaste al mundo.

Pero ella para verme
y para verte un día
atravesó los mares
y yo para abrazar
su pequeña cintura
toda la tierra anduve,
con guerras y montañas,
con arenas y espinas.

Así llegaste al mundo.

De tantos sitios vienes,
del agua y de la tierra,

THE SON

Ah, son, do you know, do you know
where you come from?

From a lake with seagulls
white and hungry.

Near the winter water
she and I raised
a red bonfire,
wearing out our lips
from kissing the soul,
casting all into the fire,
burning our lives.

That's how you came to the world.

But she, to see me
and to see you, one day
crossed the oceans,
and I, to hold
her small waist,
wandered all the earth,
across wars and mountains,
through sand and thorns.

That's how you came to the world.

You come from so many places,
from water and earth,

del fuego y de la nieve,
de tan lejos caminas
hacia nosotros dos,
desde el amor terrible
que nos ha encadenado,
que queremos saber
cómo eres, qué nos dices,
porque tú sabes más
del mundo que te dimos.

Como una gran tormenta
sacudimos nosotros
el árbol de la vida
hasta las más ocultas
fibras de las raíces
y apareces ahora
cantando en el follaje,
en la más alta rama
que contigo alcanzamos.

EXPLICO ALGUNAS COSAS

Preguntaréis: Y dónde están las lilas?
Y la metafísica cubierta de amapolas?
Y la lluvia que a menudo golpeaba
sus palabras llenándolas
de agujeros y pájaros?

Os voy a contar todo lo que me pasa.

from fire and snow,
you walk from far away
toward us two,
from the terrible love
that has bewitched us,
so we want to know
what you're like, what you say to us,
because you know more
of the world we gave you.

Like a great storm
we shake
the tree of life
to its most hidden
root fibers
and you appear now
singing in the foliage,
in the highest branch
we reach with you.

*Translated by
Ilan Stavans
and Alison Sparks*

I EXPLAIN A FEW THINGS

You will ask: But where are the lilacs?
And the metaphysics covered with poppies?
And the rain that often struck
his words, filling them
with holes and birds?

Let me tell you what's happening with me.

Yo vivía en un barrio
de Madrid, con campanas,
con relojes, con árboles.

Desde allí se veía
el rostro seco de Castilla
como un océano de cuero.
                    Mi casa era llamada
la casa de las flores, porque por todas partes
estallaban geranios: era
una bella casa
con perros y chiquillos.
                    Raúl, te acuerdas?
Te acuerdas, Rafael?
                    Federico, te acuerdas
debajo de la tierra,
te acuerdas de mi casa con balcones en donde
la luz de junio ahogaba flores en tu boca?
                    Hermano, hermano!

Todo
eran grandes voces, sal de mercaderías,
aglomeraciones de pan palpitante,
mercados de mi barrio de Argüelles con su estatua
como un tintero pálido entre las merluzas:
el aceite llegaba a las cucharas,
un profundo latido
de pies y manos llenaba las calles,
metros, litros, esencia
aguda de la vida,
                    pescados hacinados,
contextura de techos con sol frío en el cual

I lived in a barrio
of Madrid, with bells,
with clocks, with trees.

From there you could see
the parched face of Castile
like an ocean of leather.
                              My house was called
the house of flowers, because from everywhere
geraniums burst: it was
a beautiful house,
with dogs and children.
                              Raul, do you remember?
Do you remember, Rafael?
                              Federico, do you remember?
Under the ground,
do you remember my house with balconies
where the June light drowned the flowers in your mouth?
                              Brother, brother!

Everything
was loud voices, salt of goods,
crowds of pulsating bread,
marketplaces in my barrio of Arguelles with its statue
like a pale inkwell set down among the hake:
oil flowed into spoons,
a deep throbbing
of feet and hands filled the streets,
meters, liters, the hard
edges of life,
                    heaps of fish,
geometry of roofs under a cold sun in which

la flecha se fatiga,
delirante marfil fino de las patatas,
tomates repetidos hasta el mar.

Y una mañana todo estaba ardiendo
y una mañana las hogueras
salían de la tierra
devorando seres,
y desde entonces fuego,
pólvora desde entonces,
y desde entonces sangre.

Bandidos con aviones y con moros,
bandidos con sortijas y duquesas,
bandidos con frailes negros bendiciendo
venían por el cielo a matar niños,
y por las calles la sangre de los niños
corría simplemente, como sangre de niños.
Chacales que el chacal rechazaría,
piedras que el cardo seco mordería escupiendo,
víboras que las víboras odiarán!

Frente a vosotros he visto la sangre
de España levantarse
para ahogaros en una sola ola
de orgullo y de cuchillos!

Generales
traidores:
mirad mi casa muerta,
mirad España rota:
pero de cada casa muerta sale metal ardiendo

the weathervane grew tired,
delirious fine ivory of potatoes,
tomatoes, more tomatoes, all the way to the sea.

And one morning it all was burning,
and one morning bonfires
sprang out of the earth
devouring humans,
and from then on fire,
gunpowder from then on,
and from then on blood.

Bandidos with planes and Moors,
bandidos with rings, and duchesses,
bandidos with black friars signing the cross
coming down from the sky to kill children,
and in the streets the blood of the children
ran simply, like blood of children.
Jackals the jackals would despise,
stones the dry thistle would bite on and spit out,
vipers the vipers would abominate.

Facing you I have seen the blood
of Spain rise up
to drown you in a single wave
of pride and knives.

Traitors,
generals:
look at my dead house,
look at Spain broken:
from every house burning metal comes out

en vez de flores,
pero de cada hueco de España
sale España,
pero de cada niño muerto sale un fusil con ojos,
pero de cada crimen nacen balas
que os hallarán un día el sitio
del corazón.

Preguntaréis por qué poesía
no nos habla del sueño, de las hojas,
de los grandes volcanes de su país natal?

Venid a ver la sangre por las calles,
venid a ver
la sangre por las calles,
venid a ver la sangre
por las calles!

ODA A LA SANDÍA

El árbol del verano
intenso,
invulnerable,
es todo cielo azul,
sol amarillo,
cansancio a goterones,
es una espada
sobre los caminos,
un zapato quemado

instead of flowers,
from every crater of Spain
comes Spain
from every dead child comes a rifle with eyes,
from every crime bullets are born
that one day will find out in you
the site of the heart.

You will ask: Why doesn't his poetry
speak to us of dreams, of leaves,
of the great volcanoes of his native land?

Come and see the blood in the streets,
come and see
the blood in the streets,
come and see the blood
in the streets!

*Translated by
Galway Kinnell*

ODE TO THE WATERMELON

The tree of summer,
intense,
invulnerable,
is all blue sky,
yellow sun,
exhaustion dripping.
It's a sword
above the roads,
a burnt shoe

en las ciudades:
la caridad, el mundo
nos agobian,
nos pegan
en los ojos
con polvareda,
con súbitos golpes de oro,
nos acosan
los pies
con espinitas,
con piedras calurosas,
y la boca
sufre
más que todos los dedos:
tienen sed
la garganta,
la dentadura,
los labios y la lengua:
queremos
beber las cataratas,
la noche azul,
el polo,
y entonces
cruza el cielo
el más fresco de todos
los planetas,
la redonda, suprema
y celestial sandía.

Es la fruta del árbol de la sed.
Es la ballena verde del verano.

in the cities:
clarity and the world
overwhelm us,
hit us
in the eye
with dust,
with sudden blows of gold;
they harass
our feet
with thorns,
with heated stones,
and the mouth
suffers
more than all the toes:
the throat
is thirsty,
the teeth,
the lips and tongue:
we want
to drink waterfalls,
the blue night,
the pole.
Just then
the coolest of all
planets
crosses the sky,
the rounded, supreme
and celestial watermelon.

It's the fruit from the tree of thirst.
It's the green whale of summer.

El universo seco
de pronto
tachonado
por este firmamento de frescura
deja caer
la fruta
rebosante:
se abren sus hemisferios
mostrando una bandera
verde, blanca, escarlata,
que se disuelve
en cascada, en azúcar,
en delicia!

Cofre del agua, plácida
reina
de la frutería,
bodega
de la profundidad, luna
terrestre!
Oh pura,
en tu abundancia
se deshacen rubíes
y uno
quisiera
morderte
hundiendo
en ti
la cara,
el pelo,
el alma!

The dry universe,
suddenly
marked
by this firmament of coolness,
allows
the fruit
to drop:
its hemispheres open,
showing a flag
—green, white, scarlet—
dissolving itself
in cascades, sugar,
delight!

Water coffer,
placid fruit
queen,
warehouse
of depth,
earthly moon!
Oh, purity
incarnate,
rubies fall apart
in your abundance.
We would like
to bite you,
sinking
the face,
the hair,
the soul
into you!

Te divisamos
en la sed
como
mina o montaña
de espléndido alimento,
pero
te conviertes
entre la dentadura y el deseo
en sólo
fresca luz
que se deslíe,
en manantial
que nos tocó
cantando.
Y así
no pesas
en la siesta
abrasadora,
no pesas,
sólo
pasas
y tu gran corazón de brasa fría
se convirtió en el agua
de una gota.

Thirsty,
we see you
like
a mine or mountain
of splendid food,
but
you transform
between our teeth and desire
only into
fresh light that unleashes us,
becoming
fresh light
that touched us,
a spring
singing.
And then
you're weightless
in the all-embracing
siesta,
you're weightless
only passing by,
and your great heart of cold embers
is transformed into water
contained in a single drop.

Translated by
Ilan Stavans

RETRATO DE JOSÉ CEMÍ

No libró ningún combate, pues jadear
fue la costumbre establecida entre su hálito
y la brisa o la tempestad.
Su nombre es también Thelema Semí,
su voluntad puede buscar un cuerpo
en la sombra, la sombra de un árbol
y el árbol que está a la entrada del Infierno.
Fue fiel a Orfeo y a Proserpina.
Reverenció a sus amigos, a la melodía,
y la que se oculta, o la que hace temblar
en el estío a las hojas.
El arte lo acompañó todos los días,
la naturaleza le regaló su calma su fiebre.
Calmoso como la noche,
la fiebre le hizo agotar la sed
en ríos sumergidos,
pues él buscaba un río y no un camino.
Tiempo le fue dado para alcanzar la dicha,
pudo oírle a Pascal:

JOSÉ LEZAMA LIMA

Cuba **1910–1976**

PORTRAIT OF JOSÉ CEMÍ

No combat did he unleash, as panting
was the custom set between his breath
and the breeze or tempest.
His name was also Thelema Semí,
his will can seek a body
in the shade, the shadow of a tree
and the tree that is at the gates of hell.
He was faithful to Orpheus and Proserpina.
He revered his friends, the melody,
both the one that is hidden and the one that shakes
the summer leaves.
Art went with him every day,
nature bestows her calm, her fever.
Calming as the night,
the fever made him quench his thirst
in sunken rivers,
for he sought a river, not a path.
Time to come to happiness was given him,
he could hear Pascal:

los ríos son caminos que andan.
Así todo lo que creyó en la fiebre,
lo comprendió después calmosamente.
Es en lo que cree, está donde conoce,
entre una columna de aire y la piedra del sacrificio.

rivers are walking paths.
So that everything he believed in fever
he later understood in calm.
Within what he believes, he is where he knows,
between a column of air and the sacrificial stone.

Translated by
Gregory Rabassa

EL JÍCARO

En memoria de Pedro Joaquín Chamorro
cuya sangre preñó a Nicaragua de libertad

Un héroe se rebeló contra los poderes de la Casa Negra.
Un héroe luchó contra los señores de la Casa de los Murciélagos.
Contra los señores de la Casa Oscura

                         —Quequma-ha—

en cuyo interior sólo se piensan siniestros pensamientos.
Los mayas lo llamaron "Ahpú," que significa "jefe" o "cabeza"
porque iba adelante. Y era su pie osado el que abría el camino
y logró muchas veces con astucia burlar a los opresores
pero al fin cayó en sus manos.

    (¡Oh sombras! ¡He perdido un amigo!
Ríos de pueblo lloran junto a sus restos.
Los viejos agoreros profetizaron un tiempo de desolación.
"Será—dijeron—el tristísimo tiempo
en que sean recogidas las mariposas"
cuando las palabras ya no trasmitan el dorado polen.

PABLO ANTONIO CUADRA

Nicaragua 1912–2002

THE CALABASH TREE

In memory of Pedro Joaquín Chamorro,

whose blood made Nicaragua conceive her freedom

A hero rebelled against the powers of the Black House.
A hero struggled against the lords of the House of Bats,
against the lords of the House of Darkness
                                        —Quequma-ha—
where, inside, there are only sinister thoughts.
The Mayas called him Ahpú, which means "chief" or "head"
because he led the way. And it was his bold foot that broke new ground.
Often he succeeded in ridiculing the oppressors,
but finally he fell into their hands.

(Shadows! I have lost a friend!
Rivers of people cry beside his remains.
The old fortune-tellers prophesied a time of desolation.
"It will be," they said, "a sad, sad time
in which butterflies will be gathered"
and words will no longer transmit the golden pollen.

285

Yo imaginé ese tiempo de luz alevosa—un sol frío
y moribundo y las aves de largos graznidos
picoteando el otoño—
pero fue una mañana, un falso brillo
del celeste júbilo, trinos
todavía frescos y entonces

¡la trampa!
ese golpe seco de la pesada loza que atrapa de pronto
al desprevenido y sonriente héroe.)

—"Seréis destruido, seréis despedazado
y aquí quedará oculta vuestra memoria"
dijeron los señores de la Casa de las Obsidianas
(el cuartel—la Casa de las Armas).
Y decapitaron al libertador.
Y mandaron colocar su cabeza en una estaca
y al punto la estaca se hizo árbol
y se cubrió de hojas y de frutos
y los frutos fueron como cabezas de hombre.
     Sobre este árbol escribo:
"Crescentia cújete"
"Crescentia trifolia"
"Xicalli" en náhuatl
jícaro sabanero
de hojas como cruces:
fasciculadas, bellas
hojas de un diseño sacrificial,
memorial de mártires
"árbol de las calaveras."

Esta es la planta
que dignifica la tierra de los llanos.

I imagined it as a time of treacherous light—
a cold, dying sun and the long caws of birds
pecking at autumn.
But it was a morning, a false shining
of blue joy, the fresh
songs of the birds and then

                                        the trap!
The dry blow of the deadfall that suddenly crushes
the smiling, unaware hero.)

"You will be destroyed, broken to pieces,
and here your hidden memory will remain,"
said the lords of the House of Obsidian
(whose barracks was the House of Weapons).
And they beheaded the liberator.
And they ordered that his head be placed on a sharpened pole,
and suddenly the pole became a tree
covered with leaves and fruit
and the fruit resembled human heads.
    On this tree, I write:
"Crescentia cújete"
"Crescentia trifolia"
"Xicalli" in the Nahuatl tongue,
the calabash tree
with leaves like crosses:
fasciculated, beautiful
leaves with a sacrificial design,
a memorial to martyrs,
"the tree of skulls."

This is the plant
that gives dignity to the plains.

Su fruto es el vaso del indio
su fruto es el guacal o la jícara

—la copa de sus bebidas—

que el campesino adorna con pájaros incisos

—porque bebemos el canto—

su fruto suena en nuestras fiestas en las maracas y las sonajas

—porque bebemos la música—

ya desde antiguo en el dialecto maya de los Chortis
la palabra "Ruch" significaba indistintamente
—como entre nosotros—jícara o cabeza

—porque bebemos pensamientos—

Pero los señores de las Tinieblas

(los que censuran)

dijeron: "Que nadie se acerque a este árbol."
"Que nadie se atreva a coger de esta fruta."

Y una muchacha de nombre Ixquic supo la historia.
Una doncella cobró valor y dijo:
—¿Por qué no he de conocer el prodigio de este árbol?
Y saltó sobre la prohibición de los opresores
y se acercó al árbol.
Se acercó para que el mito nos congregara en su imagen:
porque la mujer es la libertad que incita
y el héroe, la voluntad sin trabas.
—"¡Ah!"—exclamó ella—¿He de morir o de vivir si corto uno de
estos frutos?
Entonces habló el fruto, habló la cabeza que estaba entre las ramas:
—"¿Qué es lo que quieres?"
¿No sabes que estos frutos son las cabezas de los sacrificados?
¿Por ventura los deseas?
Y la doncella contestó: —"Sí los deseo!"

Its fruit is the Indians' cup.
The campesinos call its fruit *el guacal* or *la jícara*

                              —*the cup of all we drink*—
and carve birds on it for decoration

                              —*because we drink the song*—
The fruit rattles in our fiestas as maracas and *sonajas*

                              —*because we drink the music*—
Since ancient times, in the dialect of the Chori Maya,
the word *Ruch* meant both
"calabash" and "head" (just as it does for us)

                              —*because we drink thoughts.*—

   But the lords of Darkness

                              (the censors)
said, "Let no one approach this tree.
Let no one dare pick this fruit."

And a girl whose name was Blood Girl knew this history.
The maiden bravely asked,
"Why can't I know this tree's miracle?"
And she jumped over the oppressors' words of warning
and approached the tree.
She approached the tree so that the myth
could bring us together in its image:
because the woman is the freedom that provokes action
and the hero is the unhindered will.
"Ah!" she exclaimed. "Will I live or die if I pick this fruit?"
Then the fruit spoke, one of the heads among the branches spoke.
"What do you want?
Don't you know that these are the heads of the sacrificed?
Could it be that you want them?"
And the maiden replied, "Yes, I want them!"

—"Extiende entonces hacia mí tu mano!"—dijo la cabeza—
y extendió la doncella su mano
y escupió la calavera sobre su palma
y desapareció al instante la saliva y habló el árbol:
—"En mi saliva te he dado mi descendencia.
Porque la palabra es sangre
y la sangre es otra vez palabra."

Y así comenzó nuestra primera civilización
—un árbol es su testimonio—
así comienza, así germina cada vez la aurora
como Ixquic, la doncella
que engendró del aliento del héroe
a Hunahpú e Ixbalanqué
los gemelos inventores del Maíz:
el pan de América, el grano
con que se amasa la comunión de los oprimidos.

"Then you must reach out your right hand!" said the head.
And the maiden reached out her hand
and the skull spit on her palm.
The saliva disappeared at once and the tree spoke.
"In my saliva, I have given you my ancestry.
Because the word is blood
and blood is once again the word."

And this is how our first civilization began
—a tree bore witness—
this is how the dawn begins and germinates each time
like Blood Girl, the maiden who begat
Hunter and Jaguar Deer
from the hero's courage.
They were the twins who invented Corn—
the bread of America, the grain
that becomes the communion of the oppressed.

Translated by
Steven F. White

AMÉN DE MARIPOSAS

El autor
y bajo el título de

Amén de mariposas

A LA EMBAJADORA NORTEAMERICANA
EN MÉXICO, EL AÑO DE 1914

porque, durante la ocupación de Veracruz por tropas
de su propio país, exclamó:

"¡Ésta es la danza de la muerte
y creo que nosotros tocamos el violín!"

y por lo que en sus palabras suena de admonitorio,
de desgarrador y quién sabe si hasta de maternal,

dedica
este poema
cincuenta años después

PEDRO MIR

Dominican Republic 1913–2000

AMEN TO BUTTERFLIES

The author
under the title

Amen to Butterflies

TO THE AMERICAN AMBASSADOR'S WIFE
IN MEXICO, 1914

because, during the occupation of Veracruz
by her country's troops,
she said:

"This is the dance of death
and I believe we play the violin!"

and for the warning that those words contain,
for all they have of heartbreak and perhaps even of the maternal,

dedicates
this poem of
fifty years later

cuando es más alegre el gatillo del violín,
cuando más tumultuoso el delirio de la danza.

Mariposa:
caricatura de aeroplano.
Pulso de abismo,
erudita de pétalos.
Antes que las manos
en la pared te mataron
... los ojos de los niños ...

        PEDRO MA. CRUZ, *Raíces iluminadas*

PRIMER TIEMPO

Cuando supe que habían caído las tres hermanas Mirabal
me dije:
        la sociedad establecida ha muerto.
        (Lapislázuli a cuento de todo emblema ruidoso
        mentís en A referido a un imperio en agonía
        y cuanto ha sido conocido desde entonces
                me dije
        y cuanto ha sido comprendido desde entonces
                me dije
        es que la sociedad establecida ha muerto)

Comprendí
que muchas unidades navales alrededor del mundo
        inician su naufragio
        en medio de la espuma
        pensadora
y que grandes ejércitos reconocidos en el planeta

when the trigger on the violin is gayer still,
much more tumultuous the frenzy of the dance.

Butterfly:
caricature of an airplane.
Pulse of the abyss,
scholar among blossoms.
Before those hands
smashed you on the wall
. . . the children's eyes . . .

    PEDRO MA. CRUZ, *Raíces iluminadas*

ACT 1

When I heard the three sisters Mirabal had fallen
I said to myself:
          society as it is is dead.
          (Lapis lazuli in place of pompous emblems
          negation in A of a moribund empire
          and everything that has been known since
                    I said to myself
          and everything that has since been understood
                    I said to myself
          society as it is is dead)

I understood
that several naval units around the world
          have started to sink
          within the thinking spume
and that huge armies famed throughout the globe

comienzan a derramarse

en el regazo de la duda

pesarosa

Es que

hay columnas de mármol impetuoso no rendidas al tiempo

y pirámides absolutas erigidas sobre las civilizaciones

que no pueden resistir a la muerte de ciertas mariposas

Cuando supe que tres de los espejos de la sociedad

tres respetos del brazo y orgullo de los hombres

tres y entonces madres

y comienzo del día

había caído

asesinadas

oh asesinadas

a pesar de sus telares en sonrisa

a pesar de sus abriles en riachuelo

a pesar de sus neblinas en reposo

(y todo el día lleno de grandes ojos abiertos)

roto el cráneo

despedazado el vientre

partida la plegaria

oh asesinadas

comprendí que el asesinato como bestia incendiada por la cola

no se detendría ya

ante ninguna puerta de concordia

ante ninguna persiana de ternura

ante ningún dintel ni balaustrada

ni ante paredes

ni ante rendijas

ni ante el paroxismo

de los progenitores iniciales

                    have started to collapse
                    in the lap of heavy doubts
Because
there are columns of impetuous marble that surrender not to time
and mighty pyramids built upon civilizations
that cannot but succumb to certain butterflies

When I heard that three pillars of society
three courtesies taken by the arm three times the pride of men
three and mothers then
                              and day's beginning
                    fell
                    murdered
                    O murdered
          despite their smiling looms
          despite the Aprils in a little spring
          despite their mists in repose
(and the day filled with great wide-open eyes)
                    a fractured skull
                    a mangled womb
                    a prayer cut short
                    O murdered ones
I understood that murder like a beast whose tail is on fire
                    would no longer be stopped
          by any door of peace
          by any shade of tenderness
          by any beam or any balustrade
                    or any walls
                    or any bars
                    or any spasms
                    of the first ancestors

porque a partir de entonces el plomo perdió su rumbo

y el sentido su rango

y sólo quedaba en pie

la Humanidad

emplazada a durar sobre este punto

escandaloso

de la inmensidad

del Universo

supe entonces que el asesinato ocupaba el lugar del pensamiento

que en la luz de la casa

comenzaba a aclimatarse

el puerco cimarrón

y la araña peluda

que la lechuza se instalaba en la escuela

que en los parques infantiles

se aposentaba el hurón

y el tiburón en las fuentes

y engranaje y puñal

y muñón y muleta

en los copos de la cuna

o que empezaba entonces la época rotunda

del bien y del mal

desnudos

frente a frente

conminados a una sola

implacable definitiva

decidida victoria

muerte a muerte

Oh asesinadas

no era una vez

porque no puedo contar la historia de los hombres

forever since the bullet lost its way
         and reason lost its rank
         and only Humanity was still
         left standing
called to endure on this scandalous spot
         in the immensity
         of space
I knew then that murder held the place of thought
         that the wild boar
         and the black widow spider
         were starting to make themselves
         at home in the light of the house
that the owl had put itself in school
         that now the ferret lodged
         in children's playgrounds
         the shark in water fountains
         and gears and daggers
         and stumps and crutches
         in the corners of the crib
or that the crucial epoch was beginning
         of good and evil
         stripped
         face to face
         menaced with a single
implacable final
    decisive victory
         death to death

O murdered ones
         it did not happen once
because I cannot tell the story of the men

que cayeron en Maimón
y Estero Hondo
a unos pocos disparos de Constanza
en el mismo corazón del año de 1959
puesto que todo el mundo sabe que somos el silencio
aún en horas de infortunio

No era una vez porque no puedo contar la historia
de este viejo país del que brotó la América Latina
puesto que todo el mundo sabe que brotó de sus vértebras
en una noche metálica denominada
                              silencio
        de una vértebra llamada Esclavitud
        de otra vértebra llamada Encomienda
        de otra vértebra llamada Ingenio
y que de una gran vértebra dorsal le descendió completa
                la Doctrina de Monroe

No contaré esta historia porque era una vez no la primera
                que los hombres caían como caen los hombres
                con un gesto de fecundidad
para dotar de purísima sangre los músculos de la tierra

La espada tiene una espiga
la espiga tiene una espera
la espera tiene una sangre
que invade a la verdadera

que invade al cañaveral
litoral y cordillera
y a todos se nos parece
de perfil en la bandera

who fell at Maimón
and at Estero Hondo
a few shots from Constanza
in the very heart of 1959
because everybody knows that we are silence
even in our hours of misfortune

It did not happen once because I cannot tell the story
of this ancient country from which Latin America was born
for everybody knows it came forth from her vertebrae
in a metallic night called
                              silence
                    from a vertebra called Slavery
                    from another vertebra called Dominion
                    from another called Plantation
and that from a great spinal column there came down intact
                    the Monroe Doctrine

I will not tell this story because it happened once and not the first time
                    that men fell as men fall
                    with a fecund gesture
to endow with purest blood the muscles of the earth

Each sword has a handle
each handle has a wait
each wait will have its blood
then true blood inundate

this blood that inundates
the canefield coast and crag
and to us all appears
in profile on the flag

la espiga tiene una espada
la espada una calavera

Pero un día se supo que tres veces el crepúsculo
tres veces el equilibrio de la maternidad
tres la continuación de nuestro territorio
sobre la superficie de los niños adyacentes
reconocidas las tres en la movida fiebre
                    de los regazos y los biberones
protegidas las tres por la andadura
                    de su maternidad navegadora navegable
                    por el espejo de su matrimonio
                    por la certeza de su vecindario
                    por la armonía de su crecimiento
                    y su triple escuela de amparo
habían caído en mismo silencio asesinadas
                    y eran las tres hermanas Mirabal
                        oh asesinadas
entonces se supo que ya no quedaba más
                    que dentro de los cañones había pavor
                    que la pólvora tenía miedo
                    que el estampido sudaba espanto
                    y el plomo lividez
y que entrábamos de lleno en la agonía de una edad
                    que esto era el desenlace de la Era Cristiana

Oh dormidas
oh delicadas
qué injuria de meditar

            El mes de noviembre descendía sobre los hombros
            como los árboles aún debajo de la noche y aún

each handle has a sword
each sword a skull its tag

But one day we heard that three times the dusk
three times the equilibrium of maternity
three times the extension of our territory
on the faces of children nearby
all three recognized in the feverish movement
                of laps and feeding bottles
all three protected by the amble
                of their navigating navigable maternity
                by the mirror of their matrimony
                by the self-assurance of their neighborhood
                by the harmony of their development
                and by their triple school of charity
had fallen in an identical silence assassinated
                and that they were the three sisters Mirabal
                    O murdered ones
then we knew that there was nothing left
                that terror lurked within the cannons
                that the gunpowder was afraid
                that the bombs sweat fear
                and lead lividity
and that we were fully entering the death throes of an age
                that this was the end of the Christian Era

O sleeping
O delicate ones
what a wrong to meditate upon

The month of November fell upon the shoulders
like trees still beneath the night and still

dando

sombra

Oh eternas

El péndulo palpitaba las horas del municipio
y el pequeño reloj destilaba en silencio gota a gota
veinticinco visiones de un día llamado de noviembre

Pero aún no era el fin
oh dormidas
aún no era el fin

no era el fin

SEGUNDO TIEMPO

Cuando supe que una pequeña inflamación del suelo
en el Cementerio de Arlington
se cubría de flores y manojos de lágrimas
con insistencia de pabellones y caballos nocturnos
alrededor de un toque de afligida trompeta
cuando todo periódico se abría en esas páginas
cuando se hicieron rojas todas las rosas amarillas

en Dallas

Texas

me dije

como era presidencial

el nuevo mes de noviembre

ya millones de seres tocaron lo imposible

ya millones de seres ya millones de estatuas ya millones
de muros de columnas y de máquinas

giving
shade

O immortal ones

The pendulum ticks out the hours of the municipality
and the small clock silently filters drop by drop
twenty-five visions of a day they say is of November

But still it was not the end
O sleeping ones
it was not yet the end
not yet the end

ACT II

When I heard a small inflammation of the earth
in Arlington Cemetery
was being cloaked in flowers and clusters of tears
with the insistence of banners and black horses
by the moan of a grief-stricken trumpet
when every paper opened on those pages
when every yellow rose turned red
in Dallas
Texas
I said to myself
how presidential
the new month of November
now millions of people touched the impossible
now millions of people now millions of statues now millions
of walls columns and machines

comprendieron de súbito

que el asesinato

no ha sido

ni un fragmento de minuto

calculado solamente para las cabezas semicoloniales y sustantivas

de las tres hermanas Mirabal

sino

que este inédito estilo de la muerte

producto de las manos de los hombres

de manos de hermanos

(por todo el siglo)

muerte sana y artesana

(por todo el mundo),

provista de catálogo

(por todo el tiempo)

de número de serie o serial number

y venida de fuera o made in usa

fría inalterable desdeñosa desde arriba desde entonces

esta muerte

esta muerte

esta muerte

asume contenido universal

forzosamente adscrita a la condición

del ser humano

en cuyo espectro solar figural todas la fórmulas personales

y todas las instancias puras

del individuo

tal

como va por la calle

como habitante de la ciudad con todo su derecho como

continuador esencial del índice de población o séase

representante manufacturero indiferente agente de

understood suddenly
that assassination
was not
even a fragment of a minute
measured merely for the semicolonial and prominent heads
of the three sisters Mirabal
but that
this unexpected style of death
the product of men's hands
of brother's hands
(throughout the century)
a death clean and craftsmanlike
(throughout the world)
provided with a catalogue
(throughout all time)
a *número de serie* or "serial number"
and imported or "made in U.S.A."
cold unalterable disdainful above us from then on
this death
this death
this death
assumes universal meaning
affixed by force to the condition
of human beings
whose solar ghost includes every personal formula
and every pristine state
of the individual
just as
he moves through the street
a city dweller having every right
essential perpetuator of the population index
or as a representative indifferent manufacturer insurance agent

307

seguros repartidor de leche asalariado guarda
campestre administrador o sabio o poeta o portador
de una botella de entusiasmo etílico donde están
convocados todas las palabras
    ciclamen platabanda metempsicosis
    canícula claudia clavicémbalo
    cartulario venático vejiga
    trepa caterva mequetrefe
    primicia verdulero postulante
        palabras todas sustitutivas
        palabras pronunciables
        en lugar de presuntas actitudes
        y todas las maldiciones y protestas
        y las posiciones geométricas igual
        que la rotura del sentido igual
        que la rotura de una biela igual
        que el desgarrón de la barriga igual
        mente todo desquiciado y rompido
        todo maligno y amargo
        todo reducido a sombra
          y nadidad y oscuridad
            y estadidad
        palabras mentirosas llenas
        de contenido impronunciable
        y desechos del organismo
        de cualquier muchacha igual
        que de cualquier cochero igual
        que el choque de la portezuela
        del catafalco igual
fue esta universal investidura de la que no está exento
        nadie nadie
        ni yo

milkman wage-earner rural guard
administrator or scholar or poet or bearer
of a bottle of ethylic enthusiasm where
all words come together
      cyclamens boundary metempsychosis
      canicule claudia clavichord
      spleen cartulary cranky
      cretin social-climber crowd
      first-fruits postulant provider
          substitute words all
          words one can say
          in place of presumed attitudes
          and every curse and protest
          and geometrical positions just like
          the rupture of a sense just like
          the fracture of an axle just like
          the belly's laceration and everything
          identically become unhinged and broken
          and perverse and bitter and
          reduced to shadow
             and nothingness and darkness
               and suspension
          lying words full of
          unspeakable meaning
          and the remains of
          any young girl's body
          like to that of any coachman
          like to the slamming of the door
          of the funeral carriage like too
was this universal investiture from which no one is exempt
          no one no one
          not me

ni tú
ni nosotros ni ellos ni nadie
podridamente nadie
nadie
desde el mismo momento en que fueron golpeadas
ciertamente
profesionalmente
maquinalmente
tres de las hermanas Mirabal
hasta llegar
en punto
exactamente
al fin fin fin
de la Era
Cristiana

(Oigamos
oigamos
esto retumba en el
más
absoluto silencio

muchas unidades navales en todos los océanos inician
su hundimiento después
de deglutir los archipiélagos
de miel envenenada
grandes ejércitos destacados en la entrada del mundo
comienzan a reintegrarse
a sus viejos orígenes
de sudor y clamor
en el seno de las masas
populares

not you
                not us not them no one
                damning decay no one
                        no one
from the very moment the three sisters Mirabal were
                skillfully
                professionally
                mechanically
        struck down
                to our arrival
                exactly
                on time
                at the
                end end end
                of the Christian Era

(Listen
listen
it resounds
in the most
absolute silence

several naval units on every ocean are beginning
                to sink after
                swallowing archipelagos
                of poisoned honey
huge armies stationed at the door to the world
                are starting to return
                to their ancient beginnings
                of sweat and noise
                in the heart of the popular
                masses

en el más
en el más categórico y el más
absoluto
silencio)

Porque
hay columnas de mármol impetuoso no rendidas al tiempo
y pirámides absolutas erigidas sobre las civilizaciones
que no pueden resistir la muerte de ciertas mariposas

y calles enteras de urbes imperiales llenas de transeúntes
sostenidas desde la base por tirantes y cuerdas de armonía
de padre a hija de joven a jovenzuela de escultor a modelo

y artilleros atormentados por la duda bajo el cráneo
cuyas miradas vuelan millares de leguas sobre el horizonte
para alcanzar un rostro flotante más allá de los mares

y camioneros rubios de grandes ojos azules obviamente veloces
que son los que dibujan o trazan las grandes carreteras
y transportan la grasa que engendra las bombas nucleares

y portaaviones nuevos de planchas adineradas invencibles
insospechablemente unidos al rumbo del acero y del petróleo
y gigantes de miedo y fronteras de radar y divisiones aéreas
y artefactos electrónicos y máquinas infernales dirigidas
de la tierra hacia el mar y del cielo a la tierra y viceversa
que no pueden
       resistir
           la muerte
               de ciertas
                    mariposas

in the most
in the most categorical and most
absolute
silence)

Because
there are columns of impetuous marble that surrender not to time
and mighty pyramids built upon civilizations
that cannot but succumb to certain butterflies

and whole streets of imperial cities full of passersby
supported at the base by suspenders and cords of harmony
from father to daughter from young man to younger woman from
     sculpture to model

and gunners tormented by doubt under the skull
whose glances fly thousands of miles beyond the horizon
to reach a floating face beyond the seas

and blond blue-eyed truck drivers manifestly swift
who are the ones that outline or lay out the great highways
and carry the grease created by nuclear bombs

and new aircraft carriers with heavy armor-plate impregnable
unsuspectingly joined to the destiny of steel and oil
and giants of fear and frontiers of radar and aircraft divisions
electronic artifacts and infernal machines launched
from land to sea from the air to the ground and viceversa
which cannot
        avoid
            succumbing
                    to certain
                            butterflies

porque la vida entera se sostiene sobre un eje de sangre
y hay pirámides muertas sobre el suelo que humillaron
porque el asesinato tiene que respetar si quiere ser respetado

y los grandes imperios deben medir sus pasos respetuosos
porque lo necesariamente débil es lo necesariamente fuerte
cuando la sociedad establecida muere por los cuatro costados
cuando hay una hora en los relojes antiguos y los modernos
que anuncia que los más grandes imperios del planeta
no pueden resistir la muerte muerte
       de ciertas ciertas
              debilidades amén
                    de mariposas

because all of life is sustained on an axis of blood
and there are pyramids dead on the ground that they humiliated
because murder must have respect to be respected

and the greatest empires must measure their steps with some respect
because the necessarily weak are the necessarily strong
when society as it is dying on all sides
when there is one hour on the old and modern clocks
that says the world's great empires
cannot avoid succumbing succumbing
      to certain certain
            weaknesses amen
                to butterflies

Translated by
Robert Márquez

CANÇÃO

Não leves nunca de mim
A filha que tu me deste
A doce, úmida, tranqüila
Filhinha que tu me deste
Deixa-a, que bem me persiga
Seu balbucio celeste.
Não leves; deixa-a comigo
Que bem me persiga, a fim
De que eu não queira comigo
A primogênita em mim
A fria, sêca, encruada
Filha que a morte me deu
Que vive dessedentada
Do leite que não é seu
E que de noite me chama
Com a voz mais triste que há
E pra dizer que me ama
E pra chamar-me de pai.
Não deixes nunca partir

VINÍCIUS DE MORAES

Brazil **1913–1980**

SONG

Never take her away,
The daughter whom you gave me,
The gentle, moist, untroubled
Small daughter whom you gave me;
O let her heavenly babbling
Beset me and enslave me.
Don't take her; let her stay,
Beset my heart, and win me,
That I may put her away,
The firstborn child within me,
That cold, petrific, dry
Daughter whom death once gave,
Whose life is a long cry
For milk she may not have,
And who, in the nighttime, calls me
In the saddest voice that can be,
Father, Father, and tells me
Of the love she feels for me.
Don't let her go away,

A filha que tu me deste
A fim de que eu não prefira
A outra, que é mais agreste
Mas que não parte de mim.

Her whom you gave—my daughter—
Lest I should come to favor
That wilder one, that other
Who does not leave me ever.

Translated by
Richard Wilbur

PARA LEER EN FORMA

INTERROGATIVA

Has visto
verdaderamente has visto
la nieve los astros los pasos afelpados de la brisa
Has tocado
de verdad has tocado
el plato el plan la cara de esa mujer que tanto amás
Has vivido
como un golpe en la frente
el instante el jadeo la caída la fuga
Has sabido
con cada poro de la piel sabido
que tus ojos tus manos tu sexo tu blando corazón
había que tirarlos
había que llorarlos
había que inventarlos otra vez.

JULIO CORTÁZAR

Argentina 1914–1986

TO BE READ IN THE
INTERROGATIVE

Have you seen
have you truly seen
the snow the stars the felt steps of the breeze
Have you touched
really have you touched
the plate the bread the face of that woman you love so much
Have you lived
like a blow to the head
the flash the gasp the fall the flight
Have you known
known in every pore of your skin
how your eyes your hands your sex your soft heart
must be thrown away
must be wept away
must be invented all over again.

Translated by
Stephen Kessler

DECLARACIÓN DE ODIO

Estar simplemente como delgada carne ya sin piel,
como huesos y aire cabalgando en el alba,
como un pequeño y mustio tiempo
duradero entre penas y esperanzas perfectas.
Estar vilmente atado por absurdas cadenas
y escuchar con el viento los penetrantes gritos
que brotan del océano:
agonizantes pájaros cayendo en la cubierta
de los barcos oscuros y eternamente bellos,
o sobre largas playas ensordecidas, ciegas
de tanta fina espuma como miles de orquídeas.
Porque, ¡qué alto mar, sucio y maravilloso!
Hay olas como árboles difuntos,
hay una rara calma y una fresca dulzura,
hay horas grises, blancas y amarillas.
Y es el cielo del mar, alto cielo con vida
que nos entra en la sangre, dando luz y sustento
a lo que hubiera muerto en las traidoras calles,
en las habitaciones turbias de esta negra ciudad.
Esta ciudad de ceniza y tezontle cada día menos puro,
ciudad de acero, sangre y apagado sudor.

EFRAÍN HUERTA

Mexico 1914–1982

DECLARATION OF HATRED

To exist simply like delicate meat without a hide,
like bones and air riding on the dawn,
like a petty and wilted time
endured among sorrows and perfect expectations.
To exist shabbily inhibited by absurd bonds
and to listen with the wind to the piercing screams
that spring up from the ocean:
dying birds falling onto the decks
of dark, eternally beautiful ships
or upon long deaf beaches,
blind from so much pure foam like thousands of orchids.
Because the sea is so high, dirty, and wonderful!
There are waves like dead trees,
there is a rare calm and a fresh sweetness,
there are gray, white, and yellow hours.
And it's the sky above the dead, the tall, vivid sky
that enters into our blood, giving light and sustenance
to what had died in the treacherous streets,
and in the confused hotel rooms of this dark city.
This city of ash and volcanic stone less pure every day,
city of pavement, blood, and lifeless sweat.

Amplia y dolorosa ciudad donde caben los perros,
la miseria y los homosexuales,
las prostitutas y la famosa melancolía de los poetas,
los rezos y las oraciones de los cristianos.
Sarcástica ciudad donde la cobardía y el cinismo son alimento diario
de los jovencitos alcahuetes de talles ondulantes,
de las mujeres asnas, de los hombres vacíos.

Ciudad negra o colérica o mansa o cruel,
o fastidiosa nada más: sencillamente tibia.
Pero valiente y vigorosa porque en sus calles viven los
días rojos y azules
de cuando el pueblo se organiza en columnas,
los días y las noches de los militantes comunistas,
los días y las noches de las huelgas victoriosas,
los crudos días en que los desocupados adiestran su rencor
agazapados en los jardines o en los quicios dolientes.

¡Los días en la ciudad! Los días pesadísimos
como una cabeza cercenada con los ojos abiertos.
Estos días como frutas podridas.
Días enturbiados por salvajes mentiras.
Días incendiarios en que padecen las curiosas estatuas
y los monumentos son más estériles que nunca.
Larga, larga ciudad con sus albas como vírgenes hipócritas,
con sus minutos como niños desnudos,
con sus bochornosos actos de vieja díscola y aparatosa,
con sus callejuelas donde mueren extenuados, al fin,
los roncos emboscados y los asesinos de la alegría.

Ciudad tan complicada, hervidero de envidias,
criadero de virtudes deshechas al cabo de una hora,

Spacious and sorrowful city where dogs,
misery, homosexuals, prostitutes,
the famous sadness of poets,
prayers and speeches of the Christian fit right in.
Sarcastic city where cowardliness and cynicism are daily nourishment
for young gossipers over women's undulating figures,
for silly women and vain men.

Black city or angry city or gentle city or cruel
or boring city; nothing more: simply tepid.
But bold and vigorous, because in its streets live
the red and blue days
for organizing the people into columns,
the days and nights of militant Communists,
the days and nights of victorious labor strikes,
the crude days in which the unemployed teach their bitterness
crouched down in the gardens or beside doorposts, suffering.

Days in the city! Nightmarish days
like a head sliced off with the eyes open.
Those days like rotten fruit.
Days made muddy on account of savage lies.
Inflammatory days in which the curious statues suffer
and the monuments are more sterile than ever.
Big, big city with its dawns like hypocrite virgins,
its minutes like naked children,
with its thunderous acts of a showy disobedient old woman,
with its narrow streets where the weak,
the ambushed raucous, and the assassins of happiness finally die.

Such a complicated city, seething with desires,
breeding ground for virtues undone at last in a single hour,

páramo sofocante, nido blando en que somos
como palabra ardiente desoída,
superficie en que vamos como un tránsito oscuro,
desierto en que latimos y respiramos vicios,
ancho bosque regado por dolorosas y punzantes lágrimas,
lágrimas de desprecio, lágrimas insultantes.

Te declaramos nuestro odio, magnífica ciudad.
A ti, a tus tristes y vulgarísimos burgueses,
a tus chicas de aire, caramelos y filmes americanos,
a tus juventudes *ice cream* rellenas de basura,
a tus desenfrenados maricones que devastan
las escuelas, la plaza Garibaldi,
la viva y venenosa calle de San Juan de Letrán.

Te declaramos nuestro odio perfeccionado a fuerza
de sentirte cada día más inmensa,
cada hora más blanda, cada línea más brusca.
Y si te odiamos, linda, primorosa ciudad sin esqueleto,
no lo hacemos por chiste refinado, nunca por neurastenia,
sino por tu candor de virgen desvestida,
por tu mes de diciembre y tus pupilas secas,
por tu pequeña burguesía, por tus poetas publicistas,
¡por tus poetas, grandísima ciudad!, por ellos
y su enfadosa categoría de descastados,
por sus flojas virtudes de ocho sonetos diarios,
por sus lamentos al crepúsculo y a la soledad interminable,
por sus retorcimientos histéricos de prometeos sin sexo
o estatuas del sollozo, por su ritmo de asnos en busca de una flauta.

Pero no es todo, ciudad de lenta vida.
Hay por ahí escondidos, asustados, acaso masturbándose,

stifling bleak wasteland, sensual hotbed in which we're
like a burning disregarded word,
surface upon which we walk as if a dark passageway,
desert upon which we throb and breathe vices,
wide forest watered by sorrows and caustic tears,
scornful tears, insulting tears.

We declare our hatred for you, splendid city.
For you, for your sad and vulgar bourgeoisie,
for your girls made of air, caramels, and American films,
for your young ones of "ice cream" stuffed full of garbage,
for your uncontrolled queers who devastate
the schools and Plaza Garibaldi,
the lively, poisonous street called San Juan Letrán.

We declare our hatred for you perfected by the force
of feeling you more immense each day,
more bland every hour, more violent every line.
And if we hate you, fine artistic city without skeleton,
we don't do it through a refined joke, never because of
nervous exhaustion, but because of your innocence of a naked virgin,
because of your month of December and your dry eyes,
because of your petty bourgeoisie, because of your publicist poets,
because of your poets, enormous city! Because of them
and their annoying category as alienated ones,
because of their feeble virtues in eight sonnets daily,
because of their laments in the twilight and their interminable solitude,
because of their hysterical twistings of sexless promises
or tearful statues, because of their asinine rhythms in search of a flute.

But that isn't all, city of slow lifestyles.
There're hidden ones around here, frightened, perhaps masturbating,

varias docenas de cobardes, niños de la teoría,
de la envidia y el caos, jóvenes del "sentido práctico de la vida,"
ruines abandonados a sus propios orgasmos,
viles niños sin forma mascullando su tedio,
especulando en libros ajenos a lo nuestro.
¡A lo nuestro, ciudad!, lo que nos pertenece,
lo que vierte alegría y hace florecer júbilos,
risas, risas de gozo de unas bocas hambrientas,
hambrientas de trabajo,
de trabajo y orgullo de ser al fin varones
en un mundo distinto.
Así hemos visto limpias decisiones que saltan
paralizando el ruido mediocre de las calles,
puliendo caracteres, dando voces de alerta,
de esperanza y progreso.

Son rosas o geranios, claveles o palomas,
saludos de victoria y puños retadores.
Son las voces, los brazos y los pies decisivos,
y los rostros perfectos, y los ojos de fuego,
y la táctica en vilo de quienes hoy te odian
para amarte mañana cuando el alba sea alba
y no chorro de insultos, y no río de fatigas,
y no una puerta falsa para huir de rodillas.

diverse dozens of cowards, children of theory,
envy and chaos, young ones with a "practical sense of life,"
runts left to their own orgasms,
rotten children without means mumbling about their boredom,
speculating about books alien to what is ours.
To what is ours, city! That which belongs to us,
that which pours forth joy and makes joys flourish:
laughter, joyful laughter from mouths that are hungry,
hungry from work,
from work, and with the pride of finally being worthy men
in a well-defined world.
So we've seen clear judgments leap up,
paralyzing this mediocre noise in the streets,
polishing the letters, giving voice to alarm
and hope and progress.

There are roses or geraniums, carnations or doves,
victory salutes and defiant fists.
There are voices and arms and decisive feet,
and perfect faces, and eyes of fire,
and the tentative tactics of those who hate you now
in order to love you tomorrow when the dawn is the dawn
and not a torrent of insults, and not a river of troubles,
and not a false door for fleeing on one's knees.

Translated by
Jim Normington

EL TÚNEL

Pasé una época de mi juventud en casa de unas tías
A raíz de la muerte de un señor íntimamente ligado a ellas
Cuyo fantasma las molestaba sin piedad
Haciéndoles imposible la vida.

En el principio yo me mantuve sordo a sus telegramas
A sus epístolas concebidas en un lenguaje de otra época
Llenas de alusiones mitológicas
Y de nombres propios desconocidos para mí
Varios de ellos pertenecientes a sabios de la antigüedad
A filósofos medievales de menor cuantía
A simples vecinos de la localidad que ellas habitaban.

Abandonar de buenas a primeras la universidad
Romper con los encantos de la vida galante
Interrumpirlo todo
Con el objeto de satisfacer los caprichos de tres ancianas histéricas
Llenas de toda clase de problemas personales

NICANOR PARRA

Chile 1914 –

THE TUNNEL

In my youth I lived for a time in the house of some aunts
On the heels of the death of a gentleman with whom they had been
  intimately connected
Whose ghost tormented them without pity
Making life intolerable for them.

At the beginning I ignored their telegrams
And their letters composed in the language of another day
Larded with mythological allusions
And proper names that meant nothing to me
Some referring to sages of antiquity
Or minor medieval philosophers
Or merely to neighbors.

To give up the university just like that
And break off the joys of a life of pleasure
To put a stop to it all
In order to placate the caprices of three hysterical old women
Riddled with every kind of personal difficulty

Resultaba, para una persona de mi carácter,
Un porvenir poco halagador
Una idea descabellada.

Cuatro años viví en El Túnel, sin embargo,
En comunidad con aquellas temibles damas
Cuatro años de martirio constante
De la mañana a la noche.
Las horas de regocijo que pasé debajo de los árboles
Tornáronse pronto en semanas de hastío
En meses de angustia que yo trataba de disimular al máximo
Con el objeto de no despertar curiosidad en torno a mi persona,
Tornáronse en años de ruina y de miseria
¡En siglos de prisión vividos por mi alma
En el interior de una botella de mesa!

Mi concepción espiritualista del mundo
Me situó ante los hechos en un plano de franca inferioridad:
Yo lo veía todo a través de un prisma
En el fondo del cual las imágenes de mis tías se entrelazaban como
     hilos vivientes
Formando una especie de malla impenetrable
Que hería mi vista haciéndola cada vez más ineficaz.

Un joven de escasos recursos no se da cuenta de las cosas.
El vive en una campana de vidrio que se llama Arte
Que se llama Lujuria, que se llama Ciencia
Tratando de establecer contacto con un mundo de relaciones
Que sólo existen para él y para un pequeño grupo de amigos.

Bajo los efectos de una especie de vapor de agua
Que se filtraba por el piso de la habitación

This, to a person of my character, seemed
An uninspiring prospect
A brainless idea.

Four years, just the same, I lived in the Tunnel
In the company of those frightening old ladies
Four years of uninterrupted torture
Morning, noon, and night.
The delightful hours that I had spent under the trees
Were duly replaced by weeks of revulsion
Months of anguish which I did my best to disguise
For fear of attracting their curiosity.
They stretched into years of ruin and misery.
For centuries my soul was imprisoned
In a bottle of drinking water!

My spiritualist conception of the world
Left me obviously inferior to every fact I was faced with:
I saw everything through a prism
In the depths of which the images of my aunts intertwined like living
    threads
Forming a sort of impenetrable chain mail
Which hurt my eyes, making them more and more useless.

A young man of scanty means can't work things out.
He lives in a bell jar called Art
Or Pleasure or Science
Trying to make contact with a world of relationships
That exist only for him and a small group of friends.

Under the influence of a sort of water vapor
That found its way through the floor of the room

Inundando la atmósfera hasta hacerlo todo invisible
Yo pasaba las noches ante mi mesa de trabajo
Absorbido en la práctica de la escritura automática.

Pero para qué profundizar en estas materias desagradables
Aquellas matronas se burlaron miserablemente de mí
Con sus falsas promesas, con sus extrañas fantasías
Con sus dolores sabiamente simulados
Lograron retenerme entre sus redes durante años
Obligándome tácitamente a trabajar para ellas
En faenas de agricultura
En compraventa de animales
Hasta que una noche, mirando por la cerradura
Me impuse que una de ellas
¡Mi tía paralítica!
Caminaba perfectamente sobre la punta de sus piernas
Y volví a la realidad con un sentimiento de los demonios.

EL PEQUEÑO BURGUÉS

El que quiera llegar al paraíso
Del pequeño burgués tiene que andar
El camino del arte por el arte
Y tragar cantidades de saliva:
El noviciado es casi interminable.

Lista de lo que tiene que saber.

Anudarse con arte la corbata
Deslizar la tarjeta de visita

Flooding the atmosphere till it blotted out everything
I spent the nights at my work table
Absorbed in practicing automatic writing.

But why rake deeper into this wretched affair?
Those old women led me on disgracefully
With their false promises, with their weird fantasies,
With their cleverly performed sufferings.
They managed to keep me enmeshed for years
Making me feel obliged to work for them, though it was never said:
Agricultural labors
Purchase and sale of cattle
Until one night, looking through the keyhole
I noticed that one of my aunts—
The paralytic!—
Was getting about beautifully on the tips of her toes
And I came to, knowing I'd been bewitched.

*Translated by
Mark Strand*

LITANY OF THE LITTLE BOURGEOIS

If you want to get to the heaven
Of the little bourgeois you must go
By the road of Art for Art's sake
And swallow a lot of saliva:
The apprenticeship is almost interminable.

A list of what you must learn how to do:

Tie your necktie artistically
Slip your card to the right people

Sacudirse por lujo los zapatos
Consultar el espejo veneciano
Estudiarse de frente y de perfil
Ingerir una dosis de cognac
Distinguir una viola de un violín
Recibir en pijama a las visitas
Impedir la caída del cabello
Y tragar cantidades de saliva.

Todo tiene que estar en sus archivos.
Si su mujer se entusiasma con otro
Le recomiendo los siguientes trucos:
Afeitarse con hojas de afeitar
Admirar las bellezas naturales
Hacer crujir un trozo de papel
Sostener una charla por teléfono
Disparar con un rifle de salón
Arreglarse las uñas con los dientes
Y tragar cantidades de saliva.

Si desea brillar en los salones
El pequeño burgués
Debe saber andar en cuatro pies
Estornudar y sonreír a un tiempo
Bailar un vals al borde del abismo
Endiosar a los órganos sexuales
Desnudarse delante del espejo
Deshojar una rosa con un lápiz
Y tragar toneladas de saliva.

A todo esto cabe preguntarse
¿Fue Jesucristo un pequeño burgués?

Polish shoes that are already shined
Consult the Venetian mirror
(Head-on and in profile)
Toss down a shot of brandy
Tell a viola from a violin
Receive guests in your pajamas
Keep your hair from falling
And swallow a lot of saliva.

Best to have everything in your kit.
If the wife falls for somebody else
We recommend the following:
Shave with razor blades
Admire the Beauties of Nature
Crumple a sheet of paper
Have a long talk on the phone
Shoot darts with a popgun
Clean your nails with your teeth
And swallow a lot of saliva.

If he wants to shine at social gatherings
The little bourgeois
Must know how to walk on all fours
How to smile and sneeze at the same time
Waltz on the edge of the abyss
Deify the organs of sex
Undress in front of a mirror
Depetal a rose with a pencil
And swallow tons of saliva.

And after all that we might well ask:
Was Jesus Christ a little bourgeois?

337

Como se ve, para poder llegar
Al paraíso del pequeño burgués
Hay que ser un acróbata completo:
Para poder llegar al paraíso
Hay que ser un acróbata completo.

¡Con razón el artista verdadero
Se entretiene matando matapiojos!

Para salir del círculo vicioso
Recomiendan el acto gratuito:
Aparecer y desaparecer
Caminar en estado cataléptico
Bailar un vals en un montón de escombros
Acunar un anciano entre los brazos
Sin despegar la vista de su vista
Preguntarle la hora al moribundo
Escupir en el hueco de la mano
Presentarse de frac en los incendios
Arremeter con el cortejo fúnebre
Ir más allá del sexo femenino
Levantar esa losa funeraria
Ver si cultivan árboles adentro
Y atravesar de una vereda a otra
Sin referencias ni al porqué ni al cuándo
Por la sola virtud de la palabra
Con su bigote de galán de cine
A la velocidad del pensamiento.

As we have seen, if you want to reach
The heaven of the little bourgeois,
You must be an accomplished acrobat:
To be able to get to heaven,
You must be a wonderful acrobat.

And how right the authentic artist is
To amuse himself killing bedbugs!

To escape from the vicious circle
We suggest the *acte gratuite*:
Appear and disappear
Walk in a cataleptic trance
Waltz on a pile of debris
Rock an old man in your arms
With your eyes fixed on his
Ask a dying man what time it is
Spit in the palm of your hand
Go to fires in a morning coat
Break into a funeral procession
Go beyond the female sex
Lift the top from that tomb to see
If they're growing trees in there
And cross from one sidewalk to the other
Without regard for when or why
For the sake of the word alone
With his movie-star mustache
With the speed of thought.

Translated by
Mark Strand

339

SOLILOQUIO DEL INDIVIDUO

Yo soy el Individuo.
Primero viví en una roca
(Allí grabé alguna figuras).
Luego busqué un lugar más apropiado.
Yo soy el Individuo.
Primero tuve que procurarme alimentos,
Buscar peces, pájaros, buscar leña,
(Ya me preocuparía de los demás asuntos),
Hacer una fogata,
Leña, leña, dónde encontrar un poco de leña,
Algo de leña para hacer una fogata,
Yo soy el Individuo.
Al mismo tiempo me pregunté,
Fui a un abismo lleno de aire;
Me respondió una voz:
Yo soy el Individuo.
Después traté de cambiarme a otra roca,
Allí también grabé figuras,
Grabé un río, búfalos,
Grabé una serpiente.
Yo soy el Individuo.
Pero no. Me aburrí de las cosas que hacía,
El fuego me molestaba,
Quería ver más,
Yo soy el Individuo.
Bajé a un valle regado por un río,
Allí encontré lo que necesitaba,
Encontré un pueblo salvaje,
Una tribu,

THE INDIVIDUAL'S SOLILOQUY

I'm the individual.
First I lived by a rock
(I scratched some figures on it).
Then I looked for some place more suitable.
I'm the individual.
First I had to get myself food,
Hunt for fish, birds, hunt up wood
(I'd take care of the rest later),
Make a fire,
Wood, wood, where could I find any wood,
Some wood to start a little fire,
I'm the individual.
At the time I was asking myself,
Went to a canyon filled with air;
A voice answered me back:
I'm the individual.
So then I started moving to another rock,
I also scratched figures there,
Scratched out a river, buffaloes,
Scratched a serpent.
I'm the individual.
But I got bored with what I was doing,
Fire annoyed me,
I wanted to see more,
I'm the individual.
Went down to a valley watered by a river,
There I found what I was looking for,
A bunch of savages,
A tribe,

Yo soy el Individuo.
Vi que allí se hacían algunas cosas,
Figuras grababan en las rocas,
Hacían fuego, ¡también hacían fuego!
Yo soy el Individuo.
Me preguntaron que de dónde venía.
Contesté que sí, que no tenía planes determinados,
Contesté que no, que de ahí en adelante.
Bien.
Tomé entonces un trozo de piedra que encontré en un río
Y empecé a trabajar con ella,
Empecé a pulirla,
De ella hice una parte de mi propia vida.
Pero esto es demasiado largo.
Corté unos árboles para navegar,
Buscaba peces,
Buscaba diferentes cosas
(Yo soy el Individuo).
Hasta que me empecé a aburrir nuevamente.
Las tempestades aburren,
Los truenos, los relámpagos,
Yo soy el Individuo.
Bien. Me puse a pensar un poco,
Preguntas estúpidas se me venían a la cabeza,
Falsos problemas.
Entonces empecé a vagar por unos bosques.
Llegué a un árbol y a otro árbol,
Llegué a una fuente,
A una fosa en que se veían algunas ratas:
Aquí vengo yo, dije entonces,
¿Habéis visto por aquí una tribu,
Un pueblo salvaje que hace fuego?

I'm the individual.
I saw they made certain things,
Scratching figures on the rocks,
Making fire, also making fire!
I'm the individual.
They asked me where I came from.
I answered yes, that I had no definite plans,
I answered no, that from here on out.
O.K.
I then took a stone I found in the river
And began working on it,
Polishing it up,
I made it a part of my life.
But it's a long story.
I chopped some trees to sail on,
Looking for fish,
Looking for lots of things
(I'm the individual.)
Till I began getting bored again.
Storms get boring,
Thunder, lightning,
I'm the individual.
O.K.
I began thinking a little bit,
Stupid questions came into my head,
Double-talk.
So then I began wandering through forests.
I came to a tree, then another tree,
I came to a spring,
A hole with a couple of rats in it;
So here I come, I said,
Anybody seen a tribe around here,
Savage people who make fire?

De este modo me desplacé hacia el oeste
Acompañado por otros seres,
O más bien solo.
Para ver hay que creer, me decían,
Yo soy el Individuo.
Formas veía nubes veía relámpagos,
A todo esto habían pasado ya varios días,
Yo me sentía morir;
Inventé unas máquinas,
Construí relojes,
Armas, vehículos,
Yo soy el Individuo.
Años más tarde concebí unas cosas,
Unas formas,
Crucé las fronteras
Y permanecí fijo en una especie de nicho,
En una barca que navegó cuarenta días,
Cuarenta noches,
Yo soy el Individuo.
Luego vinieron unas sequías,
Vinieron unas guerras,
Tipos de color entraron al valle,
pero yo debía seguir adelante,
Debía producir.
Produje ciencia, verdades inmutables,
Produje tanagras,
Dí a luz libros de miles de páginas,
Se me hinchó la cara,
Construí un fonógrafo,
La máquina de coser,
Empezaron a aparecer los primeros automóviles,

That's how I moved on westward
Accompanied by others,
Or rather alone.
Believing is seeing, they told me,
I'm the individual.
I saw shapes in the darkness,
Clouds maybe,
Maybe I saw clouds, or sheet lightning,
Meanwhile several days had gone by,
I felt as if I were dying;
Invented some machines,
Constructed clocks,
Weapons, vehicles,
I'm the individual.
Years later I conceived a few things,
A few forms,
Crossed frontiers
And got struck in a kind of niche,
In a barque that sailed forty days,
Forty nights,
I'm the individual.
Then came the droughts,
Then came the wars,
Colored guys entered the valley,
But I had to keep going,
Had to produce.
Produced science, immutable truths,
Produced tanagers,
Hatched up thousand-page books,
My face got swollen,
Invented a phonograph,
The sewing machine,
The first automobiles began to appear,

Yo soy el Individuo.
Alguien segregaba planetas,
¡Arboles segregaba!
Pero yo segregaba herramientas,
Muebles, útiles de escritorio,
Yo soy el Individuo.
Se construyeron también ciudades,
Rutas,
Instituciones religiosas pasaron de moda,
Buscaban dicha, buscaban felicidad,
Yo soy el Individuo.
Después me dediqué mejor a viajar,
A practicar, a practicar idiomas,
Idiomas,
Yo soy el Individuo.
Miré por una cerradura,
Sí, miré, qué digo, miré,
Para salir de la duda miré,
Detrás de unas cortinas,
Yo soy el Individuo.
Bien.
Mejor es tal vez que vuelva a ese valle,
A esa roca que me sirvió de hogar,
Y empiece a grabar de nuevo,
De atrás para adelante grabar
El mundo al revés.
Pero no: la vida no tiene sentido.

I'm the individual.
Someone set up planets,
Trees got set up!
But I set up hardware,
Furniture, stationery,
I'm the individual.
Cities also got built,
Highways,
Religious institutions went out of fashion,
They looked for joy, they looked for happiness,
I'm the individual.
Afterward I devoted myself to travel,
Practicing, practicing languages,
Languages,
I'm the individual.
I looked into a keyhole,
Sure, I looked, what am I saying, looked,
To get rid of all doubt looked,
Behind the curtains,
I'm the individual.
O.K.
Perhaps I better go back to that valley,
To that rock that was home,
And start scratching all over again,
Scratching out everything backward,
The world in reverse.
But no: life doesn't make sense.

Translated by
Lawrence Ferlinghetti
and Allen Ginsberg

NOCTURNO DE SAN ILDEFONSO

1

Inventa la noche en mi ventana
                              otra noche,
otro espacio:
              fiesta convulsa
en un metro cuadrado de negrura.
                              Momentáneas
confederaciones de fuego,
                              nómadas geometrías,
números errantes.
                    Del amarillo al verde al rojo
se desovilla la espiral.
                    Ventana:
lámina imantada de llamadas y respuestas,
caligrafía de alto voltaje,
mentido cielo/infierno de la industria
sobre la piel cambiante del instante.

OCTAVIO PAZ

Mexico 1914-1998

SAN ILDEFONSO NOCTURNE

I

In my window night
              invents another night,
another space:
              carnival convulsed
in a square yard of blackness.
                            Momentary
confederations of fire,
                       nomadic geometries,
errant numbers.
              From yellow to green to red,
the spiral unwinds.
                  Window:
magnetic plate of calls and answers,
high-voltage calligraphy,
false heaven/hell of industry
on the changing skin of the moment.

Signos-semillas:

                la noche los dispara,

suben,

          estallan allá arriba,

                    se precipitan,

ya quemados,

           en un cono de sombra,

                      reaparecen,

lumbres divagantes,

               racimos de sílabas,

incendios giratorios,

              se dispersan,

                    otra vez añicos.

La ciudad los inventa y los anula.

Estoy a la entrada de un túnel.

Estas frases perforan el tiempo.

Tal vez yo soy ese que espera al final del túnel.

Hablo con los ojos cerrados.

                Alguien

ha plantado en mis párpados

un bosque de agujas magnéticas,

                alguien

guía la hilera de estas palabras.

              La página

se ha vuelto un hormiguero.

              El vacío

se estableció en la boca de mi estómago.

                Caigo

interminablemente sobre ese vacío.

              Caigo sin caer.

Sign-seeds:
>> the night shoots them off,
they rise,
>> bursting above,
>>>> fall
still burning
>> in a cone of shadow,
>>>> reappear,
rambling sparks,
>> syllable-clusters,
spinning flames
>> that scatter,
>>>> smithereens once more.
The city invents and erases them.

I am at the entrance to a tunnel.
These phrases drill through time.
Perhaps I am that which waits at the end of a tunnel.
I speak with eyes closed.
>>>> Someone
has planted
>> a forest of magnetic needles
in my eyelids,
>> someone
guides the thread of these words.
>>>> The page
has become an ants' nest.
>>>> The void
has settled at the pit of my stomach.
>>>> I fall
endlessly through that void.
>>>> I fall without falling.

351

Tengo las manos frías,

                los pies fríos

—pero los alfabetos arden, arden.

                        El espacio

se hace y se deshace.

                 La noche insiste,

la noche palpa mi frente,

                    palpa mis pensamientos.

¿Qué quiere?

2

Calles vacías, luces tuertas.

                   En una esquina,

el espectro de un perro.

                Busca, en la basura,

un hueso fantasma.

              Gallera alborotada:

patio de vecindad y su mitote.

                  México, hacia 1931.

Gorriones callejeros,

               una bandada de niños

con los periódicos que no vendieron

                   hace un nido.

Los faroles inventa,

            en la soledumbre,

charcos irreales de luz amarillenta.

                Apariciones,

el tiempo se abre:

         un taconeo lúgubre, lascivo:

bajo un *cielo de hollín*

My hands are cold,

                         my feet cold—

but the alphabets are burning, burning.

                                         Space

makes and unmakes itself.

                           The night insists,

the night touches my forehead,

                                touches my thoughts.

What does it want?

2

Empty streets, squinting lights.

                         On a corner,

the ghost of a dog

                   searches the garbage

for a spectral bone.

                       Uproar in a nearby patio:

cacophonous cockpit.

                       Mexico, circa 1931.

Loitering sparrows,

                   a flock of children

builds a nest

                 of unsold newspapers.

In the desolation

                 the streetlights invent

unreal pools of yellowish light.

                       Apparitions:

time splits open:

                   a lugubrious, lascivious clatter of heels,

beneath *a sky of soot*

la llamarada de una falda.
C'est la mort—ou la morte . . .

El viento indiferente
arranca en las paredes anuncios lacerados.

A esta hora
            los muros rojos de San Ildefonso
son negros y respiran:
                        sol hecho tiempo,
tiempo hecho piedra,
                        piedra hecha cuerpo.
Estas calles fueron canales.
                        Al sol,
las casas eran plata:
                        ciudad de cal y canto,
luna caída en el lago.
                        Los criollos levantaron,
sobre el canal cegado y el ídolo enterrado,
otra ciudad
            —no blanca : rosa y oro—
idea vuelta espacio, número tangible.
                        La asentaron
en el cruce de las ocho direcciones,
                        sus puertas
a lo invisible abiertas:
                        el cielo y el infierno.

Barrio dormido.
            Andamos por galerías de ecos,
entre imágenes rotas:
                        nuestra historia.

                              the flash of a skirt.
C'est la mort—ou la morte . . .
                                        The indifferent wind
rips posters from the walls.

At this hour,
              the red walls of San Ildefonso
are black, and they breathe:
                                        sun turned to time,
time turned to stone,
                              stone turned to body.
These streets were once canals.
                                        In the sun,
the houses were silver:
                              city of mortar and stone,
moon fallen in the lake.
                                        Over the filled canals
and the buried idols
                    the *criollos* erected
another city
              —not white, but red and gold—
idea turned to space, tangible number.
                                                  They placed it
at the crossroads of eight directions,
                                        its doors
open to the invisible:
                    heaven and hell.

Sleeping district.
                    We walk through galleries of echoes,
past broken images:
                    our history.

Callada nación de las piedras.

                Iglesias,
vegetación de cúpulas,

            sus fachadas
petrificados jardines de símbolos.

                Embarrancados
en la proliferación rencorosa de casas enanas,
palacios humillados,

          fuentes sin agua,
afrentados frontispicios.

            Cúmulos,
madréporas insubstanciales:

                se acumulan
sobre las graves moles,

          vencidas
no por la pesadumbre de los años,
por el oprobio del presente.

            Plaza del Zócalo,
vasta como firmamento:

          especio diáfano,
frontón de ecos.

         Allí inventamos,
entre Aliocha K. y Julián S.,

            sinos de relámpago
cara al siglo y sus camarillas.

           Nos arrastra
el viento del pensamiento,

          el viento verbal,
el viento que juega con espejos,

            señor de reflejos,

Hushed nation of stones.
                    Churches,
dome-growths,
                    their facades
petrified gardens of symbols.
                    Shipwrecked
in the spiteful proliferation of dwarf houses:
humiliated palaces,
                            fountains without water,
affronted frontispieces.
                    Cumuli,
insubstantial madrepore,
                            accumulate
over the ponderous bulks,
                            conquered
not by the weight of the years,
but by the infamy of the present.

                    Zócalo Plaza,
vast as the heavens:
                    diaphanous space,
court of echoes.
                    There,
with Alyosha K. and Julien S.,
                            we devised bolts of lightning
against the century and its cliques.
                            The wind of thought
carried us away,
                    the verbal wind,
the wind that plays with mirrors,
                            master of reflections,

357

constructor de ciudades de aire,

                      geometrías

suspendidas del hilo de la razón.

                          Gusanos gigantes:

amarillos tranvías apagados.

                      Eses y zetas:

un auto loco, insecto de ojos malignos.

                       Ideas,

frutos al alcance de la mano.

                      Frutos: astros.

                         Arden.

Arde, árbol de pólvora,

                el diálogo adolescente,

súbito armazón chamuscado.

             12 veces

golpea el puño de bronce de las torres.

                   La noche

estalla en pedazos,

             los junta luego y sí misma,

intacta, se une.

            Nos dispersamos,

no allá en la plaza con sus trenes quemados,

                    aquí,

sobre esta página: letras petrificadas.

3

El muchacho que camina por este poema,

entre San Ildefonso y el Zócalo,

builder of cities of air,
>   geometries
hung from the thread of reason.

Shut down for the night,
>   the yellow trolleys,
giant worms.
>   S's and Z's:
a crazed auto, insect with malicious eyes.
>   Ideas,
fruits within an arm's reach,
>   like stars,
>   burning.
The girandola is burning,
>   the adolescent dialogue,
the scorched hasty frame.
>   The bronze fist
of the towers beats
>   12 times.
>   Night
bursts into pieces,
>   gathers them by itself,
and becomes one, intact.
>   We disperse,
not there in the plaza with its dead trains,
>   but here,
on this page: petrified letters.

3

The boy who walks through this poem,
between San Ildefonso and the Zócalo,

es el hombre que lo escribe:

                esta página

también es una caminata nocturna.

                    Aquí encarnan

los espectros amigos,

              las ideas se disipan.

El bien, quisimos el bien:

                enderezar al mundo.

No nos faltó entereza:

          nos faltó humildad.

Lo que quisimos no lo quisimos con inocencia.

Preceptos y conceptos,

             soberbia de teólogos:

golpear con la cruz,

           fundar con sangre,

levantar la casa con ladrillos de crimen,

decretar la comunión obligatoria.

                  Algunos

se convirtieron en secretarios de los secretarios

del Secretario General del Infierno.

                  La rabia

se volvió filósofa,

           su baba ha cubierto al planeta.

La razón descendió a la tierra,

tomó la forma del patíbulo

            —y la adoran millones.

Enredo circular:

          todos hemos sido,

en el Gran Teatro del Inmundo;

jueces, verdugos, víctimas, testigos,

             todos

is the man who writes it:
                              this page too
is a ramble through the night.
                                        Here the friendly ghosts
become flesh,
                    ideas dissolve.

Good, we wanted good:
                              to set the world right.
We didn't lack integrity:
                              we lacked humility.
What we wanted was not innocently wanted.
Precepts and concepts,
                              the arrogance of theologians,
to beat with a cross,
                              to institute with blood,
to build the house with bricks of crime,
to declare obligatory communion.
                                        Some
became secretaries to the secretary
to the General Secretary of the Inferno.
                                        Rage
became philosophy,
                              its drivel has covered the planet.
Reason came down to earth,
took the form of a gallows
                              —and is worshiped by millions.
Circular plot:
                    we have all been,
in the Grand Theater of Filth,
judge, executioner, victim, and witness,
                                        we have all

hemos levantado falso testimonio

               contra los otros

y contra nosotros mismos.

            Y lo más vil: fuimos

el público que aplaude o bosteza en su butaca.

La culpa que no se sabe culpa,

              la inocencia,

fue la culpa mayor.

          Cada año fue monte de huesos.

Conversiones, retracciones, excomuniones,

reconciliaciones, apostasías, abjuraciones,

zig-zag de las demonolatrías y las androlatrías,

los embrujamientos y las desviaciones:

mi historia,

        ¿son las historias de un error?

La historia es el error.

         La verdad es aquello,

más allá de las fechas,

          más acá de los nombres,

que la historia desdeña:

           el cada día

—latido anónimo de todos,

           latido

único de cada uno—,

         el irrepetible

cada día idéntico a todos los días.

           La verdad

es el fondo del tiempo sin historia.

           El peso

del instante que no pesa:

         unas piedras con sol,

given false testimony
                                against others
and against ourselves.
                                And the most vile: we
were the public that applauded or yawned in its seats.
The guilt that knows no guilt,
                                innocence
was the greatest guilt.
                                Each year was a mountain of bones.

Conversions, retractions, excommunications,
reconciliations, apostasies, recantations,
the zigzag of the demonolatries and the androlatries,
bewitchments and aberrations:
my history.
                Are they the histories of an error?
History is the error.
                        Beyond dates,
before names,
                truth is that
which history scorns:
                        the everyday
—everyone's anonymous heartbeat,
                                the unique
beat of every one—
                        the unrepeatable
everyday, identical to all days.
                                Truth
is the base of a time without history.
                                The weight
of the weightless moment:
                        a few stones in the sun

vistas hace ya mucho y que hoy regresan,
piedras de tiempo que son también de piedra
bajo este sol de tiempo,
sol que viene de un día sin fecha,
                       sol
que ilumina estas palabras,
                  sol de palabras
que se apaga al nombrarlas.
                  Arden y se apagan
soles, palabras, piedras:
               el instante los quema
sin quemarse.
          Oculto, inmóvil, intocable,
el presente—no sus presencias—está siempre.

Entre el hacer y el ver,
              acción o contemplación,
escogí el acto de palabras:
               hacerlas, habitarlas,
dar ojos al lenguaje.
          La poesía no es la verdad:
es la resurrección de las presencias,
              la historia
transfigurada en la verdad del tiempo no fechado.
La poesía,
       como la historia, se hace;
             la poesía,
como la verdad, se ve.
          La poesía:
            encarnación
del sol-sobre-las-piedras en un nombre,
             disolución

seen long ago,
today return,
stones of time that are also stone
beneath this sun of time,
sun that comes from a dateless day,
sun
that lights up these words,
that burns out when they are named.
Suns, words, stones,
burn and burn out:
that moment burns them
without burning.
Hidden, unmoving, untouchable,
the present—not its presences—is always.

Between seeing and making,
contemplation or action,
I chose the act of words:
to make them, to inhabit them,
to give eyes to the language.
Poetry is not truth:
it is the resurrection of presences,
history
transfigured in the truth of undated time.
Poetry,
like history, is made;
poetry,
like truth, is seen.
Poetry:
incarnation
of the sun-on-the-stones in a name,
dissolution

del nombre en un más allá de las piedras.
La poesía,

      puente colgante entre historia y verdad,
no es camino hacia esto o aquello:

          es ver
la quietud en el movimiento,

        el tránsito
en la quietud.

      La historia es el camino:
no va a ninguna parte,

      todos lo caminamos,
la verdad es caminarlo.

      No vamos ni venimos:
estamos en las manos del tiempo.

      La verdad:
sabernos,

    desde el origen,

      suspendidos.
Fraternidad sobre el vacío.

4

Las ideas se disipan,

      quedan los espectros:
verdad de lo vivido y padecido.
Queda un sabor casi vacío:

      el tiempo
—furor compartido—

     el tiempo
—olvido compartido—

     al fin transfigurado

of the name in a beyond of stones.
Poetry,
            suspension bridge between history and truth,
is not a path toward this or that:
                        it is to see
the stillness in motion,
                  change
in stillness.
            History is the path:
it goes nowhere,
                  we all walk it,
truth is to walk it.
                  We neither go nor come:
we are in the hands of time.
                        Truth:
to know ourselves,
                  from the beginning,
                              hung.
Brotherhood over the void.

4

Ideas scatter,
                  the ghosts remain:
truth of the lived and suffered.
An almost empty taste remains:
                        time
—shared fury—
                  time
—shared oblivion—
                  in the end transfigured

en la memoria y sus encarnaciones.

Queda
el tiempo hecho cuerpo repartido: lenguaje.

En la ventana,

simulacro guerrero,

se enciende y apaga
el cielo comercial de los anuncios.

Atrás,
apenas visibles,

las constelaciones verdaderas.
Aparece,

entre tinacos, antenas, azoteas,
columna líquida,

más mental que corpórea,
cascada de silencio:

las luna.

Ni fantasma ni idea:
fue diosa y es hoy claridad errante.

Mi mujer está dormida.

También es luna,
claridad que transcurre

—no entre escollos de nubes,
entre las peñas y las penas de los sueños:
también es alma.

Fluye bajo sus ojos cerrados,
desde su frente se despeña,

torrente silencioso,
hasta sus pies,

en sí misma se desploma

in memory and its incarnations.

What remains is

time as portioned body: language.

In the window,

transvestites of battle:

the commercial sky of advertisements

flares up, goes out.

Behind,

barely visible,

the true constellations.

Among the water towers, antennas, rooftops,

a liquid column,

more mental than corporeal,

a waterfall of silence:

the moon.

Neither phantom nor idea:

once a goddess,

today an errant clarity.

My wife sleeps.

She too is a moon,

a clarity that travels

not between the reefs of the clouds,

but between the rocks and wracks of dreams:

she too is a soul.

She flows below her closed eyes,

a silent torrent

rushing down

from her forehead to her feet,

she tumbles within,

y de sí misma brota,

                     sus latidos la esculpen,

se inventa al recorrerse,

                        se copia al inventarse,

entre las islas de sus pechos

                           es un brazo de mar,

su vientre es la laguna

                    donde se desvanecen

la sombra y sus vegetaciones,

                         fluye por su talle,

sube,

         desciende,

                 en sí misma se esparce,

                            se ata

a su fluir,

           se dispersa en su forma:

también es cuerpo.

              La verdad

es el oleaje de una respiración

y las visiones que miran unos ojos cerrados:

palpable misterio de la persona.

La noche está a punto de desbordarse.

                          Clarea.

El horizonte se ha vuelto acuático.

                     Despeñarse

desde la altura de esta hora:

                 ¿morir

será caer o subir,

             una sensación o una cesación?

bursts out from within,
                              her heartbeats sculpt her,
traveling through herself
                              she invents herself,
inventing herself
                   she copies it,
she is an arm of the sea
                              between the islands of her breasts,
her belly a lagoon
                   where darkness and its foliage
grow pale,
              she flows through her shape,
rises,
       falls,
              scatters in herself,
                                        ties
herself to her flowing,
                         disperses in her form:
she too is a body.
                   Truth
is the swell of a breath
and the visions closed eyes see:
the palpable mystery of the person.

The night is at the point of running over.
                                        It grows light,
The horizon has become aquatic.
                                   To rush down
from the heights of this hour:
                              will dying
be a falling or a rising,
                         a sensation or a cessation?

Cierro los ojos,

oigo en mi cráneo

los pasos de mi sangre,

oigo

pasar el tiempo por mis sienes.

Todavía estoy vivo.

El cuarto se ha enarenado de luna.

Mujer:

fuente en la noche,

Yo me fío a su fluir sosegado.

LA LLAVE DE AGUA

Delante de Rishikesh
el Ganges es todavía verde.
El horizonte de vidrio
se rompe entre los picos.
Caminamos sobre cristales.
Arriba y abajo
grandes golfos de calma.
En los espacios azules
rocas blancas, nubes negras.
Dijiste:

Le pays est plein de sources.
Esa noche mojé mis manos en tus pechos.

I close my eyes,
                    I hear in my skull
the footsteps of my blood,
                    I hear
time pass through my temples.
                              I am still alive.
The room is covered with moon.
                              Woman:
fountain in the night.
                    I am bound to her quiet flowing.

*Translated by
Eliot Weinberger*

THE KEY OF WATER

After Rishikesh
the Ganges is still green.
The glass horizon
breaks between the peaks.
We walk upon crystals.
Above and below
great gulfs of calm.
In the blue spaces
white rocks, black clouds.
You said:
          Le pays est plein de sources.
That night I dipped my hands into your breasts.

*Translated by
Elizabeth Bishop*

OBJETOS Y APARICIONES

A Joseph Cornell

Hexaedros de madera y de vidrio
apenas más grandes que una caja de zapatos.
En ellos caben la noche y sus lámparas.

Monumentos a cada momento
hechos con los desechos de cada momento:
jaulas de infinito.

Canicas, botones, dedales, dados,
alfileres, timbres, cuentas de vidrio:
cuentos del tiempo.

Memoria teje y destejo los ecos:
en las cuatro esquinas de la caja
juegan al aleleví damas sin sombra.

El fuego enterrado en el espejo,
el agua dormida en el ágata:
solos de Jenny Lind y Jenny Colon.

"Hay que hacer un cuadro," dijo Degas,
"como se comete un crimen." Pero tú construiste
cajas donde las cosas se aligeran de sus nombres.

Slot machine de visiones,
vaso de encuentro de las reminiscencias,
hotel de grillos y de constelaciones.

OBJECTS AND APPARITIONS

To Joseph Cornell

Hexahedrons of wood and glass,
scarcely bigger than a shoebox,
with room in them for night and all its lights.

Monuments to every moment,
refuse of every moment, used:
cages for infinity.

Marbles, buttons, thimbles, dice,
pins, stamps, and glass beads:
tales of the time.

Memory weaves, unweaves the echoes:
in the four corners of the box
shadowless ladies play at hide-and-seek.

Fire buried in the mirror,
water sleeping in the agate:
solos of Jenny Colonne and Jenny Lind.

"One has to commit a painting," said Degas,
"the way one commits a crime." But you constructed
boxes where things hurry away from their names.

Slot machines of visions,
condensation flask for conversations,
hotel of crickets and constellations.

Fragmentos mínimos, incoherentes:
al revés de la Historia, creadora de ruinas,
tú hiciste con tus ruinas creaciones.

Teatro de los espíritus:
los objetos juegan al aro
con las leyes de la identidad.

Grand Hotel Couronne: en una redoma
el tres de tréboles y, toda ojos,
Almendrita en los jardines de un reflejo.

Un peine es un harpa
pulsada por la mirada de una niña
muda de nacimiento.

El reflector del ojo mental
disipa el espectáculo:
dios solitario sobre un mundo extinto.

Las apariciones son patentes.
Sus cuerpos pesan menos que la luz.
Duran lo que dura esta frase.

Joseph Cornell: en el interior de tus cajas
mis palabras se volvieron visibles un instante.

Minimal, incoherent fragments:
the opposite of History, creator of ruins,
out of your ruins you have made creations.

Theater of the spirits:
objects putting the laws
of identity through hoops.

"Grand Hotel de la Couronne": in a vial,
the three of clubs, and very surprised,
Thumbelina in gardens of reflection.

A comb is a harp strummed by the glance
of a little girl
born dumb.

The reflector of the inner eye
scatters the spectacle:
God all alone above an extinct world.

The apparitions are manifest,
their bodies weigh less than light,
lasting as long as this phrase lasts.

Joseph Cornell: inside your boxes
my words became visible for a moment.

Translated by
Elizabeth Bishop

A JULIA DE BURGOS

Ya las gentes murmuran que yo soy tu enemiga
porque dicen que en verso doy al mundo tu yo.

Mienten, Julia de Burgos. Mienten, Julia de Burgos.
La que se alza en mis versos no es tu voz: es mi voz
porque tú eres ropaje y la esencia soy yo;
y el más profundo abismo se tiende entre las dos.

Tú eres fría muñeca de mentira social,
y yo, viril destello de la humana verdad.

Tú, miel de cortesanas hipocresías; yo no;
que en todos mis poemas desnudo el corazón.

Tú eres como tu mundo, egoísta; yo no;
que en todo me lo juego a ser lo que soy yo.

Tú eres sólo la grave señora señorona;
yo no; yo soy la vida, la fuerza, la mujer.

JULIA DE BURGOS

Puerto Rico 1917–1953

TO JULIA DE BURGOS

Already the people murmur that I am your enemy
because they say that in verse I give the world your me.

They lie, Julia de Burgos. They lie, Julia de Burgos.
Who rises in my verses is not your voice. It is my voice
because you are the dressing and the essence is me;
and the most profound abyss is spread between us.

You are the cold doll of social lies,
and me, the virile starburst of the human truth.

You, honey of courtesan hypocrisies; not me;
in all my poems I undress my heart.

You are like your world, selfish; not me,
who gambles everything on betting on what I am.

You are only the ponderous ladylike lady;
not me; I am life, strength, woman.

Tú eres de tu marido, de tu amo; yo no;
yo de nadie, o de todos, porque a todos, a todos,
en mi limpio sentir y en mi pensar me doy.

Tú te rizas el pelo y te pintas; yo no;
a mí me riza el viento; a mí me pinta el sol.

Tú eres dama casera, resignada, sumisa,
atada a los prejuicios de los hombres; yo no;
que yo soy Rocinante corriendo desbocado
olfateando horizontes de justicia de Dios.

Tú en ti misma no mandas; a ti todos te mandan;
en ti mandan tu esposo, tus padres, tus parientes,
el cura, la modista, el teatro, el casino,
el auto, las alhajas, el banquete, el champán,
el cielo y el infierno, y el qué dirán social.

You belong to your husband, your master; not me;
I belong to nobody, or all, because to all, to all
I give myself in my clean feeling and in my thought.

You curl your hair and paint yourself; not me;
the wind curls my hair, the sun paints me.

You are a housewife, resigned, submissive,
tied to the prejudices of men; not me;
unbridled, I am a runaway Rocinante
snorting horizons of God's justice.

You in yourself have no say; everyone governs you;
your husband, your parents, your family,
the priest, the dressmaker, the theater, the dance hall,
the auto, the fine furnishings, the feast, champagne,
heaven and hell, and the social "what will they say."

Translated by
Jack Agüeros

GRACIAS A LA VIDA

Gracias a la vida que me ha dado tanto.
Me dio dos luceros, que cuando los abro
perfecto distingo lo negro del blanco,
y en el alto cielo su fondo estrellado
y en las multitudes al hombre que yo amo.

Gracias a la vida que me ha dado tanto.
Me ha dado el oído, que en todo su ancho
graba noche y día grillos y canarios;
martillos turbinas, ladridos, chubascos,
y la voz tan tierna de mi bienamado.

Gracias a la vida que me ha dado tanto.
Me ha dado el sonido y el abecedario,
con él las palabras que pienso y declaro,
madre, amigo, hermano y luz alumbrando
la ruta del alma del que estoy amando.

Gracias a la vida que me ha dado tanto.
Me ha dado la marcha de mis pies cansados,

VIOLETA PARRA

Chile **1917-1967**

HERE'S TO LIFE!

Thanks to life that has given me so much.
It has given me two eyes; when I open them
I can tell black and white clearly apart,
the star-covered depths of the lofty sky,
the man I love among all the crowd.

Thanks to life that has given me so much.
It has given me hearing that in all its breadth
night and day records crickets and canaries,
hammers, turbines, barking, squalls,
and the soft voice of my beloved.

Thanks to life that has given me so much.
It has given me sound and the alphabet
and with it the words I think and speak:
mother, friend, brother, and light that brightens
the way of the soul of the one I love.

Thanks to life that has given me so much.
It has given me the step of my tired feet;

con ellos anduve ciudades y charcos,
playas y desiertos, montañas y llanos
y la casa tuya, tu calle y tu patio.

Gracias a la vida que me ha dado tanto.
Me dio el corazón que agita su marco
cuando miro el fruto del cerebro humano,
cuando miro al bueno tan lejos del malo,
cuando miro el fondo de tus ojos claros.

Gracias a la vida que me ha dado tanto.
Me ha dado la risa y me ha dado el llanto,
así yo distingo dicha de quebranto,
los dos materiales que forman mi canto,
y el canto de ustedes que es el mismo canto
y el canto de todos que es mi propio canto.

with them I walk around cities and puddles,
beaches and deserts, mountains and plains,
and your house, your street, and your courtyard.

Thanks to life that has given me so much.
It gave me the heart, which shakes its frame
when I look at the fruit of the human brain,
when I look at the good so far from the bad,
when I look at the bottom of your clear eyes.

Thanks to life that has given me so much.
It has given me laughter and it has given me tears
so I can tell happiness from grief,
the two things my song is made of,
and the song of yours that is the same song
and everyone's song that is my own song.

*Translated by
Joan Baez and
John Upton*

385

LOS LETRADOS

Lo prostituyen todo
con su ánimo gastado en circunloquios.
Lo explican todo. Monologan
como máquinas llenas de aceite.
Lo manchan todo con su baba metafísica.

Yo los quisiera ver en los mares del sur
una noche de viento real, con la cabeza
vaciada en el frío, oliendo
la soledad del mundo,
sin luna,
sin explicación posible,
fumando en el terror del desamparo.

GONZALO ROJAS

Chile 1917–

THE LITERATI

They prostitute us all,
waste their spirit on circumlocution,
explain it all. They ramble on
like machines full of oil,
and slobber metaphysics on everything.

I would like to see them on the southern seas
on a night of royal wind, their heads
emptied into the cold, sniffing
at the world's loneliness,
with no moon,
and no possible explanation,
smoking, helpless, terrified.

*Translated by
Christopher Maurer*

LATÍN Y JAZZ

Leo en un mismo aire a mi Catulo y oigo a Louis Armstrong, lo reoigo
en la improvisación del cielo, vuelan los ángeles
en la latín augusto de roma con las trompetas libérrimas, lentísimas,
en un acorde ya sin tiempo, en un zumbido
de arterias y de pétalos para irme en el torrente con las olas
que salen de esta silla, de esta mesa de tabla, de esta materia
que somos yo y mi cuerpo en el minuto de este azar
en que amarro la ventolera de estas sílabas.

Es el parto, lo abierto de lo sonoro, el resplandor
del movimiento, loco el círculo de los sentidos, lo súbito
de este aroma áspero a sangre de sacrificio Roma
a África, la opulencia y el látigo, la fascinación
del ocio y el golpe amargo de los remos, el frenesí
y el infortunio de los imperios, vaticinio
o estertor: éste es el jazz,
el éxtasis
antes del derrumbe, Armstrong; éste es el éxtasis,
Catulo mío,
            ¡Tánatos!

LATIN AND JAZZ

In the same air I read my Catullus and listen to Louis Armstrong,
hear him again
in an impoverished heaven, angels soar
in the august Latin of Rome, with their trumpets, free and slow,
in a chord now timeless, in the buzz
of arteries and petals so I can float away on the torrent, on the waves
that come out of this chair, this wooden table, this material
that is me and my body in the moment of this chance,
to which I lash the gust of these syllables.

It is the birth, the aperture of sound, the splendor
of movement, crazy the circle of the senses, the suddenness
of this rough odor of sacrificial blood: Rome
and Africa, opulence and the whip, the fascination
of leisure and the bitter lash of the oars, the frenzy
and the misfortunes of empires, vaticination
or death rattle: this is jazz,
the ecstasy
before the crash, Armstrong; this is ecstasy,
my Catullus,
          Thanatos!

Translated by
Christopher Maurer

CONTRA LOS PUENTES LEVADIZOS

1

Nos han contado a todos
cómo eran los crepúsculos
de hace noventa o novecientos años

cómo al primer disparo los arrepentimientos
echaban a volar cómo palomas
cómo hubo siempre trenzas que colgaban
un poco sucias pero siempre hermosas
cómo los odios eran antiguos y elegantes
y en su barbaridad venturosa latían
cómo nadie moría de cáncer o de asco
sino de tisis breves o de espinas de rosa

otro tiempo otra vida otra muerte otra tierra
donde los pobres héroes iban siempre a caballo
y no se apeaban ni en la estatua propia

MARIO BENEDETTI

Uruguay **1920–2009**

AGAINST DRAWBRIDGES

1

We've all of us been told
how the sunsets were
ninety or nine hundred years ago

how at the first shot regrets
would fly like doves
how there were always dangling braids
a little soiled but always beautiful
how there were hatreds old and elegant
that throbbed in their prosperous barbarity
how no one ever died of cancer or of nausea
but of galloping consumption or rose thorns

another time another life another death another land
where the poor heroes always rode on horseback
never dismounting even onto their own statues

otro acaso otro nunca otro siempre otro modo
de quitarle a la hembra su alcachofa de ropas

otro fuego otro asombro otro esclavo otro dueño
que tenía el derecho y además del derecho
la propensión a usar sus látigos sagrados

abajo estaba el mundo
abajo los de abajo
los borrachos de hambre
los locos de miseria
los ciegos de rencores
los lisiados de espanto
comprenderán ustedes que en esas condiciones
eran imprescindibles los puentes levandizos.

2

No sé si es el momento
de decirlo
en este punto muerto
en este año desgracia

por ejemplo
decírselo a esos mansos
que no pueden
resignarse a la muerte
y se inscriben a ciegas
caracoles de miedo
en la resurrección
qué garantía

another perhaps another never another always another way
of stripping a woman of her artichoke of clothes

another fire another fear another slave another master
who had the right and besides the right
the tendency to use his holy whip

below there was the world
below there were the underdogs
those drunk with hunger
those crazed by misery
those blinded by resentment
those crippled by fear
you will understand that under such conditions
drawbridges were indispensable.

2

I don't know if this is the time
to say it
on this dead spot
in this year of affliction

to tell it for example
to those gentle souls
who can't
resign themselves to death
and blindly enroll
the snails of fear
in the resurrection
with what guarantee?

por ejemplo
a esos ásperos
no exactamente ebrios
que alguna vez gritaron
y ahora no aceptan
la otra
la imprevista
reconvención del eco

o a los espectadores
casi profesionales
esos viciosos
de la lucidez
esos inconmovibles
que se instalan

en la primera fila
así no pierden
ni un solo efecto
ni el menor indicio
ni un solo espasmo
ni el menor cadáver

o a los sonrientes lúgubres
los exiliados de lo real
los duros
metidos para siempre en su campana
de pura sílice
egoísmo insecto
esos los sin hermanos
sin latido
los con mirada acero de desprecio
los con fulgor y labios de cuchillo

for example
to the harsh ones
not drunk exactly
who once shouted
and now do not accept
the other
the unforeseen
accusation of the echo

or to the nearly
professional spectators
those addicts
of lucidity
the unmovable ones
who take a place

in the front row
to avoid losing
a single effect
or the slightest sign
or a single spasm
or the least important corpse

or to the gloomy smiling ones
those exiled from the real
the stubborn ones
forever sunk into their
bell of purest quartz
an insect egoism
the brotherless ones
without a pulse
those with the steely look of scorn
those intellects with knife-sharp lips

en este punto muerto
en este año desgracia
no sé si es el momento
de decirlo
con los puentes a medio descender
o a medio levantar
que no es lo mismo.

3

Puedo permanecer en mi baluarte
en ésta o en aquella soledad sin derecho
disfrutando mis últimos
racimos de silencio
puedo asomarme al tiempo
a las nubes al río
perderme en el follaje que está lejos

pero me consta y sé
nunca lo olvido
que mi destino fértil voluntario
es convertirme en ojos boca manos
para otras manos bocas y miradas

que baje el puente y que se quede bajo

que entren amor y odio y voz y gritos
que venga la tristeza con sus brazos abiertos
y la ilusión con sus zapatos nuevos
que venga el frío germinal y honesto
y el verano de angustias calcinadas

in this dead spot
in this year of affliction
I don't know if this is the time
to say it
with the bridge half lowered
or half raised
which is not exactly the same thing.

3

I can stay here in my bulwark
in this or that solitude without any right
enjoying my last
clusters of silence
I can look out look on time
on the clouds the river
vanish in the far foliage

but I'm aware I know
never forget
that my fertile voluntary destiny
is to become the eyes the mouth and hands
for other hands and mouths and eyes

lower the bridge and keep it down

let love and hate and voice and shouting in
let sadness in with its arms open wide
and hope with its new shoes
let in the germinal and honest cold
and the summer with its scorched sufferings

que vengan los rencores con su niebla
y los adioses con su pan de lágrimas
que venga el muerto y sobre todo el vivo
y el viejo olor de la melancolía

que baje el puente y que se quede bajo

que entren la rabia y su ademán oscuro
que entren el mal y el bien
y lo que media
entre uno y otro
o sea
la verdad ese péndulo
que entre el incendio con o sin la lluvia
y las mujeres con o sin historia
que entre el trabajo y sobre todo el ocio
ese derecho al sueño
ese arcoíris

que baje el puente y que se quede bajo

que entren los perros
los hijos de perra
las comadronas los sepultureros
los ángeles si hubiera
y si no hay
que entre la luna con su niño frío

que baje el puente y que se quede bajo

que entre el que sabe lo que no sabemos
y amasa pan

let resentments with their mists come in
and farewells with their bread of tears
let the dead come and above all the living
and the old smell of melancholy

lower the bridge and keep it down

let rage and its dark gestures in
let in good and evil
and that which mediates
between them
which is to say
the truth this pendulum
let fire in with or without rain
and women with or without a past
let work in and above all leisure
that right to dream
that rainbow

lower the bridge and keep it down

let in the dogs
the sons of bitches
the midwives and gravediggers
the angels if they exist
and if not
let in the moon and her icy child

lower the bridge and keep it down

let in the one who knows what we don't know
who kneads the bread

o hace revoluciones
y el que no puede hacerlas
y el que cierra los ojos

en fin
para que nadie se llame a confusiones
que entre mi prójimo ese insoportable
tan fuerte y frágil
ése necesario
ése con dudas sombra rostro sangre
y vida a término
ése bienvenido

que sólo quede afuera
el encargado
de levantar el puente

a esta altura
no ha de ser un secreto
para nadie

yo estoy contra los puentes levadizos.

or who makes revolutions
and the one who can't make them
and the one who shuts his eyes

in short
to avoid confusion
let in my fellow the insufferable
so strong and fragile one
the necessary one
the one with doubts shadow face blood
and a life that ends
the welcome one

keep out no one but the man
in charge
of raising the bridge

at this point
it should be no secret
to anyone

I'm against drawbridges.

*Translated by
Robert Márquez and
Elinor Randall*

A EDUCAÇÃO PELA PEDRA

Uma educação pela pedra: por lições;
para aprender de pedra, freqüentá-la;
captar sua voz inenfática, impessoal
(pela de dicção ela começa as aulas).
A lição de moral, sua resistência fria
ao que flui e a fluir, a ser maleada;
a de poética, sua carnadura concreta;
a de economia, seu adensar-se compacta:
lições da pedra (de fora para dentro,
cartilha muda), para quem soletrá-la.

Outra educação pela pedra: no Sertão
(de dentro para fora, e pré-didática).
No Sertão a pedra não sabe lecionar,
e se lecionasse, não ensinaria nada;
lá não se aprende a pedra: lá a pedra,
uma pedra de nascença, entranha a alma.

JOÃO CABRAL DE MELO NETO

Brazil **1920–1999**

EDUCATION BY STONE

An education by stone: through lessons,
to learn from the stone: to go to it often,
to catch its level, impersonal voice
(by its choice of words it begins its classes).
The lesson in morals, the stone's cold resistance
to flow, to flowing, to being hammered;
the lesson in poetics, its concrete flesh;
in economics, how to grow dense compactly:
lessons from stone (from without to within,
dumb primer), for the routine speller of spells.

Another education by stone: in the backlands
(from within to without and predidactic place).
In the backlands stone does not know how to lecture,
and, even if it did, would teach nothing:
you don't learn the stone, there: there, the stone,
born stone, penetrates the soul.

*Translated by
James Wright*

TECENDO A MANHÃ

1

Um galo sòzinho não tece uma manhã:
êle precisará sempre de outros galos.
De um que apanhe êsse grito que êle
e o lance a outro; de um outro galo
que apanhe o grito que um galo antes
e o lance a outro; e de outros galos
que com muitos outros galos se cruzem
os fios de sol de seus gritos de galo,
para que a manhã, desde uma teia tênue,
se vá tecendo, entre todos os galos.

2

E se encorpando em tela, entre todos,
se erguendo tenda, onde entrem todos,
se entretendendo para todos, no tôldo
(a manhã) que plana livre de armação.
A manhã, toldo de um tecido tão aéreo
que, tecido, se eleva por si: luz balão.

WEAVING THE MORNING

1

One rooster does not weave a morning,
he will always need the other roosters.
One to pick up the shout that he
tossed to another; another rooster
to pick up the shout that a rooster before him
tossed to another; and other roosters
with many other roosters to criss-cross
the sun-threads of their rooster-shouts,
so that the morning, starting from a frail cobweb,
may go on being woven, among all the roosters.

2

And growing larger, becoming cloth,
pitching itself a tent where they all may enter,
inter-unfurling itself for them all, in the tent
(the morning), which soars free of ties and ropes.
The morning, tent of a weave so light
that, woven, it lifts itself through itself: balloon light.

Translated by
Galway Kinnell

405

UMA FACA SÓ LÂMINA

Para Vinícius de Moraes

Assim como uma bala
enterrada no corpo,
fazendo mais espesso
um dos lados do morto;

assim como uma bala
do chumbo mais pesado,
no músculo de um homem
pesando-o mais de um lado;

qual bala que tivesse
um vivo mecanismo,
bala que possuísse
um coração ativo

igual ao de um relógio
submerso em algum corpo,
ao de um relógio vivo
e também revoltoso,

relógio que tivesse
o gume de uma faca
e tôda a impiedade
de lâmina azulada;

assim como uma faca
que sem bôlso ou bainha

A KNIFE ALL BLADE

For Vinícius de Moraes

Like a bullet
buried in flesh
weighing down one side
of the dead man,

like a bullet
made of a heavier lead
lodged in some muscle,
making the man tip to one side,

like a bullet fired
from a living machine,
a bullet that had
its own heartbeat,

like a clock's
beating deep down in the body
of a clock who once lived
and rebelled,

clock whose hands
had knife-edges
and all the pitilessness
of blued steel.

Yes, like a knife,
without pocket or sheath

se transformasse em parte
de vossa anatomia;

qual uma faca íntima
ou faca de uso interno,
habitando num corpo
como o própio esqueleto

de um homem que o tivesse,
e sempre, doloroso,
de homem que se ferisse
contra seus próprios ossos.

OS VAZIOS DO HOMEM

1

Os vazios do homem não sentem ao nada
do vazio qualquer: do do casaco vazio,
do da saca vazia (que não ficam de pé
quando vazios, ou o homem com vazios);
os vazios do homem sentem a um cheio
de uma coisa que inchasse já inchada;
ou ao que deve sentir, quando cheia,
uma saca: todavia não, qualquer saca.
Os vazios do homem, êsse vazio cheio,
não sentem ao que uma saca de tijolos,
uma saca de rebites; nem têm, o pulso
que bate numa de sementes, de ovos.

transformed into part
of your anatomy,

a most intimate knife,
a knife for internal use
inhabiting the body
like the skeleton itself

of the man who would own it,
in pain, always in pain,
of the man who would wound himself
against his own bones.

*Translated by
Galway Kinnell*

THE EMPTINESS OF MAN

1

The emptiness of man is not like
any other: not like an empty coat
or empty sack (things that do not stand up
when empty, such as an empty man),
the emptiness of man is more like fullness
in swollen things that keep on swelling,
the way a sack must feel
that is being filled, or any sack at all.
The emptiness of man, this full emptiness,
is not like a sack of bricks' emptiness
or a sack of rivets', it does not have the pulse
that beats in a seed bag or bag of eggs.

2

Os vazios do homem, ainda que sintam
a uma plenitude (gôra mas presença)
contêm nadas, contêm apenas vazios:
o que a esponja, vazia quando plena;
incham do que a esponja, de ar vazio,
e dela copiam certamente a estrutura:
tôda em grutas ou em gotas de vazio,
postas em cachos de bolha, de não-uva.
Êsse cheio vazio sente ao que uma saca
mas cheia de esponjas cheias de vazio;
os vazios do homem ou vazio inchado:
ou o vazio que inchou por estar vazio.

O SERTANEJO FALANDO

1

A fala a nível do sertanejo engana:
as palavras dêle vem, como rebuçadas
(palavras confeito, pílula), na glace
de uma entonação lisa, de adocicada.
Enquanto que sob ela, dura e endurece
o caroço de pedra, a amêndoa pétrea,
dessa árvore pedrenta (o sertanejo)
incapaz de não se expressar em pedra.

2

The emptiness of man, though it resembles
fullness, and seems all of a piece, actually
is made of nothings, bits of emptiness,
like the sponge, empty when filled,
swollen like the sponge, with air, with empty air;
it has copied its very structure from the sponge,
it is made up in clusters, of bubbles, of nongrapes.
Man's empty fullness is like a sack
filled with sponges, is filled with emptiness:
man's emptiness, or swollen emptiness,
or the emptiness that swells by being empty.

Translated by
Galway Kinnell

THE MAN FROM

UP-COUNTRY TALKING

1

The man from up-country disguises his talk:
the words come out of him like wrapped-up candy
(candy words, pills) in the icing
of a smooth intonation, sweetened.
While under the talk the core of stone
keeps hardening, the stone almond
from the rocky tree back where he comes from:
it can express itself only in stone.

Daí porque o sertanejo fala pouco:
as palavras de pedra ulceram a bôca
e no idioma pedra se fala doloroso;
a natural dêsse idioma fala à fôrça.
Daí também porque êle fala devagar:
tem de pegar as palavras com cuidado,
confeitá-las na língua, rebuçá-las;
pois toma tempo todo êsse trabalho.

O FIM DO MUNDO

No fim de um mundo melancólico
os homens lêem jornais.
Homens indiferentes a comer laranjas
que ardem como o sol.

Me deram uma maçã para lembrar
a morte. Sei que cidades telegrafam
pedindo querosene. O véu que olhei voar
caiu no deserto.

O poema final ninguém escreverá
dêsse mundo particular de doze horas.
Em vez de juízo final a mim me preocupa
o sonho final.

2

That's why the man from up-country says little:
the stone words ulcerate the mouth
and it hurts to speak in the stone language;
those to whom it's native speak by main force.
Furthermore, that's why he speaks slowly:
he has to take up the words carefully,
he has to sweeten them with his tongue, candy them;
well, all this work takes time.

Translated by
W. S. Merwin

THE END OF THE WORLD

At the end of a melancholy world
men read the newspapers.
Men indifferent to eating oranges
that flame like the sun.

They gave me an apple to remind me
of death. I know that cities telegraph
asking for kerosene. The veil I saw flying
fell in the desert.

No one will write the final poem
about this particular twelve o'clock world.
Instead of the last judgment, what worries me
is the final dream.

Translated by
James Wright

BALADA DE LOS
LUGARES OLVIDADOS

Mis refugios más bellos,
los lugares que se adaptan mejor a los colores últimos de mi alma,
están hechos de todo lo que los otros olvidaron.

Son sitios solitarios excavados en la caricia de la hierba,
en una sombra de alas; en una canción que pasa;
regiones cuyos límites giran con los carruajes fantasmales
que transportan la niebla en el amanecer
y en cuyos cielos se dibujan nombres, viejas frases de amor,
juramentos ardientes como constelaciones de luciérnagas ebrias.

Algunas veces pasan poblaciones terrosas, acampan roncos trenes,
una pareja junta naranjas prodigiosas en el borde del mar,
una sola reliquia se propaga por toda la extensión.
Parecerían espejismos rotos,
recortes de fotografías arrancados de un álbum para orientar a la
    nostalgia,
pero tienen raíces más profundas que este suelo que se hunde,
estas puertas que huyen, estas paredes que se borran.

OLGA OROZCO

Argentina 1920–1999

BALLAD OF

FORGOTTEN PLACES

My most beautiful hiding places,
places that best fit my soul's deepest colors,
are made of all that others forgot.

They are solitary sites hollowed out in the grass's caress,
in a shadow of wings, in a passing song;
regions whose limits swirl with the ghostly carriages
that transport the mist in the dawn,
and in whose skies names are sketched, ancient words of love,
vows burning like constellations of drunken fireflies.

Sometimes earthly villages pass, hoarse trains make camp,
a couple piles marvelous oranges at the edge of the sea,
a single relic is spread through all space.
My places would look like broken mirages,
clippings of photographs torn from an album to orient nostalgia,
but they have roots deeper than this sinking ground,
these fleeing doors, these vanishing walls.

Son islas encantadas en las que sólo yo puedo ser la hechicera.

¿Y quién si no, sube las escaleras hacia aquellos desvanes entre nubes
donde la luz zumbaba enardecida en la miel de la siesta,
vuelve a abrir el arcón donde yacen los restos de una historia
        inclemente,
mil veces inmolada nada más que a delirios, nada más que a espumas,
y se prueba de nuevo los pedazos
como aquellos disfraces de las protagonistas invencibles,
el círculo de fuego con el que encandilaba al escorpión del tiempo?

¿Quién limpia con su aliento los cristales y remueve la lumbre del
        atardecer
en aquellas habitaciones donde la mesa era un altar de idolatría,
cada silla, un paisaje replegado después de cada viaje,
y el lecho, un tormentoso atajo hacia la otra orilla de los sueños;
aposentos profundos como redes suspendidas del cielo,
como los abrazos sin fin donde me deslizaba hasta rozar las plumas de
        la muerte,
hasta invertir las leyes del conocimiento y la caída?

¿Quién se interna en los parques con el soplo dorado de cada Navidad
y lava los follajes con un trapito gris que fue el pañuelo de las
        despedidas,
y entrelaza de nuevo las guirnaldas con un hilo de lágrimas,
repitiendo un fantástico ritual entre copas trizadas y absortos
        comensales,
mientras paladea en las doce uvas verdes de la redención
—una por cada mes, una por cada año, una por cada siglo de vacía
        indulgencia—
un ácido sabor menos mordiente que el del pan del olvido?

They are enchanted islands where only I can be the magician.

And who else, if not I, is climbing the stairs toward those attics in the
    clouds
where the light, aflame, used to hum in the siesta's honey,
who else will open again the big chest where the remains of an
    unhappy story lie,
sacrificed a thousand times only to fantasy, only to foam,
and try on the rags again
like those costumes of invincible heroes,
circle of fire that inflamed time's scorpion?

Who cleans the windowpane with her breath and stirs the fire of the
    afternoon
in those rooms where the table was an altar of idolatry,
each chair, a landscape folded up after every trip,
and the bed, a stormy shortcut to the other shore of dreams,
rooms deep as nets hung from the sky,
like endless embraces I slid down till I brushed the feathers of death,
until I overturned the laws of knowledge and the fall of man?

Who goes into the parks with the golden breath of each Christmas
and washes the foliage with a little gray rag that was the handkerchief
    for waving good-bye,
and reweaves the garlands with a thread of tears,
repeating a fantastic ritual among smashed wineglasses and guests
    lost in thought,
while she savors the twelve green grapes of redemption
—one each month, one for each year, one for each century of empty
    indulgence—
a taste acid but not as sharp as the bread of forgetfulness?

¿Por qué quién sino yo les cambia el agua a todos los recuerdos?
¿Quién incrusta el presente como un tajo ante las proyecciones del
    pasado?
¿Alguien trueca mis lámparas antiguas por sus lámparas nuevas?

Mis refugios más bellos son sitios solitarios a los que nadie va
y en los que sólo hay sombras que se animan cuando soy la hechicera.

Because who but I changes the water for all the memories?
Who inserts the present like a slash into the dreams of the past?
Who switches my ancient lamps for new ones?

My most beautiful hiding places are solitary sites where no one goes,
and where there are shadows that come to life only when I am the
magician.

Translated by
Marcy Crow

POEMA DE LÁSTIMAS A LA

MUERTE DE MARCEL PROUST

¿En qué rincón de tu alcoba, ante qué espejo,
tras qué olvidado frasco de jarabe,
hiciste tu pacto?
Cumplida la tregua de años, de meses,
de semanas de asfixia,
de interminables días del verano
vividos entre gruesos edredones,
buscando, llamando, rescatando
la semilla intacta del tiempo,
construyendo un laberinto perdurable
donde el hábito pierde su especial energía,
su voraz exterminio;
la muerte acecha a los pies de tu cama,
labrando en tu rostro milenario
la máscara letal de tu agonía.
Se pega a tu oscuro pelo de rabino,
cava el pozo febril de tus ojeras
y algo de seca flor, de tenue ceniza volcánica,

ÁLVARO MUTIS

Colombia 1923-

LAMENT FOR THE DEATH

OF MARCEL PROUST

In what corner of your alcove, before which mirror,
behind what forgotten medicine bottle,
did you make a pact?
With a truce fulfilled that took years, months,
weeks of asphyxia,
of interminable days of summer
lived through thick duvet covers,
searching, calling, rescuing
the intact seed of time,
building a durable labyrinth
where habit loses its special energy,
its voracious extermination;
death lies in wait at the bottom of your bed,
sculpting in your millenarian face
your agony's lethal mask.
It sticks to your dark rabbi's hair,
digging the feverish well of your dark circles
and something of a dry flower, of light volcanic ash,

de lavado vendaje de mendigo,
extiende por tu cuerpo
como un leve sudario de otro mundo
o un borroso sello que perdura.
Ahora la ves erguirse, venir hacia ti,
herirte en pleno pecho malamente
y pides a Celeste que abra las ventanas
donde el otoño golpea como una bestia herida.
Pero no te oye ya, no te comprende,
e inútilmente acude con presurosos dedos de hilandera
para abrir aun más las llaves del oxígeno
y pasarte un poco del aire que te esquiva
y aliviar tu estertor de supliciado.
Monsieur Marcel ne se rend compte de rien,
explica a tus amigos
que escépticos preguntan por tus males
y la llamas con el ronco ahogo del que inhala
el último aliento de su vida.
Tiendes tus manos al seco vacío del mundo,
rasgas la piel de tu garganta,
saltan tus dulces ojos de otros días
y por última vez tu pecho se alza
en un violento esfuerzo por librarse
del peso de la losa que te espera.
El silencio se hace en tus dominios,
mientras te precipitas vertiginosamente
hacia el nostálgico limbo donde habitan,
a la orilla del tiempo, tus criaturas.
Vagas sombras cruzan por tu rostro
a medida que ganas a la muerte
una nueva porción de tus asuntos
y, borrando el desorden de una larga agonía,

of a pauper's washed-out bandage,
extends through your body
like a light, out-of-this world shroud
and an enduring foggy seal.
Now you see it standing, coming to you,
injuring you malignantly in the chest,
and you ask Celeste to open the windows
where autumn beats like an injured beast.
But it no longer hears you, it doesn't understand you,
and, needlessly, it comes with its spinner's hurried fingers
to open even more the oxygen valves
and bring to you a bit of the air that evades you
and alleviate your supplicant's death.
Monsieur Marcel ne se rend compte de rien,
she explains to your friends
who ask skeptically about your ailment,
and you call her with the hoarse breathlessness of he who breathes
the last sigh of life.
You extend your hands to the dry emptiness of the world,
you rip the skin of your throat,
your sweet eyes of yesteryear jump up
and for the last time your chest emerges
in a violent effort seeking to liberate
itself of the weight of the loss that awaits you.
Silence takes over your dominion,
While you precipitate yourself dizzily
toward the nostalgic limbo habituated,
at the edge of time, by your creatures.
Vague shadows cross your face
while you reclaim from death
a new portion of your affairs
and, erasing the disdain of a long agony,

surgen tus facciones de astuto cazador babilónico,
emergen del fondo de las aguas funerales
para mostrar al mundo
la fértil permanencia de tu sueño,
la ruina del tiempo y las costumbres
en la frágil materia de los años.

your facial gestures of astute Babylonian hunter come up,
emerging from the bottom of the funeral waters
to show the world
the fertile endurance of your dream,
the ruin of time and the routine
of the fragile matter that makes time.

Translated by
Ilan Stavans

DESTINOS

Somos las furias
las erinias
las de siniestras alas
de murciélago.
Nacimos de la tierra
de tres gotas de sangre
que Urano derramó
sobre la tierra.
Son negros nuestros cuerpos
tenemos serpientes por cabellos
y cabezas de perro.
En nuestras manos brillan
azotes tachonados de metal.
Ingrato nuestro oficio
perseguidoras somos
vengadoras
con afán de justicia.
Enloquecimos a Orestes
le dimos muerte a Edipo
y lo lloramos.

CLARIBEL ALEGRÍA

El Salvador 1924-

DESTINIES

We are the Furies
the Erinyes
they of the sinister
bat wings.
We are born of the earth
of three drops of blood
Uranus spilled
onto the earth.
Black are our bodies
serpents writhe
on our doglike heads.
Metal-studded scourges
flash in our hands.
Our office is thankless
we are pursuers
avengers
we thirst for justice.
We drove Orestes mad
we killed Oedipus
and we weep for him.

427

Hicimos penitencia:
en el fuego sagrado
quemamos nuestras alas
que brotaron de nuevo
agigantadas.
Somos las más temidas
por temor nos adulan
nos llaman bondadosas
y en susurros pronuncian
nuestros nombres.
Cumplimos un destino
¿pero quién lo fraguó?
un oscuro destino
que golpea
que impele
hacemos nuestra ronda
no hay perdón.
Somos las tres furias solitarias
las más viejas
en los confines del Olimpo.
¿Quién habló de piedad?
Sólo el destino existe
ese destino-abismo
nos succiona
nos lanza
no nos deja escapar.

We did our penance:
in the sacred fire
we burned our wings
which budded anew
made large.
We are feared above all others
adulated out of fear
called generous
our names spoken
in whispers.
We fulfilled a destiny
but who forged it?
A dark destiny
that spurs
and incites us
we make our rounds
without forgiveness.
We are the three solitary Furies
the oldest here on Olympus.
Who spoke of mercy?
Nothing exists but destiny
that destiny-abyss
that engulfs us
draws us in
thrusts us out
refuses us escape.

Translated by
Margaret Sayers Peden

MÁSCARAS

Cuanto fui
cuanto no fui
todo eso soy.

FERNANDO PESSOA

Soy todo lo que fui
lo que pude haber sido
lo que soñé y no fui
todos esos retazos incongruentes
que componen mi máscara
y me arañan el rostro
en mis noches de insomnio.
Soy todo lo que amo
los que me aman
y también mis fracasos
y mis lloros
y mis ángeles mudos
y mis antepasados silenciosos.
Soy este oscuro tedio
que me opaca las horas
que me roe los huesos
que me atrapa
y me impide soltarme
y danzar hacia ti.

MASKS

All I was
all I was not
all that am I.

FERNANDO PESSOA

I am all that I was
all that I could have been
what I dreamed but was not
all the mismatched scraps
that compose my mask
and claw my face
through sleepless nights.
I am everything I love
all those who love me
and also my failures
my weeping
my mute angels
my silent ancestors.
I am this dark tedium
that clouds my hours
that gnaws my bones
that traps me
and prevents my breaking loose
to dance my way toward you.

Translated by
Margaret Sayers Peden

431

ANTÍGONA

Sepultaré a mi hermano
aunque yo muera
ignorando las leyes
del desamor.
Se equivoca Creonte
jamás lo dejaré
como pasto de aves.
He ungido mis brazos
de cólera
y dureza
para encender la hoguera
que ha de borrar su cuerpo.
Se equivoca Creonte
no somos timoratas las mujeres
ni envenenamos la razón
ni esquivamos el riesgo.
Sepultaré a mi hermano
sin miedo
y con amor.

ANTIGONE

I shall bury my brother
though it mean my death
and ignore the laws
of enmity.
Creon is mistaken
I will never leave Polyneices
as food for the birds.
I have anointed my arms
with anger
and strength
to light the pyre
that will consume his body.
Creon is mistaken
we women are not fainthearted
we do not poison reason
neither do we shy from risk.
I shall bury my brother
without fear
and with love.

Translated by
Margaret Sayers Peden

ORACIÓN POR MARILYN MONROE

Señor
recibe a esta muchacha conocida en toda la tierra con el nombre de
    Marilyn Monroe
aunque ése no era su verdadero nombre
(pero Tú conoces su verdadero nombre, el de la huerfanita violada a
    los 9 años
y la empleadita de tienda que a los 16 años se había querido matar)
y que ahora se presenta ante Ti sin ningún maquillaje
sin su Agente de Prensa
sin fotógrafos y sin firmar autógrafos
sola como una astronauta frente a la noche espacial.

Ella soñó cuando niña que estaba desnuda en una iglesia
                (según cuenta el *Time*)
ante una multitud postrada, con las cabezas en el suelo
y tenía que caminar en puntillas para no pisar las cabezas.
Tú conoces nuestros sueños mejor que los psiquiatras.
Iglesia, casa, cueva, son la seguridad del seno materno
pero también algo más que eso . . .
Las cabezas son los admiradores, es claro

434

ERNESTO CARDENAL

Nicaragua 1925–

PRAYER FOR MARILYN MONROE

Lord
accept this girl called Marilyn Monroe throughout the world
though that was not her name
(but You know her real name, that of the orphan raped at nine,
the shopgirl who tried to kill herself aged just sixteen)
who now goes into Your presence without makeup
without her press agent
without her photographs or signing autographs
lonely as an astronaut facing the darkness of outer space.

When she was a child, she dreamed she was naked in a church
                (according to *Time*)
standing in front of a prostrate multitude, heads to the ground,
and had to walk on tiptoe to avoid the heads.
You know our dreams better than the psychiatrist.
Church, house, or cave all represent the safety of the womb
but also something more . . .
The heads are admirers, so much is clear (that

435

(las masa de cabezas en la oscuridad bajo el chorro de luz).
Pero el templo no son los estudios de la 20th Century–Fox
El templo—de mármol y oro—es el templo de su cuerpo
en el que está el Hijo del Hombre con un látigo en la mano
expulsando a los mercaderes de la 20th Century–Fox
que hicieron de Tu casa de oración una cueva de ladrones

Señor
en este mundo contaminado de pecados y radioactividad
Tú no culparás tan sólo a una empleadita de tienda.
Que como toda empleadita de tienda soñó ser estrella de cine.
Y su sueño fue realidad (pero como la realidad del tecnicolor).
Ella no hizo sino actuar según el script que le dimos.
—El de nuestras propias vidas—. Y era un script absurdo.
Perdónala Señor y perdónanos a nosotros
por nuestra 20th Century
por esta Colosal Super-Producción en la que todos hemos trabajado.

Ella tenía hambre de amor y le ofrecimos tranquilizantes.
Para la tristeza de no ser santos
                                se le recomendó el Psicoanálisis.
Recuerda Señor su creciente pavor a la cámara
y el odio al maquillaje—insistiendo en maquillarse en cada escena—
y cómo se fue haciendo mayor el horror
y mayor la impuntualidad a los estudios.

Como toda empleadita de tienda
soñó ser estrella de cine.
Y su vida fue irreal como un sueño que un psiquiatra interpreta y
    archiva.
Sus romances fueron un beso con los ojos cerrados
que cuando se abren los ojos

mass of heads in the darkness below the beam to the screen).
But the temple isn't the studios of 20th Century–Fox.
The temple, of gold and marble, is the temple of her body
in which the Son of Man stands whip in hand
driving out the money-changers of 20th Century–Fox
who made Your house of prayer a den of thieves.

Lord
in this world defiled by radioactivity and sin
surely You will not blame a shopgirl
who (like any other shopgirl) dreamed of being a star.
And her dream became "reality" (Technicolor reality).
All she did was follow the script we gave her,
that of our own lives, but it was meaningless.
Forgive her Lord and forgive all of us
for this our twentieth century
and the Mammoth Superproduction in whose making we all shared.

She was hungry for love and we offered her tranquilizers.
For the sadness of our not being saints
                                        they recommend psychoanalysis.
Remember Lord her increasing terror of the camera
and hatred of makeup (yet her insistence on fresh makeup
for each scene) and how the terror grew
and how her unpunctuality at the studios grew.

Like any other shopgirl
she dreamed of being a star.
And her life was as unreal as a dream an analyst reads and files.
Her romances were kisses with closed eyes
which when the eyes are opened

se descubre que fue bajo reflectores

y apagan los reflectores!
y desmontan las dos paredes de aposento (era un set cinematográfico)
mientras el Director se aleja con su libreta

porque la escena ya fue tomada.
O como un viaje en yate, un beso en Singapur, un baile en Río,
la recepción en la mansión del Duque y la Duquesa de Windsor

vistos en la salita del apartamento miserable.

La película terminó sin el beso final.
La hallaron muerta en su cama con la mano en el teléfono.
Y los detectives no supieron a quién iba a llamar.
Fue
como alguien que ha marcado el número de la única voz amiga
y oye tan sólo la voz de un disco que le dice: WRONG NUMBER.
O como alguien que herido por los gángsters
alarga la mano a un teléfono desconectado.

Señor
quienquiera que haya sido el que ella iba a llamar
y no llamó (y tal vez no era nadie
o era Alguien cuyo número no está en el Directorio de Los Ángeles)

contesta Tú el teléfono!

are seen to have been played out beneath the spotlights
                              and the spotlights are switched off
and the two walls of the room (it was a set) are taken down
while the director moves away notebook in hand,
                              the scene being safely canned.
Or like a cruise on a yacht, a kiss in Singapore, a dance in Rio,
a reception in the mansion of the Duke and Duchess of Windsor
                    viewed in the sad tawdriness of a cheap apartment.

The film ended without the final kiss.
They found her dead in bed, hand on the phone.
And the detectives never learned who she was going to call.
It was as
though someone had dialed the only friendly voice
and heard a prerecorded tape just saying, "WRONG NUMBER";
or like someone wounded by gangsters, who
reaches out toward a disconnected phone.

Lord
whoever it may have been that she was going to call
but did not (and perhaps it was no one at all
or Someone not in the Los Angeles telephone book),
                              Lord, You pick up that phone.

Translated by
Robert Pring-Mill

439

SI CONOCIÉRAMOS EL PUNTO

Si conociéramos el punto
donde va a romperse algo,
donde se cortará el hilo de los besos,
donde una mirada dejará de encontrarse con otra mirada,
donde el corazón saltará hacia otro sitio,
podríamos poner otro punto sobre ese punto
o por lo menos acompañarlo al romperse.

Si conociéramos el punto
donde algo va a fundirse con algo,
donde el desierto se encontrará con la lluvia,
donde el abrazo se tocará con la vida,
donde mi muerte se aproximará a la tuya,
podríamos desenvolver ese punto como una serpentina
o por lo menos cantarlo hasta morirnos.

Si conociéramos el punto
donde algo será siempre ese algo,
donde el hueso no olvidará a la carne,

ROBERTO JUARRÓZ

Argentina 1925-1995

IF WE KNEW THE POINT

If we knew the point
where something is going to break,
where the thread of kisses will be cut,
where a look will no longer meet another,
where the heart will leap toward another place,
we could all put another point on that point
or at least go with it to its breaking.

If we knew the point
where something is going to melt into something,
where the desert will meet the rain,
where the embrace will touch life itself,
where my death will come closer to yours,
we could unwind that point like a streamer,
or at least sing it till we died.

If we knew the point
where something will always be something,
where the bone will not forget the flesh,

donde la fuente es madre de otra fuente,
donde el pasado nunca será pasado,
podríamos dejar sólo ese punto y borrar todos los otros
o guardarlo por lo menos en un lugar más seguro.

(A Laura)

where the fountain is mother to another fountain,
where the past will never be past,
we could leave that point and erase all the others,
or at least keep it in a safer place.

(To Laura)

Translated by
W. S. Merwin

EL RESPLANDOR DEL SER

Sólo el silencio es sabio.
Pero yo estoy labrando, como con cien abejas,
un pequeño panal con mis palabras.

Todo el día el zumbido
del trabajo feliz va esparciendo en el aire
el polvo de oro de un jardín lejano.

En mí crece un rumor lento como en el árbol
cuando madura un fruto.
Todo lo que era tierra—oscuridad y peso—,
lo que era turbulencia de savia, ruido de hoja,
va haciéndose sabor y redondez.
¡Inminencia feliz de la palabra!

Porque una palabra no es el pájaro
que vuela y huye lejos.
Porque no es el árbol bien plantado.

ROSARIO CASTELLANOS

Mexico 1925-1974

THE SPLENDOR OF BEING

Silence alone is wise.
But with my words, as with a hundred bees,
I am building a small hive.

All day the hum
of happy work strews the air
with the gold dust of a far-off garden.

Within me a slow roar grows as in a tree
when a fruit ripens.
All that was earth—darkness and weight—
all that was turbulence of wild sage, leaves rustling,
is becoming flavor and roundness.
Sweet imminence of the word!

Because a word is not a bird
that flies and escapes far away.
Because it's not a rooted tree.

Porque una palabra es el sabor
que nuestra lengua tiene de lo eterno,
por eso hablo.

El ser eterno, único,
la redondez del círculo cumplida.

Boca que se abre para decir sí
como se abre—asintiendo—la semilla.

Baja a la inteligencia
total, sin mengua, la palabra;
y queda (como el ámbito por el que vuela un pájaro)
plena y maravillada.

En mí su voluntad no fue hermosura.
Me hizo, como a la planta del desierto,
áspera y taciturna.
Me alzó para medir la soledad
en la extensión sin término, desnuda.
El viento—herido en mis espinas—sangra.
Mi única flor es la obediencia oscura.

No ser ya más. O ser
sumisa, un instrumento.
Una flauta en los dedos de la música,
una espiga inclinada bajo el verano inmenso.

No ser ya más. Girar
disciplinadamente ceñida al universo.
Navegar sin orillas
en el amor perfecto.

A word is the taste
our tongue has of eternity;
that's why I speak.

The eternal being, unique,
the complete roundness of the circle.

Mouth that opens to say yes
as a seed—assenting—opens.

Down to intelligence
complete, undiminished, the word descends;
and remains (like the path a bird draws as it flies)
full and astonished.

In me its will was never beauty.
Like a desert plant,
it turned me taciturn and harsh.
Raised me up to measure
solitude's unending, naked span.
The wind—wounded on my thorns—bleeds.
My only flower is dark obedience.

To be no more. Or be
submissive, an instrument.
A flute in music's hands,
an ear of wheat bent beneath vast summer.

To be no more. To spin
with discipline around the universe.
To sail without shorelines
in perfect love.

Amanece en el valle. Con qué lento
resplandor se sonrosa la nieve de las cimas
y cómo se difunde la luz en el silencio.

Hechizada, contemplo el milagro de estar
como en el centro puro de un diamente.

¡Ah, despertar, vivir,
amar, amar el viento
como un amor de pájaro!

De toda la creación esta creatura,
ésta, para mi gozo.
Escogida y perfecta,
coronación del mundo más hermoso.

De su promesa viene
a ser presencia pura.
¡Oh, amor! ¡Oh, misterio,
agua donde la perla se consuma!

¡Alegría de ser dos! En dos orillas
va el río, regalándose.
En dos alas el pájaro
sube al centro del aire.

En las manos unidas
reposa, sostenido, el universo.
¡Alegría de ser dos, y entre dos
lo eterno!

Me llamas, como a Eurídice,
rompiendo la tiniebla.

Dawn in the valley. With what slow
splendor the snow blushes on the peaks
and how the light spreads in the silence.

Spellbound, I contemplate the miracle of being
as at the pure center of a diamond.

Ah, to wake, to live,
to love, to love the wind
as a bird loves!

Of all creation, this creature,
this one, for my pleasure.
Select and perfect,
coronation of the world most beautiful.

From its promise it becomes
pure presence.
Oh, love! Oh, mystery,
water where the pearl is consummated!

Joy of being two! Between two shores
the river flows, regales itself.
On two wings the bird
climbs to the center of the air.

In cupped hands
the held universe reposes.
Joy of being two, and between the two
all that is eternal!

You call me, like Eurydice,
breaking the dark.

El nombre que me das
es para que amanezca.

Sonreída, inocente,
hierba, me vuelvo al aire conmovido.
De la noche no tengo
más que el rocío.

Me alegro con la rama del almendro.
Calló todo el invierno, pero sin descansar,
pues preparaba el tiempo
de convertir lo oscuro de la tierra
en esta flor con la que hoy me alegro.

Se mecía la rama
y era una flor abierta
su única palabra.

¡Cuánta muerte vencida para alcanzar la cima
de plenitud tan breve y delicada!

No era la eternidad. Era la primavera.
La primavera que florece y pasa.

Lo supe con mi carne.
Que la vida es la flor que entre sus dedos
va deshojando el aire
para dejar sin cárcel el perfume
y sin dueño la miel temblorosa del cáliz.

Así, como a la flor del cardo, nos destruye.
Lo supe con mi carne.

The name you give me
is for breaking the dark.

Smiling, innocent,
tall grass, I return to the startled air.
Dew is all I have
of night.

I rejoice with the branch of the almond tree.
All winter it was mute, but without rest,
because it was preparing
to change earth's darkness
to this flower that today brings me such joy.

The branch swayed
and the open flower
was its only word.

How much death overcome to reach
plentitude's brief, delicate peak!

It was not eternity. It was spring.
Spring that blooms and passes.

I knew it in my flesh.
That life is the bloom the air's fingers
tear to leave
its perfume without jail,
the trembling honey of its chalice without master.

And so it destroys us, like the thistle.
I knew it in my flesh.

¡Qué amistad la del agua con su cace
y qué conversación la de la rama
cortejada del aire!

En la mano del día
resplandece un anillo de esponsales.

¡Qué nupcias de la luz y del espejo!

Nadie está solo. Nadie.

No temo por la hoja del arbusto pequeño,
aunque la oculte el árbol poderoso,
aunque la huelle el paso del becerro.

El rocío la embellece
de noche y en silencio.

¡Cómo canta la tierra cuando gira!
Canta la ligereza de su vuelo,
su libertad, su gracia, su alegría.

Así cantan los pájaros
regresando a su nido desde lejos.

El amor que nos ama
no aparta de nosotros ni un instante
la mirada.

Bajo ella estamos todos los dispersos,
como espigas en haz, en gavilla apretada.

What friendship binds the water to its source,
what conversation the branch holds
with the wooing air!

A wedding ring gleams
on the day's hand.

Nuptials of light and the mirror!

No one is alone. No one.

I do not fear for the leaf of the tiny bush,
even if the great tree hides it,
even if the lamb's hoof breaks it.

The dew adorns it
by night and in silence.

How the earth sings as it spins!
Sings the lightness of its flight,
its freedom, its grace, its joy.

So birds sing
returning to their nests from far away.

The love that loves us
does not turn its gaze from us
even for a second.

Beneath its gaze we are all gathered in
like sheaves of wheat bound tight.

La medida completa
que él alzaría en sólo una brazada.

¿Quién vivió y no lo cree?
Las palabras lo juran,
lo atestiguan los seres.

Que este don que nos dieron es don que se recibe
y ya no se devuelve.

A veces hay la noche,
pero la luz es fiel y vuelve siempre.

Al tercer día todo resucita.

Sólo la muerte muere.

No te despidas nunca.

La hoja que el otoño desprende de la rama
conoce los caminos del regreso.

La juventud recuerda su querencia.
La golondrina vuelve del destierro.

No te despidas nunca, porque el mundo
es redondo y perfecto.

The complete measure
it would raise in a single clasp.

Who has lived and does not believe?
Words swear to it,
beings bear witness to it.

That this gift they gave us is a gift received
and not returned.

Sometimes there is night,
but the light is faithful and always returns.

On the third day everything comes back to life.

Only death dies.

Never say good-bye.

The leaf autumn looses from the branch
knows the way back.

Youth remembers its affection.
The swallow returns from exile.

Never say good-bye, because the world
is round and perfect.

Translated by
Magda Bogin

ROSARIO CASTELLANOS

MURO DE LAMENTACIONES

I

Alguien que clama en vano contra el cielo:
la sorda inmensidad, la azul indiferencia,
el vacío imposible para el eco.
Porque los niños surgen de vientres como ataúdes
y en el pecho materno se nutren de venenos.
Porque la flor es breve y el tiempo interminable
y la tierra un cadáver transformándose
y el espanto la máscara perfecta de la nada.

Alguien, yo arrodillada: rasgué mis vestiduras
y colmé de cenizas mi cabeza.
Lloro por esa patria que no he tenido nunca,
la patria que edifica la angustia en el desierto
cuando humean los granos de arena al mediodía.
Porque yo soy de aquellos desterrados
para quienes el pan de su mesa es ajeno
y su lecho una inmensa llanura abandonada
y toda voz humana una lengua extranjera.

Porque yo soy el éxodo.
(Un arcángel me cierra caminos de regreso
y su espada flamígera incendia paraísos.)
¡Más allá, más allá, más allá! ¡Sombras, fuentes,
praderas deleitosas, ciudades, más allá!
Más allá del camello y el ojo de la aguja,
de la humilde semilla de mostaza
y del lirio y del pájaro desnudos.

WAILING WALL

I

Someone who cries in vain against the sky:
its deaf immensity, its blue indifference,
its emptiness inhospitable to echo.
Because children rise from wombs like coffins
and suck poison at their mothers' breasts.
Because the flower is brief and time interminable
and the earth a corpse transforming itself
and dread the perfect mask of nothingness.

Someone, myself, kneeling: I rent my clothes
and filled my head with ash.
I weep for the country I have never had,
the country anguish builds in the desert
when grains of sand smoke at noon.
Because I am one of those exiles
whose daily bread is a stranger,
whose bed is a vast abandoned plain,
and for whom each human voice is a foreign tongue.

Because I am the exodus.
(An archangel blocks all roads of return
and his flaming sword sets paradises blazing.)
Beyond, beyond, beyond! Shadows, fountains,
meadows of delight, cities, beyond!
Beyond the camel and the needle's eye,
beyond the humble mustard seed
and the naked lily and the bird.

No podría tomar tu pecho por almohada
ni cabría en los pastos que triscan tus ovejas.

Reverbera mi hogar en el crepúsculo.

Yo dormiré en la Mano que quiebra a los relojes.

II

Detrás de mí tan sólo las memorias borradas.
Mis muertos ni transcienden de sus tumbas
y por primera vez estoy mirando el mundo.

Soy hija de mí misma.
De mi sueño nací. Mi sueño me sostiene.

No busquéis en mis filtros más que mi propia sangre
ni remontéis los ríos para alcanzar mi origen.

En mi genealogía no hay más que una palabra:
Soledad.

III

Sedienta como el mar y como el mar ahogada
de agua salobre y honda
vengo desde el abismo hasta mis labios
que son como una torpe tentativa de playa,
como arena rendida
llorando por la fuga de las olas.

I could not use your breast as a pillow
nor frolic in the pastures your sheep flock.

My hearth reverberates in the dusk.

I shall sleep in the Hand that breaks the clocks.

II

Behind me, only memories erased.
My dead do not transcend their tombs
and I am looking at the world for the first time.

I am the daughter of myself.
I am born of my own dream. My dream sustains me.

Seek no more in my filters than my own blood,
do not retrace rivers for my source.

In my genealogy there is a single word:
solitude.

III

Thirsty as the sea and like the sea drowned
with salt water and deep
I come from the abyss to my own lips,
which are a clumsy attempt at a beach,
like exhausted sand
weeping for the waves' retreat.

Todo mi mar es de pañuelos blancos,
de muelles desolados y de presencias náufragas.
Toda mi playa un caracol que gime
porque el viento encerrado en sus paredes
se revuelve furioso y lo golpea.

IV

Antes acabarán mis pasos que el espacio.
Antes caerá la noche de que mi afán concluya.

Me cercarán las fieras en ronda enloquecida,
cercenarán mis voces cuchillos afilados,
se romperán los grillos que sujetan el miedo.

No prevalecerá sobre mí el enemigo
si en la tribulación digo Tu nombre.

V

Entre las cosas busco Tu huella y no la encuentro.
Lo que mi oído toca se convierte en silencio,
la orilla en que me tiendo se deshace.

¿Dónde estás? ¿Por qué apartas tu rostro de mi rostro?
¿Eres la puerta enorme que esconde la locura,
el muro que devuelve lamento por lamento?

Esperanza,
¿eres sólo una lápida?

My whole sea is white kerchiefs,
deserted piers and shipwrecked presences.
My whole beach a seashell moaning
because the wind locked in its walls
batters it with unrelenting rage.

I V

My footsteps will sooner end than space.
Night will sooner fall than my eagerness wane.

The beasts will encircle me in a crazed round,
sharp knives will shear off my voices,
the shackles that hold fear in check will snap.

The enemy will not prevail over me
if in my tribulation I speak Your name.

V

Among all things I seek Your trace and do not find it.
What my ear touches becomes silence,
the shore on which I lie is coming undone.

Where are you? Why do you turn your face from mine?
Are you the gaping door that covers madness,
the wall that answers one grief with another?

Hope,
are you nothing but a tomb?

VI

No diré con los otros que también me olvidaste.
No ingresaré en el coro de los que te desprecian
ni seguiré al ejército blasfemo.

Si no existes
yo te haré a semejanza de mi anhelo,
a imagen de mis ansias.

Llama petrificada
habitarás en mí como en Tu reino.

VII

Te amo hasta los límites extremos:
la yema palpitante de los dedos,
la punta vibratoria del cabello.

Creo en Ti con los párpados cerrados.
Creo en Tu fuego siempre renovado.

Mi corazón se ensancha por contener Tus ámbitos.

VIII

Ha de ser tu substancia igual que la del día
que sigue a las tinieblas, radiante y absoluto.
Como lluvia, la gracia prometida

VI

I will not say with the others that You also forgot me.
I will not join the chorus of those who despise You
nor follow the blaspheming army.

If You do not exist
I will shape You after my desire,
in the image of my worry.

Petrified flame,
You will dwell in me as in Your kingdom.

VII

I love You to my farthest limits:
to the trembling tips of my fingers,
the vibrating ends of my hair.

I believe in You with my eyelids closed.
I believe in Your flame eternally renewed.

My heart expands to hold Your realm.

VIII

Your substance shall resemble the day
that follows night, radiant and absolute.
Like rain, the promised grace

descenderá en escalas luminosas
a bañar la aridez de nuestra frente.

Pues ¿para qué esta fiebre si no es para anunciarte?

Carbones encendidos han limpiado mi boca.

Canto tus alabanzas desde antes que amanezca.

will descend luminous stairs
to bathe our arid brows.

Why else this fever if not to announce You?

Blazing coals have cleansed my mouth.

I have been singing Your praises since long before dawn.

Translated by
Magda Bogin

CON LOS NERVIOS

SALIÉNDOME DEL CUERPO

Con los nervios saliéndome del cuerpo como hilachas,
como las fibras de una escoba vieja,
y arrastrando en el suelo, jalando todavía
el fardo de mi alma,
cansado, todo, más que mis propias piernas,
hastiado de usar mi corazón del diario,
estoy sobre esta cama y a estas horas
esperando el derrumbe,
la inminente caída que ha de sepultarme.
(Hay que cerrar los ojos como para dormir
y no mover ni una hoja de tu cuerpo.
Esto puede ocurrir de un momento a otro:
estarse quieto.
Pañuelos de aire giran lentamente,
sombras espesas rascan las paredes,
el cielo te chupa a través del techo.)

Mañana te has de levantar de nuevo
a caminar entre las gentes.

JAIME SABINES

Mexico 1925–1999

WITH NERVES

TRAILING

I'm out on this bed
with nerves trailing from my body like frayed threads,
like the whiskers of an old broom,
dragging on the floor, tugging
at the bundle of my soul.
I'm dead tired. More tired of using my heart
every day than my legs.
I wait at all hours for the landslide,
the scheduled collapse, that will bury me.
(You have to shut your eyes as in sleep
and hold every leaf of your body still.
This can occur from one moment to the next,
this stilling oneself.
Handkerchiefs of air are slowly being spun,
heavy shadows scrape the walls,
heaven is sucking you up through the roof.)

Tomorrow you'll rise again
and walk among your people.

Y amarás el sol y el frío,
los automóviles, los trenes,
las casas de moda, y los establos,
las paredes a que se pegan los enamorados
al entrar la noche, como calcomanías,
los parques solitarios en que se pasean las desgracias
con la cabeza baja, y los sueños se sientan a descansar,
y algún novio la busca bajo la falda,
mientras la sirena de la ambulancia de la hora
de entrar a la fábrica de la muerte.
Amarás la milagrosa ciudad y en ella el campo soñado,
el río de las avenidas iluminadas por tanta gente que quiere lo mismo,
las puertas de los bares abiertas, las sorpresas de las librerías,
el estanco de flores, los niños descalzos
que no quieren ser héroes de la miseria,
y las marquesinas, los anuncios,
la prisa de los que no tienen a dónde ir.
Amarás el asfalto y la buhardilla
y las bombas para el drenaje y las grúas
y los palacios y los hoteles de lujo
y el césped de las casas donde hay un perro guardián
y dos o tres gentes que también se van a morir.
Amarás los olores de las fritangas
que en la noche atraen como una luz a los hambrientos,
y tu cabeza se irá detrás del perfume
que alguna mujer deja en el aire como una boa suspendida.
Y amarás la ferias mecánicas
donde los pobres llegan al vértigo y a la risa,
y el zoológico, donde todos se sienten importantes,
y el hospital, donde el dolor hace más hermanos
que los que puede hacer la pobreza,
y las casas de cuna, y las guarderías en que juegan los niños,

You'll love the sun, the cold,
the cars, trains,
the fancy shops and the stables,
the walls to which lovers plaster themselves
like posters at dusk,
the empty parks where sorrow walks
head down and your dreams slump on a bench,
where the lover slides his hand under a skirt
as the ambulance whistles a new shift
into the factories of death.
You'll love the magic city and in her the land you dreamed,
the blazing streets burned by all those who love them,
the open doors of bars, the surprises of the bookshops,
the flower stands, the barefoot kids
who don't want to be the noble poor,
the movie marquees, the ads,
the rush of those who have nowhere to go.
You'll love the pavement below and the attics above,
the drainage pumps and the tow trucks,
the palaces and the first-class hotels
and the watchdogs in the yards of those houses
where two or three are going to die.
You'll love the smell of doughnuts
that signal the poor all night like a beacon,
and your head will be turned by some woman's perfume
left in the air like a floating boa.
You'll love the amusement parks
where the poor get dizzy and laugh,
the zoo where all feel superior,
the hospitals where pain
makes more brothers than poverty,
the orphanages and nurseries where the kids play,

y todos los lugares en que la ternura se asoma como un tallo
y las cosas todas te ponen a dar gracias.
Pasa tu mano sobre la piel de los muebles,
quita el polvo que has dejado caer sobre los espejos.
En todas partes hay semillas que quieren nacer.
(Como una escarlatina te va a brotar, de pronto, la vida.)

PASA EL LUNES . . .

Pasa el lunes y pasa el martes
y pasa el miércoles y el jueves y el viernes
y el sábado y el domingo,
y otra vez el lunes y el martes
y la gotera de los días sobre la cama donde se quiere dormir,
la estúpida gota del tiempo cayendo sobre el corazón aturdido,
la vida pasando como estas palabras:
lunes, martes, miércoles,
enero, febrero, diciembre, otro año, otra vida.
La vida yéndose sin sentido, entre la borrachera y la concienca,
entre la lujuria y el remordimiento y el cansancio.

Encontrarse, de pronto, con las manos vacías,
con el corazón vacío,
con la memoria como una ventana hacia la obscuridad,
y preguntarse: ¿qué hice? ¿qué fui? ¿en dónde estuve?
Sombra perdida entre las sombras,
¿cómo recuperarte, rehacerte, vida?

all those places where tenderness nudges forth like a sprout
and all things lead you to give thanks.
Run your hand over the surfaces of furniture,
wipe away the dust that has fallen on your mirror.
Everywhere there are seeds that want to be born.
(Life bursts from you, like scarlet fever, without warning.)

*Translated by
Philip Levine and
Ernesto Trejo*

MONDAY PASSES . . .

Monday passes and Tuesday passes
and Wednesday goes by and Thursday and Friday
and Saturday and Sunday also,
and again Monday and Tuesday,
the days leaking onto the bed where you search for sleep,
the dumb drip of time leaking into your stunned heart,
life passes just as these words pass:
Monday, Tuesday, Wednesday,
January, February, December, another year, still another, another life.
Life slips by without your noticing, between bouts of boozing and fits of
    conscience,
between lust, remorse, exhaustion.

Suddenly you find yourself empty-handed,
empty-hearted,
with a memory like a window that looks out on darkness,
and you ask yourself: "What happened? Who was I? Where am I?"
A shadow lost among shadows,
how can you find yourself? How can you take up your life?

471

Nadie puede vivir de cara a la verdad
sin caer enfermo o dolerse hasta los huesos.
Porque la verdad es que somos débiles y miserables
y necesitamos amar, ampararnos, esperar, creer y afirmar.
No podemos vivir a la intemperie
en el solo minuto que nos es dado.

¡Qué hermosa palabra "Dios," larga
y útil al miedo, salvadora!
Aprendamos a cerrar los labios del corazón
cuando quiera decirla,
y enseñémosle a vivir en su sangre,
a revolcarse en su sangre limitada.

No hay más que esta ternura que siento hacia ti, engañado,
porque algún día vas a abrir los ojos
y mirarás tus ojos cerrados para siempre.
No hay más que esta ternura de mí mismo
que estoy abierto como un árbol,
plantado como un árbol, recorriéndolo todo.

He aquí la verdad: hacer las máscaras,
recitar las voces, elaborar los sueños.
Ponerse el rostro del enamorado,
la cara del que sufre,
la faz del que sonríe,
el día lunes, y el martes, y el mes de marzo
y el año de la solidaridad humana,
y comer a las horas lo mejor que se pueda,
y dormir y ayuntar,
y seguirse entrenando ocultamente para el evento final
del que no habrá testigos.

Because we're weak, miserable creatures
who need love, who need secrecy, hope, belief, affirmation,
to live looking truth in the face
is to sicken, to ache down to the bones.
We can't survive in the world
for even that brief moment given us.

What a beautiful word God, so full,
so useful when you're scared, such a savior!
We must learn to still the heart
when it wants to say that word,
we must teach it to live on its own blood,
to survive on its own limit of blood.

Cheated, you feel sorry only for yourself
because someday you'll open your eyes
and see only your own eyes closed forever.
For myself alone I too feel pity,
for I am branched open like a tree,
rooted like a tree, and surveying everything.

So here's how it's done: you put on your mask,
assume your voice, embroider your dreams.
Put on the face of a lover,
the wounded face,
the contented smile,
Monday, and Tuesday, and the month of March,
and the year of human solidarity,
you eat on the hour as best you can,
and sleep and make love,
and go on rehearsing for the final act
that no one will witness.

Translated by
Philip Levine and
Ernesto Trejo

CURRICULUM VITAE

digamos que ganaste la carrera
y que el premio
era otra carrera
que no bebiste el vino de la victoria
sino tu propia sal
que jamás escuchaste vítores
sino ladridos de perros
y que tu sombra
tu propia sombra
fue tu única
y desleal competidora

BLANCA VARELA

Peru **1926–2009**

CURRICULUM VITAE

let's say you won the race
and the prize
was another race
you didn't savor the wine of victory
but your own salt
you never listened to hurrahs
but dog barks
and your shadow
your own shadow
was your only
and disloyal competitor

*Translated by
Ilan Stavans*

RECUERDOS DE MATRIMONIO

Buscábamos un subsuelo donde vivir,
cualquier lugar que no fuera una casa de huéspedes. El paraíso perdido
tomaba ahora su verdadero aspecto: unos de esos pequeños departamentos
que se arriendan por un precio todavía razonable
pero a las seis de la mañana. "Ayer, no más, lo tomó un matrimonio joven."
Mientras íbamos y veníamos en la oscuridad en direcciones capciosas.
El hombre es un lobo para el hombre y el lobo una dueña de casa de
    pensión con los dientes cariados, húmedad en las axilas, dudosamente
    viuda.
Y allí donde el periódico nos invitaba a vivir se alzaba un abismo
    de tres pisos:
un nuevo foco de corrupción conyugal.

Mientras íbamos y veníamos en la oscuridad, más distantes el uno del
    otro a cada paso
ellos ya estaban allí, estableciendo su nido sobre una base sólida,
granándose la simpatía del conserje, tan hosco con los extraños
como ansioso de inspirarles gratitud filial.
"No se les habrá escapado nada. Seguramente el nuevo ascensorista
    recibió una propina."
"La pareja ideal." A la hora justa. En el momento oportuno.

ENRIQUE LIHN

Chile **1929–1988**

MEMORIES OF MARRIAGE

We were looking for a basement to live in,
anywhere that wasn't a rooming house. Paradise lost
began to take on its true shape: one of those little flats
you can still rent for a decent price
but at six in the morning. "A young couple took it, just yesterday."
While we went back and forth in the dark on misleading streets.
Man is a wolf to man and the wolf's a landlady with rotten teeth,
    damp armpits, a dubious widow.
And there where the paper invited us to live, an abyss three stories
    deep rose up,
a new center of conjugal corruption.

While we went back and forth in the dark, farther apart with every
    step,
they were there already, building their nest on solid ground,
winning over the caretaker, a man as surly to strangers
as he is eager to evoke their filial gratitude.
"They haven't missed a thing. I'll bet the new elevator boy got a tip."
"The ideal couple." Right on time. Not a moment too soon.

De ellos, los invisibles, sólo alcanzábamos a sentir su futura
    presencia en un cuarto vacío:
nuestras sombras tomadas de la mano entre los primeros brotes del
    sol en el parquet,
un remanso de blanca luz nupcial.

"Pueden verlo, si quieren
pero han llegado tarde."
Se nos hacía tarde.
Se hacía tarde en todo.
Para siempre.

PORQUE ESCRIBÍ

Ahora que quizás, en un año de calma,
piense: la poesía me sirvió para esto:
no pude ser feliz, ello me fue negado,
pero escribí.

Escribí: fui la víctima
de la mendicidad y el orgullo mezclados
y ajusticié también a unos pocos lectores:
tendí la mano en puertas que nunca, nunca he visto;
una muchacha cayó, en otro mundo, a mis pies.

Pero escribí: tuve esta rara certeza,
la ilusión de tener el mundo entre las manos
—¡qué ilusión más perfecta! como un cristo barroco
con toda su crueldad innecesaria—

As to them, the invisible ones, all we could do was imagine them
    settled one day in the empty room:
our shadows hand in hand through the first flecks of sun on
    the parquet,
a still pool of white nuptial light.

"You can see it if you want
but you got here late."
It was getting late for us.
It was getting late for everything.
Forever.

Translated by
John Felstiner

BECAUSE I WROTE

Well, maybe in a quiet year
I'll think, Here's what poetry did for me:
kept me from being happy, that much was denied me,
but I wrote.

I wrote, was a poor kind
of beggar boggled with pride,
and also put a few readers to death,
reached my hand into doors I've never seen;
a girl, in another world, dropped at my feet.

But I wrote. I had that rare assurance,
the illusion you've got the world in your hands—
what a perfect illusion! like a baroque Christ
with all its needless cruelty.

479

Escribí, mi escritura fue como la maleza
de flores ácimas pero flores en fin,
el pan de cada día de las tierras eriazas:
una caparazón de espinas y raíces.

De la vida tomé todas estas palabras
como un niño oropel, guijarros junto al río:
las cosas de una magia, perfectamente inútiles
pero que siempre vuelven a renovar su encanto.

La especie de locura con que vuela un anciano
detrás de las palomas imitándolas
me fue dada en lugar de servir para algo.
Me condené escribiendo a que todos dudaran
de mi existencia real,
(días de mi escritura, solar del extranjero).
Todos las que sirvieron y los que fueron servidos
digo que pasarán porque escribí
y hacerlo significa trabajar con la muerte
codo a codo, robarle unos cuantos secretos.
En su origen el río es una veta de agua
—allí, por un momento, siquiera, en esa altura—
luego, al final, un mar que nadie ve
de los que están braceándose la vida.
Porque escribí fui un odio vergonzante,
pero el mar forma parte de mi escritura misma:
línea de la rompiente en que un verso se espuma
yo puedo reiterar la poesía.

Estuve enfermo, sin lugar a dudas
y no sólo de insomnio,
también de ideas fijas que me hicieron leer

I wrote, my writing was like the rot
on wilted flowers but flowers after all,
daily bread from the barren soil,
a shell of thorns and roots.

I took all these words from life
like a child after tinsel, pebbles by the river—
things with a magic to them, completely useless
but they always manage to renew their charm.

The kind of madness that makes an old man
trail along mimicking pigeons
was what I got instead of being good for something.
Writing brought it on me, everyone doubted
my real existence
(days of my writing, the stranger's home).
Those who were useful and those who did the using,
I say they'll all die off because I wrote,
and doing that means working shoulder to shoulder
with Death, stealing a few of her secrets.
At first the river is a vein of water,
at least for a moment there at that height,
then it ends in an ocean unnoticed
by those who churn through life.
Because I wrote I was an abomination,
but the sea forms part of my writing itself:
line of surf where a verse breaks into foam
I can make into poems all over again.

I was sick, no doubt about it,
and not just from insomnia,
also from fixed ideas that made me read

con obscena atención a unos cuantos sicólogos,
pero escribí y el crimen fue menor,
lo pagué verso a verso hasta escribirlo,
porque de la palabra que se ajusta al abismo
surge un poco de oscura inteligencia
y a esa luz muchos monstruos no son ajusticiados.

Porque escribí no estuve en casa del verdugo
ni me dejé llevar por el amor a Dios
ni acepté que los hombres fueran dioses
ni me hice desear como escribiente
ni la pobreza me pareció atroz
ni el poder una cosa deseable
ni me lavé ni me ensucié las manos
ni fueron vírgenes mis mejores amigas
ni tuve como amigo a un fariseo
ni a pesar de la cólera
quise desbaratar a mi enemigo.

Pero escribí y me muero por mi cuenta,
porque escribí porque estoy vivo.

a good few psychologists with obscene care,
but I wrote and the crime got less,
line by line I paid till it was written,
because words that fit in the abyss
give off a bit of dark intelligence
and by that light many a monster's life is spared.

Because I wrote I never helped the hangman
or gave way to loving God
or stood for men as gods
or ran for favorite scribbler
or found poverty disgusting
or power desirable
or washed or dirtied up my hands
or had virgin girlfriends
or pharisees for pals
or in spite of anger
tried to break my enemy.

But I wrote and I'm dying on my own,
because I wrote because I wrote I'm alive.

Translated by
John Felstiner

EPITAFIO

Un pájaro vivía en mí.
Una flor viajaba en mi sangre.
Mi corazón era un violín.

Quise o no quise. Pero a veces
me quisieron. También a mí
me alegraban: la primavera,
las manos juntas, lo feliz.

¡Digo que el hombre debe serlo!

(Aquí yace un pájaro.
                    Una flor.
                              Un violín.)

JUAN GELMAN

Argentina **1930–**

EPITAPH

A bird lived in me.
A flower traveled in my blood.
My heart was a violin.

I loved and didn't love. But sometimes
I was loved. I also
was happy: about the spring,
the hands together, what is happy.

I say man has to be!

(Herein lies a bird.
　　　　A flower.
　　　　　　　A violin.)

Translated by
Ilan Stavans

DE **DIBAXU**

I

il batideru di mis bezus/
quero dizer: il batideru di mis bezus
si sintirá in tu pasadu
cun mí in tu vinu/

avrindo la puarta dil tiempu/
tu sueniu
dexa cayer yuvia dormida/
dámila tu yuvia/

mi quedarí/quietu
in tu yuvia di sueniu/
londji nil pinser/
sin spantu/sin sulvidu/

nila caza dil tiempu
sta il pasadu/
dibaxu di tu piede/
qui balia/

XII

lu qui a mí dates
es avla qui timbla
nila manu dil tiempu
aviarta para bever/

FROM **DIBAXU**

I

the tremor in my lips/
I mean: the tremor of my kisses
will be heard in your past
with me in your wine/

opening the door of time/
your dream
allows sleeping rain to fall/
give me your rain/

I will stop you/ still
in your rain of sleep/
far inside the thinking/
without fear/ without forgetfulness/

in the house of time
is the past/
under your foot/
dancing/

XII

what you gave me
is the trembling word
in the hand of time
open for drinking/

cayada
sta la caza
ondi nus bezamus
adientru dil sol/

silent
the house is
where we kissed
inside the sun/

Translated by
Ilan Stavans

ANA FRANK

Frente a la catedral de Colonia
—dividida por dos columnas negras—
los niños
de nuevo canturrean.

Los he visto correr;
generalmente los he visto
saltar de un canto al otro,
de una música
a la otra.

Y hoy me dieron la foto
donde tu cara magra palidece,
niña llegada del alto cielo hebreo.
¡Y qué extraño
sentarme en este banco
(a unos metros del Rhin),
viendo pasar las aguas!
Yo que creí por mucho tiempo
que iba a sangrar . . .

HEBERTO PADILLA

Cuba 1932-2004

ANNE FRANK

In front of Cologne Cathedral
—divided by two black columns—
once more the children
are taking up their songs.

I have watched them playing:
mostly, I have noticed,
they jump from one song to the next,
from one tune
to another.

And today I was given the photo
of your thin fading face,
child, now arrived in your high Hebrew heaven.
And how odd
that I am now sitting on this bench
(a few steps from the Rhine)
watching the water go by,
for I had long thought
that blood would have flowed . . .

*Translated by
Alastair Reid and
Andrew Hurley*

RETRATO DEL POETA

COMO UN DUENDE JOVEN

I

Buscador de muy agudos ojos
hundes tus nasas en la noche. Vasta es la noche,
pero el viento y la lámpara,
las luces de la orilla,
las olas que te alzan con un golpe de vidrio
te abrevian, te resumen
sobre las piedras en que estás suspenso,
donde escuchas, observas, lo vives,
lo sientes todo.

Así como estás frente a esas aguas,
caminas invisible entre las cosas.
A medianoche
te deslizas con el hombre que va a Matar.
A medianoche
andas con el hombre que va a morir.
Frente a la casa del ahorcado
pones la flor del miserable.
Tu vigilia hace temblar las estrellas más altas.
Se acumulan en ti
fuerzas que no te dieron a elegir,
que no fueron nacidas de tu sangre.

En galerías
por las que pasa la noche;

PORTRAIT OF THE ARTIST

AS A YOUNG WIZARD

I

Sharp-eyed hunter,
you set your fish traps at night. The night is vast,
but the wind and the lantern,
the lights from the shore,
the waves that lift you with a slap of glass,
reduce you, sum you up
on the rocks where you are hanging,
listening, watching, living—
aware of everything.

In the way that you exist for those waters,
so you walk among things, invisible.
At midnight
you speak carelessly to the man who will kill.
At midnight
you walk with the man who will die.
In front of the hanged man's house
you lay the flower of the wretched.
Your virgin sets trembling the highest stars.
In you gather
forces not given you to choose,
not born of your blood.

On porches
where the night passes by,

en los caminos
donde dialogan los errantes;
o al final de las vías
donde se juntan los que cantan
(una taberna, un galpón derruido),
llegas con capa negra,
te sorprendes multiplicado en los espejos;
no puedes hablar
porque te inundan con sus voces amadas;
no puedes huir
sin que se quiebren de repente tus dones;
no puedes herir
porque en ti se han deshecho las armas.

II

La vida crece, arde para ti.
La fuente suena en este instante sólo para ti.
Lo que importa es llegar
(las puertas fueron abiertas con el alba y un
vientecillo nos reanima),
todo es poner las cosas en su sitio.
Los hombres se levantan
y construyen la vida para ti.
Todas esas mujeres
están pariendo, gritando, animando a sus hijos
frente a ti.
Todos esos niños
están plantando rosas enormes
para el momento en que sus padres
caigan de bruces

in the roads
where wanderers converse,
or at the end of the tracks
where singers come together
(a bar, a rundown hut),
you arrive in a black cape,
you surprise yourself multiplied in mirrors.
You cannot speak
because their dear voices drown you.
You cannot flee
without suddenly shattering your gifts.
You cannot wound
because your weapons are all undone.

I I

For you, life grows, burns.
At this moment the fountain plays for you alone.
The important thing is to arrive
(the doors were opened at dawn and a breeze revives us).
It all comes down to putting things in their places.
Men get up
and build life for you.
All those women
are giving birth, shouting, cheering their children
in front of you.
All those children
are planting huge roses
for the moment when their parents
fall headlong

en el polvo que has conocido ya.
Matan,
pero tu vientre se agita como el de ellos
a la hora del amor.
En el trapecio salta esa muchacha
(el cuerpo tenso, hermoso), sólo para ti.
Tu corazón dibuja el salto.
Ella quisiera caer, a veces, cuando no hay nadie en torno
y parece que todo ha terminado,
pero encuentra tu hombro.
Estás temblando abajo.
Duermen,
pero en la noche cuanto existe es tu sueño.
Abren la puerta
en el silencio y tu soledad los conturba.
Por la ventana a que te asomas
te alegran las hojas
del árbol que, de algún modo,
has plantado tú.

in the dust that you already know.
They kill,
but your body thrills as theirs do
at the time of love.
High on the trapeze that girl leaps
(her body tensed and sleek) for you alone.
Your heart traces the leap.
She would like to fall, sometimes, when there is no one around
and it seems as though everything is over,
but she finds your shoulder.
You are there trembling below.
They sleep,
but at night all that exists is your dream.
They open the door
in the silence and your solitude troubles them.
Through the window you lean out of
you rejoice in the leaves
of the tree that somehow or other
you have planted.

Translated by
Alastair Reid and
Andrew Hurley

KARL MARX

Desde los ojos nobles de león brillando al fondo de tus barbas
desde la humedad polvorienta en las bibliotecas mal alumbradas
desde los lácteos brazos de Jenny de Westfalia
desde el remolino de la miseria en los exilios lentos y fríos
desde las cóleras en aquellas redacciones renanas llenas de humo
desde la fiebre como un pequeño mundo de luz en las noches sin fin
le corregiste la renca labor de Dios
tú oh gran culpable de la esperanza
oh responsable entre los responsables
de la felicidad que sigue caminando

ROQUE DALTON

El Salvador 1935–1975

KARL MARX

From the noble eyes of the lion shining deep in your beard
from dank and dusty libraries dimly lit
from the milky arms of Jenny of Westphalia
from the vortex of misery in cold slow exiles
from the anger in those smoke-filled Rhenish pressrooms
from fevers like a little world of light in the endless nights
you righted the crippled work of God
yes great guilty man of hope
responsible among the responsible
O man of happiness still walking

Translated by
Elinor Randall

A TRISTEZA CORTESÃ

ME PISCA OS OLHOS

Eu procuro o mais triste, o que encontrado
nunca mais perderei, porque vai me seguir
mais fiel que um cachorro, o fantasma
de um cachorro, a tristeza sem verbo.
Eu tenho três escolhas: na primeira, um homem
que ainda está vivo à borda de sua cama me acena
e fala com seu tom mais baixo: "reza pra eu dormir, viu?"
Na outra, sonho que bato num menino. Bato, bato,
até apodrecer meu braço e ele ficar roxo. Eu bato mais
e ele ri sem raiva, ri pra mim que bato nele.
Na última, eu mesma engendro este horror:
a sirene apita chamando um homem já morto
e fica de noite e amanheçe ele não volta
e ela insiste e sua voz é humana.
Se não te basta, espia:
eu levanto o meu filho pelos órgãos sensíveis
e ele me beija o rosto.

ADÉLIA PRADO

Brazil 1935–

SEDUCTIVE SADNESS

WINKS AT ME

I'm looking for the saddest thing, which once found
will never be lost again, because it will follow me
more loyal than a dog, the ghost
of a dog, sadness beyond words.
I have three choices: the first, a man,
still alive, calls me to his bedside
and says in his softest voice: "Pray for me to sleep, will you?"
Or, I dream I'm beating a little boy. I beat him and beat him
until my arm is decomposing and he's black and blue. I beat him
    some more
and he laughs, without anger, he laughs at me who beats him.
In the last (and I personally create this horror),
the siren shrieks, calling a man who's already dead, and keeps
shrieking through the night till dawn and he doesn't return
and the siren insists and her voice is human.
If that's not enough, try this:
I lift my son by his sensitive organs
and he kisses me on the face.

Translated by
Ellen Doré Watson

O ALFABETO NO PARQUE

Eu sei escrever.
Escrevo cartas, bilhetes, lista de compras,
composição escolar narrando o belo passeio
à fazenda da vovó que nunca existiu
porque ela era pobre como Jó.
Mas escrevo também coisas inexplicáveis:
quero ser feliz, isto é amarelo.
E não consigo, isto é dor.
Vai-te de mim, tristeza, sino gago,
pessoas dizendo entre soluços:
"não aguento mais."
Moro num lugar chamado globo terrestre
onde se chora mais
que o volume das águas denominadas mar,
para onde levam os rios outro tanto de lágrimas.
Aqui se passa fome. Aqui se odeia.
Aqui se é feliz, no meio de invenções miraculosas.
Imagine que uma dita roda-gigante
propicia passeios e vertigens entre
luzes, música, namorados em êxtase.
Como é bom! De um lado os rapazes.
do outro as moças, eu louca para casar
e dormir com meu marido no quartinho
de uma casa antiga com soalho de tábua.
Não há como não pensar na morte,
entre tantas delícias, querer ser eterno.
Sou alegre e sou triste, meio a meio.
Levas tudo a peito, diz minha mãe,
dá uma volta, distrai-te, vai ao cinema.

THE ALPHABET IN THE PARK

I know how to write.
I write letters, shopping lists,
school compositions about the lovely walk
to Grandmother's farm, which never existed
because she was poor as Job.
But I write inexplicable things too:
I want to be happy, that's yellow.
And I'm not, that's pain.
Get away from me, sadness, stammering bell,
people saying between sobs:
"I can't take it anymore."
I live on something called the terrestrial globe,
where we cry more
than the volume of waters called the sea,
which is where each river carries its batch of tears.
People go hungry here. Hate each other.
People are happy here, surrounded by miraculous inventions.
Imagine a certain Ferris wheel
whose ride makes you dizzy—
lights, music, lovers in ecstasy.
It's terrific! On one side the boys,
on the other the girls—me, crazy to get married
and sleep with my husband in our little bedroom
in an old house with a wood floor.
There's no way not to think about death,
among so much deliciousness, and want to be eternal.
I'm happy and I'm sad, half and half.
"You take everything too seriously," said Mother;
"go for a walk, enjoy yourself, take in a movie."

A mãe não sabe, cinema é como diria o avô:
"cinema é gente passando.
Viu uma vez, viu todas."
Com perdão da palavra, quero cair na vida.
Quero ficar no parque, a voz do cantor açucarando a tarde . . .
Assim escrevo: tarde. Não a palavra.
A coisa.

Mother doesn't realize that movies are like Grandfather said:
"Just people going by—if you've ever seen one,
you've seen them all."
Excuse the expression, but I want to fall in life.
I want to stay in the park, the singer's voice
sweetening the afternoon.
So I write: afternoon. Not the word,
the thing.

Translated by
Ellen Doré Watson

EL POETA EN EL CAMPO

(Pintura de Marc Chagall)

Sí
también podríamos estar tendidos
en el primer plano del cuadro
con la chaqueta manchada de pasto
y de nuestro sueño
quizás surgirían
un caballo indiferente
una vaca de lento rumiar
una choza de techo de paja.

Pero
el asunto
es que las cosas sueñen con nosotros,
y al final no se sepa
si somos nosotros quienes soñamos con el poeta
que sueña este paisaje,
o es el paisaje quien sueña con nosotros
y el poeta
y el pintor.

JORGE TEILLIER

Chile **1935–1996**

THE POET IN THE COUNTRYSIDE

(After a Marc Chagall painting)

Yes
we could also be lying down
prominently in the painting
with the raincoat covered with grass
and from our dream
perhaps
an indifferent horse would emerge
a slow-chewing cow
a helmet with a hay roof.

But
the point is
that things ought to dream with us,
and at the end no one ought to know
if it is we who are dreaming with the poet
that dreams this landscape
or it is the landscape that dreams with us
and the poet
and the painter.

Translated by
Ilan Stavans

EL DESPERTAR

A León Ostrov

Señor
La jaula se ha vuelto pájaro
y se ha volado
y mi corazón está loco
porque aúlla a la muerte
y sonríe detrás del viento
a mis delirios

Qué haré con el miedo
Qué haré con el miedo

Ya no baila la luz en mi sonrisa
ni las estaciones queman palomas en mis ideas
Mis manos se han desnudado
y se han ido donde la muerte
enseña a vivir a los muertos

Señor
El aire me castiga el ser

ALEJANDRA PIZARNIK

Argentina **1936-1972**

THE AWAKENING

To León Ostrov

Lord
The cage has become a bird
and has flown away
and my heart is crazy
because it howls at death
and smiles behind the wind
at my ravings

What will I do with my fear
What will I do with my fear

Light no longer dances in my smile
nor do seasons burn doves in my ideas
My hands have undressed
and gone where death
teaches the dead to live

Lord
The air punishes my body

Detrás del aire hay monstruos
que beben de mi sangre

Es el desastre
Es la hora del vacío no vacío
Es el instante de poner cerrojo a los labios
oír a los condenados gritar
contemplar a cada uno de mis nombres
ahorcados en la nada.

Señor
Tengo veinte años
También mis ojos tienen veinte años
y sin embargo no dicen nada

Señor
He consumado mi vida en un instante
La última inocencia estalló
Ahora es nunca o jamás
o simplemente fue

¿Cómo no me suicido frente a un espejo
y desaparezco para reaparecer en el mar
donde un gran barco me esperaría
con las luces encendidas?

¿Cómo no me extraigo las venas
y hago con ellas una escala
para huir al otro lado de la noche?

El principio ha dado a luz el final
Todo continuará igual

Behind the air there are monsters
that drink my blood

It is a disaster
It is the hour of emptiness not empty
It is the moment to bolt closed the lips
to hear the screaming of the condemned
to study each one of my names
hanged by its neck in nothingness

Lord
I am twenty years old
My eyes are also twenty
Yet say nothing

Lord
I have lived out my life in an instant
The last innocence shattered
Now is never or nevermore
or simply was

How is it I don't kill myself in front of a mirror
and disappear to reappear in the sea
where a great ship would await me
with its lights burning?

How is it I don't pull out my veins
and with them build a ladder
to flee to the other side of night?

The beginning has given birth to the end
Everything will remain the same

Las sonrisas gastadas
El interés interesado

Las gesticulaciones que remedan amor
Todo continuará igual
Pero mis brazos insisten en abrazar al mundo
porque aún no les enseñaron
que ya es demasiado tarde

Señor
Arroja los féretros de mi sangre
Recuerdo mi niñez
cuando yo era una anciana
Las flores morían en mis manos
porque la danza salvaje de la alegría
les destruía el corazón

Recuerdo las negras mañanas del sol
cuando era niña
es decir ayer
es decir hace siglos

Señor
La jaula se ha vuelto pájaro
y ha devorado mis esperanzas

Señor
La jaula se ha vuelto pájaro
Qué haré con el miedo

The worn-out smiles
The concerned concern

The grimaces that mimic love
Everything will remain the same
But my arms insist on embracing the world
because they still haven't been taught
that it's already too late

Lord
Throw the coffins out of my blood
I remember my childhood
when I was an old woman
Flowers died in my hands
because the savage dance of joy
destroyed their hearts

I remember the black mornings of sun
when I was a girl
which is to say yesterday
which is to say centuries ago

Lord
The cage has become a bird
and has devoured my hopes

Lord
The cage has become a bird
What will I do with my fear

*Translated by
Frank Graziano*

EXILIO

A Raúl Gustavo Aguirre

Esta manía de saberme ángel,
sin edad,
sin muerte en qué vivirme,
sin piedad por mi nombre
ni por mis huesos que lloran vagando.

¿Y quién no tiene un amor?
¿Y quién no goza entre amapolas?
¿Y quién no posee un fuego, una muerte,

un miedo, algo horrible,
aunque fuere con plumas,
aunque fuere con sonrisas?

Siniestro delirio amar a una sombra.
La sombra no muere.
Y mi amor
sólo abraza a lo que fluye
como lava del infierno:
una logia callada,
fantasmas en dulce erección,
sacerdotes de espuma,
y sobre todo ángeles,
ángeles bellos como cuchillos
que se elevan en la noche
y devastan la esperanza.

EXILE

To Raúl Gustavo Aguirre

This mania of knowing I am an angel,
without age,
without a death in which to live,
without pity for my name
nor for my bones which roam around crying.

And who doesn't have a love?
And who doesn't rejoice among poppies?
And who doesn't have a fire, a death,

a fear, something awful,
even though it might be feathered,
even though it might be smiling?

Sinister delirium to love a shadow.
The shadow doesn't die.
And my love
hugs only what flows
like lava from hell:
a silent lodge,
ghosts in sweet erection,
priests made of foam,
and above all angels,
angels as beautiful as knives
that rise in the night
and devastate hope.

*Translated by
Frank Graziano*

515

PEREGRINAJE

A Elizabeth Azcona Cranwell

Llamé, llamé como la náufraga dichosa
a la olas verdugas
que conocen el verdadero nombre
de la muerte.

He llamado al viento,
le confié mi desea de ser.

Pero un pájaro muerto
vuela hacia la desesperanza
en medio de la música
cuando brujas y flores
cortan la mano de la bruma.
Un pájaro muerto llamado azul.

No es la soledad con alas,
es el silencio de la prisionera,
es la mudez de pájaros y viento,
es el mundo enojado con mi risa
o los guardianes del infierno
rompiendo mis cartas.

He llamado, he llamado.
He llamado hacia nunca.

PILGRIMAGE

To Elizabeth Azcona Cranwell

I called, I called to the lashing waves
which know the true name
of death
like a happy shipwrecked woman.

I have called to the wind,
I confided to it my desire to exist.

But a dead bird
flies toward despair
in the middle of the music
when witches and flowers
cut the hand of the mist.
A dead bird named blue.

It is not solitude with wings,
it is the silence of the prisoner,
the muteness of birds and wind,
the world mad at my laugh
or the guardians of hell
tearing up my letters.

I have called, I have called.
I have called toward never.

*Translated by
Frank Graziano*

NINGÚN LUGAR ESTÁ

AQUÍ O ESTÁ AHÍ

Ningún lugar está aquí o está ahí
Todo lugar es proyectado desde adentro
todo lugar es superpuesto en el espacio

Ahora estoy echando un lugar para afuera
estoy tratando de ponerlo encima de ahí
encima del espacio donde no estás
a ver si de tanto hacer fuerza si de tanto hacer fuerza
te apareces ahí sonriente otra vez

Aparécete ahí aparécete sin miedo
y desde afuera avanza hacia aquí
y haz harta fuerza harta fuerza
a ver si yo me aparezco otra vez si aparezco otra vez
si reaparecemos los dos tomados de la mano
en el espacio

donde coinciden

todos nuestros lugares

OSCAR HAHN

Chile 1938–

PLACES ARE NEITHER

HERE NOR THERE

Places are neither here nor there
Each place is projected from within
each place is superimposed on space

I am now clearing a place outside
I am trying to lay it over there
on top of the space you're not in
to see if by trying harder and harder
you appear there smiling again

Appear there appear without fear
and move from outside toward here
and try hard try hard
to see if I appear again if I appear again
if taken by the hand we both reappear
in the space

     where all our places

     come together

Translated by
James Hoggard

519

EL CENTRO DEL DORMITORIO

Un ojo choca contra las torres del sueño
y se queja por cada uno de sus fragmentos
mientras cae la nieve en las calles de Iowa City
la triste nieve la sucia nieve de hogaño

Algo nos despertó en medio de la noche
quizá un pequeño salto un pequeño murmullo
posiblemente los pasos de una sombra en el césped
algo difícil de precisar pero flotante

Y aquello estaba allí: de pie en el centro del dormitorio
con una vela sobre la cabeza
y la cera rodándole por las mejillas

Ahora me levanto ahora voy al baño ahora tomo agua
ahora me miro en el espejo: y desde el fondo
eso también nos mira
con su cara tan triste con sus ojos llenos de cera
mientras cae la nieve en el centro del dormitorio
la triste nieve la sucia nieve de hogaño

THE CENTER OF THE BEDROOM

An eye smashes against the dream's towers
and complains through all its fragments
while snow falls on Iowa City's streets
the sad snow this year's dirty snow

Something woke us up in the middle of the night
perhaps a twitch a faint murmur
possibly the steps of a shadow on the lawn
something floating but hard to pin down

It was there: standing in the center of the bedroom
with a candle on its head
and wax rolling down its cheeks

Now I get up go now to the bathroom drink water now
look at myself now in the mirror: and from behind me
it also looks at us
with its face so sad with its eyes thick with wax
while snow falls in the center of the bedroom
the sad snow this year's dirty snow

Translated by
James Hoggard

MOSQUITOS

Nacen en los pantanos del insomnio.
Son negrura afilada que aletea.
Vampiritos inermes,
                        sublibélulas,
pegasitos de pica
                     del demonio.

PERRA VIDA

Despreciamos al perro por dejarse
domesticar y ser obediente.
Llenamos de rencor el sustantivo *perro*
para insultarlos.
Y una muerte indigna
es *morir como un perro*.

Sin embargo los perros miran y escuchan
lo que no vemos ni escuchamos.

JOSÉ EMILIO PACHECO

Mexico **1939–**

Translated by
Margaret Sayers Peden

MOSQUITOES

Born in the marshland of insomnia,
they are blackness, needle-sharp and winged.
Frail vampires,
                subdragonflies,
a light brigade
             with devil's pitchforks.

BITCH LIFE

We scorn the dog for letting itself
be tamed, for its obedience.
With disdain, we mouth the noun *dog*
to insult ourselves.
An unworthy death
is *to die like a dog*.

Dogs, nevertheless, watch and hear
what we cannot see or hear.

A falta de lenguaje
(o eso creemos)
poseen un don que ciertamente nos falta.
Y sin duda piensan y saben.

Así pues,
resulta muy probable que nos desprecien
por nuestra necesidad de buscar amos,
por nuestro voto de obediencia al más fuerte.

JOSÉ ORTEGA Y GASSET

CONTEMPLA EL VIENTO

Son estos unos pensamientos de El Escorial, durante una fiesta de Resurrección
. . . Mientras que por materia entendemos lo inerte, buscamos con el concepto
de espíritu el principio que triunfa de la materia, que la mueve y agita, que la
informa y la transforma y en todo instante pugna contra su poder negativo,
contra su trágica pasividad. Y, en efecto, hallamos en el viento una criatura
que, con un mínimo de materia, posee un máximo de movilidad: su ser es
su movimiento, su perpetuo sostenerse a sí mismo, trascender de sí mismo,
derramarse más allá de sí mismo. No es casi cuerpo, es todo acción:
su escencia es su inquietud. Y esto es de uno u otro modo, en definitiva,
el espíritu: sobre la mole muerta del universo una inquietud y un temblor.
—"La vida en torno: Muerte y resurrección,"
EL ESPECTADOR, II, 1917

El Escorial inerte.
El viento pugna
por quebrantar *su trágica molicie.*

For lack of language
(or so we believe)
they possess a gift we clearly do not have.
We cannot deny that they think and know.

And being so
it is likely that they scorn us
for needing to seek masters,
for vowing obedience to the most powerful.

Translated by
Margaret Sayers Peden

JOSÉ ORTEGA Y GASSET

MEDITATES ON THE WIND

There are some thoughts on the Escorial, during the feast of the Resurrection . . .
While by the material we understand the inert, we seek through this concept of
spirit the principle that triumphs over the material, which moves and bestirs it,
which informs and transforms it, and all the time struggles against its negative
power, against its tragic passivity. And, in fact, we find in the wind an essence
that, with a minimum of material, possesses a maximum of mobility: its being
is movement, its continuous supporting of itself, transcending of itself, spilling
over beyond itself. It is hardly body, it is altogether action: its essence is its
restlessness. And this, in one sense or another, is definitively what spirit is:
over the dead mass of the universe a restlessness and a trembling.

—"About Life: Death and Resurrection,"
EL ESPECTADOR, II, 1917

The Escorial inanimate.
The wind is struggling
to mollify *its tragic passivity.*

525

Su ser es movimiento,
es su perpetuo
sostenerse a sí mismo,
derramarse
más allá de sí mismo.
No es casi cuerpo.
Su esencia es su inquietud.
Y esto de un modo u otro
es el espíritu.

Ortega piensa,
entrecierra los ojos.
Buenas frases
con su rotundidad tan castellana,
el prodigioso idioma que un día fue,
como el latín, lengua imperial del mundo
(¿o metafisiqueos, *suspirillos germánicos?*)

El Escorial inerte.
El rey Felipe
convirtió el monasterio en su parrilla
y dejó que lo asaran los gusanos
—suerte mejor que disponer del mundo.

Molicie de la mole
o bien escoria
que es lo que deja tras de sí la historia.
Molicie de la historia,
una mole de escoria,
molicie de la escoria.

Its being is movement,
is its continuous
supporting of itself,
spilling over
beyond itself.
It is hardly body.
Its essence is its restlessness.
And this, in one sense or another,
is what spirit is.

Ortega meditates,
half closing his eyes.
Ringing phrases,
so Castilian in their roundness,
the formidable language that was once,
like Latin, the imperial language of the world
(or metaphysicking, *Germanic sights?*)

The Escorial inanimate.
Philip, the king,
turned the monastery into his gridiron
and left the worms to see to the roasting—
a better fate than disposing of the world.

Softness of the mass
or rather of the dross
which is what history leaves behind.
Softness of history,
a mass of dross,
softness of dross.

Ortega piensa.
Su esencia es su inquietud,
no es casi cuerpo.

La materia despliega sus poderes,
sin pausa se transforma
y se de forma.
Inventa el mundo en que medita Ortega,
materializa en letras tanta tinta
—suerte mejor que disponer del mundo.

MALPAÍS

Malpaís*: Terreno árido, desértico e ingrato; sin agua*
ni vegetación; por lo común cubierto de lava.

FRANCISCO J. SANTAMARÍA,
Diccionario de Mejicanismos

Ayer el aire se limpió de pronto
y renacieron las montañas.
Siglos sin verlas. Demasiado tiempo
sin algo más que la conciencia de que allí están,
  circundándonos.
Caravana de nieve el Iztacíhuatl.
  Cúpula helada
o crisol de lava en la caverna del sueño,
  nuestro Popcatépetl.

Esta fue la ciudad de las montañas.
Desde cualquier esquina se veían las montañas.

Ortega meditates.
Its essence is its restlessness,
it is hardly body.

Matter unfolds its power,
endlessly it transforms itself
and takes new forms.
It invents the world in which Ortega meditates,
materializing in letters as so much ink—
a better fate than disposing of the world.

Translated by
Alistair Reid

BADLANDS

Badlands*: arid, desertlike, inhospitable land;*
without water or vegetation; commonly covered by lava.

FRANCISCO J. SANTAMARÍA,
Dictionary of Mexicanisms

Yesterday the air cleared suddenly
and the mountains were reborn.
Centuries without seeing them. Too long,
knowing only that they were there,
    surrounding us.
Iztacíhuatl—caravan of snow.
    Our Popcatépetl,
    frozen cupola
or crucible of lava in the cavern of a dream.

This was the city of mountains.
From any corner you could see mountains.

Tan visibles se hallaban que era muy raro
fijarse en ellas. Verdaderamente
nos dimos cuenta de que existían las montañas
cuando el polvo de lago muerto,
los desechos fabriles, la cruel ponzoña
de incesantes millones de vehículos
    la mierda en átomos
de muchos más millones de explotados,
bajaron el telón irrespirable
    y ya no hubo montañas.
    Contadas veces
se deja contemplar azul y enorme el Ajusco.
Aún reina sobre el valle pero lo están acabando
entre fraccionamientos, taladores y lo que es peor
    incendiarios.
    Por mucho tiempo
lo creímos invulnerable. Ahora sabemos
de nuestra inmensa capacidad destructiva.

Cuando no quede un árbol,
cuando todo sea asfalto y asfixia
o malpaís, terreno pedregoso sin vida,
esta será de nuevo la capital de la muerte.

En ese instante renacerán los volcanes.
Vendrá de lo alto el gran cortejo de lava.
El aire inerte se cubrirá de ceniza.
El mar de fuego lavará la ignominia
y en poco tiempo se hará de piedra.
Entre la roca brotará una planta.
Cuando florezca tal vez comience
la nueva vida en el desierto de muerte.

They were so visible you didn't
notice them. We truly realized
the mountains existed only when
the dust of the dead lake,
industrial wastes, the cruel toxin
from the incessant millions of vehicles
    the shit in atoms
of the many more millions of the exploited,
brought down an unbreathable curtain
    and the mountains were no more.
    Seldom
can you see the huge blue Ajusco.
It still reigns over the valley but are being done away with
among housing developments, wreckers, and what's worse
    incinerators.
    For a long time
we thought it invulnerable. Now we know
our immense destructive capacity.

When there is not one tree left,
when everything is asphalt or asphyxiation
or badlands, stony lifeless ground,
this will once again be the capital of death.

In that instant the volcanoes will be born again.
The great cortege of lava will descend from above.
The inert air will be covered by ash.
The sea of fire will wash away the ignominy
and soon become stone.
A plant will sprout among the rocks.
When it blooms, perhaps in the desert
of death new life will begin.

Allí estarán, eternamente invencibles,
astros de ira, soles de lava
indiferentes deidades,
centros de todo en su espantoso silencio,
ejes del mundo, los atroces volcanes.

Eternally invincible, there they will be fixed—
suns of lava, stars of rage,
impassive deities,
centers of everything in their frightening silence—
axes of the world, the horrible volcanoes.

Translated by
Linda Sheer

EL OJO DE LA BALLENA

Y Dios creó las grandes ballenas. GENESIS, 1:21

A Betty

Y Dios creó las grandes ballenas
allá en Laguna San Ignacio,
y cada criatura que se mueve
en los muslos sombreados del agua.

Y creó al delfín y al lobo marino,
a la garza azul y a la tortuga verde,
al pelícano blanco, al águila real
y al cormorán de doble cresta.

Y Dios dijo a las ballenas:
"Fructificad y multiplicaos
en actos de amor que sean
visibles desde la superficie

sólo por una burbuja,
por una aleta ladeada,

HOMERO ARIDJIS

Mexico 1940–

THE EYE OF THE WHALE

And God created the great whales.   GENESIS, 1:21

To Betty

And there in San Ignacio Lagoon
God created the great whales
and each creature that moves
on the shadowy thighs of the waters.

God created dolphin and sea lion,
blue heron and green turtle,
white pelican, golden eagle,
and double crested cormorant.

And God said unto the whales:
"Be fruitful and multiply
in acts of love that are visible
on the surface

only through a bubble
or a fin, flapping,

asida la hembra debajo
por el largo pene prensil;

que no hay mayor esplendor del gris
que cuando la luz lo platea.
Su respiración profunda
es una exhalación."

Y Dios vio que era bueno
que las ballenas se amaran
y jugaran con sus crías
en la laguna mágica.

Y Dios dijo:
"Siete ballenas juntas
hacen una procesión.
Cien hacen un amanecer."

Y las ballenas salieron
a atisbar a Dios entre
las estrías danzantes de las agua.
Y Dios fue visto por el ojo de una ballena.

Y las ballenas llenaron
los mares de la tierra.
Y fue la tarde y la mañana
del quinto día.

while the cow is seized on the long
prehensile penis below;

there is no splendor greater than a gray
when the light turns it silver.
Its bottomless breath is
an exhalation."

And God saw that love
between the whales
and the sporting with their calves
in the magical lagoon was good.

And God said:
"Seven whales together
make up a procession.
One hundred, a daybreak."

And the whales came up
to spot God over
the dancing grooves of the waters
and God was sighted by a whale's eye.

And whales filled
the waters of the earth.
And the evening and the morning
were the fifth day.

Translated by
George McWhirter

NAÏF

Cangrejo, me muevo de medio lado.

De lado y medio, con gran esfuerzo, soy un unicornio artrítico, la
virgen del espejo.

Este oído interno lo heredé del perro mudo de la Isla de Cuba: son
las doce y diez, el mundo está bosquejado: bosquejo del bosquejo
de Dios (se tomó su tiempo) nos dio mano izquierda (Dios,
retozón): investir a los seres de la Creación con rúbricas de
omisión, mermarlos designándolos, llamar vaca a la corneja,
asignar a la ternera el apelativo que corresponde al escarabajo:
Dios, sin duda, retozón.

Todo tiene solución (doy un ejemplo): mayor de edad (tocado) a modo
de ejercicio me propongo caminar el kilómetro que lleva en línea
recta de casa a la bodega donde por regla general me abastezco:
son las doce y diez, índice derecho en alto doy orden de detenerse
al sol, en la distancia los labriegos se vuelven de repente estatuas
(sean de bronce o fiemo o mármol): doy el primer paso; cosa
curiosa, y quizás sea lo que me irá a sostener, arranco a caminar

JOSÉ KOZER

Cuba 1940–

NAÏF

A crab, I move sideways.

Aside and then some, with enormous effort, I am an arthritic unicorn,
it's the seventieth birthday of the virgin holding the mirror.

The middle ear I inherited from the mute dog of the island of Cuba;
it's 12:10, the world is mapped out, map of the map of God (he has
taken his time), it's a free hand he gave us (a mischievous God): to
invest in Creation's beings under the rubric of omission, reducing
them, naming them, calling the crow crow and the calf beetle: God,
mischievous, certainly.

Everything has its solution (for example): older (wearing a hat), for
exercise I propose to myself to walk the kilometer that leads in a
straight line from home to the grocery store where as a rule I stock
my larder: it's 12:10, I point my index finger skyward and command
the sun to stop, in the distance peasants become suddenly statues
(bronze, manure, or marble): I take the first step, strangely—and
perhaps it's this will keep me going—I set forth at the first chord

con los primeros acordes del Septeto (*opus* 20) (movimiento tercero, *Tempo di Menuetto*) de Beethoven, fijo la vista en los puntos uno a uno que constituyen más allá de toda aporía la línea recta que lleva a la bodega: meandros; disquisiciones; la hila que se me va se me fue a bolina; el problema árabe israelí; la salud de mi madre; achaques de próstata; volunta; los seres inocentes suben al Cielo por una escalera de caracol.

Mareado (ésta es mi verdadera condición) en mí trifulcan el can con el unicornio, la hormiga festiva a la carrera a merodear al cangrejo de río que acaban de aplastar de una pedrada (querrá cerciorarse primero; hace bien): tal la función de la piedra, la hormiga, la mano, el cangrejo (incluso las pantanosas aguas de un río): ¿cómo salir de estos aprietos? Sencillo: no barruntar. En todo instante saber ahuyentar los malos pensamientos, donde dice muladar poner la imagen de una perinola, al entrar a la iglesia se nos recuerda que morir habemos (y demás retahíla) de un manotazo espantar la mosca teológica, mosca fétida de los osarios: alzar zampoñas. Y al regreso de la caminata que a diario emprendemos al atardecer detenernos (la mano en el picaporte) en el umbral de casa, cerrar los ojos (entrar, a ciegas) (ved, se trata de un juego; quizás un ejercicio mental o parte de las pruebas diversas que quedan por realizar para acceder a la vía iluminativa) concebirnos (en tinieblas) mantis ante un Libro de Horas.

of the Beethoven septet (opus 20) (third movement, *Tempo di Menuetto*), I concentrate on the view, point to point, constituting beyond all aporia the direct line to the store: wanderings, disquisitions, the thread that leads that led away from me a bowline; the Arab-Israeli conflict; my mother's health; prostate problems; volutes; the innocent climb to heaven on a spiral staircase.

Dizzy (my true condition) within me the hound and the unicorn squabble, the festive ant rushes to the river where it spies a crab that's been crushed with a stone (it will want to make sure, as it should); the function of stone, ant, hand, crab (and the river's swampy water as well): how to evade these problems? Simple: don't guess. Knowing to banish bad thoughts at each instant, when it says dung heap imagine a spinning top, when we enter the church it reminds us that to die we must (whatever) with a slap scare off the theological fly, the fetid fly of the boneyards: raise up the panpipes. Returning to our daily sunset walk we stop (hand on the doorknob) on the threshold, closing our eyes (so as to enter, blind) (see, it's about a game; maybe a mental exercise or the various tests left to make real the access to the illuminative way) we discover ourselves (in the dark) a praying mantis before a Book of Hours.

*Translated by
Mark Weiss*

CRÓNICA DE CHAPI, 1965

Para Washington Delgado

Lengua sin manos, ¿cómo osas hablar? POEMA DE MÍO CID

Oronqoy. Aquí es dura la tierra. Nada en ella
se mueve, nada cambia, ni el bicho más pequeño.
Por las dudosas huellas del Angana
a—media jornada sobre una mula vieja—
         bien recuerdo
a los 200 muertos estrujados
y sin embargo frescos como un recién nacido.
         Oronqoy.
La tierra permanece repetida, blanca y repetida
hasta las últimas montañas.
         Detrás de ellas
el aire pesa más que un ahogado.
         Y abajo,
entre las ramas barbudas y calientes:
Héctor. Ciro. Daniel, experto en huellas.
Edgardo El Viejo. El Que Dudó Tres Días.

ANTONIO CISNEROS

Peru 1942–

CHRONICLE OF CHAPI, 1965

For Washington Delgado

Tongue without hands, how durst thou speak? MÍO CID

Oronqoy. Here the earth is hard. Nothing
moves, nothing changes, not even the smallest beast.
Along the faded tracks of the Angaga
—half a day's journey on an old mule—
           I well remember
the two hundred dead crushed
yet fresh as a newborn child.
           Oronqoy.
The land continues repeated, white and repeated
up to the farthest mountains.
           Behind them
the air is heavier than a drowned man.
           And below,
between the hot and bearded branches:
Hector. Ciro. Daniel, the expert in tracking.
Edgardo the Old Man. The One Who Doubted Three Days.

Samuel, llamado el Burro. Y Mariano. Y Ramiro.
El callado Marcial. Todos los duros. Los de la rabia entera.
(Samuel afloja sus botines.) Fuman. Conversan.
Y abren latas de atún bajo el chillido
de un pájaro picudo.

"Siempre este bosque
que me recuerda al mar, con sus colinas,
sus inmóviles olas y su luz
diferente a la de todos los soles conocidos.
                    Aún ignoro
las costumbres del viento y de las aguas.
                    Es verdad,
ya nada se parece al país que dejamos y sin embargo
es todavía el mismo."

Cenizas casi verdes,
restos de su fogata ardiendo entre la nuestra:
estuvieron muy cerca los soldados.
                    Su capitán,
el de la baba inmensa, el de las púas
—casi a tiro de piedra lo recuerdo—
en pocos días ametralló
              a los 200 hombres
                    y eso fue en noviembre
(no indagues, caminante, por las pruebas:
para los siervos muertos no hay túmulo o señal)
                    y esa noche,
en los campos de Chapi,
hasta que el viento arrastró la Cruz del Sur,
se oyeron los chillidos de las viejas,
                    ayataki,

Samuel—called the Ass. And Mariano. And Ramiro.
Marcial, the quiet one. All the hard men. The men of complete rage.
(Samuel undoes his boots.) They smoke and talk.
And open tins of tuna beneath the shriek
of a sharp-beaked bird.

"Always this wood
which reminds me of the sea, with its hills
its immobile waves, and its light
unlike that of any known sun.
                    I still don't know
the customs of the wind and the waters.
                    It's true
now nothing resembles the country we left and yet
it's still the same."

Ashes almost green,
remains of their fire glowing within ours:
they got very close, the soldiers.
                    Their captain,
the one with the barbs and the great slobber
—I remember him at just a stone's throw away—
in a few days
machine-gunned
            the two hundred men
                    and that was in November
(don't inquire, passerby, for the proofs:
for dead slaves there's no tumulus or sign)
                    and that night
in the fields of Chapi
until the wind dragged away the Southern Cross
old women's screams were heard,
            ayataki,

el canto de los muertos,
pesado como lluvia

           sobre las anchas hojas de los plátanos,
duro como tambores.

           Y el halcón de tierras altas
sombra fue sobre sus cuerpos maduros y perfectos.

(En Chapi, distrito de La Mar, donde en setiembre,
Don Gonzalo Carrillo—quien gustaba
moler a sus peones en un trapiche viejo—
fue juzgado y muerto por los muertos.)
"El suelo es desigual, Ramiro, tu cuerpo
se ha estropeado entre las cuevas y corrientes submarinas.
Al principio, sólo una herida en la pierna derecha,
           después
las moscas verdes invadieron tus miembros.
Y eras duro, todavía.

           Pero tus pómulos no resistieron más
—fue la Uta, el hambriento animal de 100 barrigas—
y tuvimos, amigo, que ofrecerte
como a los bravos marinos que mueren sobre el mar."

Ese jueves, desde el Cerro Morado se aceraban.
           Eran más de cuarenta.
El capitán—según pude saber—
sólo temía al tiempo de las lluvias
y a las enfermedades que provocan
las hembras de los indios.
           Sus soldados
temían a la muerte.
Sin referirme a Tambo—5000 habitantes y naranjas—
doce pueblos del río hicieron leña tras su filudo andar.

the song of the dead,
heavy as rain

on the wide banana leaves,
hard as drums.

And the hawk from the highlands
cast his shadow on their mature and perfect bodies.

(In Chapi, district of La Mar, where in September
Don Gonzalo Carrillo—who liked
to grind his peons in an old mill—
was judged and sentenced to death by the dead.)
"The ground is rough, Ramiro, your body
has been maimed in undersea caves and currents.
At the beginning, just a wound in the right leg,

afterward
green flies invaded your limbs.
And you were strong, still.

But your cheekbones could bear no more
—it was Uta, the hungry animal with a hundred bellies—
and we had, friend, to offer you up
like a brave sailor who's died at sea."

That Thursday, they came up from Cerro Morado.

There were more than forty of them.
The captain—as far as I could tell—
feared only the time of the rains
and the diseases caused by
Indian women.

His soldiers
feared death.
Without speaking of Tambo—five thousand inhabitants and oranges—
twelve riverside villages turned firewood behind his knife-edged march.

Fueron harto botín hombres y bestias.

Se acercaban.

Junto a las barbas de la ortiga gigante
cayeron un teniente y el cabo fusilero.

(El capitán
se había levantado de prisa, bien de mañana
para combatir a los rebeldes.
Y sin saber que había una emboscada,
marchó con la jauría hasta un lugar tenido por seguro y discreto.
Y Héctor tendió la mano, y sus hombres
se alzaron con presteza.)

Y asi,
cuando escaparon, carne enlatada y armas recogimos.
El capitán huía sobre sus propios muertos
abandonados al mordisco de las moscas.

No tuvimos heridos.

Los guerrilleros entierran sus latas de pescado,
recogen su fusil, callan, caminan.

Sin más bienes
que sus huesos y las armas, y a veces la duda como grieta
en un campo de arcilla. También el miedo.

Y las negras raíces
y las buenas, y los hongos que engordan y aquellos que dan muerte
ofreciéndose iguales.

Y la yerba y las arenas y el pantano
más altos cada vez en la ruta del Este, y los días
más largos cada vez

(y eso fue poco antes de las lluvias).
Y así lo hicieron tres noches con sus días.

Y llegados al río
decidieron esperar la mañana antes de atravesarlo.

Man and beast made plentiful booty.
                    They came up close.
Beside the giant nettle's beard
fell a lieutenant and the corporal gunner.
                    (The captain
had hurried to get up early in the morning
to fight the rebels.
And not knowing there was an ambush,
he marched with his pack to a place held to be safe and discreet.
And Hector stretched out his hand, and his men
rose up rapidly.)
                    And so,
when they got away, we picked up meat and guns.
The captain fled over his own dead
abandoned to the nibbling of the flies.
                    We had no wounded.
The guerrillas bury their tins of fish,
pick up their guns, fall silent, walk on.
                    With no belongings
but their bones and guns, and sometimes doubt like a cleft
in a field of clay. Also fear.
                    And the black roots
and the good ones, and the fungi that fatten and those which bring death
proffering themselves identically.
                    And the grass and the sands and the swamp
getting higher on the eastern route, and the days
getting longer
                    (and that was a little before the rains).
And they kept on like this for three days and nights.
                    And arriving at the river
they decided to wait for morning before crossing.

549

"Wauqechay, hermanito, wauqechay,
es tu cansancio
largo como este día, wauqechay.
Verde arvejita verde,
wauqechay,
descansa en mi cocina,
verde arvejita verde,
wauqechay,
descansa en mi frazada y en mi sombra."
Daniel, Ciro, Mariano, Edgardo El Viejo,
El Que Dudó Tres Días, Samuel llamado El Burro,
Héctor, Marcial, Ramiro,
                        qué angosto corazón, qué reino habitan.

Y ya ninguno pregunte sobre el peso y la medida de los hermanos
    muertos,
y ya nadie les guarde repugnancia o temor.

"*Waukechay*, little brother, *waukechay*,
it's your weariness
long as this day, *waukechay*.
Green little pea,
waukechay,
rest in my kitchen,
green little pea,
waukechay,
rest in my blanket and in my shadow."
Daniel, Ciro, Mariano, Edgardo the Old Man,
The One Who Doubted Three Days, Samuel called the Ass,
Héctor, Marcial, Ramiro,
        what narrow heart, what kingdom do they inhabit.

And now let no man ask about the weight and height of our dead
    brothers,
let no one nurture fear or hatred for them now.

*Translated by
William Rowe*

DE **SHAJARIT**

En las migraciones de los claveles rojos donde revientan cantos de
     aves picudas
y se pudren las manzanas antes del desastre
Ahí donde las mujeres se palpan los senos y se tocan el sexo
en el sudor de los polvos de arroz y de la hora del té
Flujo de enredaderas a través de lo que siempre es lo mismo
Ciudades atravesadas por el pensamiento
Miércoles de ceniza. La vieja nana nos mira desde un haz de luz
Respiran estanques de sombras, llueve morados casi rojos
El calor abre sus fauces
Abajo, la luna se hunde en la calle
y una voz de negra, de negra triste, canta. Y crece
Incienso de gladiolos, barcas
Y tus dedos como moluscos tibios se pierden adentro de mí
Estamos en la fragilidad de la corteza del otoño
En el parque rectangular
en la canícula, cuando los colores claros son los más conmovedores
Después de Shajarit
olvidadas plegarias, ásperas

GLORIA GERVITZ

Mexico **1943–**

FROM **SHAJARIT**

In the migrations of red marigolds where songs burst from long-
   beaked birds
and apples rot before the disaster
Where women fondle their breasts and touch themselves
in the perspiration of rice powder and teatime
Climbing vines course through what remains always the same
Cities crisscrossed by thought
Ash Wednesday. Old nanny watches us from a beam of light
Pools of shadow breathe, purples rain down nearly red
The heat opens its jaws
Below, the moon sinks into the street
and a black woman's voice, a sad black woman's voice, begins to sing
The incense of gladioli and ferry boats grows
And your fingers, lukewarm mollusks, slip inside me
We are in the fragile hide of autumn
In the rectangular park
in the dog days when the pale shades are most deeply moving
After Shajarit
raw, forgotten prayers

Nacen vientos levemente aclarados por la oración, bosques de pirules
Y mi abuela tocaba siempre la misma sonata
Una niña toma una nieve en la esquina de una calle soleada
Un hombre lee un periódico mientras espera el camión
Se fractura la luz
Y la ropa está tendida al sol. Impenetrable la sonata de la abuela
Tú dijiste que era el verano. Oh música
Y la invasión de las albas y la invasión de los verdes
Abajo, gritos de niños que juegan, vendedores de nueces
respiración de rosas amarillas. Y mi abuela me dijo a la salida del cine
sueña que es hermoso el sueño de la vida, muchacha
Bajo el sauce inmerso en el verano sólo la impaciencia se demora
Dóciles nubes descienden hacia el silencio
El día se disipa en el aire caliente
Estalla el verde dentro del verde
Bajo el grifo de la bañera abro las piernas
El chorro del agua cae
El agua me penetra
Es la hora en que se abren las palabras del Zohar
Quedan las preguntas de siempre
Me hundo más y más
La luz late desordenadamente
En el vértigo de Kol Nidrei antes de comenzar el gran ayuno
En los vapores azules de las sinagogas
Después y antes de Rosh Hashaná
En el color blanco de la lluvia en la Plaza del Carmen
mi abuela reza el rosario de las cinco
y al fondo precipitándose
el eco del Shofar abre el año
En la vertiente de las ausencias al noreste
En el estupor desembocan las palabras, la saliva, los insomnios
y más hacia el este me masturbo pensando en ti

Winds rise lightly rinsed by invocation, forests of alders
And my grandmother always played the same sonata
A girl eats ice cream on a sunny corner of the street
A man reads a paper while he waits for the bus
The light fractures
And clothing hangs in the sun. My grandmother's impenetrable sonata
You said it was summer. O music
And the invasion of dawns and the invasion of greens
Below, shouts of children at play, nut vendors
yellow roses breathing. And as we left the movies my grandmother said
    to me
child, dream that the dream of life is beautiful
Beneath the summer-drenched willows only restlessness lingers
Docile clouds descend into the silence
The day evaporates in the hot air
Green erupts within green
I spread my legs beneath the bathtub faucet
The gushing water falls
Enters me
This is the hour when the words of the Zohar are spread out
Still the same questions as always
I sink deeper and deeper
The light throbs wildly
In the vertigo of Kol Nidre before the great fast begins
In the blue haze of the synagogues
Before and after Rosh Hashanah
In the whiteness of the rain in the Plaza del Carmen
my grandmother says her five o'clock rosary
And swooping in the background
the shofar's echo opens the year
Words, saliva, insomnia pour
into the northeast edge of absence, into the stupor
and farther to the east I masturbate thinking of you

Los chillidos de las gaviotas. El amanecer. La espuma en el azoro
    de ala
El color y el tiempo de las buganvillas son para ti. El polen quedó
    en mis dedos
Apriétame. Madura la lluvia, tu olor
de violetas ácidas y afiebradas por el polvo
las palabras que no son más que una oración larga
una forma de locura después de la locura
Las jaulas donde se encierran los perfumes, las alegrías interminables
la voluptuosidad de nacer una vez y otra, éxtasis inmóvil
Muévete más. Más
Pido mucho. Eres más bella, más aterradora que la noche
Me dueles
Fotografías casi despintadas por la fermentación del silencio
Corredores abiertos
Tu respiración aplasta el verano
Y la fiebre enrojeció otros cielos, las terrazas lustradas
se oscurecieron con las acacias
Y en la cocina los platos recién lavados, las frutas secas, los almíbares
En la crecida de los ríos
En la noche de los sauces
En los lavaderos del sueño desde donde se desprende ese vaho
de entrañas femeninas inconfundible y anchuroso
te dejo mi muerte íntegra, intacta
Toda mi muerte para ti
¿A quién se habla antes de morir? ¿dónde estás?
¿En qué parte de mí puedo inventarte?
Ciudades de hilo, carreteras que llevan siempre al principio
Milagros amontonados en la cal de la iglesia de Santa Clara en
    Guanajuato
Flores de tinta en un hebreo luido saliéndose de los rollos de la Toráh
Nada se mueve

Screech of seagulls. Dawn. The froth in the dazzle of the wing
The color and season of bougainvilleas are for you. The pollen stuck
    to my fingers
Holds me tight. The ripening rain, your scent
of sour violets feverish with dust
words that are nothing but an extended prayer
a kind of madness after the madness
The cages enclosing the perfumes, the limitless delights
the voluptuousness of being born again and again, fixed ecstasy
Move. More, more
I ask for a lot. You are more beautiful, more terrifying than the night
You ache in me
Photographs nearly faded in the fermentation of silence
Unscreened porches
Your breath crushes summer
And fever flushed other skies, the gleaming verandas
grew dark with the acacias
And in the kitchen the just-washed dishes, the dried fruits, the syrups
In the swelling of rivers
In the night of willows
In the washbasins of dreams from which the fumes
of female viscera rise, unmistakable and expansive
I leave you my death, entire, intact
My death for you alone
To whom does one speak before dying? Where are you?
Where within me can I invent you?
Cities of thread, highways that always lead to the beginning
Milagros crowding the calcite of that church of Santa Clara in
    Guanajuanto
Ink flowers in spent Hebrew dripping from the scrolls of the Torah
Nothing moves

Se me están perdiendo los días, van resbalando despacio
los va apretando la migraña
No me encuentro. Ni siquiera tengo cirios para velar mi muerte
ni siquiera sé las palabras del Kadish
Ya no tengo brújula. Estoy abrazada al aire
¿Dónde se rompen los latidos? ¿con qué se desprende este último
    pedazo de sueño?
Y la casa amarrada a un árbol, amarrada al viento
Las hojas y su sombra de ópalo
Espiral de ecos
Reverberación
Somos lo que pensamos
Pensamiento atrás del pensamiento
Regresan las grullas
abren con sus alas el silencio
instantáneas flores blancas en un cielo vacío
En las ciudades al mediodía
cuando el calor rodea la respiración ámbar de las montañas
siempre hacia el sur, allí donde no pasa nada
Prefiero seguir aferrada a lo que invento y no entender lo que sí existe
mejor soñar que estoy muerta y no morirme de los tantos sueños que
    me inventan
Tú y yo nos miramos
No miro más que unos ojos como todos los demás
Me vuelvo a dormir. Ya no sueño. La luz empuja los árboles
y el grito de los árboles en el filo del día ensordece
La tarde sólo dice lo mismo, no abre esa pausa entre lo real
único espacio habitable, geometría momentánea
En el frescor de anís, insomnio lento y cerrado
Un sol de abejas rompe las olas, espesa el día
Llueve mientras mi abuela reza el rosario
Llueve mientras mi hermano dice Kadish por mí

The days are slipping away from me, skid slowly
gripped by migraine
I can't find myself. I don't even have candles for my wake
I don't even know the words of the Kaddish
I no longer have a compass. I clutch the air
Where does the beating break? How can I cast off this last shred of
    sleep?
And the house lashed to a tree, lashed to the wind
The leaves and their opal shadow
A spiral of echoes
Reverberation
We are what we think
One thought after another
The cranes return
open silence with their wings
sudden white flowers in an empty sky
At midday in the cities
when heat surrounds the mountains' amber breath
always to the south, where nothing ever happens
I prefer to cling to what I invent and not to know what actually exists
better to dream that I am dead than to die of the many dreams that
    invent me
We look at each other
The eyes I see could belong to anyone
I fall asleep again, no longer dreaming. Light presses against the trees
and on the edge of the day the cry of the trees is deafening
Afternoon merely repeats, it doesn't open that pause in reality
the only inhabitable space, fleeting geometry
Slow, shuttered insomnia in the freshness of anise
A sun of bees breaks the waves, thickens the day
It rains as my grandmother says her rosary
It rains as my brother says Kaddish for me

559

Cada día estoy más lejos y no sé que hacer. No puedo salir de mí
   misma
y sólo en mí conozco y siento a los demás
invención que comienza cada mañana con el monótono aprendizaje
   de despertar
y volver a ser yo, una de las tantas que me habitan
¿Y si despierto para siempre?
Se disuelve la mañana. Lapsos de silencio caliente, espacios afilados
estructuras instantáneas, rectángulos
Puedo ver fragmentos, casi los aromas
Cada nivel tiene su propia irrigación sanguínea
Mi nana está conmigo mientras guardo mis cosas para irme
palomas alrededor del cuarto, aleteos. Abro la ventana
Pequeñísimas fisuras duelen, atrofian, inflaman la tarde, no siento lo
   que soy
soy lo que fui y lo que estoy queriendo ser
En el vuelo de las ercilias de centro abierto a la penetración
en el contorno apenas
las amigas se acarician
Porque siempre es la primera vez, porque hemos nacido muchas veces
y siempre regresamos
Crisantemos azules de Mondrian antes de su encuentro con el blanco
En junio, olas
Los pájaros están fijos, detenidos en su vuelo. Yo duermo mucho
despierto y ya casi es de noche, entro a un cine, está nevando en
   Nueva York
entro a otro cine, el presente es sólo una circunstancia
alguien me mira desde la superficie, las líneas se dispersan, parten
   ruidos
los inscriben en una lluvia alargada y desnuda apenas fría
Desciendo. Son casi las ocho de la mañana. Clarea. Es enero
Transcurrimos dentro de nosotros, cuelga una lámpara de leche

Every day I am farther away and don't know what to do. I can't
    escape myself
yet only in myself do I know and feel others
an invention that begins every morning as I tediously learn how to
    wake up
and become myself, one of many women who inhabit me
And if I were to wake once and for all?
The morning dissolves. Intervals of hot silence, sharpened spaces
momentary structures, rectangles
I can see fragments, can almost see smells
Blood irrigates every level individually
My nanny attends to me as I pack my things to go
flapping wings, the room full of doves. I open the window
The tiniest fissures ache, atrophy, inflame the afternoon, I don't feel
    what I am
I am what I was and what I now wish to be
In the flight of calendulas, centers open to penetration
barely on the perimeter
girlfriends caress themselves
Because it is always the first time, because we have been born many
    times
and always return
Mondrian's blue chrysanthemums before his encounter with white
Waves in June
The birds are still, frozen in flight. I sleep a lot
wake and find it's nearly night, enter a movie theater, it's snowing in
    New York
I enter another movie theater, the present is merely circumstantial
someone watches me from the surface, lines disperse, noises depart
are inscribed in a drawn-out naked rain, almost chilly
I descend. It's almost eight in the morning. Daylight. January
We elapse within ourselves. A milky lamp dangles

Estoy viviendo superposiciones de instantes en una perspectiva plana

Me extiendo sobre tardes que no existen más que para mí

Afuera de las ventanas queda el tiempo de hoy

Siento una libertad que abre los muros y perfora la imaginación

Este día no lo conozco, pero estoy agarrada de mis otros días

Podría vivir aquí siempre

Pero todo se acaba, hasta la costumbre

pequeños momentos saturados que se distienden

se alcanzan en la disolución

Mientras siga aquí encerrada en este cuarto, en esta ciudad

Mientras siga lloviendo y el ruido de la lluvia atraviese las paredes
    que me contienen

Mientras todavía pueda sentir que siento

y el hambre me haga ponerme un abrigo y una bufanda sobre el
    camisón

y salir a la calle

Pero, por qué creer todo esto

Al otro lado del mar a través de los encajes florean todo el año geranios

Y los grandes baúles pesados de aromas resinosos y cálidos

se derraman en habitaciones desconocidas

Y los ungüentos, los jabones de avena y de leche de cabra

los polvos de trigo, las pastas de dientes con sabor a chicle

y aquellos enjuagues para desenredar el cabello en días largos

Persianas requemadas del sol verde de Cuernavaca

una niña púber se mira el sexo en el ardor del mediodía

espeso de insectos y lagartijas

La mayor parte del tiempo duermo. No estoy segura si dormir es estar
    despierta

Me sorprendo después del mediodía, las manos me estorban, no sé
    dónde ponerlas

Lenta la lluvia casi se detiene

todo se detiene, me aprieta, pero llueve

I am experiencing the superposition of moments flattened on a plane
I stretch across afternoons that exist for me alone
Outside the windows it's still today
I feel a freedom that splits the walls and pierces the imagination
I don't recognize this day but I cling to my other days
I could live here forever
But everything ends, even habit
small saturated moments swell
and touch, dissolving
As long as I remain shut in this room, in this city
As long as the rain continues and the din of the rain passes through
    the walls that hold me
As long as I still feel myself feeling
and hunger makes me throw a coat and scarf over my nightgown and
    go out
into the street
But why believe all this
Across the sea behind lace curtains geraniums bloom all year long
And large trunks laden with warm, resinous odors
overflow in unfamiliar bedrooms
And ointments, oat and goat-milk soaps
wheat face powder, toothpaste that tastes like chewing gum
and those rinses for untangling hair on endless days
Venetian blinds scorched by the green sun of Cuernavaca
in the midday heat thick with insects and lizards
a pubescent girl gazes at her vulva
Most of the time I sleep. It may be that when I'm asleep I'm awake
Past noon I startle myself, my hands are in the way, I don't know
    where to put them
The slow rain falters, almost stops
everything stops, grips me, but the rain still falls

Se abren ventanas

Abajo, médanos

y más abajo parten los navíos como una exhalación

hacia las muchachas de los frescos del palacio de Cnosos

muchachas de agua y cal

La piel se desata, atrás, un sol de polvo, más adentro, pájaros

Nunca llegamos más que a nosotros mismos

Pero todo el año allá en la memoria florecen los geranios

y las persianas verdes también están allí en esa memoria

latidos que se fijan en un daguerrotipo, ¿dónde laten? ¿en qué parte?

Algo se desliza, va hacia una cesación

Estoy lejos de las mañanas

Lejos de los hombres y de las mujeres

Lejos de los hábitos y las costumbres

Me dejo caer. Regreso

La atmósfera se cierra

Irrecuperable el amarillo, la caída tenue, pérdida del color,
  rompimiento

Obstinación del blanco

Y se inscriben las primeras palabras de la Toráh

En la expiación del blanco

En la angustia del blanco

En la neutralidad del blanco

Estoy aferrada a la vida. Todo pasa

colibríes, sol de lluvia sobre mis pies

niebla, ramificaciones casi azul, el cabello deshecho

y ese olor, ese olor que sube desde la infancia

Pero, ¿qué sabemos de la muerte?

Todavía queda una línea de amarillo dentro de este blanco. Aletea,
  reaparece

Ahora, ondula larga, de muy lejos casi parece un principio de girasol

ahora se disloca apenas percibiéndose de ese blanco compacto

Windows open

Below them, sandbanks

and farther still ships sail forth like an exhaled breath

heading for the girls in the frescos of the palace at Knossos

girls of water and lime

The skin comes loose, behind it a dusty sun, farther in, birds

We only get as far as ourselves

But all year long geraniums bloom in distant memory

and the green blinds hang in that memory as well

beats registered on a daguerreotype. Where are they beating? Where?

Something slides toward cessation

I am far from mornings

Far from men and women

Far from habits and customs

I let myself fall. I return

The air grows heavy

The irretrievable yellow, the tenuous falling, color lost, shattering

The obstinacy of white

And the first words of the Torah are inscribed

In the atonement of white

In the anguish of white

In the neutrality of white

I cling to life. Everything passes

hummingbirds, sunlight showering my feet

fog, nearly blue ramifications, hair in disarray

and that smell, that smell which rises from childhood

But what do we know of death?

A yellow line still lies inside this white. It flutters, reappears

Now it sways, from a distance it almost seems the outline of a
    sunflower

now it separates, barely distinguishable in that dense whiteness

otra vez perfora la substancia de la nada, otra vez comienzan los
    sueños aferrados
a la línea casi todavía amarilla
No voy a ninguna parte. Aquí está todo. Aquí está allá
Siento una identificación profunda con el polvo
Paisaje hueco, amplio, inconstante, agudo. No puedo atravesar el aire
Comienzo a vivir de brisa
En las regiones donde las mujeres trenzan sus cabellos castaños
y perfuman sus axilas
En esas regiones donde el olor del sexo madura y oprime las tardes
En las juderías altas y bajas escondidas en las mañanas de Segovia
los romances de las niñas judías y los caballeros cristianos todavía
    acechan
desde los puentes
y los relatos de la Hagadá me crecen mientras espero desvelada en los
    corredores
de los aeropuertos
En los paisajes de neuronas casi en el umbral del oráculo de Delfos
Sólo hay una primera y única respuesta. No hay explicación inmediata
apenas la incisión
Adentro, blanco. Mi madre y algunas amigas juegan al bridge
El perfume de las señoras mezclado al blanco lo oscurece
en el pecho y en el cuello
A través de las ventanas casi olvidados los pirules. Pálido el viento
Vaho de mimbre en el porche deslavado
La casa se deshace
Eternidad de los jardines de arena
Perseverancia del aire. Se doblan las hojas, inician el regreso
Despierto. Las amigas tiemblan entre los sauces
No hay nadie en casa. Cepillas tus cabellos castaños
La veranda sombría, fresca en el bullicio del lino

again it pierces the substance of nothingness, again the dreams begin, clinging
to that still nearly yellow line
I'm not going anywhere. Everything is here. Here is there
I feel a deep identification with the dust
Sharp and shifting landscape, hollow and wide. Unable to cut across the air
I begin living off the breeze
In the regions where women braid their chestnut hair
and scent their armpits
In those regions where the smell of sex ripens and oppresses the afternoons
In the Jewish quarters high and low hidden within the mornings of Segovia
the love affairs of Jewish girls and Christian noblemen
still haunt the bridges
and the tales from the Haggadah grow within me as I wait bleary-eyed
in airport lobbies
In landscapes of neurons close to the threshold of the oracle of Delphi
There is only one answer. Explanations are not forthcoming
barely the incision
White inside. My mother plays bridge with some friends
Their perfume mingling with the white darkens
at their breasts and necks
The alders outside the windows are nearly forgotten. The pale wind
Breath of willow on the faded porch
The house comes apart
Eternity in the gardens of sand
The continuous wind. The leaves bend back, begin their return
I wake up. The girlfriends tremble among the willows
No one is home. You brush your chestnut hair
The shady veranda, cool in the bustling of linen

El polen cubre aquella memoria de espejos

Apenas nos movemos

Pero aparta de mí tus ojos. Son terriblemente bellos

Todavía me arde, me toco, estoy sola

Alba desaguada. De otros diluvios

Querida, lejana

Quiero llegar otra vez al lugar donde duermo

La complicidad de la voz

su persistencia

Y yo soy lo que se está cayendo

Ahora estoy en un paisaje de cenzontles

Cada vez estoy más cerca

Cuando posea esa inmensidad

apenas tendré fuerza para despertar en la brevedad de la muerte

La luz golpea el aire. Estamos donde los colores se abren

Son días largos y apretados como la migraña. Y todo se repite

Los árboles desamarrados

La noche se deshace

¿Y después?

Lo único verdadero es el reflejo del sueño que trato de fracturar

pero que ni siquiera me atrevo a soñar, continuo plagio de mí misma

Y el lugar del encuentro es sólo tiempo. Todo no es sino tiempo

Allá donde unas cuantas buganvillas en un vaso de agua

bastan para hacernos un jardín

Porque morimos solos. Y la muerte es apenas el despertar

de este sueño primero de vivir y dijo mi abuela a la salida del cine

sueña que es hermoso el sueño de la vida, muchacha

Se oxida la lumbre de las veladoras

Y yo, ¿dónde estoy?

Soy la que fui siempre. Lo inesperado de estar siendo

Llego al lugar del principio donde comienza el comienzo

Pollen coating that memory of mirrors
We barely move
Do not look upon me. Your eyes are terrible and beautiful
I still feel the burning, I touch myself, I am alone
Dawn, drained by other floods
Beloved, distant one
I want to return to the place where I sleep
The complicity of voice
its persistence
And I am what is falling
I move now through a landscape of mockingbirds
Getting closer and closer
When I've finally mastered that vastness
I will barely have the strength to wake into the brevity of death
Light strikes the air. We are where the colors open
The days are long and clutch like migraines. Everything repeats
The trees unmoored
Night comes apart
And then what?
Nothing is real but the reflection of the dream I'm trying to shatter
but don't even dare to dream, the constant plagiarism of myself
And time is the only meeting place. There is nothing but time
Where a few sprigs of bougainvillea in a glass of water
are enough to make a garden
Because we die alone. And death is just the awakening
from this first dream of living and my grandmother said as we left the
    movies
child, dream that the dream of life is beautiful
The glow of the candles grows rusty
and I—where am I?
I am the woman I always was. The unexpectedness of my being
I come to the place of origins where the beginning begins

Éste es el tiempo

Es el tiempo de despertar

La abuela enciende las velas sabáticas desde su muerte y me mira

Se extiende el sábado hasta nunca, hasta después, hasta antes

Mi abuela que murió de sueños mece interminablemente el sueño
      que la inventa

que yo invento. Una niña loca me mira desde adentro

Estoy intacta

It is time

Time to wake up

From her death Grandmother lights the Sabbath candles and looks
    at me

The Sabbath lengthens into never, after, before

My grandmother who died of dreams endlessly rocks the dream that
    invents

that which I invent. A wild girl looks at me from inside

I am intact

ANÁLISIS DE LA MELANCOLÍA

Horas que pasan
                como un soplo.
Sombras de un mundo vivo,
que pasan como un soplo,
me hacen hablar contigo.

Descoyuntadas, breves,
coloreadas de rabia,
vienen a mí las horas
y también vienes tú
expresándote,
honrándome con ellas.

Entrando a un río. Brincando
charcos. Volando
sobre un muro. Leyendo
las noticias del día. Descubriendo
la lluvia. Andando

NANCY MOREJÓN

Cuba 1944–

ANALYSIS OF MELANCHOLY

Hours passing
             like a breeze.
Shadows of a living world,
passing like a breeze,
they bring me to speak with you.

Disjointed, brief,
tinged the color of rage,
hours come to me
and you also,
expressing yourself,
honoring me with them.

Stepping into a river. Skipping
over puddles. Jumping
over a wall. Reading
the day's news. Discovering
rain. Walking under the leaves

sobre hojas de Ceiba. Cantando
en el atardecer.

Latiendo
en su erotismo: la quieta y pura melancolía.

PERSONA

¿Cuál de estas mujeres soy yo?
¿O no soy yo la que está hablando
tras los barrotes de una ventana sin estilo
que da a la plenitud de todos estos siglos?
¿Acaso seré yo la mujer negra y alta
que corre y casi vuela
y alcanza récords astronómicos,
con sus oscuras piernas celestiales
en su espiral de lunas?
¿En cuál músculo suyo se dibuja mi rostro,
clavado allí como un endecasílabo importado
de un país de nieve prohibida?

Estoy en la ventana
y cruza "la mujer de Antonio":
"la vecinita de enfrente," de una calle sin formas;
"la madre—negra Paula Valdés—."
¿Quién es el señorito que sufraga
sus ropas y sus viandas
y los olores de vetiver ya desprendidos de su andar?
¿Qué permanece en mí de esa mujer?

of the silk-cotton tree. Singing
in the afternoon.

Beating
with its erotic pulse: quiet and pure melancholy.

*Translated by
Kathleen Weaver*

PERSONA

Which of these women is me?
Or am I not the one who's talking
behind the thick bars of a nondescript window
that looks out on the abundance of all these eras?
Might I be the tall, black woman
who runs, who nearly flies,
who sets astronomical records,
with her dark celestial legs
spiraling like moons?
Which of her muscles reflects my face,
fixed there like an imported line of poetry
from a land where snow is forbidden?

I'm at the window
and there goes "la mujer de Antonio,"
"la vecinita de enfrente," crossing a shapeless street;
"la madre—negra Paula Valdés—."
Which is the young Andalusian don who pays for
her clothes and her vittles
and the smell of vetiver root she scatters as she walks?
What's left in me of this woman?

¿Qué nos une a las dos? ¿Qué nos separa?
¿O seré yo la "vagabunda del alba,"
que alquila taxis en la noche de los jaguares
como una garza tendida en el pavimento
después de haber sido cazada

    y esquilmada

    y revendida

por la Quinta de los Molinos
y los embarcaderos del puerto?
Ellas: ¿quiénes serán? ¿o soy yo misma?
¿Quiénes son éstas que se parecen tanto a mí
no sólo por los colores de sus cuerpos
sino por ese humo devastador
que exhala nuestra piel de res marcada
por un extraño fuego que no cesa?
¿Por qué soy yo? ¿Por qué son ellas?
¿Quién es esa mujer
que está en todas nosotras huyendo de nosotras,
huyendo de su enigma y de su largo origen
con una incrédula plegaria entre los labios
o con un himno cantado
después de una batalla siempre renacida?

Todos mis huesos, ¿serán míos?
¿de quién serán todos mis huesos?
¿Me los habrán comprado
en aquella plaza remota de Gorée?
¿Toda mi piel será la mía
o me han devuelto a cambio
los huesos y la piel de otra mujer
cuyo vientre ha marcado otro horizonte,
otro ser, otras criaturas, otro dios?

What holds the two of us together? What separates us?
Or might I be the "early morning wanderer"
who takes taxis in the night of jaguars
like a heron fallen to the pavement
after being hunted
    and wasted
    and resold
around the Quinta de los Molinos
and the piers of the port?
Who are they, these women? Or are they me?
Who are they, who look so much like me
not only in the color of their bodies
but in the devastating smoke
that rises from our animal hides, branded
by a strange, unceasing fire?
Why am I me? Why are they them?
Who is that woman,
the one in us all fleeing from us all,
fleeing her enigma and her long origin
with an incredulous prayer on her lips,
or singing a hymn
after a battle always being refought?

My bones: are they all mine?
Whose are all these bones?
Did they buy them for me
in that far-off plaza in Gorée?
Is all my skin my own,
or did they trade it to me
for the skin and bones of another woman
whose womb once marked another horizon,
another self, other beings, another god?

Estoy en la ventana.
Yo sé que hay alguien.
Yo sé que una mujer ostenta mis huesos y mi carne;
que me ha buscado en su gastado seno
y que me encuentra en la vicisitud y el extravío.
La noche está enterrada en nuestra piel.
La sabia noche recompone sus huesos y los míos.
Un pájaro del cielo ha trocado su luz en nuestros ojos.

I'm at the window.
I know someone's there.
I know there's a woman flaunting my bones and my flesh;
know she's looked for me in her worn-out breast
and has found me, miserable and straying.
Night is rooted in our skin.
Wise night rebuilds her bones and mine.
A bird from the sky has transposed its light into our eyes.

Translated by
David Frye

PAULOLEMINSKI

o pauloleminski
é um cachorro louco
que deve ser morto
a pau a pedra
a fogo a pique
senão é bem capaz
o filhadaputa
de fazer chover
em nosso piquenique

PAULO LEMINSKI

Brazil **1945–1989**

PAULOLEMINSKI

pauloleminski
is a mad dog
that must be beaten to death
with a rock and a stick
by a flame by a kick
or else he might very well
the sonofabitch
spoil our picnic

Translated by
Regina Alfarano

LOS AMANTES DE TLATELOLCO

Para Teresa Franco

Apenas se desprenden de la sombra.
Sus murmullos
                    alzan leves señales
al pie del contrafuerte.
Sus tenis blancos fulguran.

Ajenos a esas piedras,
vuelto uno hacia el otro,
olvidan en sus labios
el grito de las masacres,
pechos abiertos a punta de obsidiana
                                o bayoneta—

Indiferentes a la sombra que los cubre,
los jóvenes amantes murmuran
                            o quedan en silencio,
mientras la noche crece sobre las ruinas,
engulle los basamentos de los templos,
las inscripciones.

ELSA CROSS

Mexico 1946-

THE LOVERS OF TLATELOLCO

For Teresa Franco

They barely emerge from the shadow.
Their murmurs
                raise gentle signs
at the foot of the foundation.
Their white tennis shoes gleam.

Far from those stones,
returned to one another,
they forgot in their lips
the scream of the massacres,
chests opened by dint of obsidian
                        or bayonet—

Indifferent to the shadow that covers them,
the young lovers murmur
                or stay silent,
while the night grows over the ruins,
bolts down the plinths of the temples,
the inscriptions.

Y más allá, la urna
con dos esqueletos abrazados
en su lecho de polvo,
bajo el cristal donde se secan
las flores de una ofrenda.

And over there, the urn
with two skeletons embracing
in their dusty deathbed,
beneath the crystal where the flowers
                    of an offering are drying.

Translated by
Forrest Gander

TECUESO TITLACHIXTOQUE

Yeyectzi ihuan tecueso
ni titlachixtoque,
ipampa quemantica tiyolpaqui
ihuan tiyoltomoni
quen se hueyiatl.

Yeyectzi ihuan tecueso
ni titlachixtoque,
ipampa quemaya tiyolpaqui
ihuan tiyolcuitlamiqui
quen se quiahuitl.

Yeyectzi ihuan tecueso
ni titlachixtoque,
ipampa quemaya tiyolpaqui
noso tipatztlami
quen ehecatl.

NATALIO HERNÁNDEZ XOCOYOTZIN

Mexico 1947–

OUR EXISTENCE IS SAD

Our existence
is joyous and sad
because at times our hearts laugh
and at others they explode like a river,
like the sea itself.

Our existence
is joyous and sad
because at times our hearts are happy
and at others they swell with rage
like a storm.

Our existence
is joyous and sad
because at times our hearts are happy
and at others they are furious
like a hurricane.

*Translated by
Donald Frischmann*

AMO NINEQUI NIMIQUIS

Amo ninequi nimiquis
ninequi niquitas yancuic tonati
ihuan yancuic tlanextli.

Amo ninequi nimiquis
ninequi nicactehuas yancuic xochicuicatl
yancuic masehualcuicatl.

Amo ninequi nimiquis
ninequi niquipohuas
yancuic masehualamoxme,
ninequi niquitztehuas
yancuic tlalamiquilistli.

Amo ninequi nimiquis
ninequi sampa nimoyolchicahuas
ocsepa cuali nimonelhuayotis
amo quema ninequi nitlacatehuas.

I DO NOT WANT TO DIE

I do not want to die.
I want to take part in the new day
and in the new dawn.

I do not want to die.
I want to enjoy the new flowered songs,
the new songs of my people.

I do not want to die.
I long to read the new books
and admire the emergence
of the new wisdom.

I do not want to die.
I want to live a vigorous life.
I yearn to recover my roots:
I do not want to abandon my life on earth.

*Translated by
Donald Frischmann*

POEMA DE AMOR 8

Tu lengua, tu sabia lengua que inventa mi piel,
tu lengua de fuego que me incendia,
tu lengua que crea el instante de demencia, el delirio del cuerpo
    enamorado,
tu lengua, látigo sagrado, brasa dulce,
invocación de los incendios que me saca de mí, que me transforma,
tu lengua de carne sin pudores,
tu lengua de entrega que me demanda todo, tu muy mía lengua,
tu bella lengua que electriza mis labios, que vuelve tuyo mi cuerpo
    por ti purificado,
tu lengua que me explora y me descubre,
tu hermosa lengua que también sabe decir que me ama.

DARÍO JARAMILLO AGUDELO

Colombia 1947–

LOVE POEM 8

Your tongue, your wise tongue that invents my skin,
your fire tongue that burns me,
your tongue that creates the instant of insanity, delirium
of the body in love
your tongue, sacred whip, sweet ember,
invocation of fire that takes me out of myself,
that transforms me,
your tongue of unmodest flesh,
your tongue of surrender that demands everything from me,
your very mine tongue,
your beautiful tongue electrifying my lips, making yours the body
  you have purified,
your tongue exploring and discovering me,
your gorgeous tongue also knowing how to say it loves me.

*Translated by
Ilan Stavans*

VENGANZA

Ahora tú, vuelta poema,
encasillada en versos que te nombran,
la hermosa, la innombrable, luminosa,
ahora tú, vuelta poema,
tu cuerpo, resplandor,
escarcha, desecho de palabra,
poema apenas tu cuerpo
prisionero en el poema,
vuelto versos que se leen en la sala,
tu cuerpo que es pasado
y es este poema
esta pobre venganza.

VENGEANCE

Now you, turned into a poem,
imprisoned in verses naming you,
beautiful, unnamable, luminous,
now you, turned into a poem,
your body, brightness,
frost, word waste,
the poem almost your body
imprisoned in the poem,
turned into verses read in the living room,
your body that is past tense
and is this poem,
a poor vengeance.

Translated by
Ilan Stavans

DXI BIABA'

Guete', guete' biaba',
sica ndaani' ti bizé yuxi
cadá yuuba' ndaani',
cadi nisa,
dxi naa biree xquidxe'.
Ladxiduá' riuuba' casi guibane'
ne guyadxie' ra zuhuaa;
xiñee nuaa' xquidxi binni
—rabe' ndaani' ladxiduá'—
ne ma' zigatá' zigaze'
lu xluuna' xtobi
qué ganna' tu laa.

VÍCTOR DE LA CRUZ

Mexico 1948–

MY FALL

To the bottom,
all the way to the bottom I fell,
as into a dry well
where pain flows
instead of water,
ever since I left
my town behind.
My heart grieves every morning,
every time I look around.
"What am I doing in this place?"
—I say to myself—
and I go to sleep
in someone else's bed,
whose name I do not know.

Translated by
Donald Frischmann

LIDXE' CANAYUBI LII

Guluaa guiuu lidxe', naquichibé
biaana ni cabeza ni lii
dxi guiuulu' ndaani' ni gatalu' guixhe
ne guicoou ñee suudu gundubu naa,
guiladxu nisaluna naze'
ne ruaa' gudiuu ti bixidu'.
Sica ti gui'chi' quichi' biaanani
cabeza ni gucaalu' lalu' ladxidó ni,
xa'na' yaga guendadxiña
didi laaga i'queni,
ni nuaa' guixhe bigaanda' cuyubi lii.
Gudá' guiba daguuya laani ne naa,
ma' cayaca huadxi laanu;
pa guixhinni ma' qué zannu'
pa naqui'chi' ni
ne qué zannu' pabía' nadxiee' lii.
Xa'na' baca'nda' xti' ca yaga cuananaxhi
zuhuaa guidubi cue'ni
cabeza' lii ne guidubi ladxiduá'.
Gudá' guiaba,
cadi cuezu' guixhinni.
Laga nabani dxi ri'
ne nabani
ladxidua'ya'.

MY HOUSE SEEKS YOU

I have whitewashed my house and,
white as snow,
it awaits you ...
the day you wish to come in and rest in its hammock
and fan me with the edge of your skirt
to drive away my sweat
and place a kiss upon my lips.
It stands like a blank sheet of paper,
awaiting your signature upon its heart,
under the *chicozapote* beam
that spans its roof
and bears the hammock that seeks you.
Come soon, this house and I await you,
the early evening is upon us;
if night falls, you will no longer discover
its whiteness,
nor will you discover just how much I love you.
In the shade of the fruit trees
that encircle the house,
I await you with all my heart.
Come soon,
do not wait for night to set in.
The day remains alive
as does
my heart.

*Translated by
Donald Frischmann*

UNA CELDA BARROCA

Para Juan José Arreola

Habría cerrojos y círculos violetas,
rasguños dorados de borní, peñas enormes.

Habría luidas conjeturas entre los densos
tomos filosóficos, bajo los mamotretos
de teologal espesor—y una calavera jerónima
presidiéndolo todo.

Habría lienzos de sombras mitológicas
y una Biblia circundada
por una desganada devoción.

Habría—no sé—un dejo de fiebre
en todo el ámbito.

Habría, en fin, un manojo de cebollas
enviado puntualmente
para mitigar el hambre heroica
de Luis de Góngora y Argote.

DAVID HUERTA

Mexico 1949–

A BAROQUE CELL

For Juan José Arreola

There would be bolts and violet circumferences,
the marsh harrier's gilded slashes, massive crags.

There would be threadbare conjectures among the dense
philosophical tomes, under the massive volumes
of theological thickness—and a Hieronymite skull
presiding over it all.

There would be canvases of mythological shadows
and a Bible surrounded
by halfhearted devotion.

There would be—perhaps—a hint of fever
throughout.

There would be, in short, a bunch of onions
sent punctually
to appease the heroic hunger
of Luis de Góngora y Argote.

*Translated by
Mark Schafer*

599

MI TRIBU

La tierra es la misma
    el cielo es otro.
El cielo es el mismo
    la tierra es otra.

De lago en lago,
de bosque en bosque:
¿cuál es mi tribu?
   —me pregunto—
¿cuál es mi lugar?

Tal vez pertenezco a la tribu
de los que no tienen tribu;
o a la tribu de las ovejas negras;
o a una tribu cuyos ancestros
    vienen del futuro:
una tribu que está por llegar.

Pero si he de pertenecer a alguna tribu
   —me digo—

ALBERTO BLANCO

Mexico 1951–

MY TRIBE

The earth is the same
     the heavens are different.
The heavens are the same
     the earth is different.

From lake to lake,
from one forest to another:
which is my tribe?
—I ask—
which is my place?

Perhaps I belong to the tribe
of those with no tribe;
or to the tribe of black sheep;
or to a tribe whose ancestors
     come from the future:
a tribe yet to come.

But if I am to belong to a tribe
—I tell myself—

que sea a una tribu grande,
que sea una tribu fuerte,
una tribu donde nada ni nadie
quede fuera de la tribu,
donde todos,
todo y siempre
tengan su santo lugar.

No hablo de una tribu humana.
No hablo de una tribu planetaria.
No hablo siquiera de una tribu universal.
Hablo de una tribu de la que no se puede hablar.

Una tribu que ha existido siempre
pero cuya existencia está todavía por ser comprobada.

Una tribu que no ha existido nunca
pero cuya existencia
podemos ahora mismo comprobar.

MAPAS

I

Comencemos por el principio:
La Tierra no es la Tierra:
El mapa no es el territorio.
El territorio no es el mapa.

let it be a large tribe,
let it be a strong tribe,
a tribe where nothing and no one
is left outside,
where everyone,
everything, and always
have a holy place.

I don't mean a human tribe.
I don't mean a planetary tribe.
I don't even mean a universal tribe.
I mean a tribe about which one cannot speak.

I mean a tribe that forever lived
but whose existence is yet to be proved.

A tribe that has never lived
but whose existence
might now be proved.

Translated by
Ilan Stavans

M A P S

I

Let's start at the beginning:
Earth is not the earth:
The map is not the territory.
The territory is not the map.

Un mapa es una imagen.
Un mapa es un modo de hablar.
Un mapa es un conjunto de recuerdos.
Un mapa es una representación proporcional.

Los cuatro vientos, los cuatro ríos, las cuatro puertas, los cuatro
pilares de la tierra de los que hablan los mitos no son más que las
cuatro esquinas de un mapa.

Todo mapa es una imagen, un cuadro, una metáfora, una descripción . . .
Pero no toda descripción, metáfora, imagen o, para el caso, todo cuadro
es—por necesidad—un mapa.
Pero puede llegar a serlo.

II

Un mapa no es más que—como lo dijo el pintor Nabi Maurice Denis
de todos los cuadros—un arreglo de formas y colores sobre una
superficie bidimensional.

Si todo el territorio fuera homogéneo, sólo se acotaría en un mapa el
perfil de los límites del territorio.

No crecen árboles en un mapa.

Un mapa del mundo real no es menos imaginario que un mapa de un
mundo imaginario.

A map is an image.
A map is a way of speaking.
A map is a collection of memories.
A map is a proportional representation.

The four winds, the four rivers, the four doors, the four pillars of the
    earth of which myths talk about are nothing but the four corners of
    a map.

Every map is an image, a painting, a metaphor, a description . . .
But not every description, metaphor, image, or, given the case, not every
    painting is—by necessity—a map.
Although it can become one.

II

A map is nothing—as the Nabi painter Maurice Denis said of all paint-
    ings—but an arrangement of forms and colors over a bidimensional
    surface.

If a territory were homogeneous, only the profile of the limits of the terri-
    tory would be accounted for in a map.

No trees grow in a map.

A map of the real world is no less imaginary than a map of an imaginary
    world.

III

Un mapa no es más que una representación bidimensional de un
mundo tridimensional que recorre un fantasma: el tiempo.

Si hemos podido mapear un mundo de tres dimensiones en dos, ha
de ser posible mapear un mundo de cuatro en tres.

Con un mapa holográfico se podría mapear *el tiempo*.

Así como la Tierra no deja de cambiar con el tiempo, la historia de
los mapas no deja de cambiar con la historia.
Nuestra idea del espacio cambia conforme cambia nuestra idea del
tiempo.

IV

Todo mapa comienza con un viaje.
Pero, ¿todo viaje comienza con un mapa?

El mapa es al viaje lo que el mito es al lenguaje.

Los mapas, al principio, fueron relatos de viajes.
Después los mapas fueron paisajes al ras del horizonte: narraciones
visuales.
Finalmente, vistos a vuelo de pájaro: poemas geográficos.

Un mapa es una manifestación artística del miedo a lo desconocido.

III

A map is nothing but a bidimensional representation of a
tridimensional world visited by a ghost: time.

If we have been able to map a three-dimensional world in two
dimensions, it ought to be possible to map a four-dimensional
world in three dimensions.

With a holographic map *time* should be able to be mapped.

Just like the earth does not stop changing with time, the history
of maps does not stop changing with history.
Our idea of space changes according to the changes in our idea
of time.

IV

Every map begins with a journey.
But does every journey start with a map?

The map is to a journey what myth is to language.

At the beginning, maps were travel stories.
Later, maps were sights at the edge of the horizon: visual narratives.
Finally, seen from a bird's eye: geographical poems.

A map is an artistic manifestation of the fear of the unknown.

607

V

Ver la tierra desde arriba: arrogancia de un dios impostado.

Al principio los mapas de la tierra siempre fueron acompañados por
   los mapas del cielo.
Después los mapas se quedaron sin cielo.
De seguir las cosas como van, muy pronto los mapas se quedarán sin
   tierra.

La verdad que se puede decir no es la verdad.
Las palabras no son las cosas que designan.
Los mapas de la tierra no son la tierra.
Las cartas estelares no son el cielo.

Un punto es un pueblo.
Una línea es una carretera.
Una superficie coloreada es un país.
Un volumen debe ser un mapa de la historia.

VI

Mapas exteriores: geografía.
Mapas interiores: psicografía.
Las puertas son los sentidos.
Los límites son el cuerpo.

La moral que se deduce de los mapas tiene que ver con una idea de
dominio o—en el mejor de los casos—con una idea de conservación.

V

To look at the earth from above: arrogance of a fake god.

At the beginning the maps of the earth were accompanied by the
    maps of heaven.
Later, maps were left without a heaven.
If things go on like this, very soon maps will be left without an earth.

Any truth that can be told is no truth.
Words are not what they designate.
Maps of the earth are not the earth.
The stellar charts are not the heavens.

A dot is a town.
A line is a freeway.
A colored surface is a country.
A volume must be a map of history.

V I

Exterior maps: geography.
Interior maps: psychography.
The doors are the senses.
The limits are the body.

The moral to be drawn from maps has to do with the idea of control,
    or—in the best of cases—with an idea of conservation.

Cuando se piensa en la relación directa que existe entre los mapas,
   las ganancias, las guerras de conquista y el dominio del tiempo,
   no se puede menos que pensar en el título de aquel poema de
   Stephen Spender:
Un cronómetro y un mapa de artillería.

Un mapa a la medida de la ambición de un hombre.
La ambición de un hombre a la medida de un sistema de referencias.

Todos los puntos de referencia en un mapa ven hacia afuera.

VII

Los mapas son retratos ideales de nuestra madre.

Los mapas nos miran de frente cuando dan cuenta de las superficies.
Cuando quieren dar cuenta de las profundidades, nos miran de lado.

En la infancia de la cartografía no era posible—y tal vez, ni siquiera
   deseable—deslindar los territorios de la vigilia de los paisajes de
   los sueños.

¿Qué son los colores en un mapa sino un sueño?
El recuerdo anestesiado de nuestra infancia.
Las ventanas abiertas en el gabinete del cartógrafo.
Una fuente de la más pura y sencilla dicha.

As one thinks of the direct relation that exists between maps and
profit, wars of conquest, and the control of time, one cannot but
think of the title of that poem by Stephen Spender:
"A Stopwatch and an Ordinance Map."

A map the size of a man's ambition.
A man's ambition the size of a referential system.

All points of reference in a map look outward.

VII

Maps are ideal portraits of our mother.

Maps look at us face to face when they show us their surfaces.
When they want to account for their depth, they look at us sideways.

At the beginning of cartography it was not possible—perhaps not
even desirable—to separate the territories of wakefulness from
the landscapes of dream.

What are the colors on a map if not a dream?
The anesthetized memory of our childhood.
The open widows in the cartographer's office.
A fountain of the purest, simplest happiness.

VIII

Todo mapa es una isla.

Lo que antes era un territorio salvaje, ya es un mapa.

Toda escritura es fragmentaria.
Todo mapa es fragmentario.

En mapas no se ha andado nada.
En poesía no hay nada escrito.

VIII

Every map is an island.

What once was a savage territory is now a map.

All writing is fragmentary.
Every map is fragmentary.

On maps no travel ever takes place.
In poetry there's nothing written.

Translated by
Ilan Stavans

COMENZARON A LLAMARTE

Comenzaron a llamarte las piedras, respiraban,
sus numerosos rostros, su palpitar
gesticulante,
desde los muros. Veías
la entrada de la cueva y sabías. Tótems
fundiéndose. Una
respiración sobre otra. Es para ti. ¿Y qué habría
sido?
¿Y de ti qué habrían ganado y para qué?
Pero no entraste, sólo
te quedaste mirándolas.

CORAL BRACHO

Mexico **1951–**

THEY BEGAN TO CALL YOU

They began to call you, the rocks, breathing,
their innumerable visages, their gesticulant
throbbing,
from the cliff face. You could see
the entrance of the cave and you knew. Totems
fusing together. One
respiration over another. It's for you. And what could it
have been?
And what would they have won from you and for what?
But you didn't enter, only
stood there taking it in.

Translated by
Forrest Gander

VI

(ACCIDENTIEN)

Buenos Aires no es
la ciudad de los amantes

al viajar
las flechas se distraen
el otoño
llega a un lugar equivocado
o no llega

los barcos
como pequeños cortejos
entre palabra y palabra
se beben el viento el odio
la triste rosa sexual

es difícil alcanzar
el enigma que se es

MARÍA NEGRONI

Argentina **1951–**

VI

(ACCIDENTIEN)

Buenos Aires is not
the city of lovers

on their way
arrows grow absentminded
autumn
arrives at the wrong place
or doesn't arrive

the ships
like little flotillas
between one word and another
drink the wind, hatred
the sad sexual rose

hard to match
the riddle of the self

naturalmente
la confusión de estar en un cuerpo
nunca emigra

a lo sumo
Buenos Aires muere
como una ciudad inclinada

tienen miedo los barcos
a no poder salir
a no querer salir
de la jaula obscena del lenguaje

en realidad
nada ha empezado todavía
nada podría empezar
          cuando buscamos lo absoluto
y no encontramos sino flechas
distraídas

es así
no tan breve la cárcel
no tan breve el cadáver
de la rosa sexual

para salir hay que entrar
no por la izquierda
sino por la izquierda

los barcos mienten cuando escriben
          mienten cuando no escriben
las decisiones toman un cariz

naturally
the perplexity of living in a body
never emigrates

at worst
Buenos Aires founders
like a listing city

the ships fear
they won't be able to leave
won't want to leave
the obscene cage of language

actually
nothing has begun yet
nothing can ever begin
        as long as our search for the absolute
finds only absentminded
arrows

that's how it goes
not so brief the love lock
not so brief the death dance
of the sexual rose

to get out you have to go in
not from the left
but from the left

the ships lie when they write
        lie when they don't write
decisions take on an air

un poco
trágico

oh Sócrates
haz música

un motín
en el hogar del miedo
no resuelve el enigma
del miedo del hogar

a lo sumo
como esas flechas que llegan
y nunca han existido

las palabras
mueren como deben

luz encerrada afuera
ciudad que no he de escribir

slightly
tragic

Oh Socrates
     make music

a riot
in the home of fear
     doesn't solve the riddle
of fear of home

at worst
like those arrows that arrive
and never existed

     words
     die as they should

     light blocked out
     city I will fail to write

*Translated by
Anne Twitty*

ZURITA

Como en un sueño, cuando todo estaba perdido
Zurita me dijo que iba a amainar
porque en lo más profundo de la noche
había visto una estrella. Entonces
acurrucado contra el fondo de tablas del bote
me pareció que la luz nuevamente
iluminaba mis apagados ojos.
Eso bastó. Sentí que el sopor me invadía:

AUNQUE NO SEA MÁS

QUE TU QUIMERA

i.   Y quién diría si enverdecen de nuevo las llanuras

ii.   Quién si cantaran de un nuevo verdor estos pastos

RAÚL ZURITA

Chile 1951–

ZURITA

As in a dream, when all was lost Zurita told me
it was going to clear
because in the depths of night
he had seen a star. Then
huddled against the boat's planked deck
it seemed that the light again
lit my lifeless eyes.
That's all it took. I was invaded by sleep.

EVEN IF IT'S

JUST A CHIMERA

i.   And who could say if the prairies will again be green

ii. Who if these meadows could sing a new green

*Translated by
Jack Schmitt*

Porque quién diría si los quemados pastos florecieran con los
valles y los valles con Chile entero cantaran entonces la
gloria que deslumbra los paisajes: la quimera de estos pastos

   iii. Chile florecería así la quimera sobre sus pastos

   iv. Todos se verían escuchando entonces la gloria que les cantó
       por las llanuras

Porque muriendo verían taparse los valles con las glorias que
cantaban y todos resonarían entonces como una quimera que les
floreciese cubriendo estos paisajes: el cantar de las llanuras

   v. Chile escucharía entonces cantar los pastos de las llanuras

   vi. Hasta las piedras se abrazarían allí embelesadas sobre el pasto

   vii. Y quién diría entonces que no florecen de nuevo los
       pastos de nuestra vida aunque no sea más que una
       quimera cantándose todos de gloria la reverdecida

ALLÍ ESTÁN

Con una paz indecible lentamente sus ojos iban
recubriendo este suelo

Por el sur del nuevo mundo emergiendo llorosos de
amor desde esas malditas como si ahora sí pudieran
ser ellos los más queridos estos cabezas negras
mucho más vivos sonriéndonos entre sus lágrimas

Because who would have said that the burned meadows could blossom
with the valleys and the valleys with all Chile could then sing
the glory dazzling the landscapes: the chimera of these meadows

    iii. Chile could thus bring the chimera to blossom in its meadows

    iv. All would then be seen listening to the glory sung to them in the
         plains

Because dying they'd see the valleys covered with the glories
they sang and then they'd all echo like a chimera covering these
landscapes with flowers: the song of the plains

    v. Chile would then hear the plains meadows singing

    vi. There even the stones would embrace ecstatic upon the meadow

    vii. And who could then say that the meadows of our lives won't
         flower again even if it's just a chimera all singing the glory of
         this country green again

*Translated by
Jack Schmitt*

THERE THEY ARE

With indescribable peace slowly their eyes began to recover
this land

Through the south of the new world emerging with tears of love
from those accursed lands as if now they could really be the
most beloved these dark-colored heads far more alive
smiling at us through their tears

Maravillosos subiendo hasta la voladura final los
ojos que de puro humanos se les arrebataban allí
mismo enmudecidos con una expresión tal de paz
y de dulzura que ni el otro mundo podría igualarlos

LOS POBRES ESTÁN POBLANDO EL PARAÍSO SI TÚ MISMO ME
    LO ANUNCIASTE
LOS POBRES UNA PURA DE AMOR VOLANDO LAS BARRIADAS Y
    YO ESTA PERDIDA
DEL ALMA O "LA NIEVE" COMO ME APODAN MIRA YO MISMO
    LOS SEGUÍA TODO RESPLANDECIDO DE MÍ

Wondrous rising up in a final burst their eyes torn away
out of sheer compassion in that very place stunned
with an expression of peace and sweetness unequaled even
in the other world

THE POOR ARE FILLING PARADISE YES YOU'RE THE ONE WHO
   PROMISED ME
THE POOR A BIT OF LOVE FLYING OVER THE BARRIOS AND I
   THIS LOST
SOUL OR "THE SNOW" AS THEY NICKNAME ME LOOK I MYSELF
   FOLLOWED THEM ALL RESPLENDENT FROM ME

Translated by
Jack Schmitt

EL BAILE

Todos bailamos
sobre la orilla de un centavo.

El pobre—por ser pobre—
pierde el equilibrio,
se cae

y los demás
le caen encima.

HUMBERTO AK'ABAL

Guatemala 1952–

THE DANCE

All of us dance
on a cent's edge.

The poor—because they are poor—
lose their step,
and fall

and everyone else
falls on top.

*Translated by
Ilan Stavans*

SAQUÉ DE MI
CABEZA TU NOMBRE

Saqué de mi cabeza tu nombre
y lo dejé perdido en el monte.

Lo recogió el aire
y agarró camino
entre los barrancos.

Yo comencé a olvidar.

De repente
chocó contra los peñascos
y regresó el rebote:

la lluvia se puso a cantar
y tu nombre me llegó llorando.

I TOOK YOUR NAME

OUT OF MY MIND

I took your name out of my mind
and lost it on the mountain.

It was picked up by the air
and found its path
through the ravine.

I began to forget.

Suddenly
it crashed against the cliffs
and bounced back:

rain made it sing
and your name reached me while crying.

Translated by
Ilan Stavans

INI RUME ÑAMVM NOEL CHI LLAFE

Feyti vlkantun che mu rume
    kvmelay, pigeken
Ka fey ti mawizantu ayiwigvn
    ti pu aliwen
ñi kallfv folil mu egvn
ka ñi chagvll negvmi ti kvrvf
chalilerpuy vñvm egu
    ti Pvnon Choyke*
Feyti vlkantun alvkonchi wirarvn
    feyti pu lalu
kiñe pin ti tapvl rimv mew
feyti weñagkvn feyti wecheche
ñi petu zugu ñi kewvn
welu ñami ñi pvllv
Feyti vlkantun, ti vlkantun fey
kiñe Pewma feyti afvl chi Mapu
tami ge ka iñche ñi ge, vlcha

*Pvnon Choyke: Trace of the Ostrich.

632

ELICURA CHIHUAILAF

Chile 1952–

THE KEY NO ONE LOST

Poetry is good for nothing
   I am told
And in the forest the trees
   caress
each other with blue roots
and wave their branches in the air
greeting with birds the Southern
   Cross
Poetry is the profound whispering
   of the murdered ones
the rumor of leaves in the fall
sadness for the boy
who preserves the language
but has lost his soul
Poetry, poetry is a gesture
   a dream, the landscape
your eyes and my eyes, girl

allkvfe piwke, ka feychi
   vl zugulvn
Ka zoy pilayan, ini rume penolu
ti llafe ini rume ñamvn nolu
Ka vlkantun fey ñi vl tañi
   pu Kuyfikeche
pukem antv mu vy lu ka chonglu
feyta chi kisu zwam weñagkvn.

ears and heart, the same music
And I say no more, because
   no one will ever find
the key nobody lost
And poetry is the song of my
   Ancestors
the winter day that blazes
   and puts out
this intimate melancholy.

Translated by
John Bierhorst

DRAMATIS PERSONAE

Mi voz se fue amoldando a sus tejidos.
Se detuvo. Creyó no poder más
y continuó.
Conoció así un cauce
nunca antes descrito,
un lugar del que era parte
sin saberlo.
Al que volvió después.
Abrió sus puertas,
dio principio a los oídos.
Caracol de oleajes vigorosos,
saciaba todas las esperas
penetrando el cuerpo
en rojo intenso.

Luego tu voz ventisca,
desde las copas
de bosques invernales,
de huertos de la tundra,
desde el encino, el cedro

PURA LÓPEZ COLOMÉ

Mexico 1952–

DRAMATIS PERSONAE

My voice went on, its tones varying.
It paused. It believed it could not go on
and it continued.
In this manner it articulated a path
never before described,
a place of which it was part
without knowing it.
To which it returned afterward.
It opened its doors,
allowing a beginning for the ears.
The cochlea surging forward,
satiating all expectations,
penetrating the body
in whelming red.

Later your blizzard voice
from the bowers
of hibernal forests,
orchards in the tundra,
from the oak, the cedar,

y desde el tamarindo,
atravesaba a los despiertos
que caminan
saboreando
la melodiosa sequedad
del trueno.

and from the tamarind,
blew across the awakened ones
who continue on their way
savoring
the dry melodies
of thunder.

Translated by
Forrest Gander

EL ÚLTIMO CANTO DE AMOR
DE PEDRO J. LASTARRIA,
ALIAS "EL CHORITO"

Sudamericano en tierra de godos,
Éste es mi canto de despedida
Ahora que los hospitales sobrevuelan
Los desayunos y las horas del té
Con una insistencia que no puedo
Sino remitir a la muerte.
Se acabaron los crepúsculos
Largamente estudiados, se acabaron
Los juegos graciosos que no conducen
A ninguna parte. Sudamericano
En tierra más hostil
Que hospitalaria, me preparo
Para entrar en el largo
Pasillo incógnito
Donde dicen que florecen
Las oportunidades perdidas.

ROBERTO BOLAÑO

Chile 1953–2003

THE LAST LOVE SONG
OF PEDRO J. LASTARRIA,
ALIAS "EL CHORITO"

South American in Gothic land,
This is my farewell song
Now that hospitals race through
Breakfasts and teatimes
With an insistence I can
Only attribute to death.
The thoroughly studied
Sunsets have ended,
The amusing games leading
Nowhere have ended. South American
In a land more hostile
Than hospitable, I'm getting ready
To go down the long
Unknown hallway
Where it's said
Lost opportunities flourish.

Mi vida fue una sucesión
De oportunidades perdidas,
Lector de Catulo en latín
Apenas tuve valor para pronunciar
Sine qua non o *Ad hoc*
En la hora más amarga
De mi vida. Sudamericano
En hospitales de godos, ¿qué hacer
Sino recordar las cosas amables
Que una vez me acaecieron?
Viajes infantiles, la elegancia
De padres y abuelos, la generosidad
De mi juventud perdida y con ella
La juventud perdida de tantos
Compatriotas
Son ahora el bálsamo de mi dolor
Son ahora el chiste incruento
Desencadenado en estas soledades
Que los godos no entienden
O que entienden de otra manera.
También yo fui elegante y generoso:
Supe apreciar las tempestades,
Los gemidos del amor en las barracas
Y el llanto de las viudas,
Pero la experiencia es una estafa.
En el hospital sólo me acompañan
Mi inmadurez premeditada
Y los resplandores vistos en otro planeta
O en otra vida.
La cabalgata de los monstruos
En donde "El Chorito"
Tiene un papel destacado.

My life was a succession
Of lost opportunities,
Reader of Catullus in Latin,
I barely had the courage to pronounce
Sine qua non or *Ad hoc*
In the bitterest hour
Of my life. South American
In Gothic hospitals, what can I do
But remember the nice things
That once happened to me?
Childhood trips, the elegance
Of parents and grandparents, the generosity
Of my lost youth and with it
The lost youth of so many
Compatriots
Are now balm for my pain
Are now the bloodless joke,
Unleashed in these solitudes,
That those Gothic bastards don't get
Or understand a different way.
I, too, was elegant and generous:
I learned to appreciate storms,
Cries of love in cabins,
And the widows' weeping,
But experience is a hoax.
In the hospital I'm accompanied only by
My deliberate immaturity
And splendors glimpsed on another planet
Or in another life.
The parade of monsters
In which "El Chorito"
Has a leading role.

Sudamericano en tierra de
Nadie, me preparo
Para entrar en el lago
Inmóvil, como mi ojo,
Donde se refractan las aventuras
De Pedro Javier Lastarria
Desde el rayo incidente
Hasta el ángulo de incidencia,
Desde el seno del ángulo
De refracción
Hasta la constante llamada
Índice de refracción.
En plata: las malas cosas
Convertidas en buenas,
En apariciones gloriosas
Las metidas de pata,
La memoria del fracaso
Convertida en la memoria
Del valor. Un sueño,
Tal vez, pero
Un sueño que he ganado
A pulso.
Que nadie siga mi ejemplo
Pero que sepan
Que son los músculos de Lastarria
Los que abren este camino.
Es el córtex de Lastarria,
El entrechocar de dientes
De Lastarria, el que ilumina
Esta noche negra del alma,
Reducida, para mi disfrute
Y reflexión, a este rincón

South American in no one's
Land, I'm getting ready
To slip into the lake,
Still as my eye,
Where the adventures of
Pedro Javier Lastarria are refracted.
From the incident ray
To the angle of incidence.
From sine of the angle
Of refraction
To the so-called constant
Index of refraction.
In brief: the bad things
Turned to good,
Blunders
Into glorious apparitions,
Memory of failure
Turned into the memory
Of courage. A dream,
Maybe, but
A dream I've conquered
With a steady hand.
I hope no one has to follow my example,
But that they might know
That they are Lastarria's muscles
Opening this passage.
It's Lastarria's cortex,
The clashing of
Lastarria's teeth, that light up
This black night of the soul,
Reduced, for my enjoyment
And reflection, to this corner

De habitación en sombras,
Como piedra afiebrada,
Como desierto detenido
En mi palabra.
Sudamericano en tierra
De sombras,
Yo que siempre fui
Un caballero,
Me preparo para asistir
A mi propio vuelo de despedida.

Of a shadowy room,
Like a feverish stone,
Like a desert detained
In my word.
South American in the land
Of shadows,
I who always was
A gentleman
Am getting ready to attend
My own farewell flight.

Translated by
Laura Healy

NO HE AMADO BASTANTE

No he amado bastante
las sillas.
Les he dado siempre
la espalda
y apenas las distingo
o las recuerdo.
Limpio las de mi casa
sin fijarme,
en tres segundos,
y sólo con esfuerzo puedo
vislumbrar
algunas sillas de mi infancia,
normales sillas de madera
que estaban en la sala
y luego,
cuando se renovó la sala,
fueron a dar a la cocina.
Eran las sillas más comunes
que se han hecho,
aunque jamás

FABIO MORÁBITO

Egypt 1955–

I HAVE NOT LOVED ENOUGH

I've never been in love enough
with chairs.
I've always turned
my back on them.
I can't tell this from that
or hold one in the mind's eye long enough.
The ones at home I clean
without a glance
in seconds flat.
It takes effort now
to visualize
the chairs I sat on as a kid,
ordinary chairs of wood
belonging to our dining room
which, once we gave the place a face-lift,
were demoted to the kitchen.
The most ordinary
of ordinary chairs.
Yet we never understand
the real

se llega a lo más simple
de una silla,
se puede empobrecer
la silla más modesta,
quitarle siempre un ángulo,
una curva,
nunca se llega al arquetipo
de la silla.
No he amado bastante
casi nada,
para enterarme necesito
un trato asiduo,
nunca recojo nada al vuelo,
dejo pasar la ecrespadura
del momento, me retiro,
solo si me sumerjo en algo
existo, y cuando lo hago,
a veces ya es intútil,
se ha ido la verdad al fondo
más prosaico.
He amortiguado demasiadas
cosas para verlas,
he amortiguado el brillo
creyéndolo un ornato,
y cuando me he dejado seducir
por la más simple,
mi amor a la profundidad
me ha entorpecido.

simplicity of chairs.
We can strip down
the humblest of chairs,
cut away for good an angle here,
the curving edges there,
but never grasp the chairness
of chairs.
I've never been in love enough
with anything
to realize that it takes
assiduous lingering,
not snatching things up on the wing.
I let the moment disappear
and get no thrill from it.
I disappear myself. It's only when
submerged in things
I exist. And if I make the effort
now, it's wasted,
for truth is blunted
to banality.
I've fooled around with far too many things
to really see them,
dismissed too many things as ornaments.
Now when I let simplicity
seduce me,
a passion for profundity
has spoiled my taste.

Translated by
Geoff Hargreaves

GIANNINA BRASCHI

Puerto Rico 1953–

PELOS EN LA LENGUA

El bilingüismo es una estética bound to double business. O, tis most
sweet when in one line two crafts directly meet. To be and not to be.
Habla con la boca llena and from both sides of its mouth. Está con Dios
y con el Diablo. Con el punto y con la coma. Es un purgatorio, un signo
grammatical intermedio, entre heaven and earth, un semicolon entre
la independencia y la estadidad, un estado libre asociado, un mama-
rracho multicultural. No tiene cláusulas ni subterfugios, no anda con
gríngolas ni con muletas, no es artrítoco, no se queja—aúlla como un
perro al infinito y pide maná del cielo que caiga como lluvia—no se
ahoga en un vaso de agua, no deja que le doren la píldora—no anda
con yeso, saltando como un güimo con muletas de aquí pá allá—no es
el canario que se balancea en el columpio dentro de la jaula comiendo
los pistachos—se ha ido y se sigue yendo de todas las jaulas como
Pedro por su Casa y no ha vuelto a mirar hacia atrás. No tiene 10 man-
damientos porque no tiene pelos en la lengua, pero tiene huevos—
yo los he venido poniendo desde toda mi obra que es una sola—y la
llamo el manifesto de los huevos poéticos—se hace mostrando los
huevos, metiendo la pata, pisseando aquí y pisseando allá. Nace del
fuego popular, del pan, de la tierra, y de la libertad. Es un perro

realengo atravesando un Puente entre el norte y el sur, entre el siglo XX y el siglo XXI, entre Segismundo y Hamlet, entre Neruda y Whitman, entre Dickinson y Sor Juana, entre Darío y Stein, entre Sarmiento y Melville—entre los dos yo's en choque está mi *Yo-Yo Boing!*

LO KE FUE

akeyos polvos
trujeron estos lodos
i estas nuves
trujeron
estas luvias
i estas luvias
trujeron estos friyos
i estos friyos
trujeron estos yelos
i estos yelos trujeron
hazinura
i akeyos polvos
son lo ke fueron
ke son esto
ke más no será

MYRIAM MOSCONA

Mexico 1955–

WHAT WAS

those dusts
bring this mud
and these clouds
bring these rains
and these rains
bring this cold
and this cold
brings this ice
and this ice brings
illness
and those dusts
are what were
which are this
which no more will be

*Translated by
Jen Hofer*

LA LETRA BETH: IL MURO

ke veas, te esto pidiendo, la forma ke tiene la prima letra de la krea-
zión. La letra beth, dize la kabalá, es komo una kaza con todos los mu-
ros aviertos manko uno. Kualo hay de la otra banda del muro serado
de la prima letra del primo versíkulo, del primo kapítulo, de la prima
perashá? De la otra banda esta el saver proivido. Desta oriya no pode-
mos ver la otra. Por algo la letra beth es la prima letra del primo ver-
sikulo, del primo kapitulo de la prima *perashá*—Endelante de la letra
beth, todo esta avierto para ke puedas saziarte del saver. Estrellas,
árvoles, insektos, linguas bivas i linguas muertas, números i astros, la
struktura del ombre i de sus guesos, aínda los órganos serados por la
piel. Todo esta avierto i puede ser de estudio posivle. Atrás del muro
de la beth, nada ai ke un bivo pueda provar, i por ese silenzio los po-
etas skriven i por ese silenzio los profetas traducen las suias profezias
i por ese silenzio los geómetras de los sielos multiplican, i por ese
silenzio se han echo kadenas de orar. Ia puedes pedalear fin al fin del
mundo ke el muro de la beth, prime saverlo, kedará serado komo un
ojo kozido . . . Savrás kuala es el biervo eternidad ama no konozesh
nada de eia porke mora atrás del muro de la prima letra, del primo
kapítulo, del primo livro, de la prima *perashá*

GLOSARIO

KUALO:	Qué
PRIMA:	Primera.
MANKO:	menos.
PERASHÁ:	El Pentatueco o *La Torá*, está dividido en 52 capítulos que corresponden a las 52 semanas del año. La lectura de cada uno de estos capítulos debe completarse en una

you see, I'm asking you, the form taken by the first letter of creation. The letter beth, as the Kabbalah says, is like a house with all but one wall open. What is there on the other side of the closed wall of the first letter of the first verse, of the first chapter, of the first *parsha*? On the other side is forbidden knowledge. From this extreme we cannot see the other. For some reason the letter beth is the first letter of the first verse of the first chapter of the first *parsha*—Before the letter beth, everything is open so you might sate yourself on knowledge. Stars, trees, insects, living tongues and dead tongues, numbers and astros, the structure of man and of his bones, even the organs enclosed in the skin. Everything is open and might possibly be studied. Behind the wall of the beth, there is nothing that a living person might prove, and because of that silence poets write and because of that silence prophets translate their prophecies and because of that silence the geometries of the heavens multiply, and because of that silence chains of prayer have been made. Now you can pedal to the end of the world, as the wall of the beth, we must first know this, will remain closed like an eye sewn shut . . . You will know which is the eternal word but you will know nothing of that word because it lives behind the wall of the first letter, of the first chapter, of the first book, of the first *parsha*

GLOSSARY

PARSHA: The Pentateuch or Torah is divided into fifty-two chapters, which correspond to the fifty-two weeks of the year. The reading of each of these chapters should be com-

semana y, al cabo del año, las 52 *perashot* habrán sido leídas en la sinagoga, durante los oficios.

PERASHOT: Plural de *perashá*

BANDA: Lado, costado.

AMA: Pero

FIN AL FIN: Hasta el fin

pleted during each week, so that by the end of the year, the fifty-two *parshot* will have been read in the synagogue, during the services.

PARSHOT: Plural of parsha.

Translated by Jen Hofer

DE **DYLAN Y LAS BALLENAS**

12

No conozco tu país Dylan Thomas y sin embargo
he visto sus montañas florecidas por el sol de la mañana,
las tierras de cultivo que se levantan
desde un alba antigua a bendecir
la piel desnuda de los niños,
los riscos donde lloran viudas ciegas
y dejan escapar sus gritos
en las voces de los truenos,
las nubes espesas que esparcen su dominio
en colinas animadas por hambrientos,
las cavernas donde los hombres atesoran
sus bienes inexpugnables,
sus partes de miseria y paraíso
donde los lobos lamen la fiebre de los desvanecidos.
He visto las altas cúpulas de flacas carnes
para el que atisba los rasgos del moribundo
abominable en la sed de un lecho.

MARÍA BARANDA

Mexico 1962–

FROM DYLAN AND THE WHALES

12

I don't know your country, Dylan Thomas, and yet
I've seen its mountains bloom in the sun at morning,
the farmlands that rise out
of an ancient dawn to bless
the children's naked skin,
the cliffs where blind widows weep
and let their wailing escape
into the voice of the thunder,
the pendent clouds that extend their dominion
in lines staged by the starving,
the caverns where men hoard
their indelible treasures,
their shares of misery and paradise
where wolves lick at the fever of the banished.
I've seen the high piles of meat carved
for whomever discerns the marks of those dying,
abominable, in the thirst of a bed.

He visto al joven loco y a la mujer enferma
caminar por esas calles de tu pueblo
buscando un punto angelical, una pluma,
donde caer frente a un dios
besado en manto, en el fardo de las piedras.
He visto a tu mundo envejecer
con su estrella cayendo a la deriva,
y la palabra "Orden" y la palabra "Fe"
que tanto te despellejaban en tus sueños,
ahora son serpientes inofensivas
que se resguardan en el púlpito
del hombre ajeno.
He visto la penumbra de tus compañeros
con sus alas de cuervo espoleando los prodigios:
sus dos pies amputados, sus manos secas
por el delirio del viento prisionero.
He visto a tus país
caer en lágrimas por los desaparecidos,
a los hijos de tus hijos
alimentar su vigor eternamente de rodillas en la tierra.
He visto al lóbrego clausurar sus párpados de fuego
para que no lastimen a sus hijas.
A los necios y gigantes, escasos y nefastos,
plañideros y exaltados caer furiosos
boca a boca contra el suelo para allí,
en el grosor de su mentira rota,
roer la piel de un solo hueso.
Tal vez por eso te apartaste Dylan Thomas,
tal vez quizás no vuelvas por aquí
donde la muchedumbre forma un solo cerro,
donde un corazón llameante

I have seen the crazy kid and the sick woman
lurching through the streets of your town
searching for an angelical place, a feather,
where they might fall before a god
whose cloak is kissed, on a bale of rocks.
I have seen your world age,
its star falling off course,
and the word "Order" and the word "Faith,"
which slandered you so badly in your dreams,
now they are guileless serpents
shielded behind the pulpit
of an alien man.
I've seen the shadow of your friends
with their raven wings spurring on the prodigals:
their two feet amputated, their hands dried
in the delirium of an imprisoned wind.
I've seen your country
turn into tears for the disappeared,
seen the children of your children
feeding your endless vitality on the earth's very knees.
I've seen the lugubrious closing of your eyelids of fire
so that they don't shame your daughters.
Seen fools and giants, the barely there and the awful,
the mournful and exalted falling furious,
mouth to mouth against the floor,
in the thickness of its broken lie,
gnawing at the skin of a single bone.
Maybe that's why you stand apart, Dylan Thomas,
perhaps maybe you won't pass this way again
where the crowds make a lone hill,
where a blazing heart

está Escondido en la palabra "Secreto."
Quizás pienses que todo esto es vida de ficción
y que el mundo urde su conjura.

Quizás tengas razón y nosotros,
los hombre solos, los huecos
capaces de cargar con la esperanza ajena,
hemos ido anocheciendo poco a poco.

is Ensconced in the word "Secret."
Perhaps you think it's all a life of fiction
and the world plots its conspiracy.

Maybe you're right and we,
the solitary men, the bones
loaded with an alien hope,
we've been benighted bit by bit.

*Translated by
Forrest Gander*

UMANTUU

maytaña riqtiykipas, k'uychi sirina
sillwi tinyachaykiwan qan
sut'inta waqyaripay
k'ita puriq almayta
uri manchali
salqay salqay erqe
t'anpa chukchan kaq
rutusqankumpanta pacha

kutichimuy takiq challwa sipas
waqtaykita waqyapayaspa

hunt'a ñuñuykitamanta lluy
phoqchirimuq q'ata ñuqñuykita
qhawa qhawaychispa

maypiña tupaspaykipas, rit'iy rit'iy
mana rikhuriq phuyuq t'ikan goya
kutichimuy q'osti

ODI GONZALES

Peru **1962-**

UMANTUU

wherever it is you go,
my rainbow siren,
with your tenacious tambourine
call my soul that wanders frightened
wild, silent
since first its hair was cut

lure it, diva of the depths,
with your wiles and your caresses

revealing, perverse,
your fertile breasts
of turbid milk

wherever it is that you encounter, invisible
flower of the mist,
harness my spirit that flees
with its asthma and its imaginary armies

ch'usaq phuyuman t'inkisqa
ayqeq almayta

ñawpachimuy yaw mana puñuq
siwiq warmi, chakinpamuy
ch'ayñakunaq ñanninman
qhatakunaq patanman

maytaña chayaqtiykipas lluy pureq
wayray wayray qoya
tusuq wayra qoto
pusarimuy chinkaq almayta
aysarimuy chakinpanamanta sichus
mana hamuyta munaqtinqa
kay khutu waqsi
aya hayt' ayman

guide it now, sleepless siren whistling
by the narrow street of goldfinches by the path
of the cliffs

wherever it is that you arrive, wanderer
nymph of the stormy gales, lead my stray soul
companion of pristine air,
drag it if it does not want to come
to this my deathbed

Translated by
Alison Krogel and
José Ramón Ruiz Sánchez

XINGÁ CHI'UN

Xingá chi'un*
asiyáxun ixti.
¿Kjtáni s'uína?† katsoxun.
Bíxun kim'ínie nguije:
Jé ndibua nixtjin xingá,
jé má ndibula sa nijan
nga kamanda ngasandié.
Indáxun s'uín'e nguije.
Iskjindayáxun kjua xió.
Kats' enkjaniexun nguindie‡
nangui, atichayáxun ndi kjín,
ko kicha inimáxun
kats'en ndijo chi'un.
¿Kótjin nixtjin chijangasen'e?

---

* En mazateco *xingá* es "Viejo," "anciano"; *chi'un* es "trueno" o "rayo." Por
tanto, literalmente es "El Viejo Trueno." Quizás corresponde al mismo sentido que
la divinidad prehispánica "Trueno Viejo" del antiguo centro ceremonial de El Tajín.
Los mazatecos lo llaman solamente "El viejo" y lo ubican en el fondo del océano.

† Literalmente, "mi día," "mi momento."

‡ Este dato de su ubicación subterránea es semejante a la tradición de El Tajín.

JUAN GREGORIO REGINO

Mexico 1962–

THE LORD OF THUNDER

The Lord of Thunder asked his children,
"When is my day?"
They responded,
"Your day is coming, Father,
the ninth moon
of the world's creation is drawing near."
He then prepared his celebration.
He broke the eternal silence.
He sent lightning bolts to the depths of the earth.
He broke up the masses of clouds
and he turned flintstone into mortal darts.
"How many more days?" he constantly asked.
"Not many, Father," his children responded.
The ninth moon arrived,

Kjit'a, kjit'axun busiya.
Chijá nguichí, tsoxun ixtí.
Jachóxun xi nijan saá
ko tay'ajixuni xi íya,
ngat'e jé bautso 'en
nga ngansandiexun si'ikjié.
¿Kjiáni nixtjínan'e?
Ti asiyáxungani.
Jé ja'a ngujñáma ja'a kim'íxun.
Kats'enxchan tonxun nguije,
ku kjuatamaxun ts'axté.
Bi'e k'e, bi'e jánxun,
b'ití, yáb'iti ndijo,
b'ití nangui.
S'e nguijé xixió,
kjae no ts'askuyánguini.

and no one told him
because, as is recorded in time,
he would spark a cataclysm.
"When is my day?" he again asked.
"It is over, Father, it was just yesterday," they responded.
He becomes filled with rage,
and unleashes his fury.
He thunders here and there,
he burns the tree,
he burns the stone,
he burns the earth.
Afterward calm returns . . .
He again awaits his day.

*Translated by
Donald Frischmann*

Called by Juana de Ibarbourou "the lay saint" of Latin America, *Delmira Agustini* (Uruguay, 1886–1914) belongs to the Modernista movement. Embracing standard poetic forms, she meditated on female sensuality in a way that was far ahead of her time. Her life and work were defined by an essential contradiction, since Agustini, who was part of the Uruguayan upper class—her family called her "*la Nena*," the spoiled girl—followed the social mores while exploring in her writing a female eroticism that put her at odds with her contemporaries. This contradiction brought her a tragic end when, two months after marrying a conventional husband not known for his intelligence and with little interest in her poetry, she abandoned him and filed for divorce. But almost simultaneously she started a series of secret sexual encounters with him while keeping a passionate correspondence with the Argentine writer Manuel Ugarte. In one of their encounters, her ex-husband shot and killed Agustini and then committed suicide. She is the author of *El libro blanco* (1907), *Cantos de la mañana* (1910), *El rosario de Eros* (1913), and *Los astros del abismo* (1924). A representative selection of her work in English is called *Poetics of Eros* (2003), edited and translated by Alejandro Cáceres.

Humberto Ak'Abal (Guatemala, 1952–) writes in the Mayan language K'iche' as well as in Spanish. He is the author of, among other books, *Guardián de la caída del agua* (1993) and *Tejedor de palabras* (1998). In 2004 he declined Guatemala's National Prize in Literature because it is named after Nobel Prize winner Miguel Ángel Asturias, known for his representations of indigenous cultures. According to Ak'Abal, Asturias encouraged racism. Ak'Abal's poetry in English is featured in *Poems I Brought Down from the Mountain* (1999), translated by Miguel Rivera with Robert Bly, as well as in the anthology *In the Language of Kings* (2001), edited by Miguel León-Portilla and Earl Shorris.

An activist and prolific poet, *Claribel Alegría* (El Salvador, 1924–) has been profusely translated into English. Her work includes *Flowers from the Volcano* (1982), translated by Carolyn Forché (1982); *Family Album* (1991), translated by Amanda Hopkinson; *Thresholds* (1996), translated by Alegría's husband, Darwin J. Flakoll (1996); and *Casting Off* (2003), translated by Margaret Sayers Peden. She is the author of essays and novels like *Ashes of Izalco* (1989). Alegría was awarded the Casa de las Américas Prize in 1978 and the Neustadt International Prize for Literature in 2006.

Born Mário Raul de Morais Andrade, the polymath *Mário de Andrade* (Brazil, 1893–1945), one of the founders of Brazilian Modernismo, was a musicologist, art historian, literary critic, and photographer, in addition to being a poet and novelist. He was the director of the *Semana de Arte Moderna* (Week of Modern Art) in 1922, a cultural event that reshaped both literature and the visual arts in Brazil. In the 1920s, Andrade, who befriended Claude Lévi-Strauss, traveled throughout Brazil, studying folklore. The result was a theory of folk music, paying attention to highbrow as well as popular manifestations. His impressions were showcased, at times accompanied by his own photographs, in a newspaper column in *O Diario Nacional*, in which he introduced readers to indigenous Brazil. The experience defined Andrade's poetry as well as his work as an ethnographer. His masterpiece, *Macunaíma: o herói sem nenhum caráter* (1928), about an indigenous protagonist described as "a hero without a character" who goes to São Paulo, learns its languages, and departs, is described as a forerunner of magical realism. The novel was turned into a successful 1968 film directed by Joaquim Pedro de Andrade. It was translated into English from the Portuguese by E. A. Goodland in 1984. Also available in English is Andrade's *Hallucinated City* (1968), translated by Jack E. Tomlins. Andrade's *Poesias completas* appeared in São Paulo in 1966.

Oswald de Andrade (Brazil, 1890–1954), born José Oswald de Andrade Souza, was one of his nation's leaders of Modernismo and a member of the *Grupo dos Cinco* (Group of Five), along with Mário de Andrade, Anita Malfatti, Tarsila do Amaral, and Menotti del Picchia, which renewed Brazilian culture at the turn of the twentieth century. He published the "Manifesto Antropófago" in 1928 in the *Revista de Antropofagia*, which included the famous line: "Tupi or not Tupi: that is the question," a reference to the Tupi tribe, who were portrayed as cannibals. Andrade's thesis is that Brazil thrives by cannibalizing other cultures, an argument not only endearing to the Modernistas in Brazil fascinated with indigenous civilization but central to the way the Americas since the age of independence have understood their hemispheric identity as a process of transculturation that absorbs the European heritage by metamorphosing it. Andrade is the author, among other books, of *Meu testamento* (1944), *A arcádia e a inconfidência* (1945), *Um aspecto antropofágico da cultura brasileira: O homem cordial* (1950), and *A marcha das utopias* (1953). The most representative sample of his work in English is *Seraphim Grosse Pointe* (1979), translated by Kenneth D. Jackson and Albert Bork.

Born in a village near where the monarch butterflies swarm yearly after their flight from Canada, *Homero Aridjis* (Mexico, 1940–) is an eco-activist whose career has been devoted to protecting whales, butterflies, and other animals from the precariousness of the post-industrialized environment. In English the most representative anthology of Aridjis's work is *Eyes to See Otherwise: Selected Poems, 1960–2000* (2002), selected and edited by Betty Ferber and George McWhirter. Aridjis is equally known for his fiction. His numerous novels include *Persephone* (1986), *1492: The Life and Times of Juan Cabezón of Castile* (1991), and *The Lord of the Last Days: Visions of the Year 1000* (1995). He serves as Mexico's ambassador in the Netherlands and Switzerland as well as ambassador at UNESCO and for six years was president of PEN International.

María Baranda (Mexico, 1962–) is the author of, among other books, *El jardín de los encantamientos* (1989) and *Dylan y las ballenas* (2003). A sample of Baranda's work in English appears in *Connecting Lines: New Poetry from Mexico* (2006), edited by Luis Cortés Bargalló. In 2002 Baranda received Mexico's Aguascalientes National Poetry Prize.

Mario Benedetti (Uruguay, 1920–2009) is known for novels like *The Truce* (1969), although he was also a prolific essayist, editor, and columnist. His poetry is collected in *Inventario: Poesía Completa, 1950–1985* (1986). The most representative samples of his work in English appear in *Little Stones at My Window* (2003), translated by Charles Dean Hatfield, and *Only in the Meantime & Office Poems* (2006), translated by Harry Morales. Benedetti wrote studies on the *Modernista* essayist José Enrique Rodó and edited anthologies of the poetry of Roque Dalton and Jaime Sabines, among others. His *Unstill Life: An Introduction to the Spanish Poetry of Latin America*, translated by Darwin J. Flakoll and Claribel Alegría, was released in 1969.

Alberto Blanco (Mexico, 1951–), an architect by profession, is known not only as a poet but as an art critic. His themes are the passage of time and the constructs of the mind. He is the author of, among other books, *El corazón del instante: 1973–1993* (1998) and *La hora y la neblina: 1968–2004* (2005). The most representative sample of his work available in English is *Dawn of the Senses* (1995).

Self-described as an enfant terrible, *Roberto Bolaño* (Chile, 1953–2003) spent his adolescence in Mexico and moved to Spain in his adulthood. He retained a passion for poetry throughout his life, although he is best known for his noir fictional narratives in the tradition of Borges and Cortázar in Spanish and the Beat Generation in English. His short stories are collected in *Last Evenings on Earth* (2006). Bolaño's best work might be his novellas, such as *Distant Star* (2004), although he is best known for the mega-novels *The Savage Detectives* (2006), awarded the Rómulo Gallegos Prize in Venezuela, and *2666* (2008), released posthumously. In English a selection of Bolaño's poetry appeared in *The Romantic Dogs* (2008). In it he maintained an intellectual dialogue with Nicanor Parra and Enrique Lihn.

Arguably the most influential Latin American poet ever, *Jorge Luis Borges* (Argentina, 1899–1986) wrote essays, fiction, and poetry, often erasing the lines between these genres. He was a distinguished conversateur as well, granting an enormous number of interviews through the years that are an invaluable source to understand his aesthetics. In "An Autobiographical Essay" he described how he first learned English and then Spanish, reading *Don Quixote* in Shakespeare's tongue. While he mostly wrote his oeuvre in Spanish, he crafted a couple of poems in English (they are featured in this anthology) and wrote part of his correspondence in French and German. Borges started his career as a poet in volumes like *Luna de enfrente* and *Fervor de Buenos Aires*, supporting movements like *Ultraísmo*, which sought to go a step beyond Futurism. He was a fecund essayist as well as book and movie reviewer, producing collections such as *Inquisiciones* and *A Universal History of Infamy*. Yet Borges always said he wanted to be remembered as a poet. However, in the late 1930s, he suffered a life-threatening accident that pushed him to write "Pierre Menard, Author of the *Quixote*" and ultimately encouraging him to devote his talents to fiction. (The accident is fictionalized in "El Sur.") His work, characterized by hyper-intellectualism, inspired literary critics like Paul de Man, Michael Foucault, Roland Barthes, and Jacques Derrida. Borges has been translated into English numerous times. A passionate reader, he was close to Victoria Ocampo's magazine *Sur* and was named director of Argentina's Biblioteca Nacional. His poetry embraced standard rhyme forms, especially the sonnet. As blindness defined his later career, he stuck to the sonnet, visualizing a new poem in his mind before he dictated it to his colleagues and students. To commemorate the centennial of Borges's birth, Viking published three omnibus volumes in the United States: *Collected Fictions* (1999), translated by Andrew Hurley; *Selected Non-Fiction* (1999), edited by Eliot Weinberger; and *Selected Poems* (2000), edited by Alexander Coleman.

Coral Bracho (Mexico, 1951–) is the author of, among other books, *El ser que va a morir* (1982), *La voluntad de ámbar* (1998), and *Trazo del tiempo* (2000). The most representative sample of Bracho's work in English appears in *Firefly Under the Tongue* (2008), translated by Forrest Gander.

Poet and novelist *Giannina Braschi* (Puerto Rico, 1953–) lives in New York City and writes in Spanglish. Her books include *Empire of Dreams* (1994) and *Yo-Yo Boing!* (1998). Her poem "Pelos en la lengua," included in this anthology, is a manifesto that endorses a hybrid identity nationally, culturally, and linguistically.

Julia de Burgos (Puerto Rico, 1917–1953) lived in New York City, where she died anonymously on the street, after which it took several days for her remains to be identified. Burgos's work was described as "a bridge [that] extends from the later vanguardism of the thirties to the anguishing existentialism of the fifties." Burgos is the author of, among other books, *Poemas exactos a mí misma* (1937), *Canción de la vida sencilla* (1939), and *El mar y tú* (1954). The most representative sample of her work in English is *Song of the Simple Truth* (1997), edited by Jack Agüeros.

Considered one of Brazil's most important twentieth-century poets, *João Cabral de Melo Neto* (Brazil, 1920–1999) is known for his reluctance to overemphasize emotion, a stand he summarized in his oft-repeated quote: "I try not to perfume the flower." Part of the post–World War II generation, among his most famous works is *Morte e vida Severina* (1956), a dramatic poem about a poor country man in Brazil's northeastern region that made use of *literatura de cordel*, a popular narrative in verse. He is also the author of, among other books, *Pedra de sono* (1942), *Terceira feira* (1961), and *A educação pela pedra* (1966). His *Obras completas* appeared in 1994. The most representative sample of his work in English appears in *Selected Poetry: 1937–1990* (1994), edited by Djelal Kadir, and *Education by Stone* (2005), translated by Richard Zenith. In 1945 he joined the diplomatic service and was stationed in posts on four continents until his retirement in 1990. He became blind shortly after his retirement. Cabral de Melo Neto was awarded the Camões Prize in 1990 and the Neustadt International Prize for Literature in 1992.

A Roman Catholic priest by calling and a disciple of Thomas Merton, *Ernesto Cardenal* (Nicaragua, 1925–) was active during the Sandinista uprising and was Minister of Culture while the Sandinistas were in office. He is the founder of the contemplative commune Our Lady of Solentiname. His oeuvre ranges from early romantic epigrams and experiments in landscape (an approach known as *exteriorismo*) to a poetry of outright political engagement and spiritual search, one in which he tackles the past as well as religious texts like the Bible and pop icons like Marilyn Monroe. Not accidentally, Allen Ginsberg once called Cardenal "a major epic-historical poet, in the grand lineage of Central American prophet Rubén Darío." Generously translated into English, his work is available in the following collections: *Apocalypse* (1977), edited by Robert Pring-Mill and Donald D. Walsh; *The Gospel in Solentiname* (1982), translated by Donald D. Walsh; *From Nicaragua with Love* (1986), translated by Jonathan Cohen; *Cosmic Canticle* (1993), translated by Jonathan Lyons; and *Pluriverse* (2009), edited by Jonathan Cohen.

Rosario Castellanos (Mexico, 1925–1974) wrote about indigenous culture and women in Mexico. Having studied philosophy and literature, she wrote puppet shows, was a journalist, worked for Mexico's National Indigenous Institute, and held various diplomatic posts, including that of Ambassador of Israel. Castellanos is the author of the novels *Balún-Canán* (1957), *Oficio de tinieblas* (1962), and *Álbum de familia* (1971), as well as numerous essays on feminist issues and other topics. The most representative samples of her work in English appear in *The Nine Guardians* (1960), translated by Irene Nicholson; *Another Way to Be* (1990), translated by Myralyn F. Allgood; *City of Kings* (1993) translated by Robert S. Rudder and Gloria Chacón de Arjona; and *The Book of Lamentations* (1996), translated by Esther Allen.

Elicura Chihuailaf (Chile, 1952–) is the author of, among other books, *Winter and Its Image* (1997) and *Of Blue Dreams and Counter Dreams* (2000). He writes in Mapuche and Spanish. He has been secretary general of the Association of Writers in Indigenous Languages Writers of America. He has translated into Mapuche the poetry of Pablo Neruda. Chihuailaf's work is unknown in English.

Antonio Cisneros (Peru, 1942–) is the author of, among other books, *Agua que no has de beber* (1971), *Crónicas del Niño Jesús de Chilca* (1982), *El arte de envolver pescado* (1990), and *Un crucero a las Islas Galápagos* (2005). The most representative sample of his work in English appears in *The Spider Hangs Too Far from the Ground* (1970) and *At Night the Cats* (1985), both translated by Maureen Ahern, William Rowe, and David Tipton.

Julio Cortázar (Argentina, 1914–1986), a leading voice of El Boom, is best known for his experimental fiction. His short stories, such as those included in the collections *Blow-Up* (1968), *End of the Game* (1978), and *We Loved Glenda So Much* (1983), along with epoch-making novels like *Hopscotch* (1975) and its sequel *62: A Model Kit* (1972), turned him into an international literary cult figure. His early work is defined by an apolitical aesthetics. The second half of his career was defined by activism, as is clear from, among other material, *Nicaraguan Sketches* (1989), in which he established his commitment to the Sandinista Revolution. His poetry is comparatively less known. It is available in English in anthologies like *Save Twilight* (1997), translated by Stephen Kessler. Cortázar translated into Spanish the complete works of Edgar Allan Poe.

Elsa Cross (Mexico, 1946–), who studied Eastern philosophy in India and the United States, teaches literature at UNAM (Universidad Nacional Autónoma de México). Known for the complexity of her thought and the clarity of her diction, she is the author of, among other books, *Canto Malavar* (1987) and *El diván de Antar* (1989). Cross has translated the poetry of Saint-John Perse into Spanish.

Víctor de la Cruz (Mexico, 1948–) writes in Zapotec and Spanish. He received a doctorate in Mesoamerican Studies from the Universidad Nacional Autónoma de México. He is the author of, among other books, *Jardín de cactus* (1991) and edited the anthology of Zapotec literature, *Guie' sti'didxazá/La flor de la palabra* (1983, 1999). The most representative sample of de la Cruz's work in English appears in *Words of the True Peoples: Anthology of Contemporary Mexican Indigenous-Language Writers* (2004), edited by Carlos Montemayor and Donald Frischmann.

Pablo Antonio Cuadra (Nicaragua, 1912–2002) is the author of, among other books, *Poemas nicaragüenses* (1934), *Canto temporal* (1943), *La tierra prometida* (1956), *El jaguar y la luna* (1959), and *Cantos de Cifar* (1960, 1971, 1979). The most representative samples of his work in English are included in *The Birth of the Sun* (1988) and *Seven Trees Against the Dying Light* (2007), both translated by Steven F. White.

Roque Dalton (El Salvador, 1935–1975), an outspoken political activist, joined his country's Communist Party in 1955. He participated in several guerrilla movements and was imprisoned numerous times. Accused of complicity with the CIA, he was assassinated under obscure circumstances, presumably by a Maoist faction within the Communist Party. He sought to reach the masses and move them into action, becoming an inspiration for the young generation that came of age during the 1980s. His poems were released under pseudonym. Dalton is the author of *La ventana en el rostro* (1961), *Taberna y otros lugares* (1969), and *Las historias prohibidas de Pulgarcito* (1974). His most representative work is available in English in the anthology *Small Hours of the Night* (1997), translated by Jonathan Cohen, Paul Pines, Hardie St. Martin, et al.

Along with José Martí, *Rubén Darío* (Nicaragua, 1867–1916) was the leader of the Modernista literary movement that renovated Latin American poetry between

1885 and 1915. In that role, he defined the way the Spanish language was used, moving away from the mannerisms that prevailed in the Iberian Peninsula at the time and embracing a more fluid, refreshing approach. Influenced by Parnassianism and other French artistic modes, Darío's poetic style was evocative and precise. His interests oscillated from anti-imperialism to Orientalism and the grotesque. His favorite symbol was the swan, which he saw as an emblem of beauty. For instance, in one of Darío's poems the swan's neck takes the form of a question mark. The subsequent poetic generations that rebelled against Modernismo ridiculed Darío's swan as an affected, artificial icon. His contemporaries derided him too, for instance the late Modernistas poet Enrique González Martínez in "Wring the Swan's Neck." Darío's most important books are *Azul* . . . (1888), *Cantos de vida y esperanza* (1905), *El cisne y otros poemas* (1905), *El canto errante* (1907), and *Canto a la Argentina* (1914). *Rubén Darío: Selected Writings* (2005), edited by Ilan Stavans, is the most representative anthology of his work in English and includes, in addition to his poems, a sample of his short stories, essays, and travelogues. Children in Nicaragua memorize his poems in elementary school.

Arguably Brazil's most important poet of the second half of the twentieth century, *Carlos Drummond de Andrade* (Brazil, 1902–1987) showcased a variety of poetic styles, from an early endorsement of the type of Modernismo exposed by Mário de Andrade, to a Whitmanian free verse, to a Socialist epoch defined by political commitment as well as a move toward metaphysical poetry. All in all, his most distinguishable quality is the fluid nature of his language and its capacity to articulate crystalline thought. The influence of Dante and T. S. Eliot is equally palpable in him. Drummond de Andrade is the author of, among other books, *Brejo das almas* (1934), *A rosa de povo* (1944), *Claro enigma* (1951), and *A vida pasada a limpo* (1959). The most representative sample of his work in English appears is *In the Middle of the Road* (1965), translated by John Nist. Mark Strand rendered Drummond de Andrade's poems in the volume *Looking for Poetry* (2002), which includes a selection from the work of the Spanish poet Rafael Alberti as well as songs from the Quechua. His poem "Canção Amiga" was printed on Brazil's currency: the bill for fifty *cruzados*.

Part of the Modernista movement, *Ricardo Jaimes Freire* (Bolivia, 1868–1933) is known for having introduced free verse into the Spanish-American literary tradition. The child of journalists and magazine editors, he himself founded a few short-lived yet important periodicals, such as *Revista de América*. Though he wrote fiction and theater, Freire is best known for his poetry, which has a melancholic current and abounds in symbolism. His books include *Castalia bárbara* (1899) and *Los sueños son vida* (1917). He is also the author of *Leyes de la versificación castellana* (1912), a popular study in which he explored the rules of poetic rhyme. Freire's *Obras completas* appeared in Buenos Aires in 1944.

Juan Gelman (Argentina, 1930–), the child of Ukrainian immigrants, is known for a poetry that showcases its political engagement while striving to recover the loss of collective memory. He is the author of, among other books, *Violín y otras cuestiones* (1956), *Gotán* (1962), *Cólera buey* (1971), and *Carta a mi madre* (1989). The most representative anthology of his work in English is *Unthinkable Tenderness: Selected Poems of Juan Gelman*, edited and translated by Joan Lindgren. He is also the author of *Dibaxu* (1994), a volume of poetry written in Ladino, the Judeo-Spanish language, which he learned in order to write the book.

The author of, among other books, *Shajarit* (1979) and *Yiskor* (1987), which showcase her Jewish heritage, *Gloria Gervitz* (Mexico, 1943–) is known as the translator, into Spanish, of Anna Akhmatova, Marguerite Yourcenar, Samuel Beckett, Clarice Lispector, Nadezdha Mendlestam, and Rita Dove.

Odi Gonzales (Peru, 1962–) is the author of, among other books, *Juego de niños* (1988), *El libro de las sirenas* (2002), and *Vírgenes urbanas* (2007). He writes in Spanish and Quechua, the latter being the language in which the two poems published in this anthology were written.

Though he participated in the Modernista movement, *Enrique González Martínez* (Mexico, 1871–1952) rebelled against Rubén Darío's mannerism and French-style symbols such as the swan. He was a journalist and a diplomat, living in Argentina, Chile, Portugal, and Spain, and adapted into Spanish the works of Charles Baudelaire, Paul Verlaine, and Maurice Maeterlinck. Known for his poetry possessing a meditative quality, he is the author of, among other books, *La muerte del cisne* (1915), *Las señales furtivas* (1925), *Poemas truncos* (1935), and *El nuevo narciso* (1952). He wrote two autobiographical volumes: *El hombre del búho* (1944) and *La apacible locura* (1951). He remains almost totally unknown in English. His *Obras completas* appeared in Mexico in 1971, edited by Antonio Castro Leal. He was the Modernista who lived the longest into the twentieth century.

Born Francisco de Asís León Bogislao de Greiff, *León de Greiff* (Colombia, 1895–1976) introduced his country to the literary movement known as Modernismo, which renewed Latin American poetry between 1885 and 1915. Toward the end of his life Greiff divided his oeuvre into eight *mamotretos*, including *Fárrago* (1954), *Bárbara Charanga* (1957), and *Nova et vetera* (1973). His *Obra completa*, edited by Hjalmar de Greiff, began appearing in Medellín in 1985.

Nicolás Guillén (Cuba, 1902–1989) was the father of the Negrista movement, an aesthetic effort that sought to affirm the place of blackness, its culture and parlance, in Caribbean civilization. In his poetry he used slang to legitimate street speech. Guillén was the author of, among other books, *Motivos del son* (1930), *Sóngoro cosongo* (1931), *West Indies, Ltd.* (1937), *Cantos para solados y sones para turistas* (1937), *El gran zoo* (1967), and *Diario de a diario* (1972). There are a number of his works available in English: *Man-Making Words* (1972), translated by Robert Márquez and David Arthur McMurray; *The Daily Daily* (1989), translated by Vera M. Kutzinski; *New Love Poetry in Some Springtime Place* (1994), translated by Keith Ellis; and *The Great Zoo* (2002), translated by Roberto Márquez. Guillén worked as a Minister of Culture under Fidel Castro's Communist regime. He befriended Langston Hughes, building a bridge between Caribbean poetry and the Harlem Renaissance.

Born Oscar Arturo Hahn Garcés, *Oscar Hahn* (Chile, 1938–) belongs to the so-called *Generación del Setenta*, the generation of the 1970s known for having been dispersed as the result of the 1972 coup. For years he taught at the University of Iowa, and is the author of, among other books, *Esta rosa negra* (1961), *Agua final* (1967), *Arte de morir* (1977, 1979, 1981), *Mal de amor* (1981), and *Magias de la escritura* (2001). *Antología retrospectiva* appeared in 1998, and *Obras selectas* in 2003. The most representative volumes of Hahn's work in English are *The Art of Dying* (1987), *Love Breaks* (1991), and *Stolen Verses and Other Poems* (2000), all translated by James Hoggard. He received the Altazor Prize in 2003.

Natalio Hernández (Mexico, 1947–), whose occasional pseudonym is Xocoyotzin, writes in Nahuatl and Spanish. He is the author of, among other books, *Xochikoskatl/Collar de flores* (1985), *Papalocuicatl/Canto a las mariposas* (1996). Some of his essays are included in *Queman tlachixque totlahtolhuan/El despertar de nuestras lenguas* (2002). The most representative sample of Hernández Xocoyotzin's work in English appears in *Words of the True Peoples: Anthology of Contemporary Mexican Indigenous-Language Writers* (2004), edited by Carlos Montemayor and Donald Frischmann.

Connected with the Modernista movement, *Julio Herrera y Reissig* (Uruguay, 1875–1910) nurtured anarchist ideals. Most of his life was spent in Montevideo, where he worked as a public servant. In his house he built a Torre de los Panoramas (Tower of Sights), where he and his friends not only gave public readings and organized political debates but practiced fencing, the guitar, and performed séances. He is the author of, among other books, *Los éxtasis de la montaña* (1904, 1907), *Los peregrines de piedra* (1909), *Los parques abandonados* (1919), and *Las pascuas del tiempo* (1920). An anthology of his complete poetry with a selection of his prose appeared in Caracas under the aegis of Biblioteca Ayacucho in 1978, introduced by Idea Vilariño. He died of a heart ailment at the age of thirty-five.

David Huerta (Mexico, 1949–), the son of Efraín Huerta, is the author of, among other books, *Versión* (1978, 2005), *Incunable* (1987), *La sombra de los perros* (1996), and *La calle blanca* (2006). A representative selection of his poetry in English appears in *Before Saying Any of the Great Words* (2009), translated by Mark Schafer.

Like that of Pablo Neruda, the work of *Efraín Huerta* (Mexico, 1914–1982), the father of David Huerta, was defined by his passionate Communism. He is the author of, among other books, *Poemas de guerra y esperanza* (1943), *La rosa primitiva* (1950), *¡Mi país, oh mi país!* (1959), and *La raíz amarga* (1962). The most representative sample of Huerta's work in English appears is 500,000 *Azaleas* (2001), edited by Jack Hirschman.

Born Vicente García-Huidobro Fernández, *Vicente Huidobro* (Chile, 1893–1948) was the leader of the *Creacionista* movement in Spanish-language poetry, which looks at a poem not as a reflection of nature but as a new item in the universe. His inspiration was the work of Tristan Tzara, Paul Éluard, Juan Larrea, and Gerardo Diego. Having lived in Paris for a long time, Huidobro wrote in Spanish and French, as "Globe-trotter," one of the poems included in this anthology, testifies. His books include, among other titles, *La gruta del silencio* (1913), *Saisons choises* (1921), and *El ciudadano del olvido* (1941). Huidobro's most important work is *Altazor, o el viaje en paracaídas* (1931), translated into English by Eliot Weinberger as *Altazor: A Voyage in a Parachute. A Poem in VII Cantos* (1988).

Born Juana Fernández Morales, *Juana de Ibarbourou* (Uruguay, 1895–1979) is a poet of eroticism and overt emotionalism. Her vision is considered to have opened the door to a type of feminism that emphasizes women's passions. She is the author of, among other books, *Raíz salvaje* (1922), *Mensajes de escriba* (1953), and *La pasajera* (1967). Ibarbourou's *Obra completa*, published in five volumes in Montevideo in 1992, edited by Jorge Arbeleche. Ibarbourou's work remains unknown in English.

Darío Jaramillo Agudelo (Colombia, 1947–) is the author of, among other books, *Historias* (1974), *Poemas de amor* (1986), *Del ojo a la lengua* (1995), and *Can-*

tar por cantar (2001). An anthology of his work, *Libros de poemas*, appeared in Bogotá in 2003 but is unknown in English. He received Colombia's National Poetry Prize in 1978.

Under the title of *Poesía vertical*, *Roberto Juarróz* (Argentina, 1925–1995) published fourteen volumes of poetry numbered successively from 1 to 14, the first appearing in 1958, the last posthumously in 1997. His style is known for its cryptic nature. The most representative anthology of his work in English is *Vertical Poetry* (1988), translated by W. S. Merwin.

The child of immigrants from Poland and Czechoslovakia, and the grandchild of a founder of Cuba's first Ashkenazi synagogue, *José Kozer* (Cuba, 1940–), after studying in Havana, left for New York in 1960. His poetry is rich with diverse Spanish language vernaculars, as well as other languages, including Yiddish and Ladino. For years he taught at Queens College. Astonishingly prolific, Kozer is the author of, among other books, *Ánima* (2002). The most representative sample of his work in English appears in *Stet* (2006), translated by Mark Weiss.

Paulo Leminski (Brazil, 1945–1989) led a marginal life working temporarily in advertising while collaborating with newspapers and magazines. He died from alcohol abuse. He is the author of, among other books, *Catatau* (1975), *Agora é que são elas* (1986), and *Metamorfose* (1994). His nonfiction includes *Basho* (1983) and *Leon Trotski, a paixão segundo a revolução* (1986). The most representative sample of his work in English appears in *Nothing the Sun Could Not Explain* (1997), edited by Michael Palmer, Régis Bonvicino, and Nelson Ascher.

A novelist with an exuberant baroque style who fought the dictatorship of Gerardo Machado, *José Lezama Lima* (Cuba, 1910–1976) is the author of the semiautobiographical novel *Paradiso* (1966), from which the poem "Portrait of José Cemí" is taken. His cosmopolitanism was already evident in his first published work, the long poem "Muerte de Narciso." One of his topics was his beloved city Havana; another was authenticity in the literary output of the Americas. Although Lezama Lima was supportive of Fidel Castro's Communism, his identity as a homosexual put him at odds with the regime. He wrote essays, poems, stories, and another novel, published posthumously, called *Oppiano Licario* (1977). His two-volume *Obras completas* was released in Mexico between 1975 and 1977.

Known for his experimental bent, *Enrique Lihn* (Chile, 1929–1988) was, aside from being a poet, an art critic and a playwright as well as a novelist and the editor of the press at the Universidad de Santiago. He despised the military junta that ruled Chile under General Augusto Pinochet, and this animosity is evident in the social, political, and religious commentary that runs through his work. A strong psychoanalytic symbolism permeated his oeuvre. Lihn was the author of, among other books, *La pieza oscura* (1963), *Poesía de paso* (1967), and *La musiquilla de los pobres* (1969). The most representative anthology of his work in English is *The Dark Room and Other Poems*, edited by Patricio Lerzundi. His last book, *Diario de muerte* (1988), was written during the six weeks preceding his death from cancer.

Born Jon Mateus de Lima and raised in a sugar plantation, in the 1920s *Jorge de Lima* (Brazil, 1895–1953) broke away from the prevailing European influences and endorsed the Modernista movement, collaborating with the anthropologist Gilberto Freyre and becoming the foremost representative of Afro-Brazilian poetry. In 1935 he converted to Catholicism and sought to "restore poetry in Christ." His works include the novels *Calunga* (1935) and *A mulher obscura* (1939), as well as the collections of poems *A túnica inconsútil* (1938) and *A invenção de Orfeu* (1952). Lima is unknown in English.

The ancestry of *Pura López Colomé* (Mexico, 1952–) is Mayan, Irish, and Catalan. She is the author of, among other books, *Aurora* (1994) and *Santo y seña* (2007). The most representative sample of her work in English appears in *No Shelter* (2002), translated by Forrest Gander. López Colomé has translated into Spanish the work of Samuel Beckett, Seamus Heaney, Gertrude Stein, T. S. Eliot, Robert Hass, Philip Larkin, Robert Creeley, Malcolm Lowry, and Louise Glück, among others. She was awarded the Xavier Villaurrutia Prize in 2008.

Born in Jeréz, Zacatecas, *Ramón López Velarde* (Mexico, 1888–1921), a leading figure in the response against Modernismo, looked to produce a less cosmopolitan, more authentically Mexican poetry. Inspired by the Mexican Revolution, his poetry underwent a transformation after he became infatuated with the legacy of Rubén Darío but later on rejected it to embrace a nostalgic mode that rotated around his desire to return to Jeréz, which he had left in order to enroll in a seminary in the state's capital. His infatuation was also connected to his adolescent love toward Josefa de los Ríos, a distant relative eight years his senior whom he called Fuensanta in his poetry. He explored the limits of Mexican Spanish by creating his own language. Considered Mexico's national poet, he is the author of, among other books, *La sangre devota* (1916); *Zozobra* (1919), his most accomplished work; and *El son del corazón* (1932). His fiction appears in *El minutero* (1923) and *El don de febrero*

(1952). *Suave Patria: Sweet Land* is López Velarde's most famous poem. Xavier Villaurrutia called him "un Baudelaire mexicano." The most representative anthology of his work in English is *Song of the Heart* (1995), translated by Margaret Sayers Peden. His *Obras* appeared in Mexico in 1971, and was edited by José Luis Martínez. He died at the age of thirty-three.

Dulce María Loynaz (Cuba, 1902–1997) was the daughter of General Enrique Loynaz del Castillo, a hero of the Cuban Liberation Army and author of the lyrics of the Cuban national anthem. A lawyer by profession, she published her work in periodicals until the arrival of Fidel Castro's revolution, at which point she remained on the island but opted for the silence of an internal exile. It wasn't until she was in her eighties when her oeuvre was embraced by an enthusiastic following. In 1987 she received the Cuban National Award of Literature. The apex of her career came in 1992 when was awarded the Premio Cervantes. The most representative sample of Loynaz's work in English appears in *A Woman in Her Garden* (2002), translated by Judith Kerman, and *Against Heaven* (2007), translated by James O'Connor.

A prolific man of letters whose ideological loyalties defined him as a Socialist early on and right-wing with a Fascist bent later in his life, *Leopoldo Lugones* (Argentina, 1874–1938) was a member of the Modernista generation, whose influence on his country's literature is substantial. (Borges's embrace of the moon as a symbol comes from him.) He spent several years in Europe. In 1930 he supported a coup d'état against President Hipólito Yrigoyen. Lugones wrote impressionistic booklong meditations on the war against the Gauchos in Argentina and another on the Jesuit presence in Paraguay during colonial times. He committed suicide at a tourist resort by taking a mixture of whiskey and cyanide. A journalist, poet, essayist, and novelist as well as a public speaker, Lugones is the author of *Los crepúsculos del jardín* (1905), *Lunario sentimental* (1909), and *El payador* (1916). His *Obras completas* appeared in Madrid between 1952 and 1962. Lugones's poetry remains unavailable in English, but some of his fiction is featured in *Strange Forces*, translated into English by Gilbert Alter-Gilbert in 2001.

In the figure of *José Martí* (Cuba, 1853–1895), poetry and politics come together. His books include *Versos sencillos* (1891), exalting the plain aspects of rural life, and *Ismaelillo* (1882), which he wrote for his son. He was a journalist with a powerfully descriptive voice. His dispatches from New York, where he lived in exile, to newspapers across the Spanish-speaking Americas became famous for the way he explored social issues like racism and poverty. In them he explored the dilemmas of contemporary urban centers in Whitmanian fashion, announcing the trend of poetry that would be produced a couple of decades later by the Andalucian poet Federico García Lorca. Considered an iconic figure by Fidel Castro's Communist regime in Havana, Martí died in the battlefield fighting for the liberation of his native island. Along with that of Rubén Darío, his work was instrumental in bringing the Modernista movement in the Spanish-speaking Americas to the fore. The most authoritative anthology of Martí's poetry and prose in English is *José Martí: Selected Writings* (2002), edited and translated by Esther Allen.

Born Cecília Benevides de Carvalho Meireles, *Cecília Meireles* (Brazil, 1901–1964) is the author, among other books, of *Espectros* (1919), *Viagem* (1939), *Romanceiro de inconfidencias* (1953), and *Solombra* (1963). The most representative sample of her work in English appears in *Poemas em tradução* (1977), translated by Henry Hunt Keith and Raymond S. Sayers. Elizabeth Bishop and Emanuel Brazil include some of her poems in *An Anthology of Twentieth-Century Brazilian Poetry.*

Born Pedro Julio Mir Valentín, *Pedro Mir* (Dominican Republic, 1913–2000) is the author of, among other books, *Amén de mariposas* (1969), about the assassination of the Mirabal sisters during the Trujillo dictatorship in the Dominican Republic. (The episode is explored in Julia Alvarez's novel *In the Time of the Butterflies*.) Mir is also the author of *Viaje a la muchedumbre* (1971). His work showcases two major influences: Whitman and Neruda. In 1947 his anti-Trujillo politics drew him to exile in Cuba, where he remained until Trujillo fell in 1961. He was named poet laureate of the Dominican Republic in 1984. In English his work is available in *Countersong to Walt Whitman and Other Poems* (1993), translated by Jonathan Cohen and Donald D. Walsh.

Born Lucila de María del Perpetuo Socorro Godoy Alcayaga of Basque and of indigenous descent, *Gabriela Mistral* (Chile, 1889–1957) won the Nobel Prize for Literature in 1945, a first for a Latin American writer and at that time the only one awarded to a woman. In addition to being a poet, she was a teacher and diplomat and an ardent feminist. Mistral is the author of, among other books, *Sonetos de la muerte* (1914), *Tala* (1954), and *Lagar* (1954). The most representative sample of her work in English appears in *A Gabriela Mistral Reader* (1993), translated by Maria Giachetti and edited by Marjorie Agosín. Also available is the fable *Crickets and Frogs* (1972), adapted by Doris Dana and illustrated by Antonio Frasconi. Mistral's central themes are motherly love, sorrow, and repentance. In Chile she is perceived as the nation's motherly figure. Her apparent lesbianism is the subject of controversy.

Born in Alexandria to Italian parents, *Fabio Morábito* (Egypt, 1955–) spent his childhood in Milan. He emigrated to Mexico at the age of fifteen. He is the author of, among other books, *Lotes baldíos* (1984), *Caja de herramientas* (1989), *La vida ordenada* (2000), and *También Berlín se olvida* (2004). His book *Toolbox* (1999), translated by Geoff Hargreaves, is an instruction manual to reacquaint ourselves with mundane objects. Morabito is the translator into Spanish of Eugenio Montale's poetry.

Born Marcus Vinícius da Cruz de Mello de Moraes, and nicknamed "o poetinha" (The Little Poet), *Vinícius de Moraes* (Brazil, 1913–1980) wrote lyrics for numerous classic Brazilian songs. He was a composer of bossa nova, a playwright, and a diplomat. Marcel Camus's award-winning 1959 film *Black Orpheus* was inspired by de Moraes' piece *Orfeu*. For a time he worked as a film censor for the Ministry of Education and Health. His songs *"Para uma menina com uma flor"* and *"Samba da Bênção"* were included on the sound track of Claude Lelouch's *Un homme et une femme* (1966). He collaborated with important musicians, like Baden Powell, João Gilberto, and Chico Buarque. Moraes's poetry is principally concerned with love and is composed in decasyllables, influenced by the work of sixteenth-century Portuguese poet Luís de Camões. Elizabeth Bishop and Emanuel Brazil include some of his poems in *An Anthology of Twentieth-Century Brazilian Poetry*.

The work of *Nancy Morejón* (Cuba, 1944–) addresses nationalism, slavery, and the experience of women of African descent in Cuba. She is the author of, among other books, *Amor, ciudad atribuída* (1964), *Octubre imprescindible* (1983), and *La quinta de los molinos* (2000). The most representative volumes of her work in English are *Grenada Notebook* (1984), translated by Lisa Davis; *Looking Within: Selected Poems, 1954–2000* (2003), translated by Gabriel Abudu and others; and *With Eyes and Soul: Images of Cuba* (2004), translated by Pamela Carmell and David Frye. Associated with Fidel Castro's regime, Morejón received Cuba's Critics' Prize in 1986 and the National Prize for Literature, the first for a black woman, in 2001.

Myriam Moscona (Mexico, 1955–) writes in Spanish as well as Ladino, the language of Iberian Jews before and after the expulsion from the peninsula in 1492. The daughter of Bulgarian immigrants who left the Ottoman Empire for the New World, she is the author of, among other books, *Las visitantes* (1989), *El árbol de los nombres* (1992), and *Negro marfil* (2006). The most representative sample of her work in English appears in *Mouth to Mouth: Twelve Contemporary Mexican Women* (1993), edited by Forrest Gander.

Álvaro Mutis (Colombia, 1923–) is primarily known for his novellas about a fictional sailor character called Maqroll. They are collected in English in *The Adventures and Misadventures of Maqroll* (2002), translated by Edith Grossman. A close friend of Gabriel García Márquez, whom he helped support during the writing of *One Hundred Years of Solitude*, Mutis worked for various corporations, including the Standard Oil Company, 20th Century Fox, and Columbia Pictures. He spent most of his life in Mexico City. As a poet, he is the author of, among other books, *La balanza* (1948), *Los elementos del desastre* (1953), and *Los trabajos perdidos* (1961). He was awarded the Cervantes Prize in 2001 and the Neustadt International Prize for Literature in 2003.

María Negroni (Argentina, 1951–) received a doctorate from Columbia University and teaches at Sarah Lawrence College. She is the author of, among other books, *La jaula bajo el trapo* (1991), *Camera delle Meraviglie* (2002), and *Andanza* (2009). The most representative samples of her work in English are *Islandia* (2001) and *Night Journey* (2002). Negroni has translated into Spanish the works of Louise Labé, Valentine Penrose, Georges Bataille, H.D., and Charles Simic.

Arguably the most popular Spanish-language poet of all time, *Pablo Neruda* (Chile, 1904–1973), born Naftalí Ricardo Reyes Basualto, received the Nobel Prize for Literature in 1970. Neruda was a diplomat and a senator before running for the presidency of Chile, eventually dropping out of the race to strengthen the candidacy of his friend Salvador Allende. His oeuvre oscillates between the intimate, private, and domestic tone of *Twenty Love Poems and a Song of Despair*, *Elementary Odes*, and *One Hundred Love Sonnets*, and the sweeping epic voice of *Canto General*, in which he attempted to retell the history of Latin America from the Neolithic period to the 1950s. Neruda was prolific, producing approximately 3,500 poems in total. In Chile, known for its poets (other celebrated figures include Gabriela Mistral, Enrique Lihn, Gonzalo Rojas, and Raúl Zurita), he is considered the nation's poet. The most representative anthology of his work in English is *The Poetry of Pablo Neruda* (2003), edited by Ilan Stavans. Neruda translated into Spanish the works of Shakespeare, Charles Baudelaire, William Blake, Rainer Maria Rilke, and James Joyce.

Amado Nervo (Mexico, 1870–1919) was a devout Catholic whose religiosity is a leitmotif in his oeuvre, although there is a certain Buddhist bent running through it. (*Amado* in Spanish means beloved.) Nervo was a cofounder of the influential *Revista Moderna*. A close friend of Rubén Darío, he was the secretary of the Mexican diplomatic delegation in Madrid from 1905 to 1918. Nervo is the author of, among other books, *Serenidad* (1914) and *Elevación* (1917). His work remains almost unknown in English. His *Obras completas* were published in Madrid in 1935.

Born Olga Noemí Gugliotta, *Olga Orozco* (Argentina, 1920–1999) believed that the poet finds her material even in the most mundane. She was born in La Pampa and moved to Buenos Aires at the age of sixteen. Working as a journalist for years, she belonged to the *Tercera vanguardia*, a generation defined by Surrealism, although she was equally influenced by Rimbaud, Nerval, Baudelaire, and Rilke. She is the author of, among other books, *Las muertes* (1951), *Los juegos peligrosos* (1962), and *Museo salvaje* (1974). The most representative anthology of Orozco's work in English is *Engravings Torn from Insomnia* (2002), translated by Mary Crow. She received Argentina's National Poetry Prize in 1988 and the Juan Rulfo Award in Mexico in 1998.

Known also as a lucid essayist, *José Emilio Pacheco* (Mexico, 1939–) is a poet who focuses in the ordinary and mundane elements of life. In English his poetry is available in *Don't Ask Me How the Time Goes By: Poems, 1964–1968* (1978), translated by Alistair Reid; *Selected Poems* (1987), edited by George McWhirter in collaboration with the author; *An Ark for the Next Millennium* (1993), translated by Margaret Sayers Peden; and *City of Memory and Other Poems* (1997), translated by Cynthia Steele and David Lauer. Pacheco is the editor of anthologies and the author of essays, screenplays, and fiction, such as the stories included in *Battles in the Desert* (1987). In 2003 he received the Octavio Paz prize, a year later the Pablo Neruda and the Alfonso Reyes Prizes, and in 2009 he was awarded the Premio Reina Sofía de Poesía Iberoamericana.

Heberto Padilla (Cuba, 1932–2004), a coveted poet in Cuba, was at the center of an ideological storm in the late 1970s known as "the Padilla affair," which divided Latin American intellectuals when Fidel Castro's government forced him to publicly confess crimes against the country. As a result, a number of writers, among them Susan Sontag and Octavio Paz, broke with Cuba's Communist regime. Padilla was imprisoned and then allowed to leave the country, settling in the United States in 1980. His memoir in English is called *Self-Portrait with the Other* (1989). Padilla is also the author of *Las rosas audaces* (1948), *El justo tiempo humano* (1960), *Fuera del juego* (1966), *Por el momento* (1970), and *El hombre junto al mar* (1980). In English his work is available in *Sent Off the Field* (1972), translated by J. M. Cohen; *Legacies* (1982), translated by Alistair Reid and Andrew Hurley; and *A Fountain, a House of Stone* (1991), translated by Reid along with Alexander Coleman.

A leading voice of the Negrista movement, which is concerned with Afro-Caribbean rhythms and motifs and the beauty of black parlance in the region, *Luis Palés Matos* (Puerto Rico, 1898–1959) was the son of the distinguished poets Vicente Palés and Consuelo Matos. Having worked as a journalist for various newspapers, he began publishing poetry in the mid-1920s. His poem "Pueblo negro" is considered a cornerstone of *Negrismo*, an Afro-Antillean aesthetic that includes Nicolás Guillén's oeuvre. Palés Matos is the author of *Azaleas* (1913) and *Tuntún de pasa y grifería* (1937). Considered by many to be Puerto Rico's unofficial national poet, he had his collected works, called *Poesía: 1915–1956*, appear in Río Piedras in 1957, with an introduction by Federico de Onís. Mercedes López-Baralt edited an inclusive anthology, *La poesía de Luis Palés Matos* (1995). The most representative sample of his work in English is *Selected Poems* (2000), translated by Julio Marzán. As a white poet, he was criticized by blacks for benefiting in their place.

Nicanor Parra (Chile, 1914–), an avant-gardist and brother of Violeta Parra, is well known in the English-speaking world for his rejection of standard poetic forms. The most representative anthologies of his poems in English include four volumes of his anti-poems, the first published in 1967 and translated by, among others, Fernando Alegría, the second in 1973 in a translation by Jorge Elliott, the third in 1985 by Lawrence Ferlinghetti, and the fourth in 2004 by Liz Werner. Also available are *Sermons and Homilies of the Christ of Elqui* (1984), translated by Sandra Reyes, and *After-Dinner Declarations* (2008), translated by Dave Oliphant.

Violeta Parra (Chile, 1917–1967), a political activist and sister of Nicanor Parra, was the author of *Poesía popular y de los Andes* (1964). Her *Décimas: Autobiografía en versos chilenos* was published posthumously. Her song *"Gracias a la vida,"* translated into English as "Here's to Life!" and sung by Joan Baez and John Upton, is a flagship of the *canción de protesta* and a chant to political freedom in Latin America.

Octavio Paz (Mexico, 1914–1998) is one of Mexico's most important twentieth-century poets. As an editor and essayist, he served as a bridge between the nation's intellectual circles and international culture. As a magazine editor, he wrote for *Plural* and *Vuelta* and was extraordinarily influential, at first testing the limits of Mexico's governmental power, then becoming a compliant supporter of the decades-long ruling party, Partido Revolucionario Institucional. He discussed the Mexican psyche in *The Labyrinth of Solitude* (1961), modern poetry from Romanticism to the avant-garde in *Children of the Mire* (1974, 1991), and the life and legacy of the Marquis of Sade in *An Erotic Beyond* (1993), among scores of other books. His autobiography, called *Itinerary: An Intellectual Journey*, was released in 1999. He also wrote an intellectual biography of Sor Juana Inés de la Cruz. Paz served as a diplomat in India and France. Paz translated into Spanish work from the French, English, Portuguese, and Chinese. The most representative anthology of his poetry available in English is *The Collected Poetry of Octavio Paz: 1957–1987* (1991), edited by Eliot Weinberger. Paz won the Nobel Prize for Literature in 1990.

The daughter of Jewish immigrants from Russia, *Alejandra Pizarnik* (Argentina, 1936–1972) published her debut collection of poetry, *La tierra más ajena* (1955), within a year of enrolling at the Universidad de Buenos Aires. In the 1960s she lived in France, where she studied at the Sorbonne and socialized with the Parisian literary world. She committed suicide in Argentina. Her life and work have prompted comparisons with Sylvia Plath. Pizarnik is the author of, among other books, *La última inocencia* (1956), *Árbol de Diana* (1962), *Extracción de la piedra de la locura* (1968), and *El infierno musical* (1971). The most representative anthology of her work in English is *Alejandra Pizarnik: A Profile* (1987), edited by Frank Graziano.

The poetry of *Adélia Prado* (Brazil, 1935–) is defined by her Catholicism, female spirituality, and the regional worldview of her native Minas Gerais. Also known for her fiction, Prado is the author of, among other books, *Bagagem* (1976), *Salte os cachorros* (1979), *Terra de Santa Cruz* (1981), and *O pelicano* (1987). The most representative anthology in English of Prado's work is *The Alphabet in the Park* (1990), translated by Ellen Doré Watson. Prado started her career as a poet at the age of forty, as a "discovery" of Carlos Drummond de Andrade.

Juan Gregorio Regino (Mexico, 1962–), who writes in Mazatec and Spanish, is part of a large movement of indigenous poets of the Americas eager to reclaim their heritage through the recovery of their native language. He is the author of, among other books, *Tatsjején nga kjabuya/No es eterna la muerte* (1994) and *Ngata'ara stsee/Que siga lloviendo* (1999). The most representative sample of Regino's work in English appears in *Words of the True Peoples: Anthology of Contemporary Mexican Indigenous-Language Writers* (2004), edited by Carlos Montemayor and Donald Frischmann.

Jorge Luis Borges called the prolific *Alfonso Reyes* (Mexico, 1889–1959) "the best writer in the Spanish language." A diplomat, an essayist, a linguist, a scholar of Hellenistic and Hispanic civilizations, and an overall polymath, he was an influential thinker whose work sought to make Mexican literature more cosmopolitan. Reyes is the author of *Visión de Anáhuac* (1917), *Ifigenia cruel* (1924), and *Última*

Tule (1942). The most representative anthologies of his work in English are *The Position of America and Other Essays* (1950) and *Mexico in a Nutshell and Other Essays* (1964), translated by Charles Ramsdell. Reyes's *Obras completas*, published in Mexico starting in 1955, span twenty-two volumes.

Gonzalo Rojas (Chile, 1917–), born in the port of Lebu, was the seventh of eight children. Like most in his generation, he was deeply influenced by Surrealism, especially during his membership in the literary group *Mandrágora*. His quest was to define himself against the giants of Chilean poetry: Gabriel Mistral, Pablo Neruda, and Vicente Huidobro. Rojas's oeuvre deals with love and death, but it is in its explorations of language—he is astonishingly precise in his wording—where his mastery shines. He is the author of, among other books, *La miseria del hombre* (1948), *Oscuro* (1977), *Del relámpago* (1978), *Trastierro* (1979), and *Río turbio* (1996). The most representative anthology of his work in English is *From the Lightning: Selected Poems* (2008), translated by John Oliver Simon.

Jaime Sabines (Mexico, 1925–1999) is arguably Mexico's most popularly beloved poet of the twentieth century. He sings to love, suffering, and death in an accessible, unadorned language, breaking taboos along the way. Sabines is the author of, among other books, *Horal* (1950), *La señal* (1951), *Tarumba* (1956), and *Maltiempo* (1972). His readings regularly drew thousands of devoted fans. The most representative collections of Sabines's work in English are *Pieces of Shadow* (1995), translated by W. S. Merwin, and *Tarumba* (2007), translated by Philip Levine and Ernesto Trejo.

José Santos Chocano (Peru, 1875–1934) spent his itinerant life in Spain, the Caribbean, and the Americas, combining the writing of a Modernista–style poetry with the insatiable search for material fortune, political intrigue, and travel adventure, all of which he nurtured while dreaming to become "el poeta de América." Among the first to achieve a lucrative career as a public performer of his poems, Santos Chicano lived in Madrid between 1905 and 1908, but had to leave as a result of a nebulous business. He promoted the Socialist values of the Mexican Revolution in the United States while serving the Guatemalan dictator Manuel Estrada Cabrera. Toward the end of his life, he became a treasure hunter. His Romantic poetry, marked by hyperbole, was excessive in tone. Santos Chocano is the author of, among other books, *La selva virgen* (1893, 1898), *El canto del siglo* (1901), *Alma América* (1906), and *Poemas del amor doliente* (1937). His *Obras completas* appeared in Mexico in 1954, edited by Luis Alberto Sánchez.

Born into a wealthy family, *José Asunción Silva* (Colombia, 1865–1896) was an active member of the Modernista movement. He served as a diplomat in Caracas. The manuscript of a novel in progress was lost in a shipwreck in 1895. His sister, Elvia, died shortly after. These events led Silva to commit suicide at the age of thirty-one. His *El libro de versos: 1883–1896* appeared posthumously in 1923. He is also the author *De sobremesa* (1925), subtitled "The Diary of a Decadent." Miguel de Unamuno published an anthology of Silva's work in 1908. An edition of his *Obras completas* appeared in Caracas in 1977 under the aegis of Biblioteca Ayacucho, edited by Eduardo Camacho Guizado and Gustavo Mejía. An English version of *After-Dinner Conversation: The Diary of a Decadent* appeared in 2005, translated by Kelly Washbourne.

Alfonsina Storni (Switzerland, 1892–1938), a feminist who reacted against the Modernista movement, is the author of, among other books, *La inquietude del rosal* (1916), *Irremediablemente* (1919), *El mundo de siete pozos* (1934), and *Mascarilla y trébol* (1938). Her father was a beer industrialist, and she learned to speak Italian before Spanish. The family moved to Rosario, Argentina, when Storni was a little girl. She worked in her father's tavern and, later on, as a teacher, journalist, and actress, performing in Ibsen's *Spectres*, among other plays. She befriended intellectuals like José Enrique Rodó, Amadio Nervo, and Miguel Ugarte. Her work is known for its eroticism in the context of the industrialized society. The most representative anthology of her work in English is the bilingual selection of poems included in *Alfonsina Storni: Argentina's Feminist Poet* (1975), edited by Florence Williams Talamantes. Afflicted with breast cancer and depressed from the death of her friend Quiroga, Storni commited suicide by jumping into the sea in Mar del Plata. (The popular song "Alfonsina y el mar" is the story of her death.)

Jorge Teillier (Chile, 1935–1996) grew up in an environment of political awareness in the southern frontier of Chile. His father was a union activist who went into exile after the 1973 coup d'état in which General Augusto Pinochet deposed the elected civilian president Salvador Allende. For most of his life, Teillier was an editor at the press at the Universidad de Chile. He led his country's poetry into a post-Neruda period, focusing his attention on memory, personal and collective. He is the author of, among other books, *El cielo cae con las hojas* (1958), *Poema del país de Nunca Jamás* (1963), *Crónica del forastero* (1978), and *Cartas para reinas de otras primaveras* (1985). The most representative sample of his work in English is *From the Country of Nevermore* (1990), translated by Mary Crow, and *In Order to Talk with the Dead* (1993), translated by Carolyne Wright.

The leader of the Vanguardista movement in Spanish-language poetry intent on rebelling against Modernismo by inserting Latin American poetry into the avant-garde climate from the 1920s onward, a tortured Catholic, a begrudging friend of Pablo Neruda, and an activist connected with the Spanish Civil War, *César Vallejo* (Peru, 1892–1938) pushed the Spanish language in unforeseen directions, crafting a poetry at once religiously exalted and perplexing in its syntactical approach and its depiction of time. His book *Trilce* (1922), written for the most part in prison, where he spent three months for participating in a riot, is considered one of the most revolutionary collections of poetry in its style and content. Vallejo was the author of *Los heraldos negros* (1918) and *Spain, Take This Chalice from Me* (1940). In the former, Vallejo offered an autobiographical picture of his childhood as a *cholo*, as a racially mixed person is described in Peru, and in the latter he crafted some of the most memorable poems about war. Thomas Merton once called him "the greatest Catholic poet since Dante." In English the most representative anthologies of his work are *The Complete Poetry of César Vallejo* (2007), edited and translated by Clayton Eshleman, and *'Spain, Take This Chalice from Me' and Other Poems* (2008), edited by Ilan Stavans and translated by Margaret Sayers Peden. Vallejo also wrote theater, essays, short stories, and a proletarian novel called *Tungsten* (1931).

Born Blanca Leonor Varela Gonzales, *Blanca Varela* (Peru, 1926–2009), is the author of, among other books, *Ese puerto existe* (1959), *Ejercicios materiales* (1978–1993), *Concierto animal* (1999), and *El falso teclado* (2001). An anthology of her work, *Canto villano: 1949–1983*, appeared in 1986. Her work is unavailable in English. Varela was the first woman to receive, in 2007, the Premio Reina Sofía de Poesía Iberoamericana.

In addition to writing poetry, *Xavier Villaurrutia* (Mexico, 1903–1950) was a playwright who adapted Shakespeare into Spanish. He called his plays *Autos profanos*. He edited separate anthologies of the poetry of Sor Juana Inés de la Cruz and Ramón López Velarde. One of composer Carlos Chávez's famous *"Dos canciones,"* two songs for mezzo-soprano or baritone and piano, is based on a Villaurrutia poem. (The other is based on a López Velarde poem.) Villaurrutia's *Obras completas* appeared in Mexico in 1953, edited by Ali Chumacero. The most representative volume of his poetry in English is *Nostalgia of Death* (1993), edited by Eliot Weinberger.

As a result of his Communist beliefs, *Raúl Zurita* (Chile, 1951–) suffered under the dictatorship of General Augusto Pinochet. He is the author of, among other books, *Purgatorio* (1979), *Anteparatso* (1982), *La vida nueva* (1994), and *Las ciu-dades del agua* (2008). His work is defined by an outright experimentalism, as is clear from a performance of a series of poems composed in 1982 in the New York City sky with an airplane. (Roberto Bolaño was inspired by the idea to write his novella *Distant Star*.) The most representative anthologies of his work in English are *Anteparadise* (1986), translated by Jack Schmitt, and *Purgatory* (2009), translated by Anna Deeny. Zurita's ur-text is Dante's *Divine Comedy*. In 1990 he was Chile's cultural attaché in Rome. In 2000 he received the National Literature Prize, and in 2006 he was awarded Cuba's Casa de las Américas Award.

INDEX OF TITLES, FIRST

LINES, AND POETS

705

711

714

PERMISSIONS ACKNOWLEDGMENTS

The editor gratefully acknowledges the following sources for permission to reprint the poems in this anthology:

Delmira Agustini: "Fiera de amor," translated by Ilan Stavans. First published in *The Literary Review*, vol. 36, Summer 2009. © 2009 by Ilan Stavans. Printed by permission of Ilan Stavans.

Humberto Ak'Abal: "El baile" and "Saqué de mi cabeza tu nombre," translated by Ilan Stavans. © 2011 by Ilan Stavans. Printed by permission of Ilan Stavans.

Claribel Alegría: "Destinos," "Máscaras," and "Antígona," by Claribel Alegría. From *Soltando Amarras/Casting Off: Poems by Claribel Alegría*, translated by Margaret Sayers Peden. Willimantic: Curbstone Press, 2003. © 2003 by Margaret Sayers Peden. Printed by permission of Northwestern University Press and Margaret Sayers Peden.

Mário de Andrade: "Ode ao Burguês," "Domingo," "Anhangabaú," and "Tu," translated by Jack E. Tomlins. From *Hallucinated City*, by Mário de Andrade, translated by Jack E. Tomlins. Vanderbilt University Press, 1968. © 1968 by Vanderbilt University Press. Printed by permission of Vanderbilt University Press.

Oswald de Andrade: "Biblioteca Nacional," "Reclame," and "Procissão do entêrro," translated by Jean R. Longland. From *An Anthology of Twentieth-Century Brazilian Poetry*, edited, with an introduction, by Elizabeth Bishop and Emanuel Brasil. Middletown: Wesleyan University Press, 1972. © 1972, 1997 by Elizabeth Bishop and Emanuel Brasil. Printed by permission of Wesleyan University Press. www.wesleyan.edu/wespress.

Homero Aridjis: "El ojo de la ballena," by Homero Aridjis. © 2000 by Homero Aridjis. Printed by permission of Homero Aridjis. "The Eye of the Whale," translated by George McWhirter. From *Eyes to See Otherwise: Selected Poems, 1960–2000*, selected and edited by Betty Ferber and George McWhirter. New York: New Directions, 2001. © 2001 by Homero Aridjis. Printed by permission of New Directions Publishing Corp.

María Baranda: From "Dylan y las ballenas: 12." © 1996 by María Baranda. Printed by permission of María Baranda. From "Dylan and the Whales: 12," translated by Forrest Gander. From *Connecting Lines: New Poetry from Mexico*, edited by Luis Cortés Bargalló. Louisville: Sarabande Books. Printed by permission of Forrest Gander.

Mario Benedetti: "Contra los puentes levadizos," by Mario Benedetti. Printed by permission of Carmen Balcells. "Against Drawbridges," translated by Roberto Márquez. From *Latin American Revolutionary Poetry*, edited by Roberto Márquez. New York and London: Monthly Review Press, 1974. © 1974 by Roberto Márquez. Printed by permission of Roberto Márquez.

Alberto Blanco: "Mi tribu" and "Mapas," from *Los relojes y las horas* by Alberto Blanco. Mexico: Fondo de Cultura Económica, 2002. © 2002 by Alberto Blanco. Printed by permission of Alberto Blanco. "My Tribe" and "Maps," translated by Ilan Stavans. First published in *The Literary Review*, vol. 36, Summer 2009. © 2009 by Ilan Stavans. Printed by permission of Ilan Stavans.

Roberto Bolaño: "El último canto de amor de Pedro J. Lastarria, Alias 'El Chorito,'" by Roberto Bolaño. Printed by permission of The Wiley Literary Agency. "The Last Love Song of Pedro J. Lastarria, Alias 'El Chorito,'" translated by Laura Healy. From *The Romantic Dogs: 1980–1998*, translated by Laura Healy. New York: New Directions, 2008. © 2008 by the Heirs of Roberto Bolaño. Printed by permission of New Directions Publishing Corp.

Jorge Luis Borges: "Página para recordar al coronel Suárez, vencedor en Junín," "La noche cíclica," and "Poema conjetura," by Jorge Luis Borges, printed by permission of The Wiley Literary Agency. "A Page to Commemorate Colonel Suárez, Victor at Junín," "The Cyclical Night," and "Conjectural Poem" translated by Alistair Reid. From *Selected Poems by Jorge Luis Borges*, edited by Alexander Coleman. New York: Viking, 1999. Printed by permission of the Penguin Group, LLC.

Jorge Luis Borges: "El golem," by Jorge Luis Borges, printed by permission of The Wiley Literary Agency. "The Golem," translated by Alan S. Trueblood. From *Selected Poems by Jorge Luis Borges*, edited by Alexander Coleman. New York: Viking, 1999. Printed by permission of the Penguin Group, LLC.

Jorge Luis Borges: "Two English Poems," from *Obras completas: 1952–1972*. Buenos Aires: Emecé Editores, 1982. Printed by permission of The Wylie Literary Agency.

Jorge Luis Borges: "Spinoza," by Jorge Luis Borges, printed by permission of The Wylie Literary Agency. "Spinoza," translated by Willis Barnstone. From *Selected Poems by Jorge Luis Borges*, edited by Alexander Coleman. New York: Viking, 1999. Printed by permission of the Penguin Group, LLC.

Jorge Luis Borges: "Borges y yo," by Jorge Luis Borges, from *El hacedor*. Buenos Aires: Emecé, 1960. Printed by permission of The Wylie Literary Agency. "Borges and I," translated by Ilan Stavans. First published in *World Voices*, edited by Walter Cummins and Thomas E. Kennedy. In chapbooks.webdelsol.com, April 2009. Printed by permission of Ilan Stavans.

Coral Bracho: "Comenzaron a llamarte." © 2008 by Coral Bracho. Printed by permission of Coral Bracho. "They Began to Call You," translated by Forrest Gander. From *Firefly Under the Tongue: Selected Poems of Coral Bracho*, translated by Forrest Gander. New York: New Directions, 2008. © 2008 by Forrest Gander. Printed by permission of New Directions Publishing Corp.

Giannina Braschi: "Pelos en la lengua." From *Lengua Fresca*, edited by Harold Augenbraum and Ilan Stavans. Boston: Houghton Mifflin, 2006. Used by permission of Giannina Braschi.

Julia de Burgos: "A Julia de Burgos," from *Antología poética*, edited by Emilio A. Colón. San Juan, Puerto Rico: Editorial Coquí, 1968. "To Julia de Burgos," translated by Jack Agüeros. From *Song of the Simple Truth: Complete Poems of Julia de Burgos*, compiled and translated by Jack Agüeros. Willimantic: Curbstone Press, 1995. © 1995 by Jack Agüeros. Printed by permission of Northwestern University Press.

João Cabral de Melo Neto: "A educação pela pedra" and "O fim do mundo," translated by James Wright. From *An Anthology of Twentieth-Century Brazilian Poetry*, edited, with an introduction, by Elizabeth Bishop and Emanuel Brasil. Middletown: Wesleyan Univer-

etry, edited by Carlos Montemayor and Donald Frischmann. Austin: University of Texas Press, 2005. Printed by permission of Donald Frischman.

Pablo Antonio Cuadra: "El jícaro." © 1977 by Pablo Antonio Cuadra. Printed by permission of Pedro Xavier Solís Cuadra for the estate of Pablo Antonio Cuadra. "The Calabash Tree," translated by Steven F. White. From *Pablo Antonio Cuadra: The Birth of the Sun, Selected Poems 1935–1985*, translated by Steven F. White. Greensboro: Unicorn Press, 1988. © 1988 by Steven F. White. Printed by permission of Steven F. White.

Roque Dalton: "Karl Marx," by Roque Dalton. Printed by permission of the estate of Roque Dalton. "Karl Marx," translated by Roberto Márquez. From *Latin American Revolutionary Poetry*, edited by Roberto Márquez. New York and London: Monthly Review Press, 1974. © 1974 by Roberto Márquez. Printed by permission of Roberto Márquez.

Rubén Darío: "A Roosevelt" and "Sonatina," translated by Lysander Kemp. From *Rubén Darío: Selected Poems*, translated by Lysander Kemp. Prologue by Octavio Paz. Austin: University of Texas Press, 1965. © 1965 by the University of Texas Press. Reprinted by permission of the University of Texas Press.

Rubén Darío: "Ama tu ritmo . . . ," translated by Greg Simon and Steven F. White. From *Rubén Darío: Selected Writings*, edited by Ilan Stavans, translated by Greg Simon, Steven F. White, and Andrew Hurley. New York: Penguin Classics, 2005. © 2005 by Greg Simon and Steven F. White. Printed by permission of Steven F. White. Original is in the public domain.

Rubén Darío: "Lo fatal," translated by Ilan Stavans. First published in *The Literary Review*, vol. 36, Summer 2009. Printed by permission of Ilan Stavans.

Carlos Drummond de Andrade: "Os ombros suportam o mundo," "O elefante," and "Procura da poesia," translated by Mark Strand. From *Looking for Poetry: Poems of Carlos Drummond de Andrade and Rafael Alberti and Songs from the Quechua*, edited by Mark Strand. © 2002 by Mark Strand. Used by permission of Alfred A. Knopf, a division of Random House, Inc.

Carlos Drummond de Andrade: "Desaparecimento de Luísa Porto," translated by Thomas Colchie. From *Looking for Poetry: Poems of Carlos Drummond de Andrade and Rafael Alberti and Songs from the Quechua*, edited by Mark Strand. © 2002 by Thomas Colchie. Used by permission of Alfred A. Knopf, a division of Random House, Inc.

Carlos Drummond de Andrade: "Retrato de família," translated by Elizabeth Bizhop. From *An Anthology of Twentieth-Century Brazilian Poetry*, edited, with an introduction, by Elizabeth Bishop and Emanuel Brasil. Middletown: Wesleyan University Press, 1972. © 1972, 1997 by Elizabeth Bishop and Emanuel Brasil. Printed by permission of Wesleyan University Press.

Ricardo Jaimes Freire: "El alba," translated by Victor Tulli. From *Twentieth-Century Latin American Poetry*, edited by Stephen Tapscott. Austin: University of Texas Press. Printed by permission of Stephen Tapscott.

Juan Gelman: "Epitafio." © 1996 by Juan Gelman. Printed by permission of Juan Gelman. "Epitaph," translated by Ilan Stavans. From *Gotán*, by Juan Gelman. Buenos Aires: Seix Barral, 1996. © 2010 by Ilan Stavans. Printed by permission of Ilan Stavans.

Juan Gelman: "Dibaxu: I" and "Dibaxu: XII." © 1994 by Juan Gelman. Printed by permis-

Selected Poems of Gabriela Mistral, translated by Ursula K. Le Guin. Albuquerque: University of New Mexico Press. Printed by permission of University of New Mexico Press.

Fabio Morábito: "No he amado bastante," translated by Geoff Hargreaves. From *Reversible Monuments: Contemporary Mexican Poetry*, edited by Mónica de la Torre and Michael Wiegers. Port Townsend: Copper Canyon Press, 2002. © 2002 by Copper Canyon Press. Printed by permission of Copper Canyon Press.

Vinícius de Moraes: "Canção," translated by Richard Wilbur. From *An Anthology of Twentieth-Century Brazilian Poetry*, edited, with an introduction, by Elizabeth Bishop and Emanuel Brasil. Middletown: Wesleyan University Press, 1972. © 1972, 1997 by Elizabeth Bishop and Emanuel Brasil. Printed by permission of Wesleyan University Press.

Nancy Morejón: "Análisis de la melancolía." © by Nancy Morejón. Printed by permission of Agencia Literaria Latinoamericana, Havana, Cuba. "Analysis of Melancholy," translated by Kathleen Weaver. First published in *Where the Island Sleeps Like a Wing: Selected Poems by Nancy Morejón*, translated by Kathleen Weaver. © 1985 by Kathleen Weaver. San Francisco: Black Scholar Press, 1985. Printed by permission of Kathleen Weaver.

Nancy Morejón: "Persona," by Nancy Morejón. Printed by permission of Nancy Morejón and Agencia Literaria Latinoamericana, Havana, Cuba. "Persona," translated by David Frye. From Nancy Morejón: *Looking Within/Mirar adentro: Selected Poems, 1954–2000*. Detroit: Wayne State University Press, 2003. © 2003 by Nancy Morejón and David Frye. Printed by permission of David Frye.

Myriam Moscona: "Lo ke fue" and "La letra beth: il muro." © 2011 by Myriam Moscona. "What Was" and "The Letter Beth: The Wall," translated by Jen Hofer. © 2011 by Myriam Moscona and Jen Hofer. Printed by permission of Myriam Moscona and Jen Hofer.

Álvaro Mutis: "Poema de lástimas a la muerte de Marcel Proust," translated by Ilan Stavans. © 2011 by Ilan Stavans. Printed by permission of Ilan Stavans.

María Negroni: "VI (accidentien)," by María Negroni. © 2004 by María Negroni. Translated by Anne Twitty. From *Arte y Fuga*. Valencia, Spain: Pre-Textos, 2004. Printed by permission of María Negroni.

Pablo Neruda: "Poema XX: Puedo escribir." © 1973 by Fundación Pablo Neruda. Printed by permission of Carmen Balcells Literary Agency. "Poem XX: Tonight I Can Write," translated by W. S. Merwin. From *I Explain a Few Things: Selected Poems of Pablo Neruda*, edited by Ilan Stavans. New York: Farrar, Straus and Giroux, 2007. Printed by permission of Farrar, Straus and Giroux.

Pablo Neruda: "Pido silencio." © 1973 by Fundación Pablo Neruda. Printed by permission of Carmen Balcells Literary Agency. "I Ask for Silence," translated by Alistair Reid. From *I Explain a Few Things: Selected Poems of Pablo Neruda*, edited by Ilan Stavans. New York: Farrar, Straus and Giroux, 2007. Printed by permission of Farrar, Straus and Giroux.

Pablo Neruda: "Tu risa" and "Oda a la sandía." © 1973 by Fundación Pablo Neruda. Printed by permission of Carmen Balcells Literary Agency. "Your Laughter" and "Ode to the Watermelon," translated by Ilan Stavans. From *I Explain a Few Things: Selected Poems of Pablo Neruda*, edited by Ilan Stavans. New York: Farrar, Straus and Giroux, 2007. Printed by permission of Farrar, Straus and Giroux.

Pablo Neruda: From "Que despierte el leñador." © 1973 by Fundación Pablo Neruda. Printed by permission of Carmen Balcells Literary Agency. From "I Wish the Woodcutter Would Wake Up," translated by Robert Bly. From *I Explain a Few Things: Selected Poems of Pablo Neruda*, edited by Ilan Stavans. New York: Farrar, Straus and Giroux, 2007. Printed by permission of Farrar, Straus and Giroux.

Pablo Neruda: "El hijo." © 1973 by Fundación Pablo Neruda. Printed by permission of Carmen Balcells Literary Agency. "The Son," translated by Ilan Stavans and Alison Sparks. First published in *The Literary Review*, vol. 36, Summer 2009. © 2009 by Ilan Stavans and Alison Sparks. Printed by permission of Ilan Stavans and Alison Sparks.

Pablo Neruda: "Explico algunas cosas." © 1973 by Fundación Pablo Neruda. Printed by permission of Carmen Balcells Literary Agency. "I Explain a Few Things," translated by Galway Kinnell. From *I Explain a Few Things: Selected Poems of Pablo Neruda*, edited by Ilan Stavans. New York: Farrar, Straus and Giroux, 2007. Printed by permission of Farrar, Straus and Giroux.

Amado Nervo: "Y tú esperando . . . ," translated by Samuel Beckett. From *Anthology of Mexican Poetry*, compiled by Octavio Paz, translated by Samuel Beckett. Bloomington and London: Indiana University Press. Copyright © 1958. Reprinted by courtesy of The Beckett Estate and the Calder Educational Trust. Copyright © Indiana University Press.

Olga Orozco: "Balada de los lugares olvidados." Printed by permission of the Estate of Olga Orozco. "Ballad of Forgotten Places," translated by Mary Crow. From *Engravings Torn from Insomnia: Selected Poems by Olga Orozco*, translated and introduction by Mary Crow. BOA Editions, 2002. Printed by permission of BOA Editions, Ltd.

José Emilio Pacheco: "Mosquitos" and "Perra vida." © 1993 by José Emilio Pacheco. Printed by permission of Marcelo Uribe and Ediciones Era. "Mosquitoes" and "Bitch Life," translated by Margaret Sayers Peden. From *An Ark for the Next Millennium: Poems by José Emilio Pacheco*, translated by Margaret Sayers Peden, selection by Jorge Esquinca. Austin: University of Texas Press, 1993. © 1993 by Margaret Sayers Peden. Printed by permission of Margaret Sayers Peden.

José Emilio Pacheco: "José Ortega y Gasset contempla el viento." © 1978 by José Emilio Pacheco. Printed by permission of Marcelo Uribe and Ediciones Era. "José Ortega y Gasset Meditates on the Wind," translated by Alistair Reid. From José Emilio Pacheco: *Don't Ask Me How the Time Goes By: Poems, 1964–1968*, translated by Alistair Reid. New York: Columbia University Press, 1978. Printed by permission of Columbia University Press.

José Emilio Pacheco: "Malpaís." © 1978 by José Emilio Pacheco. Printed by permission of Marcelo Uribe and Ediciones Era. "Badlands," translated by Linda Sheer. From José Emilio Pacheco: *Don't Ask Me How the Time Goes By: Poems, 1964–1968*, translated by Alistair Reid. New York: Columbia University Press, 1978. Printed by permission of Columbia University Press.

Heberto Padilla: "Ana Frank" and "Retrato del poeta como un duende joven," translated by

Alistair Reid and Andrew Hurley. From *Legacies: Selected Poems of Heberto Padilla*, translated by Alistair Reid and Andrew Hurley. New York: Farrar, Straus and Giroux, 1982. Printed by permission of Farrar, Straus and Giroux.

Luis Palés Matos: "Preludio en boricua" and "Mulata-Antilla," translated by Roberto Márquez. From *Puerto Rican Poetry: A Selection from Aboriginal to Contemporary Times*, edited and translated by Roberto Márquez. Amherst and Boston: University of Massachusetts Press, 2007. © 2007 by Roberto Márquez. Printed by permission of Roberto Márquez.

Nicanor Parra: "El túnel" published by Editorial Universitaria de Chile. Printed by permission of Carmen Balcells Literary Agency. "The Tunnel," translated by Mark Strand. From *Another Republic: 17 European & South American Writers*, edited by Charles Simic and Mark Strand. New York: Ecco Press, 1976. Printed by permission of the publisher.

Nicanor Parra: "El pequeño burgués," published by Editorial Universitaria de Chile. Printed by permission of Carmen Balcells Literary Agency. "Litany of the Little Bourgeois," translated by Mark Strand. From *Another Republic: 17 European & South American Writers*, edited by Charles Simic and Mark Strand. New York: Ecco Press, 1976. Printed by permission of the publisher.

Nicanor Parra: "Soliloquio del individuo," published by Editorial Universitaria de Chile. Printed by permission of Carmen Balcells Literary Agency. "The Individual's Soliloquy," translated by W. S. Merwin. From *Antipoems: New and Selected*, by Nicanor Parra, edited by David Unger, introduction by Frank MacShane. New York: New Directions, 1985. © 1985 by Nicanor Parra. Printed by permission of New Directions Publishing Corp.

Violeta Parra: "Gracias a la vida," by Violeta Parra. Printed by permission of Fundación Violeta Parra. "Here's to Life!" translated by Joan Baez and John Upton. Copyright © 1966, 1974 by Chandos Music (ASCAP). Reprinted by permission.

Octavio Paz: "Nocturno en San Ildefonso." © 1991 by Octavio Paz. Printed by permission of the estate of Octavio Paz. "San Ildefonso Nocturne," translated by Eliot Weinberger. From *The Collected Poems of Octavio Paz: 1957–1987*, translated and edited by Eliot Weinberger. New York: New Directions, 1987. © 1986 by Octavio Paz and Eliot Weinberger. Printed by permission of New Directions Publishing Corp.

Octavio Paz: "La llave del agua." © 1991 by Octavio Paz. Printed by permission of the estate of Octavio Paz. "The Key of Water," translated by Elizabeth Bishop. From *The Collected Poems of Octavio Paz: 1957–1987*, translated and edited by Eliot Weinberger. New York: New Directions. Originally published in *The Collected Poems of Elizabeth Bishop*. New York: Farrar, Straus and Giroux. Printed by permission of Farrar, Straus and Giroux.

Octavio Paz: "Objetos y apariciones." © 1991 by Octavio Paz. Printed by permission of the estate of Octavio Paz. "Objects and Apparitions," translated by Elizabeth Bishop. From *The Collected Poems of Octavio Paz: 1957–1987*, translated and edited by Eliot Weinberger. New York: New Directions, 1987. Printed by permission of Farrar, Straus and Giroux.

Alejandra Pizarnik: "El despertar," "Exilio," and "Peregrinaje," translated by Frank Graziano and María Rosa Fort. From *Alejandra Pizarnik: A Profile*, edited, with an introduc-

Blanca Varela: "Curriculum Vitae," translated by Ilan Stavans. © 2011 by Ilan Stavans. Printed by permission of Ilan Stavans.

Xavier Villaurrutia: "Nocturno Grito." Mexico: Fondo de Cultura Económica, 1953. Printed by permission of Fondo de Cultura Económíca. "Nocturne: The Scream," translated by Eliot Weinberger. From *Nostalgia of Death: Poetry by Xavier Villaurrutia & Hieroglyphs of Desire: A Critical Study of Villaurrutia by Octavio Paz*, edited by Eliot Weinberger. Port Townsend: Copper Canyon Press, 2003. Printed by permission of Copper Canyon Press.

Raúl Zurita: "Zurita," "Aunque no sea más que tu quimera," and "Allí están." © 1982 by Raúl Zurita. First published in *Anteparaíso*. Santiago, Chile: Ediciones Universidad Diego Portales. Printed by permission of Matías Rivas on behalf of Ediciones Universidad Diego Portales. "Zurita," "Even If It's Just a Chimera," and "There They Are," translated by Jack Schmitt. From Raúl Zurita: *Anteparaíso*, translated by Jack Schmitt. Berkeley, Los Angeles, and London: University of California Press, 1986. © 1986 by Jack Schmitt. Printed by permission of University of California Press.

A NOTE ABOUT THE EDITOR

ILAN STAVANS IS THE LEWIS-SEBRING
PROFESSOR IN LATIN AMERICAN AND
LATINO CULTURE AT AMHERST COLLEGE.

4/11